Advances
in COMPUTERS
VOLUME 59

Advances in
COMPUTERS

EDITED BY

MARVIN V. ZELKOWITZ

Department of Computer Science
and Institute for Advanced Computer Studies
University of Maryland
College Park, Maryland

VOLUME 59

ACADEMIC PRESS

An imprint of Elsevier Science

Amsterdam Boston Heidelberg London New York Oxford
Paris San Diego San Francisco Singapore Sydney Tokyo

Academic Press
An imprint of Elsevier Science
525 B Street, Suite 1900, San Diego, California 92101-4495, USA
http://www.academicpress.com

© 2003 Elsevier USA All rights reserved.

This work is protected under copyright by Elsevier Science, and the following terms and conditions apply to its use:

Photocopying
Single photocopies of single chapters may be made for personal use as allowed by national copyright laws. Permission of the Publisher and payment of a fee is required for all other photocopying, including multiple or systematic copying, copying for advertising or promotional purposes, resale, and all forms of document delivery. Special rates are available for educational institutions that wish to make photocopies for non-profit educational classroom use.

Permissions may be sought directly from Elsevier's Science & Technology Rights Department in Oxford, UK: phone: (+44) 1865 843830, fax: (+44) 1865 853333, e-mail: permissions@elsevier.com. You may also complete your request on-line via the Elsevier Science homepage (http://www.elsevier.com), by selecting 'Customer Support' and then 'Obtaining Permissions'.

In the USA, users may clear permissions and make payments through the Copyright Clearance Center, Inc., 222 Rosewood Drive, Danvers, MA 01923, USA; phone: (+1) (978) 7508400, fax: (+1) (978) 7504744, and in the UK through the Copyright Licensing Agency Rapid Clearance Service (CLARCS), 90 Tottenham Court Road, London W1P 0LP, UK; phone: (+44) 207 631 5555; fax: (+44) 207 631 5500. Other countries may have a local reprographic rights agency for payments.

Derivative Works
Tables of contents may be reproduced for internal circulation, but permission of Elsevier Science is required for external resale or distribution of such material.
Permission of the Publisher is required for all other derivative works, including compilations and translations.

Electronic Storage or Usage
Permission of the Publisher is required to store or use electronically any material contained in this work, including any chapter or part of a chapter.

Except as outlined above, no part of this work may be reproduced, stored in a retrieval system or transmitted in any form or by any means, electronic, mechanical, photocopying, recording or otherwise, without prior written permission of the Publisher.
Address permissions requests to: Elsevier's Science & Technology Rights Department, at the phone, fax and e-mail addresses noted above.

Notice
No responsibility is assumed by the Publisher for any injury and/or damage to persons or property as a matter of products liability, negligence or otherwise, or from any use or operation of any methods, products, instructions or ideas contained in the material herein. Because of rapid advances in the medical sciences, in particular, independent verification of diagnoses and drug dosages should be made.

First edition 2003

Library of Congress Cataloging in Publication Data
A catalog record from the Library of Congress has been applied for.

British Library Cataloguing in Publication Data
A catalogue record from the British Library has been applied for.

ISBN: 0-12-012159-X
ISSN (Series): 0065-2458

⊚ The paper used in this publication meets the requirements of ANSI/NISO Z39.48-1992 (Permanence of Paper).

Printed in Great Britain by MPG Books Ltd, Bodmin, Cornwall

Contents

CONTRIBUTORS ix
PREFACE xiii

Collaborative Development Environments

Grady Booch and Alan W. Brown

1. Introduction 2
2. The Physics of Software 3
3. A Day in the Life of a Developer 6
4. The Emergence of Collaborative Development Environments 8
5. Creating a Frictionless Surface 9
6. A Survey of Collaborative Sites 12
7. Collaborative Development Environment Features 21
8. The Evolution of Collaborative Development Environments 24
9. Summary 25
   References 27

Tool Support for Experience-Based Software Development Methodologies

Scott Henninger

1. Experience-Based Approaches for Software Engineering 30
2. Experience-Based Knowledge Management 32
3. Tool Support for Experience-Based Approaches 41
4. The BORE Software Experience Base Tool 44
5. Putting BORE into Practice: Some Starting Points 61
6. Other Related Research 65
7. Open Issues and Future Work 69
8. Conclusions 72
   Acknowledgements 73
   References 73

Why New Software Processes Are Not Adopted

Stan Rifkin

1. Change Is Harder Than We Think	84
2. The Answers	86
3. Beginning the Inquiry	93
4. Process Descriptions of Implementation	96
5. Diffusion: The Most Popular Explanation	101
6. Resistance	105
7. Path Dependence Theory	109
8. Process Studies	110
9. Factor Studies	110
10. Case Studies	115
11. Conclusion	115
Acknowledgements	116
References	116

Impact Analysis in Software Evolution

Mikael Lindvall

1. Introduction	130
2. Related Work	135
3. The PMR-Project and Its Context	143
4. Evaluation on the Class Level	151
5. Evaluation of RDIA on the Member Function Level	156
6. Summary of Statistics	162
7. Evaluation of RDIA per Requirement	163
8. Models vs. Actual Implementation	169
9. Class Size	178
10. Relations between Classes	182
11. Discussion of Findings	190
12. Comments Regarding RDIA	193
13. Summary and Conclusions	205
References	207

Coherence Protocols for Bus-Based and Scalable Multiprocessors, Internet, and Wireless Distributed Computing Environments: A Survey

John Sustersic and Ali Hurson

1. Introduction and Background 212
2. Broadcast (Bus-Based) Protocols 216
3. Message-Passing (Directory Based) Protocols 227
4. Coherence on the World Wide Web 246
5. Wireless Protocols 259
6. Summary and Conclusions 267
   Acknowledgements 273
   References 273

AUTHOR INDEX 279
SUBJECT INDEX 289
CONTENTS OF VOLUMES IN THIS SERIES 297

Contributors

Grady Booch is recognized internationally for his innovative work on software architecture, modeling, and software engineering process. His work has improved the effectiveness of software developers worldwide. He has been with Rational Software Corporation as Chief Scientist since its founding in 1980. Grady is one of the original developers of the Unified Modeling Language (UML) and was also one of the original developers of several of Rational's products including Rational Rose. Grady has served as architect and architectural mentor for numerous complex software systems around the world. Grady is a member of the Association for Computing Machinery (ACM), the Institute of Electrical and Electronics Engineers (IEEE), the American Association for the Advancement of Science (AAAS), and Computer Professionals for Social Responsibility (CPSR). He is also an ACM Fellow and a Rational Fellow. Grady received his BS in engineering from the United States Air Force Academy in 1977 and his MSEE from the University of California at Santa Barbara in 1979. He can be reached at eqb@rational.com.

Dr. Alan W. Brown is Director of the Rational Development Accelerator team at Rational, helping customers to be more productive in the application of Rational tools and services. In this capacity Alan manages intellectual property artifacts supporting Rational's desktop products, including Rational Rose and Rational XDE. Before joining Rational Software through the acquisition of Catapulse in 2001, he was Chief Technology Officer for Sterling Software's Application Development Group (ADG) where he was responsible for advanced technology activities across the organization. Previously, Alan had spent five years at the Software Engineering Institute (SEI) at Carnegie Mellon University in Pittsburgh, Pennsylvania. There he led the CASE environments project advising on a variety of U.S. government agencies and contractors on the application and integration of CASE technologies. Alan's primary research interests are in component-based development, software engineering environments, and enterprise application development tools. He has published over 40 papers, edited three books and is the author of five books. Alan received his PhD from the University of Newcastle-upon-Tyne, UK. Dr. Brown can be reached at alan.brown@rational.com.

Prof. Scott Henninger is with the Department of Computer Science and Engineering, University of Nebraska–Lincoln. Dr. Henninger received in Ph.D. in Computer Science from the University of Colorado–Boulder in 1993 and a Bachelors of Science in Electrical Engineering at the University of Southern California in 1983. He has published 50 papers in the general research areas of software engineering and human–computer interaction. His current research efforts focus on using the software process and workflow management as an organizing principle for knowledge building and management, particularly in the context of software development. Techniques are being investigated that ensures that past knowledge is used as the basis for current work and the continuous improvement of the process. His work has been funded by the National Science Foundation for the past eight years and has also received funding from various industry organizations, such as The Gallup Organization, JD Edwards Company, Union Pacific, and Microsoft. In addition, he founded the Software Design Studios for the JD Edwards Honors Program in Computer Science and Management at the University of Nebraska. He is President of the newly founded Adaptive Process Technologies company, a software process consulting firm that uses the BORE framework to develop flexible development processes that can adapt to the changing needs of organizations. Dr. Henninger can be reached at scotth@cse.unl.edu.

Prof. A. R. Hurson is on the Computer Science and Engineering Faculty at The Pennsylvania State University. His research for the past 20 years has been directed toward the design and analysis of general as well as special purpose computer architectures. His research has been supported by NSF, ONR, DARPA, NCR Corp., IBM, Lockheed Martin, and Penn State University. He has published over 200 technical papers in areas including database systems, multidatabases, object oriented databases, computer architecture and cache memory, parallel and distributed processing, dataflow architectures, and VLSI algorithms. He is the co-author of the IEEE Tutorials on Parallel Architectures for Database Systems, Multidatabase systems: An advanced solution for global information sharing, Parallel architectures for data/knowledge base systems, and Scheduling and Load Balancing in Parallel and Distributed Systems. He is also the Co-founder of the IEEE Symposium on Parallel and Distributed Processing (currently IPDPS). Professor Hurson has been active in various IEEE/ACM Conferences and has given tutorials for various conferences on global information sharing, dataflow processing, database management systems, supercomputer technology, data/knowledge-based systems, scheduling and load balancing, and parallel computing. He served as a member of the IEEE Computer Society Press Editorial Board, the editor of IEEE transactions on computers, and an IEEE Distinguished speaker. Currently, he is serving in the IEEE/ACM Computer Sciences Accreditation Board and as an ACM lecturer. Hurson can be reached at hurson@cse.psu.edu.

Dr. Mikael Lindvall is a scientist at Fraunhofer Center for Experimental Software Engineering Maryland. Dr. Lindvall specializes on experience and knowledge management in software engineering and on software architecture evaluation and evolution. He is currently working on ways of building experience bases to attract users to both contribute and use experience bases tools as well as on methods to quickly understanding an architecture and identifying architectural deviations. Dr. Lindvall received his PhD in computer science from Linköpings University, Sweden in 1997. Lindvall's PhD work focused on evolution of object-oriented systems and was based on a commercial development project at Ericsson Radio in Sweden. Contact Dr. Lindvall at mlindvall@fc-md.umd.edu.

Stan Rifkin is a principal with Master Systems Inc., an advisory services firm specializing in software improvement. Started in 1985 at the request of the National Headquarters of the American Red Cross, Master Systems serves the improvement needs of organizations for which computing is strategic. Mr. Rifkin worked at the American Red Cross, the American Association for the Advancement of Science, and the Software Engineering Institute (SEI). He was the co-chair of the Software Engineering Process Group (SEPG) Conference in 2002 and has started many SEPGs and Software Process Improvement Network (SPIN) chapters, most recently in San Diego, California. At the SEI he co-wrote the SEPG Guide and Measurement in Practice. He recently wrote articles in IEEE Software about the place of organizational strategy in improvement. He earned a BS in Business Administration (quantitative methods) from California State University at Northridge, an MS in Computer Science at UCLA, and is near a doctorate in education at the George Washington University in Washington, DC. He is a member of IEEE, ACM, Institute for Operations Research and Management Science, Academy of Management, and is a charter member of the editorial board of Empirical Software Engineering. He can be reached at sr@Master-Sytems.com.

J.P. Sustersic is a Ph.D. Candidate in the Department of Computer Science and Engineering at The Pennsylvania State University. After completing his Bachelor's in Electrical Engineering at Cleveland State in 1999, John spent a year researching and developing digitally controlled DC-DC power converter technology to be used in a distributed, cooperative environment in Space Applications. Funded by a NASA-Glenn grant, this work included helping to establish the Advanced Research Lab at Cleveland State University as that college's premier research organization. John then entered the Ph.D. program at Penn State to pursue his primary research interests of parallel and distributed computing, focusing his work on the study of caching in heterogeneous distributed computing environments. John may be reached at sustersi@cse.psu.edu.

Preface

This is volume 59 of *Advances in Computers*. This series, which has been continuously published since 1960, presents in each volume several chapters describing new developments in software, hardware, or uses of computers. In each volume we chronicle the ever-changing landscape of computer technology. In this volume, we cover five new developments that affect how computers are used. Four describe various components of how individuals or groups use computers to produce software and the fifth describes hardware features that improve a computer's performance.

The first chapter by Grady Booch and Alan W. Brown, entitled "Collaborative Development Environments" describes environments where a team of individuals, separated geographically, can work cooperatively on a single development. Previously all developers needed access to the same set of files to manage a development. Today, the World Wide Web has enabled worldwide development practices via a virtual development environment where stakeholders can gather to discuss issues, make decisions, and develop products. This chapter includes many of the features that such environments contain.

Chapter 2, "Tool Support for Experienced-Based Software Development Methodologies" by Scott Henninger, explores a different form of development environment than the one described by Booch and Brown in Chapter 1. In this chapter, Dr. Henninger uses an experience base as the mechanism for capturing and sharing knowledge among the stakeholders in a development. The ideas explored are based on Basili's Experience Factory development model and on organizational learning. The author uses his BORE (Building an Organizational Repository of Experiences) environment as an example of the approach he is describing.

There have been many chapters in previous volumes of the "Advances" which describe new technologies to help developers improve the software they are producing. Sadly, many of these technologies are ignored. Why is this so? In Chapter 3, Stan Rifkin explores this in "Why New Software Processes Are Not Adopted." The author explores many different formal models of process adoption, from general process models of Repenning and Markus, which describe the process of innovation entering the mainstream of industry, to the more software-oriented approach of Redwine and Riddle, who try and calculate the stages of innovation and compute how long it takes for a new technology to get adopted.

"Impact Analysis in Software Evolution" by Mikael Lindvall looks at the requirements process in software development, especially as that software evolves over time. Project planning requires accurate estimates on any tasks that are necessary to complete. However, as a project evolves and new versions are produced, an experience base of previous versions provides data that can be used to produce better estimates on the effort needed to produce the next version. In this chapter, a method, called Requirements-Driven Impact Analysis (RDIA), is described, which provides the necessary feedback from earlier versions looking at change data—counting those attributes of the new version that changed from the previous version. This chapter provides an in-depth case study of the effectiveness of RDIA.

In the final chapter, "Coherence Protocols for Bus-Based and Scalable Multiprocessors, Internet, and Wireless Distributed Computing Environments" by John Sustersic and Ali Hurson, the authors discuss the problems inherent in cache memory systems. Most modern computers use a cache memory, a small very fast memory that is between the central processor and the large main memory, for storing information very quickly in order to process the next instruction, while the hardware takes considerably longer to move the information from the cache into the main memory. With a single processor, there are few problems. But if a machine has multiple processors executing from the same main memory, situations arise where one processor puts information into the cache, and before it can be stored into the main memory, the other processor wants to access it. This is the cache coherence problem. This chapter discusses various solutions to this problem for various system architectures.

I hope that you find these articles of interest. Each year I try and anticipate what developments will be most important two years hence—not any easy task. If you have any suggestions of topics for future chapters or think that a given topic has been ignored for too many years, let me know. If you wish to be considered as an author for a chapter, I can be reached at mvz@cs.umd.edu.

Marvin Zelkowitz
University of Maryland,
College Park, MD, USA

Fraunhofer Center for Experimental Software Engineering
College Park, MD, USA

Collaborative Development Environments

GRADY BOOCH AND ALAN W. BROWN

IBM Rational Software
USA

Abstract

A *collaborative development environment* (CDE) is a virtual space wherein all the stakeholders of a project—even if distributed by time or distance—may negotiate, brainstorm, discuss, share knowledge, and generally labor together to carry out some task, most often to create an executable deliverable and its supporting artifacts. CDEs are particularly useful as places where engineers may collaborate to solve problems. Here we focus on software developers in their tasks of designing, implementing, deploying, and maintaining high quality software-intensive systems where they are physically separated and make use of the Internet as the basis for their interactions.

In this paper, we examine the points of friction in the software development process and the mechanisms that reduce that friction. We then survey a variety of sites, both inside and outside the software domain, which provide some of these mechanisms. We conclude with observations as to what a CDE is, what it is not, and what it can become.

1. Introduction 2
2. The Physics of Software 3
3. A Day in the Life of a Developer 6
4. The Emergence of Collaborative Development Environments 8
5. Creating a Frictionless Surface 9
6. A Survey of Collaborative Sites 12
   6.1. Non-Software Domains 12
   6.2. Asset Management 14
   6.3. Information Services 15
   6.4. Infrastructure 16
   6.5. Community 17
   6.6. Software Development 19
7. Collaborative Development Environment Features 21
8. The Evolution of Collaborative Development Environments 24
9. Summary 25
   References 27

1. Introduction

A *collaborative development environment* (CDE) is a virtual space wherein all the stakeholders of a project—even if distributed by time or distance—may negotiate, brainstorm, discuss, share knowledge, and generally labor together to carry out some task, most often to create an executable deliverable and its supporting artifacts.

Collaboration is essential to every engineering domain. What we are interested in, and what we focus on in this paper, are engineers working to solve problems collaboratively. More specifically, we are focused on software engineers in their tasks of designing, implementing, deploying, and maintaining high quality software-intensive systems where they are physically separated and make use of the Internet as the basis for their interactions. This scenario is commonplace, fueled by outsourcing, integration of third party software, increasing off-shore development, use of home offices, strategic partnerships among companies, etc. The success of distributed teams working together effectively is imperative, and is a distinguishing factor in the success or failure of many modest to large software development organizations.

From its earliest days, collaboration has been an essential part of the fabric of the Internet: email, instant messaging, chat rooms, and discussion groups are common collaborative elements that already exist, and so in one regard, there is nothing new or novel here. Furthermore, collaboration among teams is already common through the use of an increasing number of features embedded into common desktop products such as office suites (e.g., Microsoft Office Suite and Sun StarOffice), and communications packages (e.g., Microsoft Outlook and IBM LotusNotes). In both, there is ample support for shared document reviews, distribution of documents among teams, and some mechanisms for performing common collaborative tasks. In a very practical sense these tools provide the baseline of collaboration functionality for today's software developers, though typically augmented with an assortment of open source, proprietary, and commercial stand-alone point products.

However, what is different about the emergence of CDEs is the collection of these mechanisms into a virtual project space, delivered over the Web and supplemented with tools and creature comforts that are focused on the mission of that particular team, in this case, the creation of software products. Communities of practice are fragile things that can flourish only given the right balance of technology and user experience, and thus creating a CDE that enables efficient, creative teamwork is a hard thing. It is the supportive, integrated nature of a CDE that distinguishes it from the variety of disparate functional products typically in use today.

Ultimately, the purpose of a CDE is to create a frictionless surface for development by eliminating or automating many of the daily, non-creative activities of the team and by providing mechanisms that encourage creative, healthy, and high-bandwidth modes of communication among a project's stakeholders. In this paper, we examine the points of friction in the development process and the mechanisms that reduce that friction. We then survey a variety of sites, both inside and outside the software domain, which provide some of these mechanisms. We conclude with observations as to what a CDE is, what it is not, and what it can become.

2. The Physics of Software

Many aspects of software engineering have changed little in the past twenty years. Re-reading some of the seminal works in software engineering, it is striking just how much of that work remains relevant to today's challenges for developing quality software on time and within budget: abstraction, information hiding, and having a good separation of concerns are all essential principles that apply to every manner of software system; additionally, the requirements management, change control, architecture, iterative development are all well-understood principles of the software development process. However, in other ways the past two decades has witnessed many advances in the technology, the business, and the practice of software engineering.

It is useful to reflect back on the nature of software development some twenty years ago, before the creation of the Unified Modeling Language (UML), the Rational Unified Process (RUP) and the methods that preceded it. This was the time before the Web was a central part of the software development landscape and before the existence of contemporary programming languages such as Java, C++, and C#. Indeed, this was even the time before object-orientation had entered the mainstream of development, although the roots of object-orientation were already present in languages such as Simula and Smalltalk and in abstract data type theory. Integrated development environments (IDEs) were just emerging, with many developers still toiling with command line tools and WYSINWYG (What You See Is Not What You Get) editors. Methodologically, the industry was focused primarily on improving the productivity of the individual developer, although some individuals, most notably Gerald Weinberg, Tom DeMarco, Tim Lister, Larry Constantine, Ed Yourdon, and Fred Brooks were urging us to consider the human side of development.

The world of software development has clearly progressed: the Web and its related technologies are a factor in virtually every project, object-oriented methods and languages are mainstream, IDEs are far more powerful, and methods have begun to address the social dynamics of the development team. Still, as Walker Royce describes it, software development remains an industry that is marked by a diseconomy of scale. In other words, as project functionality, size, and complexity rise, the incremental cost of each new line of code or additional feature tends to increase, not

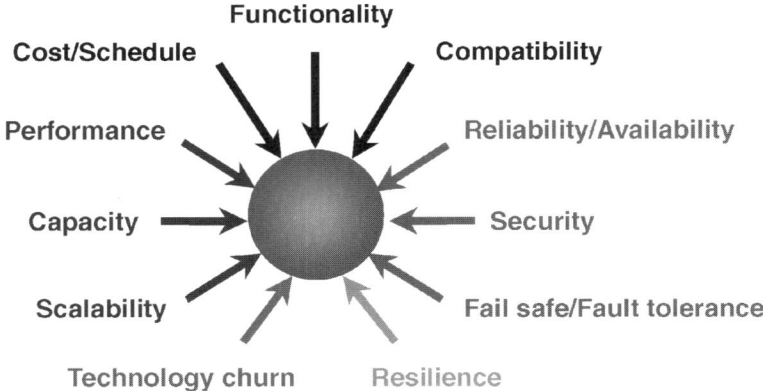

FIG. 1. Forces in software.

decrease, as we might expect in a classical engineering setting. Furthermore, economic pressures that demand faster time to market often collide with the engineering demands for higher quality.

Figure 1 illustrates a number of pressures that weigh upon and the development team as a whole. Cost, schedule, functionality, and compatibility (with legacy code and with packaged software, including operating systems and middleware, both of which are outside the primary control of the development team) are the most pressing forces. Depending upon the particular nature of the problem domain, performance, capacity, scalability, reliability, availability, security, and fault tolerance weigh in with varying amounts. Technology churn represents the force caused by the rate of change of packaged software, protocols, and hardware, also all outside the control of the development team (except for the choice of what technology to be used). Finally, resilience represents the force caused by the need to construct systems that must accommodate continuous change, with different parts of the system changing at different rates of speed.

For systems of any reasonable complexity, no one person can efficiently counteract these forces. Thus, for most systems under construction, operation, or revision, software development is a team sport. In these circumstances inter- and intra-team interaction, communication, and dynamics play as least as important a role as individual heroics in successful software development. For this reason, understanding more about optimizing software development team performance is a critical task of software engineering.

There are no hard studies that tell us the median size of a contemporary development team, but our experience, across a broad range of domains, is that teams of four to eight people are most common, with teams of one or two being the second-most common. Beyond the range of four to eight members, the existence of larger teams tends to tail off although we also find a peak in the curve of team size/occurrence somewhere around the one to two hundred mark. Some systems, such as telephony, financial, and command and control systems are so complex that they require large teams to complete the work in a timely fashion.

To be honest, these apocryphal figures are not especially useful, because they focus only upon the immediate development team. In practice, most organizations build systems, not just applications. Furthermore, for any interesting system that has deep economic value to the development organization or its users, there are a number of stakeholders beyond the core programming team who have a say in the development process. Web-centric systems are especially sensitive to this factor, for the extended team will typically involve network engineers, security architects, and content creators. If we take these elements into account, our experience is that the median team size for building systems is much larger, somewhere in the range of several dozen to one hundred or more.

Not only must an organization focus upon the efficiency of each individual team, it must also be concerned about the efficiency of its teams of teams. In even a modest size development organization, there might be a hundred or so developers perhaps organized in teams of four to eight, with most focused on point products but a few focused on infrastructure technologies that support all the other teams.[1] In practice, most of these individual teams will themselves be contiguous (that is, their cubicles are physically close to one another), which encourages the jelling of the team through the myriad of informal interactions that occur during the day. However, relative to one another, these teams will typically be physically disconnected from other teams, thus reducing the level of informal contact and in turn reducing the bandwidth and quality of inter-team communication. Indeed, one of the problems any such organization faces is simply keeping these teams of teams on the same page. That requires sharing project status, reducing duplication of work, engineering the architectural seams among groups, and sharing knowledge and experience.

In short, delivering better software faster involves the rhythms of the individual developer, the small team of developers and—for larger projects—teams of teams and even teams of teams of teams of developers.

Relative to software development two decades ago, we now better understand the best practices of software development that work and those that do not work. However, as Gerald Weinberg has noted, ultimately, programming is a human activity. All

---

[1] For example, it is common to have an architecture team that builds mechanisms upon commercial middleware such as Microsoft's .NET or IBM's WebSphere. Creating such mechanisms typically requires special knowledge, which is more efficiently managed by a centralized team than by every individual developer most of whom are domain experts, not technology experts.

meaningful development work derives from activities that beat at different rhythms: the activities of the individual developer, the social dynamics among small teams of developers, and the dynamics among teams of teams. Thus, even if we use the most expressive languages, the most comprehensive packaged software, and the best methods, it is still the manual labor of the development team that yields systems of quality.

Software developers spend a majority of their time on code-centric activities supported by an IDE offering a range of code development and manipulation features. Other aspects of their task involving interaction, communication and coordination within and across teams are generally supported by a discrete combination of capabilities including configuration management systems, issue tracking databases, instant messaging systems, project websites, and so on. Assembled in a coherent fashion, this latter set of capabilities can compose a collaborative development environment (CDE) for software engineers.

Whereas traditional IDEs focus upon improving the efficiencies of the individual developer, CDEs focus upon improving the efficiencies of the development team as a whole. While it is the case that most modern IDEs have some degree of collaborative support (for example, the ability to check in/check out an artifact from a common repository or call out to NetMeeting and whiteboards from a menu), we contend that incrementally adding such collaborative features will not transmogrify an IDE into a CDE. IDEs are essentially developer-centric, meaning that their primary user experience focuses on the individual developer, whereas CDEs are essentially team-centric, meaning that their primary user experience focuses on the needs of the team (but with points of entry for different individuals). Psychologically, this is a subtle yet very important shift of perspective.

3. A Day in the Life of a Developer

In order to best understand the requirements for a CDE, it is reasonable to first understand the social dynamics of the individual, the team and a team of teams. Surprisingly, however, there exist very few empirical studies that highlight what developers really do with their time. There are some soft studies, such as found in the experiences of Gerald Weinberg [1], Tom DeMarco [2], and Larry Constantine [3]. Larry Votta has proposed a framework for such scientific study [4], although no deep studies from that framework have yet been released.

There is one interesting empirical study that can be found, carried out by Joerg Strubing, a sociologist at the University of Berlin. In his study [5], he observed, "Being a sociologist, I have found that designing software is a highly cooperative process." His study consisted of two series of experiments. In the first series, he conducted 10 open-ended interviews and one group discussion; in the second series, he conducted 25 interviews with programmers and two other experts.

Although his sample size was relatively small, Strubing found three activities that developers consistently carried out beyond just coding: organizing their working space and process, representing and communicating design decisions and ideas, and communicating and negotiating with various stakeholders. Thus, beyond coding, Strubing declared programming to be a profession that involved very heterogeneous activities, the management of ambiguity, and a significant degree of negotiativeness.

Because of the scarcity of hard data, Booch conducted an experiment in March 2001 to obtain a snapshot of the daily life of a developer. This experiment was carried out on the Web and involved 50 developers from around the world. Artifacts generated for this experiment included a pre-day survey, timesheets during the event, a digital photo of each participant taken at noon local time on the day of the survey, and one or two snapshots of their desktop. Here we provide a short summary of the main results of that study.

Participants were 81% male and 19% female with most coming from the United States but others from countries including Austria, Germany, Canada, India, Australia, New Zealand, Venezuela, and the Russian Federation. On average, participants had nine years of experience in software development, ranging from one to 43 years. Project domains varied widely, encompassing command and control, financial, communications, and entertainment industries. 46% of the participants worked on Unix, 41% on Windows, 7% on Linux, and 5% on pure Web applications.[2] 37% of the participants worked in Java, 35% in C, C++, or C#, and 28% worked in other languages, most commonly Perl, Visual Basic, Ada, and assembly language.

In analyzing their surveys and time sheets, participants spent about 16% of their day in analysis (ranging from 5% to 40%), 14% of their day designing (ranging from 1% to 40%), 16% of their day coding (ranging from 0% to 60%), and 10% of their day testing (ranging from 0% to 50%).

Beyond these traditional activities, what's particularly interesting is the time each spent on infrastructure tasks. On average, participants spent 3% of their day on the phone and 7% reading (email, snail mail, documents, journals, and magazines). The survey asked participants to distinguish between productive and useless meetings: on average, 10% of their time was spent in productive meetings and a disturbing 7% was spent in useless ones.

This study on day in the life of a developer resonates with Strubing's research: software development is a deeply social process. Whereas IDEs such as Microsoft's VisualStudio, the open source NetBeans and eclipse, IBM's WebSphere Studio, and Borland's JBuilder are primarily individual productivity tools, there is emerging a

---

[2] These numbers add up to more than 100%, because several participants worked on multiple platforms.

genre of development environments we call collaborative, because they address the requirements of this social process.

4. The Emergence of Collaborative Development Environments

To paraphrase Abraham Lincoln, software development takes place of the Web, by the Web, and for the Web. There is considerable development *of* the Web's infrastructure; similarly, a great deal of application software is being developed *for* Web-centric systems. Relative to CDEs, however, development *by* the Web means using the Web to change the nature of software development itself.

If we project out from the most common IDEs such as Microsoft's Visual Studio and IBM's open source eclipse, we observe that emerging CDEs are and should be Web-based, artifact-centric, and multi-dimensional. The Web is an ideal platform for doing software engineering because the very nature of the Web permits the creation of virtual spaces that transcend the physical boundaries of its participants. CDEs should also be artifact-centric, meaning that they should offer up a user experience that makes work products primary and engages tools only as necessary.[3] Finally, a CDE should be multidimensional in the sense that different stakeholders should be offered different views, each adapted to that stakeholder's specific needs.

Collaborative sites both on and off the Web have existed for some time,[4] but we began to see collaborative sites focused solely on software development starting only about five years ago. Most of these sites were neither public nor reusable, but rather were one-off creations for specific projects. One of the earliest such sites we encountered was for a large command and control system. As part of an architectural review, we were placed in front of a homegrown intranet that contained literally every artifact created by the project, from vision documents to models to code to executables. Although this site offered very little in terms of collaborative mechanisms, it did offer up a virtual presence, a veritable electronic meeting place for the project's team members, many of whom were geographically distributed.

Soon after, we saw emerge commercial sites for the construction and CAD industries, both using the Web to provide a virtual project space. Similar sites grew up for the open source software development industry. Indeed, since much open source code is written by individuals who never interact with one another in person but

---

[3] This is a subtle but psychologically important shift: rather than saying "I shall open this editor so that I can cut some code" one would say "here's an aspect of code that I need to work on (and hand me the right tools to do the job)."

[4] In particular, the Well is perhaps the quintessential collaborative site.

only via email and the Web, it is natural that the Web be used to provide a sense of presence for open source projects.

Recognizing the emergence of the Web as a platform for software development, Frank Maurer, an associate professor at the University of Calgary, began sponsoring a workshop on software engineering over the Internet in conjunction with the International Conference on Software Engineering. His workshops have been conducted since 1998, and have generated several dozen important papers on the theory and practice of CDEs. Many of the mechanisms visible in the sites we survey later in this paper had their roots or were described in these workshops. In addition to Maurer's workshops, A.J. Kim[5] and Adele Goldberg [6] have independently contributed to the practice of building communities on the Web that, relative to CDEs, offer valuable insights into the social dynamics of groups and the elements necessary to make such communities flourish. Finally, the MIT Media Laboratory (www.media.mit.edu) has conducted basic research regarding collaboration and the Starfire (www.asktog.com/starfire/starfireHome.html) project, led by Bruce Tognazzini while he was at Sun Microsystems, offers a future vision of collaborative development that is worth study.

It can also be noted that collaborative development environments are beginning to get traction in traditional consumer product development [7]. Proctor & Gamble, Johnson & Johnson, Ford, SCI Systems, and The Limited, among many others, are all currently using a variety of collaborative mechanisms to manage their research, design, manufacturing, and shipping needs. Clearly, the artifacts that these companies manipulate are not the same as one would find in a software development organization, but it appears that many of the underlying collaborative mechanisms are identical. This is good news, for it means that there is likely a broad market for general CDEs, which can thus raise the level of practice for software-specific CDEs.

5. Creating a Frictionless Surface

The purpose of a CDE is to create a frictionless surface for development. Our experience suggests that there are a number of points of friction in the daily life of the developer that individually and collectively impact the team's efficiency:

- the cost of start up and on-going working space organization,
- inefficient work product collaboration,
- maintaining effective group communication, including knowledge and experience, project status, and project memory,

[5]In particular, see Kim, A.J., 2000, *Community Building on the Web: Secret Strategies for Successful Online Communities*, Peachpit Press.

- time starvation across multiple tasks,
- stakeholder negotiation,
- stuff that doesn't work.

We call these points of friction because energy is lost in their execution which otherwise could be directed to more creative activities that contribute directly to the completion of the project's mission. Addressing these points of friction represents substantial return on investment for many organizations.

The *costs of start up* are related to Strubing's observations concerning organizing the working space. As a team gets started or as new team members join a project, there is always an awkward, disorienting period of time that the member gets settled into his or her space. Finding the right tools, knowing who to talk to, knowing what documents to read first, understanding the current state of the project are activities that all take time, and are especially painful if the project or member is not offered any guidance as to where to begin.

Work product collaboration involves the friction associated with multiple stakeholders creating a shared artifact. Often, one person is given the responsibility for owning a particular artifact and so serves as its primary author. Over time, however, critical documents involve many people in their evolution. Keeping track of changes, knowing who changed things and why, synchronizing simultaneous edits, and in general handling accountability for the life of the artifact are all activities that cost time and that can create inefficiencies if not automated.

Communication is perhaps the largest point of friction. As Strubing noted, "negotiativeness" and the management of ambiguity are both critical non-programming tasks, and both are at the core of sound communication. Typically, the memory of a project, its culture, and its design decisions are locked up in the heads of a few core individuals, and part of a team's activities involve sort of a tribal sharing. Insofar as such knowledge is inaccessible, the depth of information flow will suffer. Furthermore, insofar as the communication paths among team members are noisy—such as it is within teams of teams—communication quality and hence team efficiency suffers.

Time starvation refers to the reality that there is typically never enough time to complete everything on an individual's to do list. Developers are finite in their capacity to work. Although time cannot be expanded, projects on a death march will try to squeeze out every possible cycle by pushing those human limits, typically at great human expense (which is why death marches are not sustainable) [8].

Stakeholder negotiation involves the time necessary to drive different members of the team having different worldviews to some degree of closure so that the team can make progress. Within a project, time will always be spent on explaining to various stakeholders what's being built, the precise desired structure and behavior of the system, and the semantics of design alternatives and ultimately design decision. In short, stakeholder negotiation is the process of driving out ambiguity.

Surprisingly little has been written about the impact of *technology and tools that don't work* upon the efficiency of the development team. Intermittent network outages, operating systems that behave in mysterious ways as if possessed, buggy packaged software, tools that don't work quite as advertised all eat up a teams time. Such interruptions are often small, but any loss will interrupt the concentration of the developer and, ultimately, losses will mount up, one minute at a time.

A CDE can address many of these points of friction. Making a virtual project environment just an URL away can minimize start up costs; being able to self-administer such sites also means that the team can manage its own artifacts rather than require the services of a dedicated support team. The friction associated with work product collaboration can be minimized by offering up artifact storage with integrated change management and the storage of metaknowledge. Communication can be facilitated by the use of mechanisms for discussions, virtual meetings, and project dashboards. Time starvation can be addressed not only by a hundred small creature comforts for the developer, but by making possible virtual agents that act as non-human members of the development team, responsible for carrying out scripted, tedious tasks.[6] Stakeholder negotiation can be facilitated by mechanisms that automate workflow. As for stuff that doesn't work, well, a CDE won't make much different: the best we can suggest is that you should simply refuse to buy or use products of inferior quality.[7] That notwithstanding, if stuff doesn't work for you, then it is likely that there are others in the world who have experienced the same problem and might have solved it or found a work around. In the presence of an extended community of developers, such as might interact with a CDE, mechanisms for sharing experiences can somewhat temper the problems of hard failure (and perhaps even offer a form of collective bargaining to put pressure on the vendor who has delivered up shoddy products).

Ultimately, technology is valuable to an organization insofar as it provides a meaningful return on investment. With CDEs, there exists a potential for both tangible and intangible returns.[8] Tangibly, there exist opportunities for real reduced costs in start up, tool administration, and artifact administration. In difficult economic times, a company's travel budget is invariably under pressure, yet collaborative work must

---

[6] As the classic joke (from www.cartoonbank.com) goes, "On the Internet, no one knows you are a dog." In a virtual project space, whether or not a team member is human is sometimes irrelevant.

[7] Of course, sometimes that's not so easy an edict to follow, especially if the market place offers limited choices.

[8] We say *potential* simply because there have been no hard economic studies for the ROI of CDEs in practice. However, the business value of a CDE comes from the observation that this technology can be both an aspirin as well as a vitamin: it alleviates some of the pain of development and promotes healthy project behavior.

continue. The presence of a CDE can actually reduce these company and human costs by eliminating the need for some travel. Intangibly, a CDE provides a sense of place and identity for the organization's nomadic developers who may be geographically distributed and mobile; such a space helps jell the team. Furthermore, in examining the patterns of communication within teams, it appears that healthy organizations create and collapse small tiger teams all the time for the purpose of wrestling specific problems to the ground. Facilitating the management of such teams permits greater accountability and focus of mission.

6. A Survey of Collaborative Sites

There exist only a few commercial CDEs focused primarily on the problem of software development over the Internet, but there are many more that have been generated for other domains or that address one specific element of the software CDE domain. Studying these different sites can help us understand what a CDE is, what it is not, and what it can be.

We can classify the spectrum of CDEs as follows, and examine exemplars of each in turn:

- non-software domains,
- asset management,
- information services,
- infrastructure,
- community,
- software development.

6.1 Non-Software Domains

The construction, manufacturing and electronics industries have been a fruitful place for the evolution of CDEs. In fact, it is these industries that have been the earliest adopters of collaborative technology, perhaps because many of their points of friction are directly addressed by the features of a CDE. Imagine, for example, a building being erected in Kuala Lumpur. On site, the construction supervisor might encounter a design problem whose resolution would require the interaction of the building's architect, structural engineers, and end users (and, amazingly so, lawyers). If the architect were in London, the structural engineer in New York, and the client in Hong Kong, getting these stakeholders together in real time would be problematic.

COLLABORATIVE DEVELOPMENT ENVIRONMENTS 13

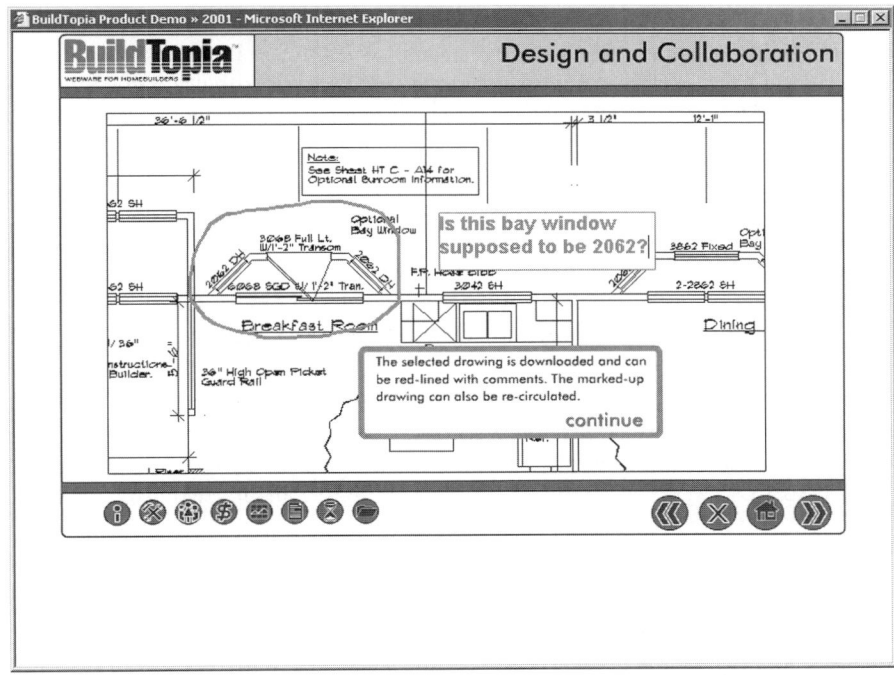

FIG. 2. BuildTopia Web-centric design collaboration.

Instead, by using the Web as a virtual meeting place for the project, resolution can take place in real time.

This kind of collaborative development is what lies behind products such as BuildTopia (www.buildtopia.com), a Web-centric system for design collaboration, project management, bidding, sales, and customer support for the homebuilding industry. As Fig. 2 shows, BuildTopia's product line permits Web-based collaboration on design artifacts such as blueprints. Within a project site, users can manipulate diagrams in real time as well as manage the workflow and artifacts of a set of building projects.

The manufacturing and electronics industries have similarly pioneered a number of Web-centric collaborative solutions. For example, CoCreate (www.cocreate.com), a subsidiary of Hewlett Packard, offers a product called OneSpace, which delivers a virtual conference room. In their words, "through the use of shared views, pointers, and annotations, product development partners can concurrently engineer through co/viewing, co/inspecting, and co/modeling." iCadence (www.cadence.com) is a similar product line directed to the collaborative engineering of electronic devices.

Sites such as these are most relevant to the problem of software development over the Internet, because they are chasing the same issues, albeit in a different domain. Thus, these CDEs contain many of the same basic elements that a software CDE requires, such as asset storage, basic mechanisms for collaboration, and multiple stakeholder views.

6.2 Asset Management

As Strubing noted, the communication of knowledge is an important task in the daily use case of developers. For software development teams in particular, a key manifestation of that knowledge is found in the project's code and components, which may be shared across releases or even across teams. Using the Web as a repository for such assets is but one feature of a full-blown CDE, but is already commercially available with vendor-neutral component vendors such as ComponentSource (www.componentsource.com, as shown in Fig. 3) and Flashline (www.flashline.com) as well as platform-specific sites such as IBM's developerWorks (www.ibm.com/developerworks) and Microsoft's MSDN (msdn.microsoft.com), both of which deliver component repositories.

From the perspective of its users, sites such as these essentially push their underlying assets outward via a fairly rigid categorized listing, but with the ability to carry out a general search for specific content. Self-publishing of content is generally not supported directly (because the site owners want to maintain control over the content).

By contrast, variations of the commercial sites, as well as homegrown solutions, are often found deployed within an organization to serve as a general repository of non-public components, parts that are either proprietary or of strategic importance to the company. In these cases, some degree of self-publication is typically possible. However, it should be noted that, without some energy applied to the process, such asset repositories could quickly turn into vast, stinking wastelands of decaying code that no one in the organization wants to touch.

Thus, asset management sites support three primary things: a public or private marketplace for assets (a primary feature of ComponentSource); an infrastructure for asset management (a primary strength of Flashline); and a source for community-contributed assets (a primary feature of MSDN and developerWorks).

In addition to these basic features, it is worth noting that most asset management sites have begun to recognize the need for a deeper user experience surrounding their assets. For example, simple features pioneered (and some patented) by Amazon (www.amazon.com), such as "top 10 lists," targeted, personalized home pages, user feedback, and discussion groups can contribute to this user experience and the creation of a vibrant community of practice surrounding these assets.

COLLABORATIVE DEVELOPMENT ENVIRONMENTS

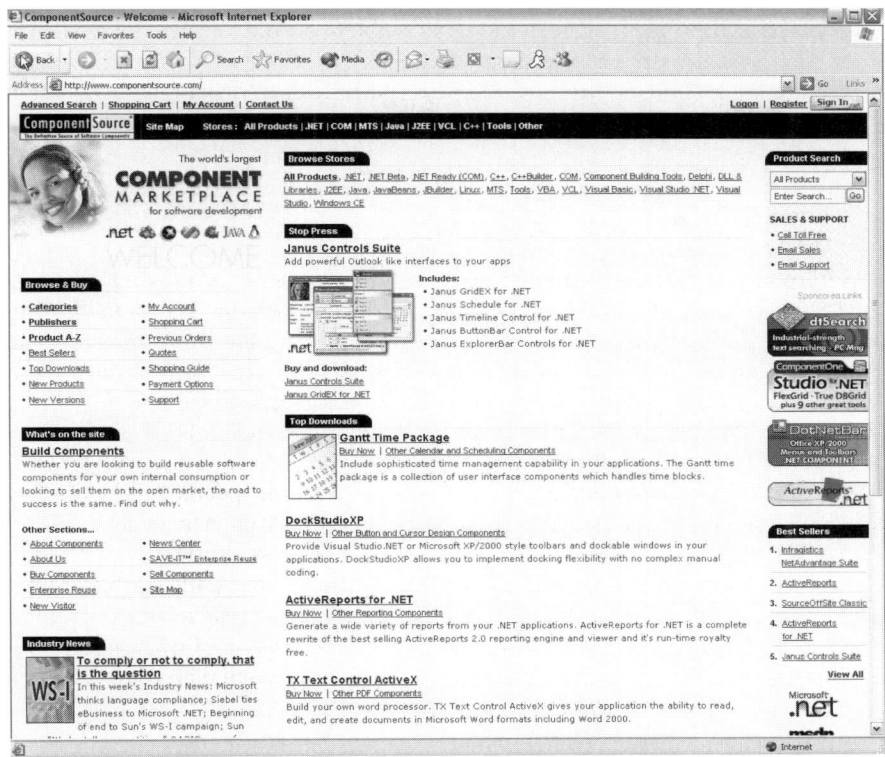

FIG. 3. ComponentSource asset management.

6.3 Information Services

Whereas asset management sites focus on the delivery of tangible code and components, information service sites focus on pure intellectual property and as such offer guidance on using particular platforms or best practices in software engineering. Information services typically come in three flavors: public sites which are either vendor-sponsored (and therefore focus on one specific platform) or vendor-neutral, and private sites, which tend to be internal project- or organization-specific. In the public categories, there are sites sponsored by the major platform vendors, including Microsoft's MSDN and IBM's developerWorks, as well as other vendor-neutral (but technology-specific) sites, such as TheServerSide (www.theserverside.com, shown in Fig. 4), Web Monkey (www.hotwired.lycos.com/webmonkey), and the Rational Developer Network (RDN) (www.Rational.net). For a subscription fee, both the

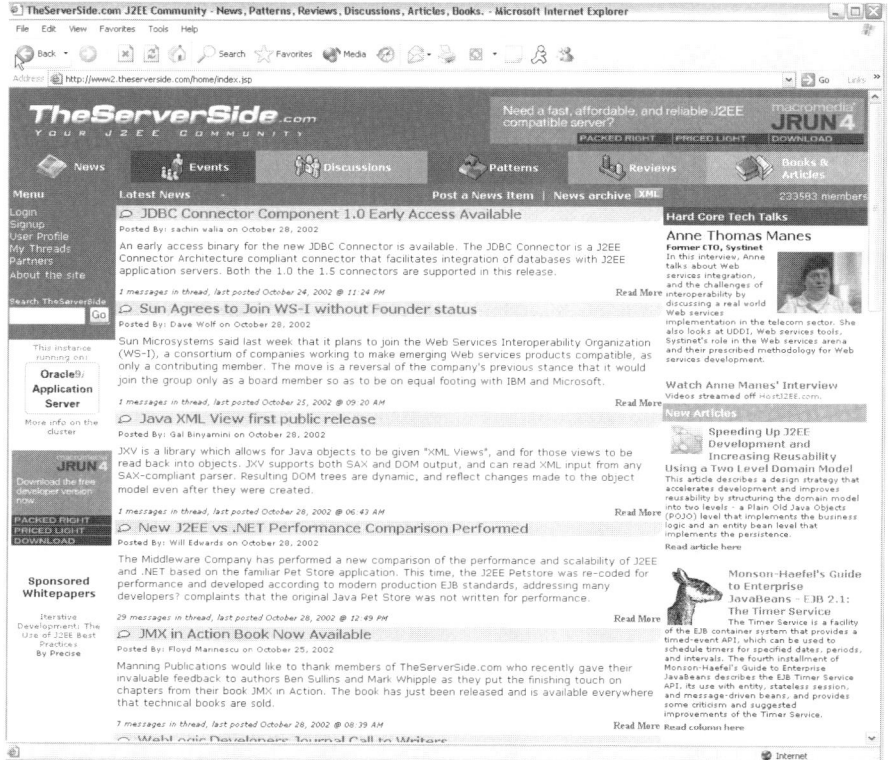

FIG. 4. TheServerSide information services.

IEEE (www.computer.org/publications/dlib) and the ACM (www.acm.org/dl) offer digital libraries, which provide access to journal articles and conference proceedings.

6.4 Infrastructure

As we will discuss shortly, a CDE is not so much a single killer app as it is a coherent collection of one hundred small things. Although not really CDEs in their own right, there exist a genre of technologies that provide critical collaborative infrastructures for full-blown CDEs. Of these, instant messaging (IM) is perhaps the most pervasive mechanism for collaboration. In our day in the life experiment, a large percentage of participants reported using IM in their desktop snapshots. Microsoft's

NetMeeting (www.microsoft.com/windows/NetMeeting) is perhaps the most commonly used infrastructure for peer-to-peer video conferencing. For web conferencing that scales, there are products such as WebEx (www.webex.com) and PlaceWare (www.placeware.com). Although subtly different in their user experience, both services offer Web-centric conferencing with the ability to broadcast documents and slides (for lectures) and to share desktops (offering the moral equivalent of an electronic whiteboard).

Indeed, there really is a spectrum of infrastructure collaborative mechanisms that may be applied to a Web community, each with its own value. Specifically:

- Mailing lists are good for small groups with a common purpose, conversations that wax and wane over time, communities that are just getting started, and newsletters and announcement.
- Message boards are useful for asking and answering questions, encouraging in-depth conversations, managing high-volume conversations, and providing context, history, and a sense of place.
- Chat rooms are good for holding scheduled events, preparing for and debriefing after life events, discussing offline events in real time, and for hanging out (namely, relaxing, flirting, gossiping, and visiting).
- Whiteboards are useful for brainstorming, communicating, and discussing.
- Net meetings are useful for one-on-one discussions.
- WebEx and PlaceWare meetings are useful for group presentations and distributed discussions.

Most of these infrastructure services are quickly becoming commodities, meaning that they are already available from a variety of sources and are ultimately being bundled as a core part of operating systems and main desktop productivity tools, such as Windows XP and Microsoft Office XP.

6.5 Community

Moving closer to complete CDEs are sites that exist to build Web communities. Basically, a Web community is a collection of individuals with a shared interest and a shared identity with that group. A multitude of small things go in to growing and sustaining a vibrant community, but in turn only one or two few small things gone bad can quickly destroy that same community. Usenet newsgroups are perhaps the most elementary Internet communities, but most are generally not satisfying because their signal to noise ratio is extremely low. Lotus Notes (www.lotus.com), developed by Ray Ozzie, has proven effective in building business communities and as such serves as an electronic bulletin board for an organization. Public community services, such as the Ward Cunningham's WikiWeb (www.wikiweb.com) and Yahoo's groups (groups.yahoo.com) both offer virtual meeting spaces with the ability to share artifacts and self-administer a community's members and content.

A very vibrant community of a different sort may be found at Slashdot (www.slashdot.com). Although short on tangible artifacts but long on collaborative content, Slashdot is a Web community in a very real sense, for its participants are typically quite passionate and involved contributors to a multitude of threads of discussion. Slashdot is a good example of a jelled community; small things, such as the personal recognition given to individuals, the high rate of change of content, and the information-rich but easily navigated pages all contribute to Slashdot being a genuinely fun place to hang out.

Groove (www.groove.com) is Ray Ozzie's take on building scalable communities by using peer-to-peer technology. Groove is a for-fee Web-centric service, and is perhaps the best example of a general, domain-independent collaborative site. As Fig. 5 illustrates, the Groove user experience provides a virtual project space with the ability to share assets, conduct discussions, and manage tasks and schedules. Groove

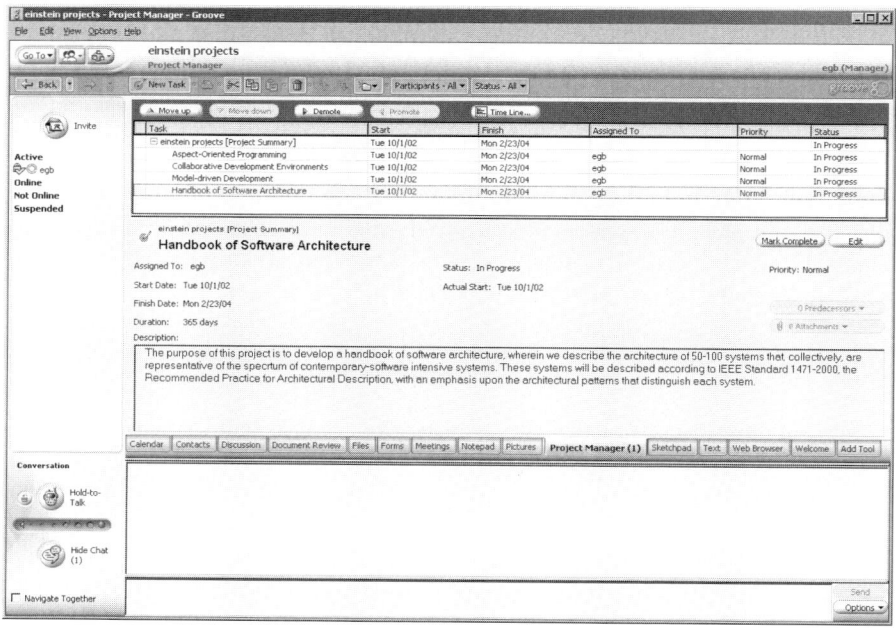

FIG. 5. A Groove workspace.

features include desktop integration with tools such as Microsoft Office, an open framework for integrating other tools, text and voice chat, and dynamic awareness of users and content.

Similar to Groove but using a very different underlying technology is Microsoft's SharePoint (www.microsoft.com/sharepoint). SharePoint comes in two flavors: SharePoint Team services (for ad hoc, small teams) and SharePoint Portal (for enterprise intranets). In Microsoft's words:

- Small or ad hoc workgroups need informal means to work together on group deliverables, share documents, and communicate status with one another. These groups need to share information easily and effortlessly and SharePoint Team Services-based Web sites allow them to do that.
- Large workgroups with structured processes need greater management over their information. They require features like formal publishing processes and the ability to search for and aggregate content from multiple data stores and file formats. For this scenario, SharePoint Portal Server 2001 is recommended.

6.6   Software Development

Currently, there exist a handful of research CDEs directed to the problem of software development, and an even smaller number of commercial sites.

Perhaps the most interesting research CDE is MILOS (Minimally Invasive Long-term Organizational Support), an effort being carried out by the Software Process Support Group at the University of Calgary and the Artificial Intelligence Group at the University of Kaiserslautern [9]. MILOS is an open source effort (under a GNU public license) and focuses primarily on software process workflow automation.

Commercially, DevX (www.devx.com) and collab.net's (www.collab.net) products fit the category of software CDEs, with DevX offering only minimal features and collab.net offering many more creature comforts. DevX is more so an information services site, although it does offer some basic tools for bug tracking.

Collab.net has both a public and a private face. Its public face is SourceForge (sourceforge.net), an open source CDE focused on, not surprisingly, the development of open source software. SourceForge is host to projects ranging from the generally useful MySQL to the more sinister BackOrfice 2000. Its private face is SourceCast (www.collab.net/products/sourcecast), in effect a private label SourceForge (but with a number of other important features, such as greater security, something that is largely a non-issue for open source development).

As Fig. 6 illustrates, the SourceForge user experience is both project- and artifact-centric. A user may enter the site via a specific project or via a personalized home page. Within a project, there are facilities for artifact storage, simple configuration

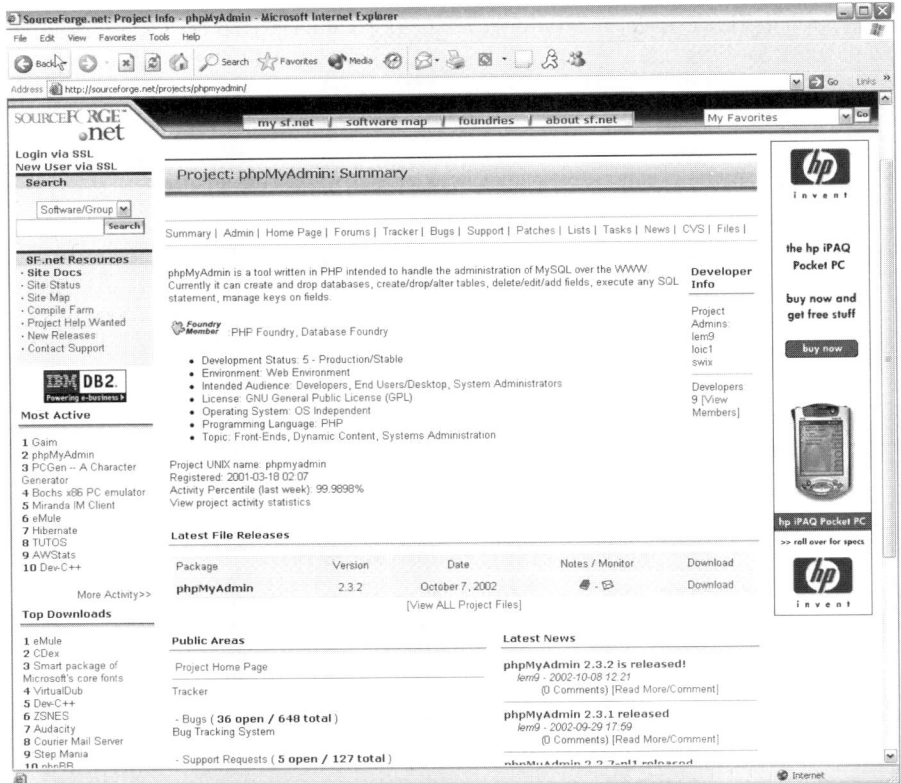

FIG. 6. SourceForge CDE.

management (via the open source CVS), simple bug tracking (also via an open source tool), task management, and discussions. SourceForge offers a number of creature comforts, such as the ability to self-publish, track changes, and manage project membership.

We cannot overemphasize the contribution made by the open source community to the creation of CDEs, recognizing that this is an emergent benefit from the open source movement. Beyond the creation of some genuinely useful software (e.g., Linux and Apache), the community has demonstrated that complex software of scale can be created by large, dispersed teams over the Internet using an interactive, fast-turnaround lifecycle, but with a core team and collaborative mechanisms that permit continuous integration and the creation of stable, intermediate releases.

7. Collaborative Development Environment Features

Our survey suggests that there does not yet exist the quintessential software-specific CDE although the prognosis for such an entity is promising, since this broad spectrum of sites and technologies offer the underlying features necessary for such a CDE. After looking at history, performing our own study of developer practices, and examining the key technical trends in the current state of the practice with collaborative solutions, we are able to synthesize the primary features of a software CDE.

The value of a CDE comes primarily in addressing the points of friction in software development. We observe that this manifests itself in features that support keeping track of project information and resources, manage tools and artifacts responsible for generating those resources, and enable communication among teams.

More specifically, Roger Fournier suggests that the following elements are essential in the creation of a virtual meeting space [10]:

- instant messaging,
- virtual meeting room,
- application sharing,
- centralized information management,
- searching and indexing,
- configuration control of shared artifacts,
- co-browsing,
- electronic document routing and workflow,
- calendaring and scheduling,
- online event notification,
- project resource profiling,
- whiteboards,
- online voting and polling.

We would add to this list the following features:

- tools for both connected and disconnected use,
- threaded discussion forum,
- project dashboards and metrics,
- self-publication of content,
- self-administration of projects,
- multiple levels of information visibility,

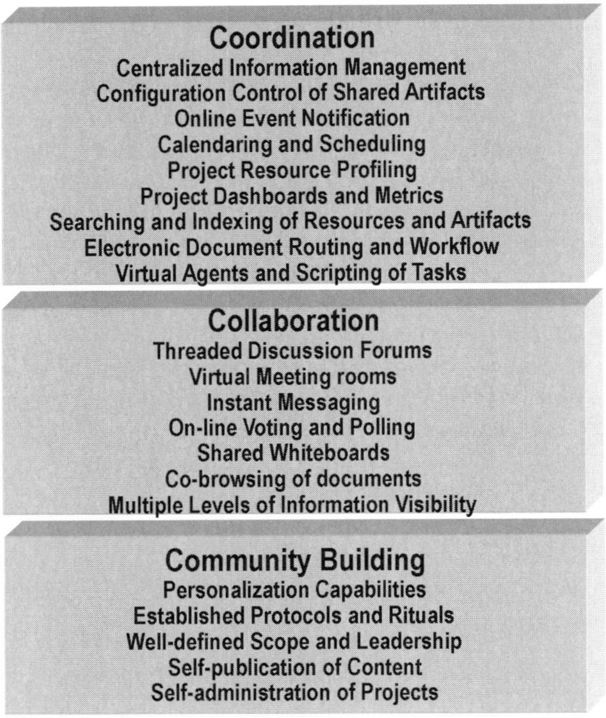

Coordination
Centralized Information Management
Configuration Control of Shared Artifacts
Online Event Notification
Calendaring and Scheduling
Project Resource Profiling
Project Dashboards and Metrics
Searching and Indexing of Resources and Artifacts
Electronic Document Routing and Workflow
Virtual Agents and Scripting of Tasks

Collaboration
Threaded Discussion Forums
Virtual Meeting rooms
Instant Messaging
On-line Voting and Polling
Shared Whiteboards
Co-browsing of documents
Multiple Levels of Information Visibility

Community Building
Personalization Capabilities
Established Protocols and Rituals
Well-defined Scope and Leadership
Self-publication of Content
Self-administration of Projects

FIG. 7. A categorization of CDE features.

- personalization of content,
- virtual agents that can be scripted to manage daily project hygiene and other repetitive tasks.[9]

As illustrated in Fig. 7, we can organize these features into three categories of capabilities necessary for any CDE. Informally known as the "Three Cs", these categories are based on the coordination, collaboration, and community building nature of a CDE.

---

[9]It's not a great leap to imagine anthropomorphized agents such as found at www.annanova.com serving as extended team members. Such virtual agents could be tasked with regular tedious administrative activities, such as providing meeting reminders, driving common workflows such as a document review cycle, or nagging developers to assemble components for daily releases.

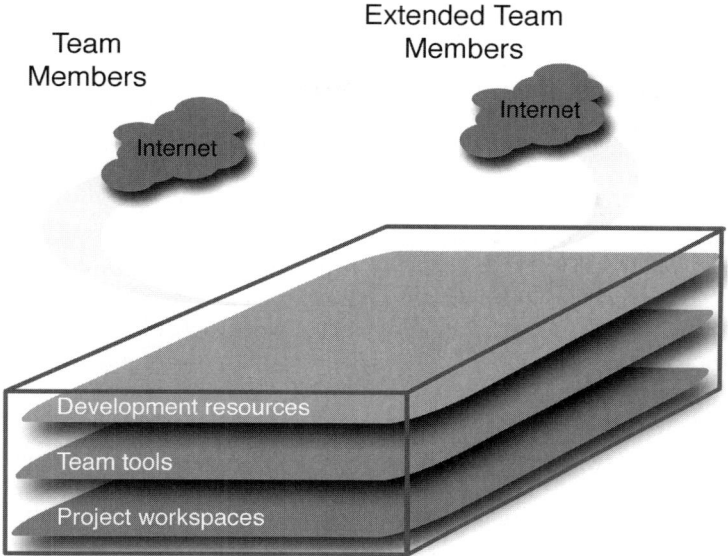

FIG. 8. Conceptual model of a Collaborative Development Environment. Adapted from a model first drawn by Dan Wedge and Rich Hillebrecht of Rational Software Corporation.

None of these features are, by themselves, particularly complex or difficult to implement.[10] For this reason, we observe that a rich CDE is the emergent creature that rises from a hundred small things, using the Web as the center of the user experience. Collectively, however, this set of capabilities offers significant challenges in the technical integration of these features, and the creation of a satisfying user experience for teams and individuals routinely employing many of these features to complete a shared task. Much of the diversity seen the examples referenced in this paper are a result of different approaches taken toward addressing these challenges.

Conceptually, we may render a software development-specific CDE as shown in Fig. 8. Orbiting the CDE are team members who may or may not be geographically dispersed. The CDE itself is bounded by a secure physical and software boundary that guards the sanctity of the CDE's content and validates users (who likely have different rights that yield different views and permissible operations upon a project's artifacts). The CDE is further decomposed into three layers:

- project workspaces, which provide mechanisms for team management and collaboration,

[10] Except for the hosting of tools and the provision of strong security, both of which are inherently difficult issues.

- team tools, which provide infrastructure support for requirements management, change management/version control, and document management,
- development resources, which provide artifact-specific tools, Web-centric training, asset management, and information services.

There are some important variations upon this model that must be considered for the general case.

First, are tools hosted or non-hosted? If fully hosted, this leads to an ASP (application service provider) model with all of its benefits (ease of tool distribution and administration) as well as its challenges (delivering a meaningful user experience for highly interactive tools such as visual modeling tools). If not fully hosted, the user experience is somewhat complicated because each user's desktop must host the appropriate tools. In practice, our experience is that a mix of hosting and non-hosting is best: host core infrastructure tools, such as change management, that must be used by every stakeholder, and support desktop integration to other, more semantically rich tools.

Second, does the CDE reside in front of or behind an organization's firewall? If the CDE lives behind the organization's firewall and is therefore a captive resource, physical and soft security issues are somewhat simplified, or rather, delegated to the company's existing information technology security policies and mechanisms. If the CDE lives on the open Web, in front of a company's firewall, security issues are more complicated, although little more so than required by any public enterprise site. Indeed, once such security mechanisms are in place, the barriers are mainly emotional, not real.

Third, does the CDE support disconnected use? If its stakeholders are all directly connected to the CDE when working with its content, the management of project state is simplified. However, in practice, developers engage in project work while disconnected: long airplane flights are still a fine place to code, as is a home office. In such cases, the CDE must take into account the synchronization of changes and the cloning of a project's state. Our experience is that the presence of a solid change management system in the CDE's infrastructure can generally deal with the disconnected use case fairly well.

8. The Evolution of Collaborative Development Environments

Given this survey of the current state of the practice in collaborative solutions on the Web, and the complete set of CDE features that may be provided in any solution, we recognize that there are a number of substantial barriers to successful adoption of a CDE. These include technological, emotional, and business barriers.

First, there remain complex technical barriers. Building a highly secure, scalable, high-performance Web-centric system, no matter the problem domain, is still a challenging engineering problem. In fact, many question the whole basis of using a public (and inherently insecure), uncontrolled infrastructure such as the Internet as the basis for many kinds of collaborative tasks involving key pieces of a corporation's intellectual property. Second, there are emotional barriers: leaving a project's key assets on servers out of the immediate control of the team is potentially frightening. Additionally, communities are fragile things, easily ruined by small, meddlesome features; as such, the importance of a simple, friendly, and complete user experience cannot be discounted. Furthermore, the presence of a CDE encourages the sharing of information, and in some larger organizations, that's viewed as a political threat. Third, there are business issues surrounding the nature of a successful business model for a CDE. This includes fundamental issues such as subscription versus pay-per-use versus single fee charging, charging for tools versus charging for services versus charging for information, and loosely-coupled best-of-breed solutions versus tightly-coupled custom developed solutions.

As for the technical issues, the good news is that time is on our side, for the general trend is that mechanisms and best practices for Web-centric development are maturing. Emotional barriers are harder to overcome, although it should be pointed out that, for most modest to large organizations, project assets are already outside the direct control of each team (and instead in the hands of the company's IT department). As for business barriers, we expect that the market place will, over time, center upon the right business models for CDEs.

9. Summary

Effective teamwork is an essential part of every non-trivial software engineering effort. Collaborative capabilities are essential to support these teams, particularly as team sizes get smaller, and team interaction becomes more geographically dispersed. This paper has examined the current features required for a fully functioning CDE by surveying the current state of the practice as represented by a range of different solutions. The paper then synthesized a complete feature list from these examples, and categorized those features into three main types: coordination, collaboration, and community building mechanisms.

However, as we have already stated, no CDE currently supports all of the features we have discussed. Furthermore, few organizations find themselves in a position to readily adopt such a CDE should it be available. Thus, having read this paper many individuals and project managers are left asking what positive steps they can now take to prepare their teams for effective adoption of CDE technology. Simply stated, we believe there are 5 key steps to prepare an organization for successful CDE adoption:

1. Get some good team processes in place for coordination, collaboration, and community building within and across your organization. Document those processes, and understand some of the key inefficiencies, or points of friction, that currently exist.

   - To assist with this you can learn from, and adopt, existing process frameworks such as the Rational Unified Process (RUP), and agree on communication via standard notations for describing artifacts and processes such as the Unified Modeling Language (UML).

2. If you have existing team infrastructure technology, evaluate it against the features described in this paper. If you don't already have that technology, examine what is available and invest in some key areas.

   - A number of products are available offering many essential infrastructure features, e.g., requirements management, visual modeling, test management.

3. Standardize on a common IP approach across the teams and projects.

   - This may involve use of information portals offered by tool vendors, together with locally maintained project specific information repositories.

4. Examine current reuse practices within and across the teams. Look for opportunities to increase collaboration and sharing of IP, and provide practical guidance that facilitates this.

   - Common standards for documentation and discovery of project assets may be helpful. Examine work such as the Reusable Asset Specification (RAS) (www.rational.com/ras) for ideas on how this can practically be achieved.

5. Monitor, optimize, and iterate these 5 steps.

To conclude, we observe that CDEs may be classified in one of several stages of maturity, each of which builds upon the previous stage:

- Stage 1: Support for simple artifact storage.
- Stage 2: Availability of basic mechanisms for collaboration.
- Stage 3: Infrastructure tools for advanced artifact management.

- Stage 4: Creature comforts for team management, advanced mechanisms for collaboration, and availability of artifact-specific tools.
- Stage 5: Asset and information services that encourage a vibrant community of practice.

With regard to the state of the practice in CDEs, the current median is hovering somewhere around Stage 1 and 2, but with point solutions, as our survey indicates, for elements at advanced stages.

Indeed, the proliferation of these point solutions suggests that the prognosis for the future of CDEs is encouraging, since vibrant CDEs are primarily the sound collection of these hundred things. Even if a project's understanding of a problem were perfect, even if things always worked, even if all stakeholders were in agreement, a software development project has inherent friction. As we have examined, the core value of a vibrant CDE is to provide a frictionless surface for the development team, thereby minimizing the many daily irritants of collaboration and letting the team focus on its primary task, namely, the creation of useful software that works.

REFERENCES

[1] Weinberg G., *The Psychology of Computer Programming*, Dorset House Publishing, 1989.
[2] DeMarco T., Lister T., *Peopleware: Productive Projects and Teams*, Dorset House Publishing, 1999.
[3] Constantine L., *Peopleware Papers: Notes on the Human Side of Computing*, Prentice Hall, 2001.
[4] Votta L., "By the way, has anyone studied real programmers yet?", in: *9th International Software Process Workshop, Reston, Virginia*, 1994.
[5] Strubing J., "Designing the working process: What programmers do besides programming", in: *User-Centered Requirements for Software Engineering Environments*, Springer, Berlin, Germany, 1994.
[6] Goldberg A., "Collaborative software engineering", in: *Net Object Days, Erfurt, Germany*, 2000.
[7] Ante S., "Simultaneous software", *BusinessWeek* (August 27, 2001).
[8] Yourdon E., *Death March*, Prentice-Hall, 1997.
[9] Holtz H., Konnecker A., Maurer F., "Task-specific knowledge management in a process centred SEE", in: *Proceedings of the Workshop on Learning Software Organizations, LSO-2001*, Springer, 2001.
[10] Fournier R., *Infoworld* (March 5, 2001).

Tool Support for Experience-Based Software Development Methodologies

SCOTT HENNINGER

Department of Computer Science & Engineering
University of Nebraska–Lincoln
Lincoln, NE 68588-0115
USA

Abstract

Experience-based approaches to software development promise to capture critical knowledge from software projects that can be used as a basis for continuous improvement of software development practices. Putting these ideas into practice in the quickly evolving discipline of software engineering has proven elusive. Techniques and tools are needed that help software practitioners apply past knowledge to current projects while engaging in knowledge creation processes. This paper outlines the experience factory and organizational learning approaches, both of which explore how experience-based approaches to software development can be used to improve software development practices. A software tool is used to investigate how these two approaches can be integrated to create an approach that addresses many issues of knowledge management in the software engineering field.

1. Experience-Based Approaches for Software Engineering	30
2. Experience-Based Knowledge Management	32
2.1. The Experience Factory Approach	33
2.2. The Organizational Learning Approach	34
2.3. The Domain Lifecycle	36
2.4. Stepping Through the Lifecycle	37
3. Tool Support for Experience-Based Approaches	41
3.1. Developing Communities of Practice	42
3.2. Experience-Based Repositories	43
3.3. Continuous Feedback of Development Knowledge	43
4. The BORE Software Experience Base Tool	44
4.1. BORE Terminology	46
4.2. The BORE Approach	48

    4.3. Creating BORE Methodologies 49
    4.4. Project Instantiation 54
    4.5. Project Execution 56
    4.6. Analysis and Review Processes 57
    4.7. Experience Packaging 61
5. Putting BORE into Practice: Some Starting Points 61
    5.1. Roles and Tasks for Implementing the BORE Approach 61
    5.2. Evaluation Contexts for BORE 62
6. Other Related Research 65
    6.1. Software Process Frameworks 66
    6.2. Software Process Modeling 66
    6.3. An Analysis of Process Models and Frameworks 68
    6.4. Design Rationale 68
7. Open Issues and Future Work 69
    7.1. Future Work 70
8. Conclusions 72
    Acknowledgements 73
    References 73

1. Experience-Based Approaches for Software Engineering

The lack of a silver bullet, a single universally applicable problem solving technique for engineering software applications [36], has been the topic of much debate within the software engineering community over the past decade. Meanwhile, an arsenal of techniques have emerged that provide reasonable and sometimes revolutionary support for pieces of the overall process and/or isolated application domains. Techniques as diverse as component and object technologies, formal methods, usability techniques, end user programming environments, database technologies, an exploding array of Web technologies, and many others continue to add to the "tool mastery burden" [36] facing modern software developers.

In spite of a general agreement in the software engineering community that no single tool or technique can cover the needs of a field as diverse as software development has become, most research focuses on isolated techniques, normally involving a "new" programming language, formal model, or design notation. Little attention has been given to understanding the scope and limitations of these point solutions, causing much confusion on what should be used and when. To make matters worse, the diversity of application domains continue to proliferate while the pace of business change rivals or exceeds the pace of technology change. Software is no longer the sole dominion of technical personnel, but reach nearly every aspect of human activity [75]. Software developed for algorithm-intensive scientific applications differ significantly from database-intensive information technology applications, which in turn differ significantly from image processing, real-time systems, word processing, and other types of applications.

Techniques to develop software systems must necessarily mirror the diversity of the types of applications being developed. Recognition of this diversity has led to recent studies of software architectures [136], domain-specific component technologies [37,96], and software process diversity [108], all of which attempt to establish frameworks for understanding the conditions for which specific tools, techniques, or methodologies are best suited for a given problem setting. But these and other efforts must necessarily settle at a high level of abstraction that can be applied across many development contexts. Each organization, and each project within an organization, must refine, specialize and extend these abstract frameworks to suit their specific needs.

An experience-based approach to software development seeks to draw on past experiences as a resource for planning and executing software development efforts [21, 89]. By drawing on experiences, these techniques must necessarily be able to address diverse development needs arising from the many application needs and development approaches available in the modern software developer's toolbox. *The objective of an experience base becomes less one of trying to find a single universally applicable development approach and/or programming language, and more one of understanding the circumstances in which a given technique, tool, methodology, etc., is most appropriate.* Developing this understanding requires an empirical approach, one that carefully collects observations from experience and establishes causal relationships between contextual factors and outcomes.

The knowledge generated within each organization to specialize existing techniques to the point that software products can be developed represents a significant corporate asset. Knowing how the Capability Maturity Model is structured or how Enterprise JavaBeans can be used to create applications is one form of knowledge that is often found in textbooks. But understanding how those techniques can be used to create a payroll application for a specific corporation is a more valuable kind of knowledge that is more localized and consequently cannot be found in textbooks. This knowledge is both created by and used within the specific context of a software development organization.

While frameworks for experience-based approaches have been developed [18, 29,48], little research has been performed on how this knowledge can be captured and systematically employed within an organizational context. Tools and techniques are needed that capture software development experiences and make them available for subsequent development efforts. This paper explores the intersection of two approaches that begin to address these issues, the Experience Factory [15] and Organizational Learning [89] approaches to software development, and demonstrates these concepts through an exploratory prototype that supports the capture and use of project experiences.

2. Experience-Based Knowledge Management

An experience-based approach to software development involves using an organization's accumulated knowledge of the development process and application domains as the basis for planning, design, and implementation. While the ultimate goal may be to create automatic programming tools [130], coalescing and analyzing the necessary knowledge to achieve this goal is a difficult process that can only be accomplished in well-understood domains [10,63,145]. Intermediate methods are needed that can disseminate knowledge as it is created in the organization so people can begin to build a culture based on success, avoid duplicate efforts, and avoid repeating mistakes. These techniques provide information relevant to local development practices that "you can't learn in school" [145], such as custom languages, organization and project-specific programming conventions, policies and guidelines concerning tool usage, individuals with expertise in specific areas, and many others.

Figure 1 depicts the experience-based knowledge lifecycle as one of using software development knowledge to create new products. Knowledge can come in many forms, including guidelines, standards, experience packages, pattern languages, manuals, software development and domain ontologies, and other forms of knowledge. During product creation, new knowledge is created to meet development needs that are unique to the project [118]. This new knowledge can be synthesized and packaged in an analysis phase to create new knowledge resources. The newly formed knowledge is then used as the basis for new product development efforts.

Within product creation lies another critically important cycle, in which existing knowledge is applied and extended to create new products. Building on past experiences is a software development step missed by most development methodologies, and in practice is normally accomplished by "reusing" experienced personnel on new development efforts. But because every project is unique, past experiences can only be used as a resource, a guide that helps ensure improvement while avoiding known pitfalls. While some experiences, design artifacts, planning modules, etc., can be reused, each project has unique characteristics and requirements that extend the available store of knowledge. The result is a product creation knowledge spiral [118] (see the Product Creation step in Fig. 1) in which new ideas are built on existing knowledge, made explicit so it can be communicated to others (see the Analysis step in Fig. 1), then routinized to become part of everyday practices that serve as

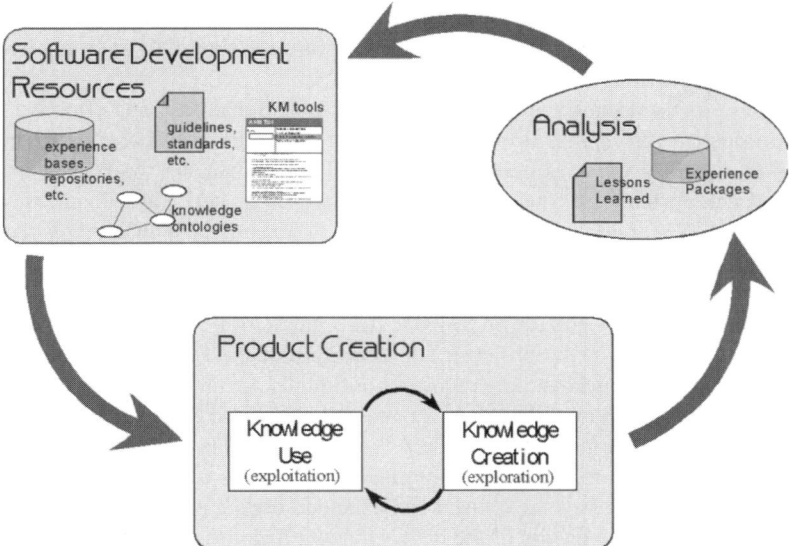

FIG. 1. The experience-based knowledge lifecycle.

the basis for future knowledge creation [118] (Software Development Resources in Fig. 1).

The exploration of how existing knowledge is brought to bear on a problem and used to create new knowledge [110] during product development has yet to be pursued in any kind of scale, particularly in the context of software engineering. The experience factory and organizational learning paradigms promise to address many of these issues. Integrating the ideas embedded in these approaches seems a worthwhile endeavor that is explored in the following sections.

2.1 The Experience Factory Approach

The Experience Factory is a framework that explicitly addresses validating processes and technologies in the context in which they are used [16,20]. This approach divides software development effort among organizations with separate responsibilities of developing projects and capturing experience. The Experience Factory unit is responsible for developing, updating and providing reusable experiences that can be utilized by product development teams. Experience artifacts can be generated either through requests by the product development units or through independent analysis of existing projects [15]. This approach addresses a widely held tenet in software reuse that a separate reusability unit is necessary for successful large-scale reuse efforts [72] and supports a kind of reflection-in-action [134] that can lead to organizational learning and improvements [4,89].

The main focus of the Experience Factory, to "make reuse easy and effective" [15] is accomplished through an infrastructure to produce, store, and reuse experience. It uses the Quality Improvement Paradigm (QIP), which consists of six steps and two feedback cycles [16]. The steps, performed within projects, are (1) characterize project goals, (2) set goals, (3) choose a process, (4) execute, (5) analyze results, and (6) package the results of analysis. The two feedback cycles are a project feedback cycle (feedback provided during the execution phase of the project) and an organizational feedback cycle (feedback provided to the organization during project execution and at the completion of the project). The definition of the QIP implies that organizational and product improvement requires continually accumulating knowledge and storing that knowledge in a form that can be easily accessed, used, and modified.

Note the close relationship between Fig. 1 and the QIP. The software development resources, captured from previous development efforts, are used to characterize and set project goals. Processes are chosen and executed during project creation. During and after execution, the results of the development effort are analyzed and packaged as new resources that can be utilized by subsequent development efforts. The two QIP feedback loops are represented in Fig. 1 by the outside cycle at the organizational level and the project level feedback in the product creation phase.

The Experience Factory is designed to support the entire process of knowledge management, including accumulating experience from the project organization, evaluating those experiences, repairing faults, and extracting items that need to be stored. But current tools to support the Experience Factory have focused almost exclusively on repository technology and experience packaging [4,18,21,49,117]. Although it is recognized that a high level of intuition is required for the analysis phase, making it extremely difficult to automate [5], analysis tools have received some attention, particularly in terms of lessons learned repositories [3,5]. Some work has also been done on tools for measuring the effectiveness of repositories [56] and using user feedback to calculate the perceived usefulness of knowledge assets [6]. But little work to date has concentrated on tools to support the (re)use of experiences and develop methodologies that explicitly integrate prior experiences and lessons learned into the development process.

2.2 The Organizational Learning Approach

The organizational learning approach to software development [89] captures project-related information during the creation of individual software products. Similar to the experience factory concept, it is designed to capture and disseminate emerging knowledge as it is created in the organization [79]. Subsequent projects can then use this information by searching for issues and problems in a repository of project experiences. The repository contains significant problems addressed in a project along with the solution and method of solution used by the project. Projects with similar characteristics can be retrieved and assessed for applicability to the problem at hand. The case-based structure of the repository can not only point to reusable solutions and code, but also suggest how novel problems can be approached by adapting similar problems, warn of possible problems with solution methods, and help designers understand the boundaries of a problem. These principles have been demonstrated through an exploratory prototype, named BORE (Building an Organizational Repository of Experiences) [83].

The experience factory and organizational learning approaches reverse the traditional methodological tendency for software development. Instead of looking at the problem from the solution perspective, the methodology itself, the experience factory facilitates viewing the problem from the perspective of the application domain [149]. Accomplishing this reversal of perspective may be a proper and more accurate way to view software development [149], but the resulting diversity of development methodologies and processes to meet diverse application needs creates another problem, one of understanding what tool, technique, methodology, and etc, are most applicable to a given application domain and its associated development needs [89]. These issues are addressed in Section 4.

Initial pilot projects using BORE addressed some of these issues [89], but feedback revealed that the approach lacked specific system support for process use and improvement. Pilot projects conducted with the tool revealed that people needed more guidance on what information should be captured and when the repository should be consulted. *In other words, having a repository and a search engine provided inadequate support for the overall approach of capturing, packaging, and disseminating experiential knowledge.* More recent activities, reported here, have begun to couple software process support with the repository. This has demonstrated promise to provide necessary guidance while ensuring that the repository is used as a significant resource in the development process. In addition, adopting an experience factory approach guides repository evolution to ensure that high quality, broadly applicable, processes are put in place and refined through use.

To accomplish these goals, the Experience Factory framework needed to be extended to show how tool support factored into the experience-based knowledge lifecycle. This has lead to a specific instance of tool support that was formalized through the "domain lifecycle" framework [77], a model of how domain knowledge evolves and is used in the software development process.

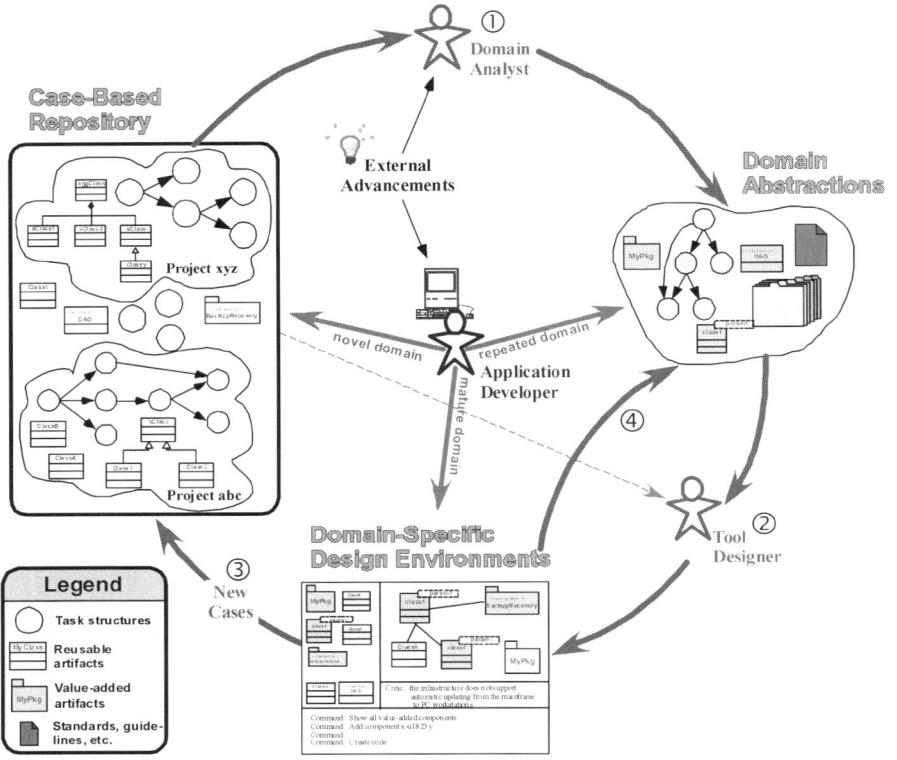

FIG. 2. The domain lifecycle as an instance of an Experience Factory.

2.3 The Domain Lifecycle

The domain lifecycle[1] (shown in Fig. 2) is a representation of two simultaneous phenomena; how knowledge evolves in an experience-based environment (the outside circle), and a model of the level of support software developers have at their disposal during the development process (inside of circle). It depicts domain analysis and the design of development tools as key experience factory concepts that con-

---

[1] The term "domain" is an overused word with multiple meanings in different contexts. In this paper, we will mainly focus on the domain of software processes (which also can, unfortunately, also have broad interpretations). Although our method is capable of maintaining other types of domain knowledge from application domain knowledge, to abstract solutions such as software design patterns [87] to specific techniques, such as the construction of Oracle configuration files [91].

tribute to the evolution of knowledge, while providing essential tools for the software developer.

The progression of knowledge in Fig. 2 proceeds clockwise (see red arrows), where knowledge begins as cases, individual pieces of highly contextualized knowledge that have little use beyond their specific setting (development tools, languages, operating systems, application domains, etc.). This is normally the project or development effort for which they were specifically created. As the situations represented in case-based knowledge recur, or are seen as key information that may be useful in other contexts, domain analysts (a specific experience factory role) perform similarity-difference analysis methods [138,139] and other domain analysis techniques designed to systematically identify objects and relationships for a class of systems [10,116,125,128]. Other techniques, such as pattern analysis [68,152], can be used to create "domain abstractions" in the form of standards, guidelines, knowledge ontologies, value-added or parameterized code pieces and other forms of knowledge. These techniques are as difficult and time consuming as software development efforts themselves, further strengthening the argument that a separate organization for this kind of analysis is crucial to the success of a software experience factory [15].

The last step of this incremental knowledge formalization process [137] is to embed the knowledge in domain-specific design environments. These environments will have limited use as a general development method, but will have high levels of reusability and utility within the domain they are designed for [63,149]. Object-oriented frameworks, although lacking the knowledge component of a design environment, are one way to develop a domain-specific development environment. Using a design environment to construct a software system will involve extending the environment's framework, creating new cases and the cycle repeats itself.

The model of developer support (blue arrows in Fig. 2) moves in the opposite direction. Development efforts start with the design environment, choosing options and receiving a partial solution to their problem. When design environment components meeting their needs are not available, they turn to domain abstractions such as guidelines to support the development of new components that may become part of the design environment once completed. If no domain abstraction exists for the problem domain, project personnel can search the case-based repository for similar components that can be used as-is, or specialized to meet their needs. Using programming languages to solve the problem is the last resort, in a similar manner that hardware designers resorting to expensive VLSI designs only when absolutely necessary.

2.4 Stepping Through the Lifecycle

Suppose a traditional IT organization begins to move towards a client-server platform. Individual projects were beginning to develop their own backup and recovery schemes, a process that had been automatic and standardized in the mainframe environment [89]. The domain analyst ① will discover this, through either requests from the development organization or an analysis of system characteristics [15]. The domain analyst evaluates these systems, begins to create a core set of best practices, and catalogs the variations between the different development contexts and the backup and recovery requirements these systems need [139]. As shown in Fig. 2, this can be characterized in a variety of ways, from documents to value added code segments (interfaces, parameterized classes, etc.), knowledge ontologies, and etc.

This knowledge, if sufficient cost–benefit ratios exist [14,107], is formulated into reusable tools, frameworks, or other reusable artifacts that can be reused, extended, and instantiated by a tool designer ② in domain-specific tools. In our example, a framework for backup and recovery, in terms of a framework, an interface, a subsystem, or parameterized classes, would be created and placed in a Domain-Specific Design Environment [58,59,63]. The knowledge embedded in this design environment, which may include hypertext-based references [8] to domain abstractions, code artifacts, and etc., would still be specific to that knowledge domain (backup and recovery, in this example), and of little use to other domains.

Suppose a new project needs a backup and recovery module. The development team begins with the design environment, choosing options that fit their specific backup and recovery needs. Although the domain-oriented tools can provide substantial coverage of the domain, they will not cover entire project domains. The rest of the project artifacts needed to complete the project would be created by the project team, creating situation-specific cases ③, or by the Experience Factory, which creates new reusable artifacts ④ and design environment (tool) extensions ② to meet the project's needs. I.e., even with the creation of knowledge environments, knowledge creation is still an essential part of software development [151], and each project *will* extend the case-based repository in some way to fill in what the environment lacks (see the Product Creation sub-cycle in Fig. 1).

Although knowledge is accumulated in specific domains, the experience factory and organizational learning paradigms assert that over time this knowledge will enhance the coverage of problem and solution domains [20,84], especially if the organization builds a fairly homogeneous product line, which is true of most organizations. Long-term empirical results provide evidences that these assertions hold [17,19,67]. Development environments with heterogeneous products will require mechanisms to differentiate between the separate application types and provide process models and information that are appropriate to the type of project (see Section 4.4.1). In addition the knowledge will be continuously refined to meet the needs of the organization and become increasingly accurate with respect to business and software development needs [81] while evolving with changing business practices and technology.

2.4.1 Case-Based Decision Support Tools

Case-based repository support collects experiences from individual projects, tool experiences, and other artifacts generated to support the development infrastructure of the organization. Project experiences and design artifacts are captured during the development process and collected in the repository as project-specific cases. The fact that knowledge in software development settings is both dynamic and situation-specific [48,83,88,143] indicates that a case-based approach is a good match in this setting [83,143]. A case is a "contextualized piece of knowledge representing an experience" [102], making case-based decision support an excellent choice to represent experience-based software engineering methodologies, lessons learned, successful, and failed techniques. Case-based decision support technology [102,101, 122], a branch of case-based reasoning that focuses more on the collection and retrieval of cases than on automated reasoning techniques [102], can be utilized for similarity matching of attributes for providing a basis for understanding the context in which specific methods will work.

The case-based reasoning cycle [1] naturally incorporates building on past experiences in a continuous learning process. The cycle advocates cases first being retrieved from a case base, which ensures knowledge use as shown in Fig. 1. The best choice is then chosen and revised or otherwise adapted to the current problem setting. Then the newly adapted case is stored to accumulate the new experiences gained.

2.4.2 Domain Abstractions and Domain Analysis

One problem with a case-based approach to software development is that cases tend to represent isolated problems that need to be adapted from one set of specifics to another. Domain analysis methods are needed that synthesize similar cases into knowledge that is applicable to a class of problems. This is precisely where organizational *learning* comes in. Most methods advocate creating a formal model of the domain [126], making domain analysis and software reuse most useful for established domains with well-known parameters [27,127,140]. But in the fast-paced world of technological advances that characterizes the computer industry, well-established domains are an increasingly rare commodity. Domain analysis methods are needed that accommodate the intrinsic forces of change stemming from the difficulty of creating well-designed systems to begin with, as well as meeting the needs of a dynamic marketplace that reflect changing and evolving user needs [44].

A key issue for domain analysis is to find commonalties and differences among systems to facilitate reusing software and other design artifacts [138,139]. From this perspective, domain analysis is a process of identifying commonly occurring patterns across a number of development efforts. The "domain" does not necessarily need to be a family of applications or a formal model, but a set of problems within applications with recurring activities and/or work products [89]. As patterns emerge, top-down domain analysis methods can be used to formalize the patterns, facilitating domain evolution from the identification of isolated patterns to formally defined domain knowledge. Identifying established patterns of system artifacts reduces the risk of costly domain analysis efforts by ensuring that the cost of analysis can be amortized over many uses.

In general, domain abstractions are domain-specific models of design problems, including domain models, design guidelines, value-added reusable artifacts, domain-specific handbooks, process models, design checklists, analysis similarities and differences between systems, formal notations or ontologies, and other forms of knowledge. It is precisely this kind of support for domain analysis that is necessary to provide "the reference assistance other types of engineers have benefited from for decades" [44, p. 5].

2.4.3 Support for Domain-Specific Design Environments

Domain-Oriented Design Environments (DODEs) [61,63] integrate a domain-oriented framework with reusable components that can be selected and configured to automatically construct systems or partial systems though the direct manipulation of visual icons representing code components. Tool designers using accumulated knowledge from the domain models, specific cases, and reusable artifacts from the case-based repository create a "seed" for the environments [65], which have mechanisms for evolving the environment to meet new needs [60].

In this paradigm, systems are composed in a work area that is monitored by "critics" [61] that display artifact-centered, domain-specific, intelligent support when sub-optimal design decisions are detected. Although knowledge accumulated in this paradigm is limited to particular domains, these systems can provide a stronger level of support because they concentrate effort on good solutions within a domain, instead of addressing universal, domain-independent methods [149]. Fischer and colleagues have also defined an incremental process of knowledge acquisition [65] where an initial seed is constructed through knowledge acquisition methods, then allowed to grow and evolve as it is used, maintaining the knowledge through "re-seeding" efforts as the knowledge base becomes outdated or unwieldy.

Frameworks are another source of domain-specific design environments that are becoming increasingly popular in systems development [34,96]. In effect, a framework or framework architecture, such as J2EE and .net define the construction kit component of a design environment [63], albeit at a lower level than Fischer's definition of a design environment. Developers use components and component constraints to compose systems by choosing options, using existing classes, and instantiating existing classes in the framework. Although wizards [22] and patterns [40] have been constructed for frameworks, the missing element in this approach is knowledge about which components should be used in a given set of circumstances and other design issues, such as conflicting components and advice on how to instantiate components. Future work in domain-specific design environments will largely take place in the context of framework architectures.

3. Tool Support for Experience-Based Approaches

Tool support for an experience-based approach to software development need to support the knowledge lifecycle shown in Fig. 1. Not only is experience-based repository technology necessary, but methodologies must also be established and practiced that ensure existing knowledge is utilized and refined in a disciplined fashion in the development process. Relationships between activities and appropriate tools, techniques, and knowledge must be established to help guide the development process. Furthermore, establishing these relationships is not a static, one-shot, endeavor. As new technologies emerge, business practices evolve, and social institutions change [100], the techniques used to address these needs will evolve. Experience-based techniques must therefore support the continuous feedback loop shown in Figs. 1 and 2.

The integration of the experience factory and organizational learning approaches show promise for addressing these issues while complementing each other. Currently, tools designed to support experience factory approaches have focused on technology for the experience base [18,29,48,55], leaving important issues unresolved, such as how the packages are acquired, used, and evolved in the context of development efforts. The organizational learning approach has focused on establishing criteria to associate knowledge with specific experiences, but lacks the kind of organizational structure found in the experience factory approach.

Bringing these two approaches together requires a combination of experience feedback techniques and repository technology. While the need to continuously evolve and improve the process is generally recognized, the problem of ensuring knowledge of best practices is used in the context of development efforts has received far less attention. Given this background, our high-level requirements for tools supporting an experience based approach is as follows:

1. An overall methodology and/or a community of practice that incorporates use of the repository in daily development practices.
2. Repository technology capable of representing both general and project-specific knowledge.
3. Means of using experience-based feedback to continuously refine and improve repository contents.

Each of these is explained in detail in the following sections.

3.1 Developing Communities of Practice

Experience reports from organizations and researchers attempting to build experience factory repositories have found that simply having a repository is not enough for success [133]. In the very least, the repository needs to be adequately seeded with a critical mass of information before people will perceive a benefit in using it [65,74,133]. But to create a repository that will grow and evolve with the dynamic needs of the organization requires that people use and are committed to the sustained growth of the repository.

The first requirement is that the repository is used, not just at the beginning (project planning) and end of the project (feedback and/or post mortem) [28,41], but throughout the development process. Work practices need to be designed that incorporate the use of existing knowledge as a normal part of the workflow. The underlying problem is not so much of capturing and storing knowledge, but using existing knowledge as the basis for current activities. Mandating the use of repositories does not solve the problem. This has been demonstrated by software reuse initiatives using various forms of incentive, most of which have failed to produce the desired results, thus demonstrating that good incentive-based solutions are not easy to create [124].

The creation of knowledge, and indeed the process of creating software systems, is a social process [153]. People work together, collaborate, challenge each other's assumptions, and generally set the knowledge creation process in motion. They create networked communities of practice [38] within the organization that disseminate and exploit existing knowledge and work together to create new knowledge when novel circumstances arise. They collaboratively adapt canonical accounts from manuals and other existing resources to novel situations to create new insights and learn. The open source community is one example that has largely used on-line communication mediums to perform work and create communities of practice [131,132].

Tool support for communities of practice must recognize that *use* of the knowledge is equally important to capturing and representing the information. Systems such as Eureka [39], the Designer Assistant [145], and others have shown that periodic review of the repository is critically important to the sustained use of the system. The Designer Assistant [145], an expert system for using a complex software component in telephone switching systems, integrated a review of the knowledge into the design and development review process. I.e., when the software developers reviewed their code, they also reviewed the adequacy and accuracy of the advice they received from the system [145]. Not only did this provide valuable feedback, but the reviews also made people take notice that using the system was valued and a necessary part of development practices at the organization.

3.2 Experience-Based Repositories

Knowledge repositories in fast evolving domains, such as software development, face becoming obsolete almost as quickly as information is captured. Experience based approaches "try to avoid this by enriching the best practice description with experience gained in its application" [117]. To accomplish this requires repository technology capable of representing both knowledge categories and associated experiences.

Relational models have been used to represent attributes of specific packages [18] and object-oriented models have also been developed [119]. These representations allow the definition of types and attribute-value pairs to describe elements of the types. Case-based technology further builds on attribute-value representations by applying similarity matching techniques [143] and a representation-adaptation-capture cycle addressing continuous knowledge acquisition. Note similarities with the general experience based knowledge framework of Fig. 1.

A problem rarely recognized in repository technology and case-based techniques are the passive nature of how they are utilized in the development process. Search is seen as an extra and optional step that is abstracted from the normal workflow and used on a discretionary basis. This is problematic for two reasons: (1) people are not able to articulate their problem in the correct terms because they are unfamiliar with terminology used in the repository [24,25], and (2) people are not always aware of the fact that information exists that may help them, and therefore do not seek assistance from repositories [50,64]. Simply having a repository of experiences and/or lessons learned is insufficient to getting the knowledge to the people that may benefit from it. Mechanisms are needed that trigger or otherwise alert people to knowledge that is available and relevant to the task at hand.

3.3 Continuous Feedback of Development Knowledge

The first step in establishing an experience-based approach is to integrate use of the repository into development practices. Once this is instituted, mechanisms are needed that ensure quality and continuous refinement of development knowledge. Knowledge acquisition cannot be viewed with an expert system mentality, where knowledge is acquired in a process separated from its use and then applied as a complete solution. Instead, knowledge must be acquired in context and in a continuous process [84] that not only keeps repository contents current with changing development needs [89], but also supports diverse development processes [108] that are necessitated by diverse application requirements.

The implication is that while a disciplined process based on past experiences is needed, there must also be a way to deviate from the process in a disciplined manner.

These deviations must not be viewed as exceptional [45] or undesired consequences, but as a normal part of the development process, one that leads to refinements in the experience base, organizational processes, etc. Because software development (and design in general) has so much variance between projects, we need to focus more on the knowledge creation process [66]. One way to look at this is as a process of improvisation, where knowledge is not constructed from a blank sheet of paper, but "involves and partly depends on the exploitation of prior routines and knowledge" [52]. In other words, knowledge creation depends on knowledge use and knowledge use leads to knowledge creation (see Fig. 1). This is particularly critical to experience-based approaches for software development, as both software technology and domain knowledge continues to evolve at a rapid pace.

4. The BORE Software Experience Base Tool

BORE (Building an Organizational Repository of Experiences) is a prototype tool designed to further explore and refine the requirements for tools supporting experience-based approaches. Its purpose has been as a proof-of-concept prototype that is used to articulate organizational learning and experience-based software development techniques. The tool has evolved from exclusively focusing on repository technology [83,80] to using defined software processes as the organizing principle of the technology [85]. It creates a framework for the experience factory by combining a work breakdown structure with repository tools for designing software process methodologies, and repository technology for capturing and applying knowledge artifacts. The BORE tool and methodology extends the experience factory concept through rule-based process tailoring, support for process modeling and enactment, and case-based organizational learning facilities.

The BORE prototype is a Web-enabled application using a three-tiered architecture with Java Swing for the interface, Java for the client application logic and server, and an SQL database back-end.[2] BORE has two main interfaces, shown in Fig. 3. The Task Manager, shown to the left in Fig. 3, displays a hierarchical arrangement of cases that define the tasks in a project's development process. In the figure, a project named "ProjectX Demo" has been chosen from the list of resources in the drop-down menu that displays projects. Each of the nodes in the project hierarchy, which are cases corresponding to project tasks, can be opened to view information about the task. In the window to the right in Fig. 3, the task named "0.10.0 Choose Project Methodology" has been opened. Status and completion of the task is indicated by the colored icon to the left of the task name in the Task Manager.

[2]Interested readers can log into BORE at http://cse-ferg41.unl.edu/bore.html. Click on the production version link and log in as 'guest' with no password.

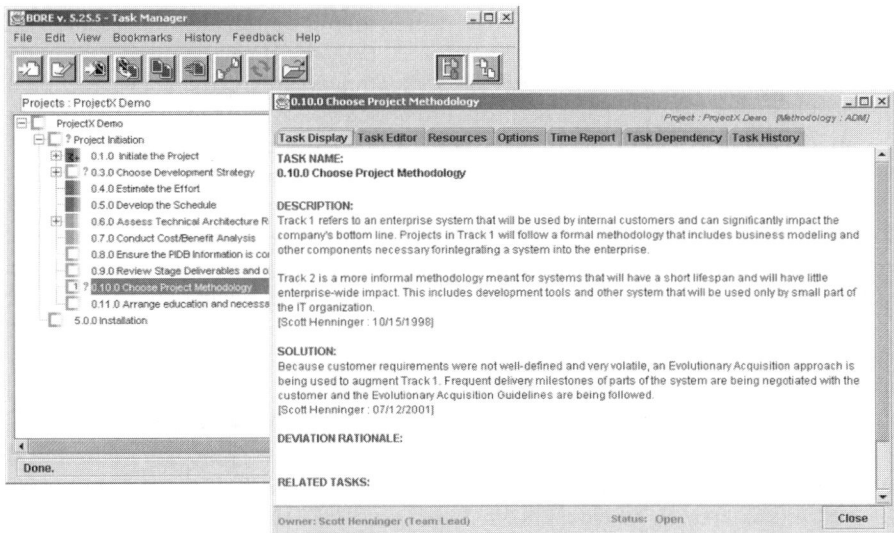

FIG. 3. The BORE Task Manager (left) and a Task Window (right).

BORE is based on a case-based architecture in which cases are used for representing all primary information sources. The primary use of cases is to represent project tasks, such as the one shown in Fig. 3. The description field of the task is normally used to describe the defined process standard while the solution field is used to document project-specific information accumulated while executing the task. The Edit tab is used to edit the task fields and the Resources tab is used to attach project documents to the task. The Options tab, which will be described in detail later, is used to choose process options available to the task. Task status is kept for each task and is displayed as a color-coded icon in the Task Manager (active, resolved, etc.), thus providing a way to get a visual overview of a project's status.

Less important for the purposes of experience-based knowledge management, but equally critical for capturing project and task metrics [32,94], and analyzing project data are the Time Reports, Task Dependency, and Task History tabs. Time Reports keeps track of time spent on a task by category. Task Dependency keep track of any kind of dependency that may exist between tasks, such as task ordering dependencies, and Task History keeps track of all changes made to the task.

These core features represent case-based organizational memory paradigm of BORE [83]. Each case represents a project-specific task that is used to help coordinate and disseminate project experiences. The project hierarchy can be used as a dynamic checklist of project tasks that captures information about projects in an organization-wide repository. A second view of the project can be created through the task dependencies, which are capable of creating Gantt Charts. A bi-directional interface between BORE and Microsoft Project has been created, and BORE has the ability to create comma-delimited files for other project scheduling programs. Effort metrics can be derived from this information that can be used for more accurate project forecasting. These features are designed to make the BORE system an integral part of project management and task enactment, which is necessary to capture the kind of experience-based knowledge necessary to implement an experience factory methodology.

4.1 BORE Terminology

Figure 4 shows a model of the major concepts used in the BORE approach to the experience-based software development. Some of these terms were introduced in the previous section and some will be used in later sections. Terminology can be difficult in this area, as researchers have used terms differently [43,54]. Therefore, the following terms only apply when we discuss BORE concepts.

Case. A case is the atomic unit of information in BORE and is used to represent all types of tasks, software patterns [68], and etc.

Task. This is a generic term for any type of task in the BORE system. In operational terms, a task is the smallest unit of work that can be represented in the system. Sets of related tasks are often referred to as *activities*. It is a subtype of a case. Although most tasks in a project are an instance of a *methodology task*, project team members can create tasks specific to a project. These tasks are tracked through a deviation process, described later (Section 4.6.1). Note that a task is unique to a project (i.e., a project can have more than one task, but a task, having been created by a project, can be part of only one project).

Methodology. A methodology in BORE is a defined or standardized set of tasks that together represent a general way of developing a software system. A methodology is more specific than a "Waterfall" or "Spiral" model in that it specifies specific activities that are required in projects. In BORE, methodologies are used as a template for creating projects. A methodology is composed of one or more methodology tasks.

Methodology Task. A methodology task is a task that is defined in a methodology. When a project is instantiated from a methodology in BORE, methodology

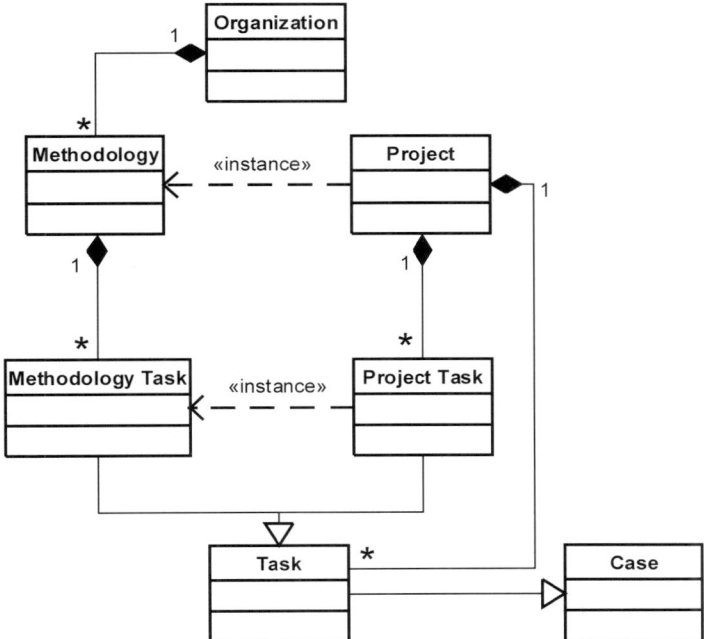

FIG. 4. UML model of BORE concepts.

tasks are copied to the project, creating project tasks. Process engineers create and edit methodology tasks to construct a methodology.

Project. A project in BORE is an instance of a defined methodology. It consists of one or more project tasks. Not all of the methodology's tasks need to be included in the project, but all tasks in the project (unless they are part of a process deviation, as explained in Section 4.6.1) are an instance of a methodology task. Projects will have one or more project tasks and/or methodology tasks.

Project Task. A project task is an instance of a methodology task that belongs to a single project. Project personnel can edit project tasks.

Organization. An organization is any business organization or unit using the BORE system to develop software and/or systems. An organization can define one or more methodology.

4.2 The BORE Approach

Using BORE to manage software development processes and methodologies can be mapped to the QIP experience-based paradigm, as shown in Fig. 5. The figure shows relationships between the steps in the methodology and, where applicable, the six QIP steps described earlier in this paper are shown in the bottom-right of the task bubbles.

To use BORE, the organization first creates a methodology by creating a work breakdown structure of tasks. Rules are also created that define when a task should be assigned to a given project. Rules and tasks define a "methodology" in BORE, which is a standard process of developing software that is defined for a specific organization, whether that organization is a company, a sub-division, or a small working group. BORE supports the representation of different organizations and methodologies within the methodology, so that many organizations can use the same BORE server securely.

Once defined, the methodology is used to create an instance of the methodology for each project using the system. This creates a set of project initiation tasks as defined in the methodology ("characterize" in QIP terminology Fig. 5). Project personnel then execute the tasks and document their progress in the tasks assigned to the project. BORE also allows tasks to be further broken down by associating tailoring options to any of the methodology tasks. Choosing options may assign other work

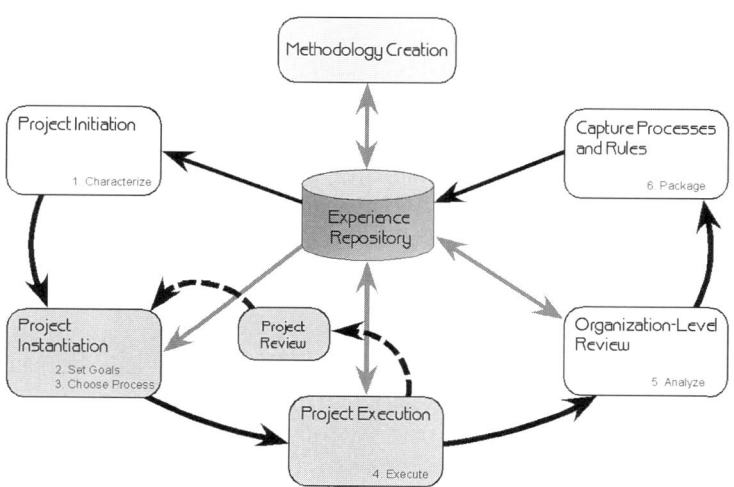

FIG. 5. The BORE experience-based methodology.

breakdown structures to the project, thereby refining the tasks that the project will undertake (Set Goals and Choose Process in QIP terms).

The result is a tailored development process consisting of tasks to be executed by the project team. For example, The Task Manager window of Fig. 3 shows the project initiation tasks that are assigned to a project when it is created from the methodology named "ADM". Once instantiated, the tasks are used to document project-specific issues (Execution in QIP terminology). Project documents and code artifacts, templates for which can be defined in the methodology and copied to projects, are attached to project tasks to act as a repository for document management. The process of choosing tailoring options, executing the assigned tasks, and periodically reviewing the project, defines the project development cycle, or spiral [33].

While executing, project members are creating and modifying project artifacts and further tailoring the development process, often through project reviews (see the Product Creation cycle in Fig. 1 and the Project Review process in Fig. 5). This may entail deviating from the process (see Section 4.6.1) as defined in the methodology, shown by the double arrow from Project Execution to the Experience Repository in Fig. 5. These deviations are knowledge creation points that can be analyzed and potentially added to the repository. This involves an organization-level review (Analysis in the QIP) that can be as lightweight as allowing project members change the process or as heavyweight as appointing task forces to analyze and change the process, which is standard in large and diverse organizations with safety critical applications, such as NASA [114], or Hughes [95]. The tasks are then packaged (see Fig. 5) and placed in the repository with appropriate rules that determine what kinds of projects should use the newly defined tasks (Package in QIP terminology). The methodology is thus modified through the modified experience base, completing the experience-based knowledge lifecycle.

Note that we have purposefully omitted an explicit link from packaging to methodology creation in Fig. 5. This is to show that projects refine the domain through the experience base. Each project therefore draws on the collective definition of the process by reusing knowledge (experience-based knowledge) placed in the repository and structured through defined methodologies. Steps in this methodology are further explained in the following sections.

4.3 Creating BORE Methodologies

Each methodology in BORE is defined by a set of methodology *tasks* in a hierarchical work breakdown structure and methodology *rules* that define when a task should be used. A methodology in BORE can be as simple as a repository of tasks related to a topic or as complex as a development methodology for a software development organization with program-level efforts that must coordinate multiple projects, contractors, and other development efforts. Projects are an instance of a single methodology, which is chosen when a project is created in BORE. All subsequent project tasks will use the tasks and rules defined for that methodology. Allowing multiple methodologies supports scalability and allows organizations to partition development tasks to meet the needs of diverse environments or product lines.

Methodology tasks define the space of possible tasks for projects within a given methodology. Tasks can be as high-level or detailed as desired. The Task Manager in the right-hand window of Fig. 6 shows a set of tasks that define a methodology using a combination of MBASE [31] and RUP (Rational Unified Process) processes. Tasks are defined in a task/subtask relationship represented in a hierarchical work breakdown. The middle window of Fig. 6 shows the Resources Tab, which both allows documents to be attached to tasks and shows all other tasks created from the same methodology task.

The defined process can be tailored to meet project-specific needs through methodology rules, which define a set of conditions under which a project is required to execute a specific task. In other words, the methodology rules choose which methodology tasks a project must follow to conform to the process standard. Therefore, the standard can define a broad set of tasks and the methodology rules determine which of those tasks are applicable to a given project. *The defined methodology is therefore more than a set of tasks or activities.* It is a representation of tasks combined with rules for when the tasks are applicable to specific project types. *In essence, the methodology is a program with data* [120], *not data alone in the form of a document.*

4.3.1 Creating Methodology Tasks

Methodology tasks are created and edited in the Task Manager using the same interface and tools available for editing project hierarchies. The window to the left in Fig. 6 shows the resource menu with 17 defined methodologies, each of which has a separate set of methodology tasks and rules. To add new tasks to the methodology, process engineers create new methodology tasks, place them in the methodology's task/subtask hierarchy (shown in the right-hand window of Fig. 6), and populate them with information about the standard. Templates, guidelines, and etc. of any document type can be attached to methodology tasks as shown in the Attached Documents field of the Resources tab (middle window of Fig. 6). The Related Projects pane displays all instances of this methodology task, which is discussed further in Section 4.4.4.

When a methodology task is assigned to a project, creating a project task, all information in the methodology task is copied to the task in the project, including creating a copy of the Attached Documents in the project's file space on the server.

TOOL SUPPORT FOR EXPERIENCE-BASED SOFTWARE 51

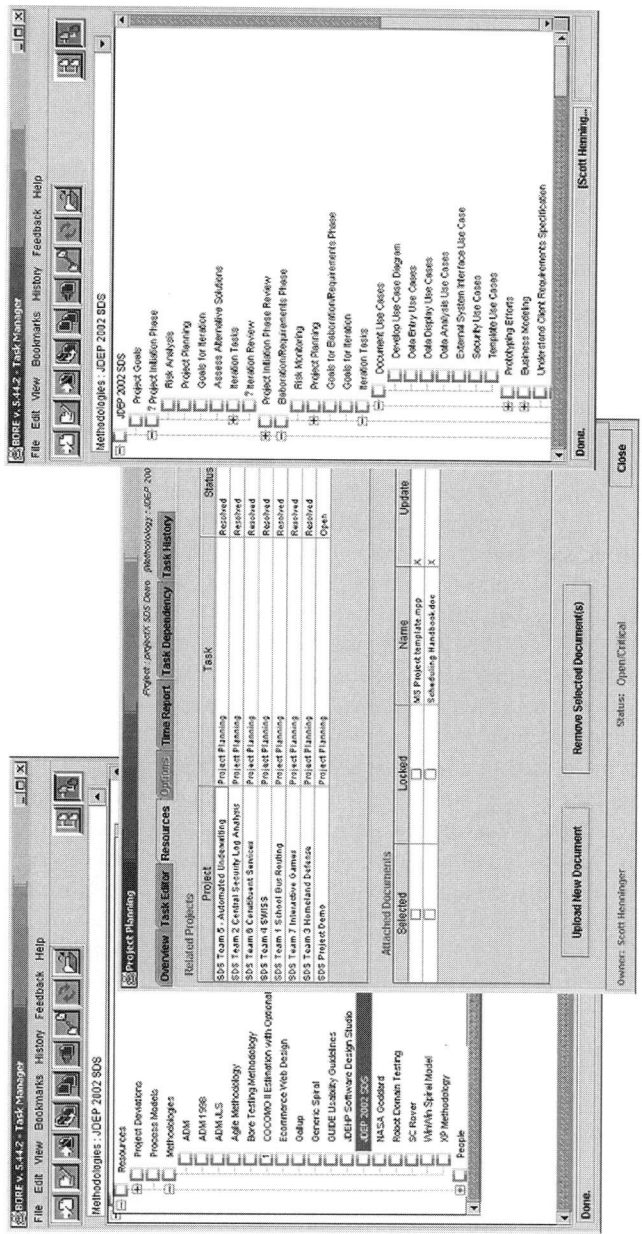

FIG. 6. Editing methodologies and attaching resources and templates.

Project personnel edit the task fields and download the templates in the Attached Documents field. During project enactment, project personnel will fill in the template with project information. The edited documents can then be uploaded to the server so others can view them. Access control is allowed by locking the document. This has been sufficient to allow version management by locking the document for editing and uploading an edited document with a new version number in the name, although more sophisticated change management may be needed in the future.

4.3.2 Editing Methodology Rules

The Rules Manager provides tools for creating and editing methodology rules and associated questions and answers (see Fig. 7). The initial window displays preconditions and actions for a given rule, as shown to the left of Fig. 7. A rule is defined through a set of preconditions, defined by question/answer pairs, and actions, that are fired when all preconditions evaluate to true. For example, following the preconditions of the figure, when the size if the team is medium, the type of project is new software development, the software is critical to mission success, and there is a significant level of hardware/software integration, the rule will fire, causing the actions to be executed. In this instance, rule actions, shown both in the Action(s) pane of the Rules Manager and Edit Actions windows execute to add three tasks to the project. In addition, when choosing options to tailor the project during process enactment (see Fig. 8), questions can be added to and removed from the New Question pane, allowing for the implementation of decision trees. The actions defined in Fig. 7 show that two questions will be added and one question removed from the New Questions stack when the rule's preconditions are met.

Preconditions are edited in a separate window (not shown) that choose the question/answer pairs for the rule (other types of preconditions, such as status change for completion of a task and others are currently under consideration). Actions are edited through the Edit Actions window shown to the right in Fig. 7. Choosing the action, type, and task to be added creates actions that add tasks to, or remove tasks from a project. Other options for the task, such as the initial status and task owner, can also be chosen (small window to the right in Fig. 7). Actions can be designed by choosing the proper Action and Type in the Edit Actions window, defining actions such as adding or removing questions from the New Questions pane, e-mail can be sent, and other actions. The list of actions is executed in the order shown in the Actions field, and can be moved through the arrow buttons.

The rule system is implemented as a simple forward-chaining rule engine that is persistently stored in a relational database. Full backtracking (undoing a fired rule) is supported, allowing people to play what-if scenarios, by choosing different options in the Options pane of a Task Window (see Fig. 8) to observe the impact of selecting different options.

TOOL SUPPORT FOR EXPERIENCE-BASED SOFTWARE

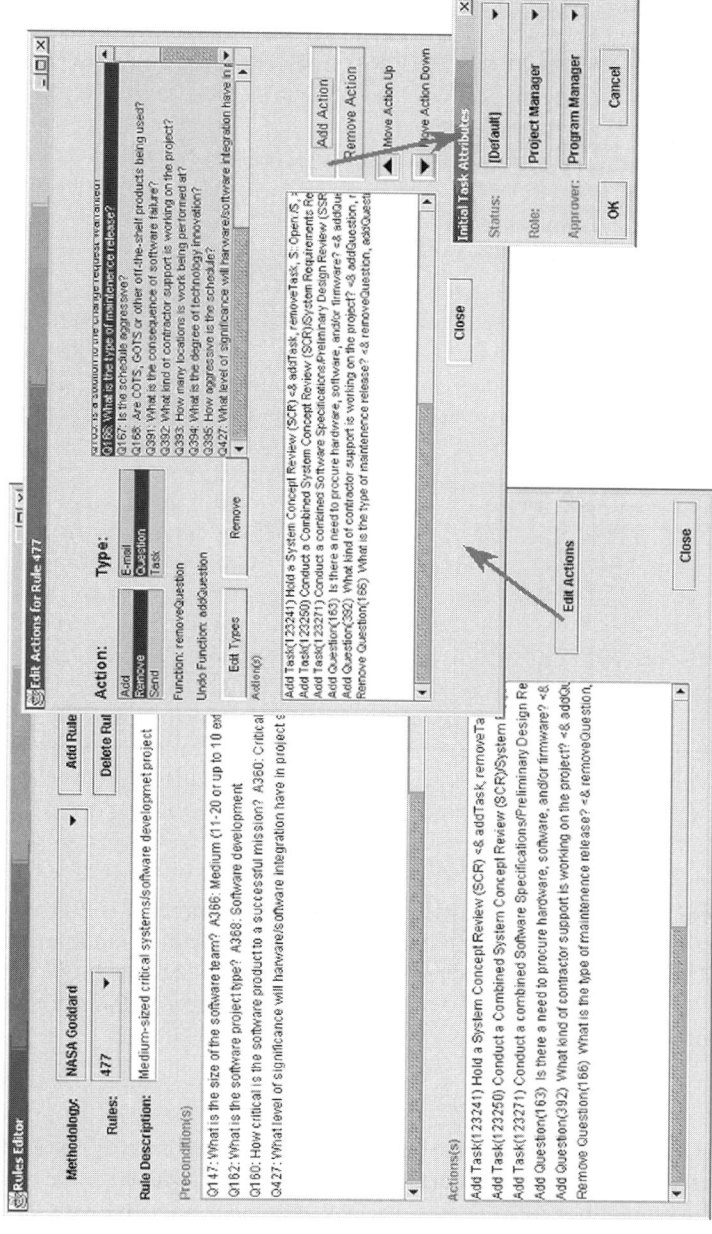

FIG. 7. Editing rules with the Rules Manager.

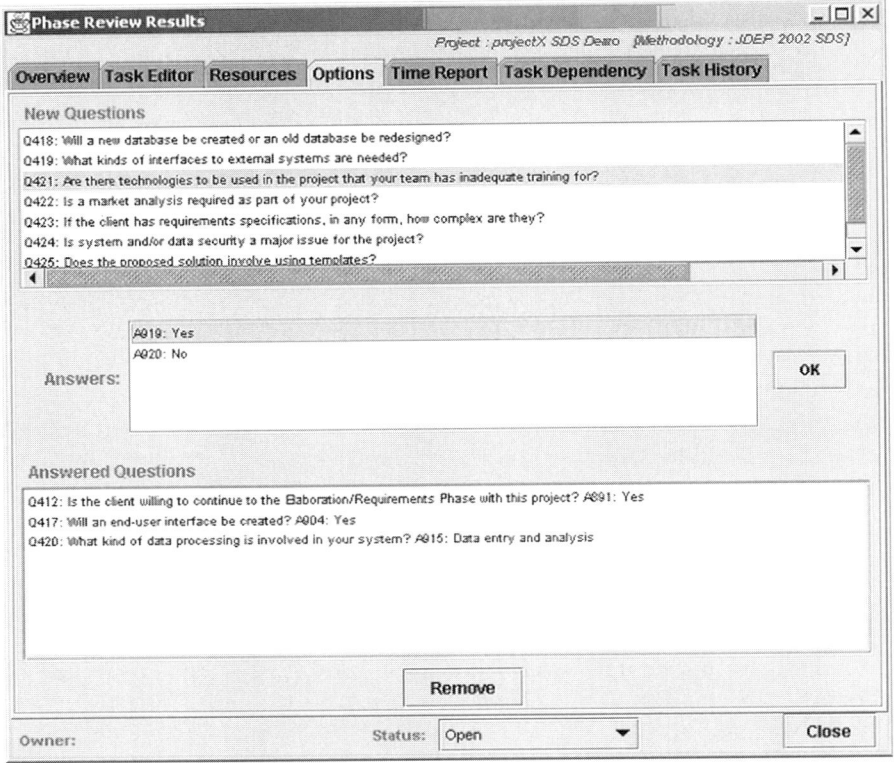

FIG. 8. The Options tab.

4.4 Project Instantiation

When a project is created in BORE, an instance of the process is created. This involves creating a set of project initiation tasks that are specified in the methodology's "rule 0" and copying the associated methodology tasks into the project hierarchy. From these initial tasks and the options designed into tasks by the methodology designer, a tailored project is created.

4.4.1 Tailoring the Process

In most BORE methodologies, the initial tasks represent a first pass to define project tasks than can be further broken down through options that can be attached to any of the methodology tasks. Tasks that have options associated with them are denoted by the "?" in the icon next to the task label in the Task Manager (see the project hierarchy in Figs. 3 or 7). The options are found by opening the Options tab (Fig. 8) and are used to tailor the process to the project's unique characteristics, usually through rules that break down the task into constituent sets of subtasks.

For example, the Software Design Studio methodology defines a number of tailoring options for the elaboration phase that indicate key areas where the project may want to look for Use Cases (as shown in Fig. 8). Three questions have been answered and more remain in the New Questions stack. When a question is chosen, possible answers are displayed in the Answers field in the middle of the window. Selecting the answer moves the question/answer pair to the Answered Questions field. Choosing a different answer causes BORE to backtrack the actions previously executed and executing the actions required by any rules fired by the new question/answer pair.

A key feature of this tailoring process is the flexibility offered by allowing options to be associated with any methodology task. This allows processes to be defined that iteratively expand each part of the project's process as they gain the knowledge necessary to address process issues [120]. Initial projects can define tasks with options that add new tasks that can in turn have options to further refine the process and provide resources for the project. In this way, the project tailors the overall process to its needs when it is able to address the issues involved. In addition, varying levels of detail can be supported by defining options as deeply in the tree of methodology tasks as desired.

4.4.2 The Rule-Based System

When an option is chosen, the rule engine is invoked to find satisfied rules. When all preconditions for a rule evaluate to true, the rule "fires," causing the rule's actions to be executed. The actions associated with process tailoring take one of three main forms: (1) A question can be removed from the question stack (displayed in the New Questions field of the Options tab of a task), (2) a question can be added to the question stack, and (3) a task or set thereof is added to the project in the proper places in the hierarchy as defined by the process domain. Other actions, such as adding information to a database, automatically alerting people of events through e-mail, and other types of actions as required by corporate standards can also be designed into a rule.

Users may exit the Options tab at any point in the session. The state of the project and its tasks will be stored in the database and restored when the user opens the Options tab for that task. BORE maintains a separate rule space for each project so that multiple projects can choose individual options.

4.4.3 Knowledge Access vs. Knowledge Delivery

Note that by creating a tailored instance of the development methodology for each project, we have changed the paradigm of following a methodology from one of manual search and determining whether process conformance is being achieved (knowledge access) to one of knowledge delivery. Through the tailoring rules, BORE has *assigned* activities to the project in an agent-like fashion that assures conformance. The software developer or manager does not have to fumble through dozens or three-ring binders or Web pages to find the information they need to perform the activity. It is *delivered* to the user in the activity.

4.4.4 Delivering Development Resources

BORE provides not just process support, but also templates and cross-references to task instances in other projects. Because each project is an instance of the methodology, it is easy to cross-reference a project's task to all other project instances of the associated methodology task. The Related Projects window of the task Resources tab, shown in Fig. 6, displays a list of all cross referenced projects using that task. Double-clicking on the project will display that project in the Task Manager hierarchy and double-clicking on the task name will open a task window for the specific project.

There is thus a level of project transparency, constrained by some access control permissions not discussed here, which allows projects within an organization to view how others have addressed the task, how long it has taken to finish the task, and view any artifacts associated with the task. This is a direct conduit to the reuse of software development artifacts that can be used to build upon and improve known best practices.

4.5 Project Execution

As project personnel perform the work specified in the tasks, work is documented using features in the Task window. This includes editing the task (in the solution field, shown in the task window of Fig. 3) or attaching work products to the task. Although many formalisms have been created for software process automation [12, 69,142], this has not been the focus of our work. Instead, we have created tools that focus on supporting parts of the process requiring human interpretation and effort by helping managers and developers make informed decisions.

Editing the Solution field of the Task Window (see Fig. 3) is intended as a quick and easy way to annotate a task, although any amount of documentation is allowed. This field is represented HTML, as are the other Overview fields, so that multimedia objects can be embedded in the text. A second method of project documentation is found in the Attached Documents pane of the Resources tab (see middle window in Fig. 6), which allows documents of any type to be attached to a task. Using the browser's HTTP facilities, the document can then be downloaded and opened with a simple mouse click, as discussed in Section 4.3.1.

BORE also supports assigning project personnel to tasks. When methodology rules are created, roles can be assigned to tasks when they are instantiated in a project, as shown in the Initial Task Attributes window in the lower right of Fig. 7. Each methodology defines a set of roles and projects can assign one or more persons to the role. Tasks can thus be assigned to specific project personnel assigned to the role for execution. The task owner can also be manually set for each task. A privilege manager allows different methodologies to define privileges for the roles in that domain. All of these features combine to allow organizations to define which personnel can have access to sensitive actions, such as deleting tasks in projects a person does not belong to, or editing the methodology tasks and rules.

4.6 Analysis and Review Processes

Once options have been chosen, and rules fired to assign the set of defined tasks, the project tasks should be reviewed for accuracy. Analysis and review of process tasks can occur at two distinct levels. The first is at the project level (see Fig. 5), where it is anticipated that each project has unique characteristics and will therefore need to deviate from the process in some way. Note that the assumption here is that more detailed process definitions are possible with this technology than with traditional, high-level, process definitions. Instead of stopping at stating that a requirements definition document is required, this approach allows organizations to define best practices for eliciting and defining requirements, potentially for different kinds of user populations. For example, the organizational standard and code for a Web-based login screen could be attached to a low-level user interface task. With this level of detail, one that can truly support software developers and managers in their daily activities, tool support for finding appropriate tasks becomes crucial with this level of detail. Therefore, the unique characteristics of each project will necessitate extensions to the process. Note that this approach is a combination of knowledge management and process support.

4.6.1 Project-Level Deviations

At the project level, process deviations are used to allow projects to define new tasks for their project and remove tasks that are deemed inappropriate. As shown in left-hand window of Fig. 9, the project has deleted the task "1.3 COTS/GOTS Evaluation..." and its subtasks, shown by the status box with a red box inside of

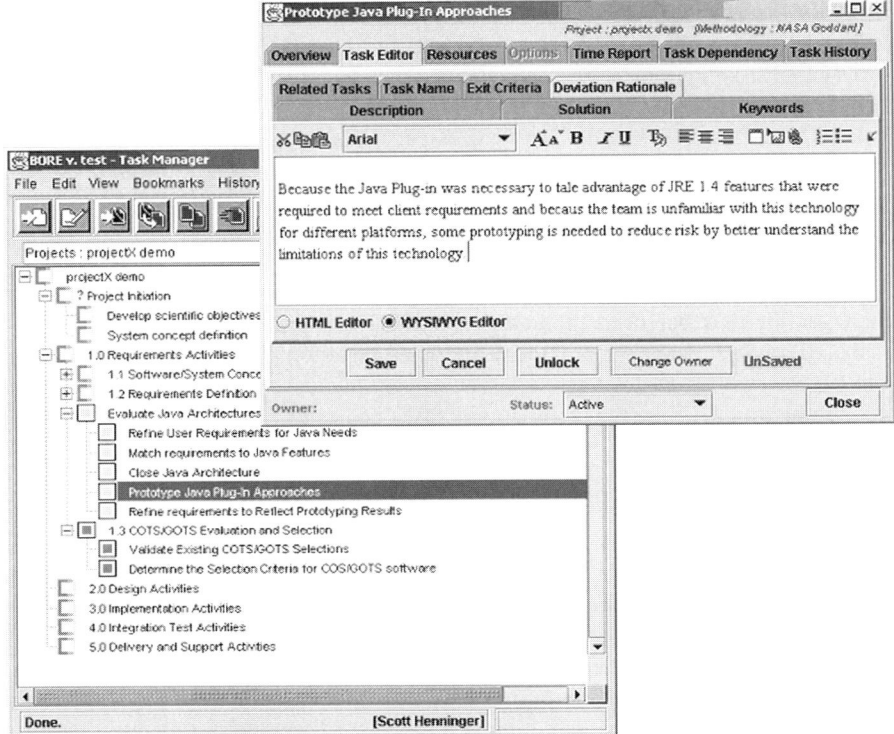

FIG. 9. Project-level Deviation Rationale.

it. In addition, a new task for evaluating Java Architectures had been added, along with a number of subtasks supporting this activity. Deviations are freely allowed, being seen as a breakdown of normal operations that leads to new knowledge of the process [153]. Each time a project deviates from the process, the task either being added or removed opens the task's Design Rationale tab (right-hand window in Fig. 9). The user must provide some information into this tab or the add/delete operation will not be completed. The purpose of this deviation rationale is to provide information about the project's specific circumstances, or context, in which the deviation should occur. The project is allowed full editing privileges for the task after rationale is entered and while it is being reviewed. If no rationale is provided, the operation is cancelled.

At the process management level, the deviations are placed in a Project Deviation resource area (see Fig. 10) where an analyst can look at the deviations to find

TOOL SUPPORT FOR EXPERIENCE-BASED SOFTWARE 59

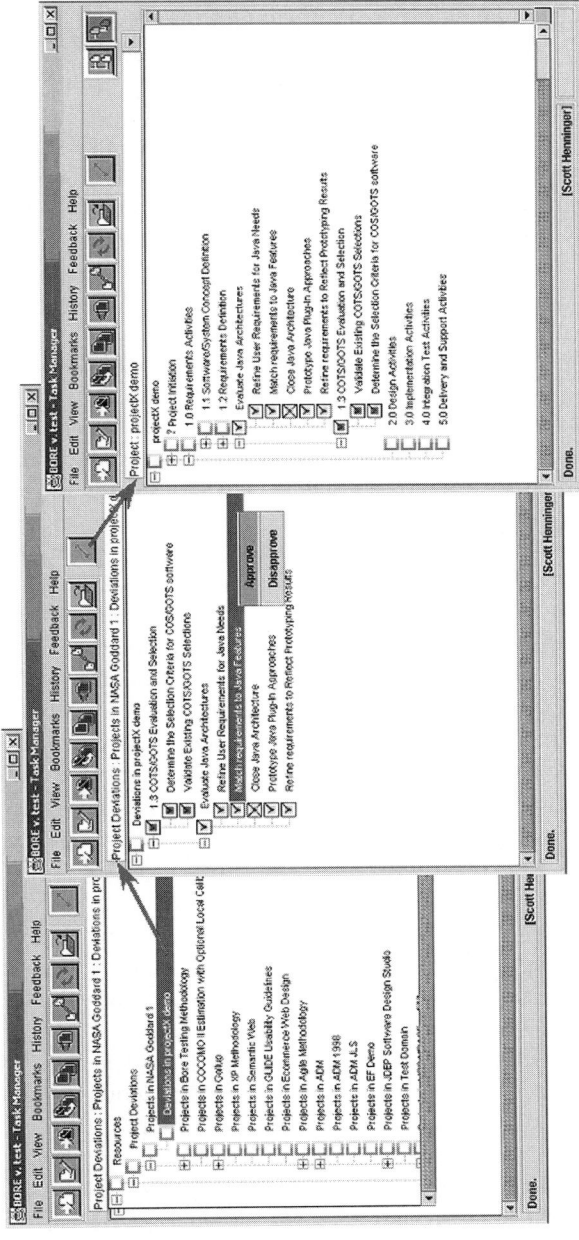

FIG. 10. Analyzing and approving process deviations.

emerging best practices. For example, if all the projects are adding a "Backup and Recovery Strategy" to their project, the analyst can detect this and begin the process of creating an organization-wide standard for this activity. In addition, since the deviation rationale is stated in terms of "under these circumstances" the analyst should be able to turn the deviation rationale into rules for when the new processes should apply. The same can happen for outdated processes that most projects remove. The analyst can determine that the information is outdated or no longer needed, either updating the task(s) or removing them from the process.

4.6.2 Process-Level Reviews

In a disciplined environment, deviations from the process would be escalated to a project-level review, as shown in the Analysis/Organizational Review step in Fig. 5. In BORE, the approval process begins after deviation rationale has been entered. The task is marked as a process deviation in the Task Manager by changing the status to "Needing Approval," represented by a square icon with a smaller square inside (see left-hand window of Fig. 9). If the deviation is a deletion, the square is red, if it is an added task the square is green. The outcome of the approval procedure, whether lightweight (the manager or developer approves their own deviations) or heavyweight (an SEPG committee must review all deviations), can have one of a number of implications. For example, discussion can take place on the appropriateness of the chosen options, perhaps requesting that one or more of them are changed. Another is that the deviations are deemed inappropriate and the project is directed toward accepted development practices that project personnel may have been unaware of. For example, note that the "Choose Java Architecture" deviation has been rejected. This can occur because the organization already has a standard that the process engineer will alert the project to, etc. One-time deviations can also be allowed by simply approving the deviation.

The most significant result, one that *all* projects will encounter, is that the methodology needs to be extended to meet emerging software development needs. Using Java architecture example in Fig. 9, the person or team with organization-wide responsibility for the process can approve the deviation (see the middle window of Fig. 10), putting a check mark in the icon that appears both in the project deviation window (shown in the Task Manager) to track whether or not deviations are accepted, and in the project, to notify project members that the deviation has been approved. Declining the deviation ('Disapprove' in the middle window of Fig. 10) causes a cross out of the icon. The task is then deleted or its status set to 'Open' when the task name is selected, depending on whether the deviation was an approved addition (status set to 'Open'), an approved task removal (task deleted), and etc.

4.7 Experience Packaging

Packaging project experience is a two-step process of creating the work breakdown structure of tasks and defining rules for when tasks should be applied to a project, bringing us back to the methodology definition phase. In the scenario depicted in Fig. 10, new methodology tasks such as "Evaluate Java Architectures" and "Prototype Java Plug-in Approaches" are created by the process manager along with attached documents, task dependencies, estimated task durations, and etc. The deviation rationale, for example, the Java Plug-In rationale in the right-hand window of Fig. 9, could be turned into an option asking whether user requirements constrain the choices for choosing a Java Plug-in version, providing a list of known choices, one of them being the 1.4 version. The actions for this rule would be the tasks created by the process manager, and guided by the project creating the deviation, to address Java Plug-in 1.4 issues. In this manner, the project's experiences are used to pave a new path that other projects can follow as part of the refined process.

5. Putting BORE into Practice: Some Starting Points

As has been stated numerous times in this document and elsewhere [15,73,147], successful experience factory and software programs require separate organizations that focus on the separate concerns of the application and technical domains [47]. Figure 11 shows how the BORE methodology accomplishes this separation between experience factory and project organization concerns. The figure shows the flow of events to create, use, and modify software development knowledge through feedback from project experiences.

5.1 Roles and Tasks for Implementing the BORE Approach

Using any experience factory approach is not a simple matter of installing software. As depicted in Fig. 11, the BORE approach is only partly a matter of keeping a repository of tasks and tailoring rules. It also involves people, reviews, and processes. In part Fig. 11 is a re-drawing of Fig. 5, but focusing on the actors and process involved. It shows that a process engineer (or Software Engineering Process Group (SEPG), etc.) must first create a methodology consisting of methodology tasks and tailoring rules. Project personnel then choose project options that fire tailoring rules, resulting in a tailored set of activities. This is normally the project manager but BORE can allow policies in which designers and developers can choose options for different kinds of tasks. The options and results of tailoring rules are then reviewed at the project level, potentially with process engineers present. This leads to

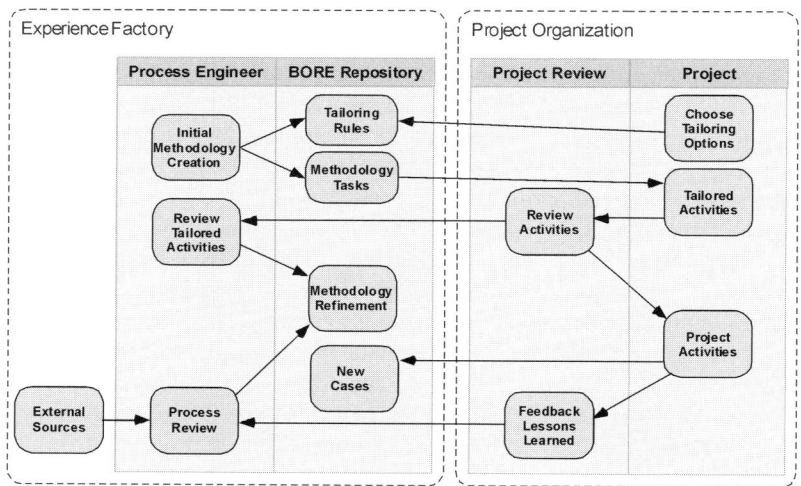

FIG. 11. Actors and processes involved in implementing the BORE approach.

the set of project activities that will be used by the project. Also, because each project creates an instance of the methodology, new cases are created in the repository. At any point in project execution, or at a project post-mortem [28], information is gathered in the form of feedback and lessons learned. This information is reviewed at the process level by the process manager and/or SEPG group, resulting in methodology refinement, including both changes to methodology tasks and tailoring rules. External sources can also prompt methodology refinements and/or be combined with project experiences to refine the methodology.

Another role needed to implement the BORE approach is a rule designer. Although interfaces have been designed to make rule creation as easy as possible, the rule system is, in effect, a type of program. This means careful design and testing of rules is necessary to ensure the proper actions are taken when options are chosen. It is perfectly reasonable, particularly in small organizations, that one person performs both roles of process manager and rules manager.

5.2 Evaluation Contexts for BORE

BORE has currently been evaluated in three contexts, each quite different in the scope of problems the system is used to address, ranging from process discovery to implementing and ensuring conformance to, well-defined processes. Other implementation and evaluation efforts are in inception processes and we hope to continue to use feedback from these projects to refine the methodology and begin to systematically study contextual factors that impact software development efforts and mitigate between success and failure.

5.2.1 Process Discovery

We have worked at bringing BORE to three separate IT organizations responsible for software development and integration for two large and one small company in three different industries. In these settings, process knowledge tends to be scattered throughout many data stores and file systems, with much of the process knowledge being held in the minds of individual workers. In these cases, process discovery is necessary to construct an initial seed repository for BORE.

We began by systematically studying software development at both macro and micro levels. The macro level was revealed through a series of interviews with developers and key management personnel. We coalesced ideas from the interviews into a prototype methodology that led to further feedback and a refinement of the process. The micro level was explored by using contextual inquiry techniques [93], in which we followed developers and project managers for a partial day and interviewed them about their work while they performed their daily activities. This technique helps uncover details and reveal aspects of one's job that they tend to abstract out in a formal interview setting. These studies were used to elicit tailoring criteria and refine methodology tasks to meet the needs of representative projects we observed.

This led to prototype methodologies that could be piloted in small projects that are currently underway. We purposefully chose projects that were partially completed so we could demonstrate to team member how the system could and should be used. We created a project with our initial methodology representation and seeded it with project artifacts and any deviations we could elicit from the team. We then held group-training sessions and visited key personnel working with BORE to assist with problems and explain approaches to their needs. While it is too early to have any systematic data on these efforts, we are collecting survey data before, during, and after the pilot study and have been collecting information, much of it encoded in BORE, on the actual practices we observe. While some missing features and marginal system quality are preventing the full empirical results we have hoped for, the efforts have been invaluable at eliciting the features and processes needed to make this kind of approach work. Feedback on the concept has been largely positive, supporting the hypothesis that we are filling a gap that is needed in IT organizations.

5.2.2 Implementing the MBASE Process

BORE has also been used to implement the MBASE (Model-Based Architecting and Software Engineering) [30] methodology as it is practiced in a yearlong software engineering course, CS577a and CS577b, at the University of Southern California [148]. The MBASE CS577 guidelines exist as document with close to 200 pages of text, plus a myriad of associated documents (templates, procedures, etc.), models (UML, COCOMO, etc.), tools (cost estimation, Rational products, etc.) and other resources. A unique aspect of MBASE is the creation of five main documents in three defined milestones, or anchor points [30]. Each anchor point specifies an iteration of partially completed documents, starting with high-level definitions and refining them as the project progresses, with some sections being more important in different phases. In addition, there are numerous cross-references throughout the guidelines that represent different parts of coherent models. The problem is that MBASE is specified in a monolithic document. There is no good way to view the guidelines or documents created to reflect the specific needs of a given milestone, which are specified in a separate exit criteria document.

USC students implemented MBASE in BORE in the 2001–2002 academic year. The approach taken was to place each MBASE section in a BORE task and create a project hierarchy to mirror the MBASE cs577 guidelines structure. This involved the creation of over 300 tasks, performed over the Internet using the BORE server at the University of Nebraska. The advantage of having MBASE in this form in BORE is that it is easier to change tasks in the methodology, and all information from the various models, templates, and etc. are placed in one location—the BORE repository represented as methodology tasks. This has proven to be much more effective than each team attempting to keep their own Web page or project files (see Section 5.2.3). To address some of the model agreement issues, which are central to the MBASE methodology, we have also created a document generation system that allows users to create custom views of task hierarchies. This replaces the many cross-references currently used in MBASE documentation to ensure agreement with custom-built documents for each model that can show an individual model or portion thereof so people can more easily assess agreement issues.

Initial investigations demonstrate that BORE already addresses many of the issues identified in implementing MBASE, but work is needed to enhance current features so BORE can be used as an empirical testbed for software project data collection. Work is currently underway to begin implementing the metrics-based CeBASE methodology [32] in BORE so that tailoring rules and other BORE features can help projects benefit from the use of metrics collected during software development efforts [90].

5.2.3 The Software Design Studio Implementation

The Software Design Studio is the centerpiece of the curriculum for the JD Edwards Honors Program in Computer Science and Management (http://jdedwards.unl.

edu) at the University of Nebraska–Lincoln (UNL), a program that integrates business concerns and technology. It is a two-year (four consecutive semesters) course in which students use software engineering principles and business practices to develop software for clients external to UNL. The development process taught and used in this course is based on MBASE and implemented in BORE, complete with tailoring criteria that have been created by analyzing the previous year's projects and anticipating the needs of this year's seven projects. This is a bottom-up experience factory strategy [146], where experiences are packaged for future development efforts [18, 21,90].

The Software Design Studio (SDS) also integrates some agile methods into MBASE. The teams work on three-week iterations that are independent of the four MBASE milestones, which are also used by RUP (Inception, Elaboration, Construction, and Transition). Every three weeks, the team starts a new iteration by performing risk and project planning activities. As in the SCRUM method [2,135], an iteration list and a backlog list are kept for each iteration. When a new iteration is created, all tasks not marked "Resolved" are automatically moved to the new iteration's iteration list. As part of the planning process, team members re-prioritize the tasks and plan the tasks that can be accomplished and/or started in the three-week iteration. All other tasks are added to the backlog list. Creating this methodology involved the development of methodology tasks and rules that implement the iterations. The fit here was not perfect, and we are working on techniques to better support some of these features, such as iteratively reusing the same set of methodology tasks while preserving rule and task scoping in the iterations.

5.2.4 CMMI Compliance

We are also working on implementing an existing CMMI guidebook to support the process of auditing for CMMI compliance. This has involved no new enhancements to BORE. By simply adding sections of the guidebook as BORE tasks, and adding a few tailoring rules, we have created a much more powerful guidebook than what was previously available on the Web. In addition, creating projects as methodology instances makes auditing much faster, easier, and cheaper. An auditor can do much of their work by remotely viewing project conformance and deviations from a Web browser, thus doing much of the "legwork" before visiting the site.

6. Other Related Research

The experience factory and organizational learning approaches lie at the intersection of a number of software development and management disciplines. Perhaps most central is the perspective of software reuse [21,85], where reusable assets are not limited to source code or frameworks, but also levels of artifacts generated in the development of large-scale software development.

6.1 Software Process Frameworks

Much of the current research on software development processes have focused on defining the parameters that define software development practices. These approaches, including CMM [121], CMMI [32], SPICE [53,103], ISO 9000 [99], Bootstrap [104] and others, aim to define the process elements that constitute good software development processes, leaving implementation and enactment of the processes to individual organizations and development efforts.

While advocated as important by most process framework and modeling frameworks, none have defined guidelines for how disciplined tailoring can or should be achieved. A significant contribution of this work, both experience factories and the BORE approach, is to define not only the process, but also how the process evolves with the changing needs of the development organization. In addition, the process can be defined at many levels of detail, allowing projects to adopt the process at an appropriate level of detail for the organization and project types within an organization.

The approaches described here define process tailoring and evolution at both the organizational and project levels. The BORE approach tailors processes through tailoring options and a review process to look over deviations to the methodology. Organization-level evolution is addressed through techniques and processes for refining, evolving, and improving the development process. No "Level 5" process is assumed as advocated by the CMMI staged model. Rather, feedback from actual projects is used to define the best-known methods within the development context and application requirements of a specific development organization. In addition, instead of stating that "Configuration Management" is a required process, these approaches provide the means to create experience-based resources for how this should be accomplished.

6.2 Software Process Modeling

Integrating languages and formal process models into environments has been researched in a number of contexts [7]. These process-based environments, often referred to as Process-centered Software Engineering Environments (PSEEs), often cover process modeling and process enactment phases of the process engineering lifecycle [69,76]. Some of these environments have investigated different formalisms, such as knowledge-based [26,97] and Petri net [11,12] approaches, while others have focused on elements of software development, such as hierarchical decomposition of activities [23,57], collaboration and coordination [51,70], and analysis and simulation of software processes [111].

The observation that developing software process definitions is similar to developing software systems [120] has given rise to a number of approaches based on programming languages [43,46,98,105] that provide language constructs for creating processes and automatable process actions, such as running test scripts when a changed file is checked in. The process representations that can be created by these languages, especially where process automation is concerned, have not been the focus of BORE and the experience factory approaches, where more emphasis is placed on supporting the human aspects of the software process. Also, the same problems facing programming language-based software development also trouble process programming. One of the problems is the difficulty of reusing program components. The entire BORE tool and methodology is designed to identify reusable processes and define them for reuse [85]. Not only does this support the modeling process, it ensures a degree of conformance with known best practices and enhances organizational learning. Nonetheless, the use of a process language would enable the integration of many automation features and future work will look into this, perhaps by embedding language support in the BORE rule engine.

A number of process notations and methods for defining processes have been researched [12,123], often using entrance criteria, task, validation, and exit criteria (the so-called ETVX method [129]) as a means to formally define a process. The purpose of these languages is often to create models that "detect inconsistencies, ambiguities, incompleteness, and opportunities for improvement for both the software process and its documentation" [13]. Frameworks and process languages are also a common research topic [35,92]. For example, Hollenbach and Frakes report on a diagram notation that creates a process definition and tailoring methodology [92]. They report that the methodology significantly reduced the time and effort to create project-specific processes in an industry setting.

The Endeavors system [35] is a flexible workflow environment that allows users to create and evolve processes while a project is in progress. It uses a visual environment to connect process elements together in a pipeline that represents a workflow. Endeavors supports most of the features found in process definition languages, and can raise warnings and notify personnel of events in the workflow. This kind of reactive process control fits into our view that modification of the process is necessary, but conflicts with the principle of drawing on current best practices. If users are able to change the process dynamically with no accountability, then we are back to documenting an ad-hoc process that can lead to chaotic and disorganized development processes. We wish to take a step further to combine reactive and proactive process control, and it is our strong opinion that some kind of process reuse will prove necessary to ensure a degree of discipline in developing large software systems.

6.3 An Analysis of Process Models and Frameworks

Although it is desirable to describe processes in a precise and unambiguous manner, most of these approaches fall on either side of a dichotomy. On one side are the Universalists, such as the CMM family and the Rational Unified Process (RUP), which wish to define a one-size-fit-all comprehensive process to be followed by all development organizations. On the other side are the Constructors [120] that provide primitives to define a process, but little guidance on whether a given process will lead to desired results.

The experience factory approach and the BORE implementation discussed here are positioned to span this dichotomy. While the focus of this research has not been on process representations, the tailoring rules, methodology instantiations, and case-based architecture of BORE can support, and could benefit from, a wide variety of formal representations. For example, the ability to specify activity precedence has recently been added to BORE by representing task dependencies and durations. This previously missing element of BORE was easily added to the task representation and is implemented through an add-on module to import and export MS Project Gantt Chart representations. Rules can be used to determine which dependencies and durations should be used that best fit a project's need and schedule constraints. The dependencies and durations are inherited by projects, facilitating the creation of first drafts of schedules that provide dependencies and estimates of task durations that are a significant aid to project managers.

6.4 Design Rationale

The BORE approach also has some roots in the design rationale field [42,62,106, 109,112]. Similar to organizational memory approaches [141,150], the motive for capturing design rationale is to avoid repeating common pitfalls or re-discussion of design decisions by describing the alternatives debated and decisions made for a given effort. Many schemes, from straightforward Procedural Hierarchy of Issue structures [42,62] to more complex structures designed to capture logical relationships for computation [106] have been devised. All have the same basic structure of a set of hierarchically arranged questions posed to flesh out issues. Alternatives and rationale for the alternatives can be attached to the questions to document discussion paths.

While a valuable brainstorming tool that organizes alternative solutions, design rationale techniques have not focused on how past rationale can be used to drive a reuse-based software development process. Furthermore, there is no mechanism to ensure the rationale is used to improve future efforts, and therefore risks becoming a form of write-only memory [42]. Our approach is more principled, using a push model to ensure conformance with known best practices and putting explicit procedures in place to compare past and present design contexts as an impetus for continuous improvement. The approach described here also differs from the current trend in design rationale research to motivate developers to use the approach by lowering the cost of collecting information. This has led to the development of a plethora of retrieval or filter-based systems that work on existing documents, such as e-mail messages or discussion databases, that tend to suffer from both information overload and knowledge paucity [9]. Our motivator for using the system is part conformance and part self-motivating. The approach embodies corporate procedures that need to be followed, but the extent to which the approach can be tailored to real project needs and provide developers and managers with valuable information will determine its fate as a development strategy.

7. Open Issues and Future Work

BORE was originally designed as a knowledge management tool for software reuse [78]. The work became involved in process modeling and process improvement out of necessity because we observed that for a knowledge management system to be used it must become part of the defined work activities—it is not sufficient to have a repository and hope people will go to it [133], much less use it effectively. Use of the experience base must become part of the development process. The experience factory and organizational learning approaches advocates knowledge management that facilitates the reuse of software artifacts. In spite of many years of research, few tools have been built to explicitly support experience factories, and all have supported repository aspects (the experience base), with little to no support for the processes involved in the experience factory, the project development organization, and the interactions between them. The research described here explores a specific approach for tools supporting these processes and other types of experience-based methods, such as the organizational learning method for software development.

Developing an understanding of the impact of experience-based approaches requires an empirical approach that both refines the approach through feedback and establishes causal relationships between contextual factors and outcomes. Early evaluations of BORE [82,86] have indicated that progress has been made on our overall goals of creating a medium for flexible software process definitions, capturing development practices from experience, and ensuring those practices are applied in a disciplined manner. The BORE system is beginning to move out of the prototyping phase and become a production-quality system, enabling evaluations in realistic software development settings, as described in Section 5.2. Through these evaluations, we hope to gain an increased understanding in the overall approach and how experience-based tools such as BORE can be used to improve software development practices.

Some of the research questions we will continue to explore with BORE include designing work practices centered on experience-based organizational learning processes. Design tools must reward users for use in the current project as well as leaving information for subsequent development and maintenance efforts. We believe these are compatible goals, as long-term projects need to track their progress and decision making process. Some major research questions include: designing methodologies based on standards set by previous projects yet flexible enough to accommodate changes in business needs and technology; creating a development process that begins by using the resources supplied by the repository and updates the repository as the project progresses; finding the "right" level of documentation that doesn't impede progress yet leaves a trace for subsequent efforts; and organizational changes needed to make such techniques work in the organization (i.e., the technology transfer and tool adoption problems).

The most important next steps include the difficult task of getting organizations to take part in efforts to evaluate emerging research in realistic settings. This involves both moving beyond the fragile system prototype stage, and finding realistic contexts for evaluation. Empirical evaluations are continuing and will provide additional sources of feedback on the approach and tool. More importantly, the potential for BORE to serve as a repository for software development phenomenon, indexed by project characteristics, will continue to be evaluated and refined. To this end, we will continue to employ a mixture of ethnographic studies and laboratory experiments to study software process improvisation and the impact of delivering process and product knowledge sources during software development efforts. This strategy will not only yield innovative system building efforts, but to also improve the field's overall understanding of software development practices.

7.1 Future Work

The overall purpose of BORE is not to restrict creativity through strict enactment of rules, but to enable creativity by identifying resources and best practices that people can build on. Rules in the rule-based system serve *only* as a means of representing contextual factors that determine whether or not tasks, or sets of related tasks, are appropriate for the specific circumstances of a project. Better tools are needed that help process engineers insert new processes and the associated rules into methodologies.

This is essentially a knowledge acquisition problem, and we are looking into using agents and critics to flag knowledge base inconsistencies and gaps [144] and ensure that complete and consistent processes are assigned to projects. One means we intend to investigate is the formal definition of entrance and exit criteria for tasks and sets of tasks.

Although our approach does not specifically call for a separate Experience Factory organization, the roles necessary to implement BORE in an organization are easily broken into experience factory and project organizations, as shown in Fig. 11. We are in full agreement that "In order to practice reuse effectively, an organization is needed whose main focus is to make reuse easy and effective." [15], and we will continue to create tools and techniques that are compatible with this methodology. Another aspect of the Experience Factory and QIP approaches is the use of metrics and project data in the project decision-making process and for process improvement. Apart from collecting task-based effort data, metric collection and analysis is currently lacking in BORE. A configuration management system has been created and we are collecting data on BORE versions, but this has not been fully integrated into the task-based structure. Defect tracking and links to change management and BORE tasks is also lacking. These are recognized deficits that we are actively working on in an integrated strategy to address them [90].

Beyond the creation of experience-based tools, our research group is involved in the CeBASE effort, which has developed a next-generation development process that focuses on integrating project-level and organizational-level processes [32]. This effort will integrate a general QIP and Experience Factory framework with the MBASE methodology [31]. The BORE tool has been designed to integrate organizational and project level concerns, and we are working on enhancements and demonstrations to illustrate BORE compatibility with the CeBASE method [90].

The BORE system currently relies on rules to find relevant activities for projects. To the extent that the activities can be designed properly, this will work. But there may be instances where a search for related activities may be useful. BORE has a simple search tool to find activities when people can specify what tasks are needed. Drawing on the observation that software development processes are a type of planning activity, we are working on using hierarchical case-based planners [115], which generate plans based on case-based search criteria and options, to find sets of tasks meeting criteria set by options. Integrating rule-based and case-based planning systems [71,113] to find work breakdowns that are relevant to the characteristics of a project holds promise to find software development processes that meet certain criteria, but do not exactly match the rule criteria designed into BORE rules.

Currently, BORE methodologies are designed using individual tasks. While this is adequate for many methodologies, rule actions (see Fig. 7) that add many tasks can become tedious to implement and maintain. In addition, many processes, such as bug tracking and the risk-based iterative process used in the Software Design Studio and MBASE (see Section 5.2), involve reusing the same or similar sets of tasks. We are therefore in the process of adding a "process model" layer between methodologies and tasks. Each process model in this layer would have its own rule and task scoping for tailoring the model, depending on evolving project needs. Methodologies would then be created with a mixture of tasks and process models, which can be repeated in projects while allowing process developers to specify the methodology at a higher level of abstraction. This will enhance methodology creation and maintenance in the BORE system.

8. Conclusions

A goal of the organizational learning and experience factory approaches is to turn development methodologies into a resource, something that truly supports the development process as actually practiced. *These approaches, an example of which is implemented in BORE, allow necessary degrees of formal procedures that ensure high-quality products while allowing the necessary freedom to improvise, innovate, and adapt to specific needs of a software development effort.* This involves not only defining a process, but also using feedback from projects using the defined process to refine and improve its procedures. To date, little research has been done to create support tools and interfaces for using the process to disseminate and organize software development knowledge. This work attempts to fill this gap with the organizational learning perspective, process tailoring techniques, case-based decision support, and the BORE prototype.

QIP and Experience Factory are experience-based techniques that advocate capturing project data as the basis for creating artifacts that can be reused in subsequent efforts. The BORE research effort takes the next step to turn the concept into a software tool capable of implementing experience-based techniques, including the experience factory. The research described here investigates the problem of creating tools that push models of best practices while allowing the flexibility necessary to improvise [52] and address the needs of individual development efforts. This has been accomplished through a process-centered approach that couples a repository of process models and best practices with an organizational learning methodology and a tool designed to support the process and repository.

To achieve these goals, we have coupled process and technology to turn defined development processes into dynamic "living" resources that can be extended and improved as new project needs and application requirements emerge. General principles are captured in the process standard and cases capture situation-specific knowledge of actual practice. The BORE tool has been created to collect and disseminate project experiences as "cases" representing emerging knowledge of development practices in an organization. The emerging, case-based, knowledge can then be turned into standards representing a software development organization's best practices that can be brought to bear on individual development efforts. As the repository accumulates through principled evolution of the methodology, it improves and is able to handle a wider range of circumstances [101], while evolving toward answers to problems that fit the organization's technical and business context.

Centering the information around a single repository through an ongoing process of capturing project experiences can prevent the duplication of efforts, avoid repeating common mistakes, and help streamline the development process. Similar projects have shown that development personnel will use such a system, provided it contains relevant, useful and up-to-date information [145]. This mandates a strong tie between technology and process in which using the technology must become part of routine work activities. Such an approach will succeed to the extent that people are rewarded in the short term for their efforts and can feel a sense of ownership of the process. This work takes some first steps in this direction, and continued efforts to gather empirical data on its use will help refine the method and learn more about how to support the software development process.

Acknowledgements

We gratefully acknowledge the efforts a number of graduate students that have helped develop BORE, particularly Kurt Baumgarten, Kalpana Gujja, Ryan Kinworthy, V. Rishi Kumar, Yu Li, Sarathkumar Polireddy and Liyuan Yu. This research was funded by the National Science Foundation (CCR-9502461, CCR-9988540, ITR-0085788, and CCR-0204436).

References

[1] Aamodt A., Plaza E., "Case-based reasoning: Foundational issues, methodological variations, and system approaches", *AI Communications* **7** (1) (1994) 39–52.

[2] Agile Alliance, *Introduction to Scrum*, 2002. Available at http://www.controlchaos.com/scrumwp.htm#Introduction2002, last accessed: 4/1/02.

[3] Aha D.W., Weber R. (Eds.), *Intelligent Lessons Learned Systems: Papers from the 2000 Workshop*, AAAI Press, Menlo Park, CA, 2000.

[4] Althoff K.-D., Birk A., Hartkopf S., Müller W., "Managing software engineering experience for comprehensive reuse", in: *Proc. 11th International Conference on Software Engineering and Knowledge Engineering, Kaiserslautern, Germany*, 1999, pp. 10–19.

[5] Althoff K.-D., Birk A., Tautz C., "The experience factory approach: Realizing learning from experience in software development organizations", in: *Tenth German Workshop on Machine Learning, University of Karlsruhe*, 1997.

[6] Althoff K.-D., Nick M., Tautz C., "Improving organizational memories through user feedback", in: *2nd International Workshop on Learning Software Organizations (LSO 2000), Oulu, Finland*, 2000, pp. 27–44.

[7] Ambriola V., Conradi R., Fuggetta A., "Assessing process-centered software engineering environments", *ACM Transactions of Software Engineering and Methodology* **6** (3) (1997) 283–328.

[8] Anderson K.M., Taylor R.N., Whitehead E.J., "Chimera: Hypermedia for heterogeneous software development environments", *ACM Transactions on Information Systems* **18** (3) (2000) 211–245.

[9] Applehans W., Globe A., Laugero G., *Managing Knowledge: A Practical Web-Based Approach*, Addison-Wesley, Reading, MA, 1999.

[10] Arango G., "Domain analysis: From art form to engineering discipline", in: *Fifth International Workshop on Software Specification and Design, Pittsburgh, PA*, ACM, New York, 1989, pp. 152–159.

[11] Bandinelli S., DiNitto E., Fuggetta A., "Supporting cooperation in the SPADE-1 environment", *Transactions on Software Engineering* **22** (12) (1996) 841–865.

[12] Bandinelli S.C., Fuggetta A., Ghezzi C., "Software process model evolution in the SPADE environment", *Transactions of Software Engineering* **19** (12) (1993) 1128–1144.

[13] Bandinelli S., Fuggetta A., Lavazza L., Loi M., Picco G.P., "Modeling and improving an industrial software process", *Transaction on Software Engineering* **21** (5) (1995) 440–453.

[14] Barnes B.H., Bollinger T.B., "Making reuse cost-effective", *IEEE Software* **8** (1) (1991) 13–24.

[15] Basili V.R., Caldiera G., Cantone G., "A reference architecture for the component factory", *ACM Transactions on Software Engineering and Methodology* **1** (1) (1992) 53–80.

[16] Basili V., Caldiera G., Rombach D., "Experience factory", in: *Encyclopedia of Software Engineering*, Wiley & Sons, 1994, pp. 469–476.

[17] Basili V.R., Daskalantonakis M.K., Yacobellis R.K., "Technology transfer at Motorola", *IEEE Software* **11** (2) (1994) 70–76.

[18] Basili V., Lindvall M., Costa P., "Implementing the experience factory concepts as a set of experience bases", in: *International Conference on Software Engineering and Knowledge Engineering (SEKE '01), Buenos Aires, Argentina*, 2001.

[19] Basili V.R., McGarry F., Pajerski R., Page G., Waligora S., Zelkowitz M., *Software Process Improvement in the NASA Software Engineering Laboratory*, Software Engineering Institute, 1994.

[20] Basili V.R., Rombach H.D., "The TAME project: Towards improvement-oriented software environments", *IEEE Transactions on Software Engineering* **14** (6) (1988) 758–773.

[21] Basili V.R., Rombach H.D., "Support for comprehensive reuse", *Software Engineering Journal* **6** (5) (1991) 303–316.
[22] Batory D., Chen G., Robertson E., Wang T., "Design wizards and visual programming environments for GenVoca generators", *Transactions on Software Engineering* **26** (5) (2000) 441–452.
[23] Belkhatir N., Estublier J., Melo W.L., "Software process model and work space control in the Adele system", in: *2nd International Conference on the Software Process, Berlin, FRG*, IEEE Computer Society, 1993, pp. 2–11.
[24] Belkin N., "Helping people find what they don't know", *Comm. of the ACM* **43** (8) (2000) 58–61.
[25] Belkin N.J., Oddy R.N., Brooks H.M., "Ask for information retrieval: Parts 1 & 2", *Journal of Documentation* **38** (2, 3) (1982) 61–71, 145–163.
[26] Ben-Shaul I.Z., Kaiser G.E., "A paradigm for decentralized process modeling and its realization in the Oz environment", in: *Proc. Sixteenth International Conference on Software Engineering, Sorrento, Italy*, IEEE Computer Society Press, 1994, pp. 179–188.
[27] Biggerstaff T.J., "An assessment and analysis of software reuse", *Advances in Computers* **34** (1992) 1–57.
[28] Birk A., Dingsøyr T., Stålhane T., "Postmortem: Never leave a project without it", *IEEE Software* **19** (3) (2002) 43–45.
[29] Birk A., Kröschel F., "A knowledge management lifecycle for experience packages on software engineering technologies", in: *1st International Workshop on Learning Software Organizations (LSO 1999), Kaiserlautern, FRG*, 1999, pp. 115–126.
[30] Boehm B., "Anchoring the software process", *IEEE Software* **13** (4) (1996) 73–82.
[31] Boehm B., Port D., "Balancing discipline and flexibility with the spiral model and MBASE", *Crosstalk* (December 2001).
[32] Boehm B., Port D., Jain A., Basili V., "Achieving CMMI level 5 improvements with MBASE and the CeBASE method", *Crosstalk* (May 2002).
[33] Boehm B.W., "A spiral model of software development and enhancement", *Computer* **21** (5) (1988) 61–72.
[34] Bohrer K., Johnson V., Nilsson A., Rubin B., "The San Francisco project: An object-oriented framework approach to building business applications", in: *COMPSAC '97—21st International Computer Software and Applications Conference*, 1997, pp. 416–424.
[35] Bolcer G.A., Taylor R.N., "Endeavors: A process system integration infrastructure", in: *Proceedings of the Fourth International Conference on the Software Process, Brighton, UK*, IEEE Computer Society Press, 1996, pp. 76–85.
[36] Brooks F.P., "No silver bullet: Essence and accidents of software engineering", *Computer* **20** (4) (1987) 10–19.
[37] Brown A.W., Wallnau K.C., "The current state of CBSE", *IEEE Software* **15** (5) (1998) 37–46.
[38] Brown J.S., Duguid P., "Organizational learning and communities-of-practice: Toward a unified view of working, learning, and innovation", *Organization Science* **2** (1) (1991) 40–57.

[39] Brown J.S., Duguid P., *The Social Life of Information*, Harvard Univ. Press, 2000.
[40] Carey J., Carlson B., *Framework Process Patterns: Lessons Learned Developing Application Frameworks*, Addison-Wesley, Boston, MA, 2002.
[41] Collier B., DeMarco T., Fearey P., "A defined process for project postmortem review", *IEEE Software* **13** (4) (1996) 65–72.
[42] Conklin E.J., Yakemovic K., "A process-oriented approach to Design Rationale", *Human–Computer Interaction* **6** (3–4) (1991) 357–391.
[43] Conradi R., Liu C., "Process modeling languages: One or many?", in: *5th European Workshop on Software Process Technology (EWSPT '95), Noordwijkerhout, The Netherlands*, 1995, pp. 98–118.
[44] CSTB, *Scaling Up: A Research Agenda for Software Engineering*, Academic Press, 1989.
[45] Cugola G., "Tolerating deviations in process support systems via flexible enactment of process models", *IEEE Transactions on Software Engineering* **24** (11) (1998) 982–1000.
[46] Curtis B., Kellner M.I., Over J., "Process modeling", *Communications of the ACM* **35** (9) (1992) 75–90.
[47] Curtis B., Krasner H., Iscoe N., "A field study of the software design process for large systems", *Communications of the ACM* **31** (11) (1988) 1268–1287.
[48] Decker B., Althoff K.D., Nick M., "Integrating business process and lessons learned with an experience factory", in: *1st German Conference on Professional Knowledge Management*, 2001.
[49] Decker B., Althoff K.-D., Nick M., Jedlitschka A., Rech J., "Corporate Information Network (CoIN): Experience management at IESE", in: *Knowledge Engineering & Management (KnowTech 2001), Dresden*, 2001.
[50] Devanbu P., Brachman R.J., Selfridge P.G., Ballard B.W., "LaSSIE: A knowledge-based software information system", *Communications of the ACM* **34** (5) (1991) 34–49.
[51] Dieters W., Gruhn V., "Managing software processes in the environment MELMAC", in: *4th ACM SIGSOFT Symposium on Software Development Environments, Irvine, CA*, 1990, pp. 193–205.
[52] Dybå T., "Improvisation in small software organizations", *IEEE Software* **17** (5) (2000) 82–87.
[53] Emam K.E., Drouin J.N., Menlo W., *SPICE: The Theory and Practice of Software Process Improvement and Capability Determination*, IEEE Computer Society, Los Alamitos, CA, 1998.
[54] Feiler P.H., Humphrey W.S., "Software process development and enactment: Concepts and definitions", in: *Second International Conference on Software Process*, 1993, pp. 28–40.
[55] Feldmann R., "Developing a tailored reuse repository structure—experience and first results", in: *1st International Workshop on Learning Software Organizations (LSO 1999), Kaiserlautern, FRG*, 1999.
[56] Feldmann R., Nick M., Frey M., "Towards industrial-strength measurement programs for reuse and experience repository systems", in: *2nd International Workshop on Learning Software Organizations (LSO 2000), Oulu, Finland*, 2000, pp. 7–18.

[57] Fernström C., "PROCESS WEAVER: Adding process support to UNIX", in: *2nd International Conference on the Software Process: Continuous Software Process Improvement, Berlin, FRG*, IEEE Computer Society Press, 1993, pp. 12–26.
[58] Fischer G., "Domain-oriented design environments", *Automated Software Engineering* **1** (2) (1994) 177–203.
[59] Fischer G., "Seeding, evolutionary growth and reseeding: Constructing, capturing and evolving knowledge in domain-oriented design environments", *Journal of Automated Software Engineering* **5** (4) (1998) 447–464.
[60] Fischer G., Girgensohn A., "End-user modifiability in design environments", in: *Proc. Human Factors in Computing Systems (CHI'90), Seattle, WA*, 1990, pp. 183–191.
[61] Fischer G., Girgensohn A., Nakakoji K., Redmiles D., "Supporting software designers with integrated, domain-oriented design environments", *IEEE Transactions on Software Engineering* **18** (6) (1992) 511–522.
[62] Fischer G., Grudin J., Lemke A., McCall R., Ostwald J., Reeves B., Shipman F., "Supporting indirect collaborative design with integrated knowledge-based design environments", *Human–Computer Interaction* **7** (1992) 281–314.
[63] Fischer G., Lemke A.C., "Construction kits and design environments: Steps toward human problem-domain communication", *Human–Computer Interaction* **3** (3) (1988) 179–222.
[64] Fischer G., Lemke A., Schwab T., "Knowledge-based help systems", in: *Proc. Human Factors in Computing Systems (CHI '85)*, 1985, pp. 161–167.
[65] Fischer G., McCall R., Ostwald J., Reeves B., Shipman F., "Seeding, evolutionary growth and reseeding: Supporting the incremental development of design environments", in: *Proc. Human Factors in Computing Systems (CHI '94), Boston, MA*, ACM, New York, 1994, pp. 292–298.
[66] Fischer G., Ostwald J., "Knowledge management: Problems, promises, realities, and challenges", *IEEE Intelligent Systems* **16** (1) (2001) 60–72.
[67] Fuggetta A., Lavazza L., Morasca S., Cefriel, Cinti S., Oldano G., Orazi E., "Applying GQM in an industrial software factory", *Transactions on Software Engineering and Methodology* **7** (4) (1998) 441–448.
[68] Gamma E., Helm R., Johnson R., Vlissides J., *Design Patterns: Elements of Reusable Object-Oriented Software*, Addison-Wesley, Reading, MA, 1995.
[69] Garg P.K., Mi P., Pham T., Scacchi W., Thunquest G., "The SMART approach for software process engineering", in: *International Conference on Software Engineering (ICSE 94), Sorrento, Italy*, IEEE Computer Society, 1994, pp. 341–350.
[70] Garg P.K., Pham T., Beach B., Deshpande A., Ishizaki A., Wentzel W., Fong W., "Matisse: A knowledge-based team programming environment", *International Journal of Software Engineering and Knowledge Engineering* **4** (1) (1994) 17–59.
[71] Golding A., Rosenbloom P.S., "Improving rule-based systems through case-based reasoning", in: *Proc. 9th National Conference on Artificial Intelligence, Anaheim, CA*, 1991, pp. 22–27.
[72] Griss M.L., "Software reuse: From library to factory", *IBM Systems Journal* **32** (4) (1993) 548–565.

[73] Griss M.L., "Software reuse experience at Hewlett-Packard", in: *Proc. Sixteenth Intl. Conference on Software Engineering*, 1994, p. 270.
[74] Grudin J., "Why CSCW applications fail: Problems in the design and evaluation of organizational interfaces", in: *Proceedings of the Conference on Computer-Supported Cooperative Work (CSCW'88)*, ACM, New York, 1988, pp. 85–93.
[75] Grudin J., "The computer reaches out: The historical continuity of interface design", in: *Proc. Human Factors in Computing Systems (CHI '90), Seattle, WA*, ACM, New York, 1990, pp. 261–268.
[76] Grundy J.C., Hosking J.G., "Serendipity: Integrated environment support for process modelling, enactment and work coordination", *Automated Software Engineering: An International Journal* **5** (1) (1998) 27–60.
[77] Henninger S., "Supporting the domain lifecycle", in: *IEEE Seventh International Workshop on Computer-Aided Software Engineering—CASE '95, Toronto, CA*, IEEE Computer Society Press, 1995, pp. 10–19.
[78] Henninger S., "Accelerating the successful reuse of problem solving knowledge through the domain lifecycle", in: *Fourth International Conference on Software Reuse, Orlando, FL*, IEEE Computer Society Press, Los Alamitos, CA, 1996, pp. 124–133.
[79] Henninger S., "Building an organization-specific infrastructure to support CASE tools", *Journal of Automated Software Engineering* **3** (3/4) (1996) 239–259.
[80] Henninger S., "Supporting software development with organizational memory tools", *International Journal of Applied Software Technology* **2** (1) (1996) 61–84.
[81] Henninger S., "Capturing and formalizing best practices in a software development organization", in: *International Conference on Software Engineering and Knowledge Engineering (SEKE '97), Madrid, Spain*, 1997.
[82] Henninger S., "Tools supporting the creation and evolution of software development knowledge", in: *Proceedings of the Automated Software Engineering Conference, Lake Tahoe, NV*, 1997, pp. 46–53.
[83] Henninger S., "Case-based knowledge management tools for software development", *Journal of Automated Software Engineering* **4** (3) (1997) 319–340.
[84] Henninger S., "An evolutionary approach to constructing effective software reuse repositories", *ACM Transactions on Software Engineering and Methodology* **6** (2) (1997) 111–140.
[85] Henninger S., "An environment for reusing software processes", in: *Fifth International Conference on Software Reuse, Victoria, British Columbia*, 1998, pp. 103–112.
[86] Henninger S., "Using software process to support learning software organizations", in: *1st International Workshop on Learning Software Organizations (LSO 1999), Kaiserlautern, FRG*, 1999.
[87] Henninger S., "An organizational learning method for applying usability guidelines and patterns", in: *8th IFIP Working Conference on Engineering for Human–Computer Interaction (EHCI'01), Toronto*, in: *Lecture Notes in Computer Science*, Springer, Berlin, 2001, pp. 141–155.
[88] Henninger S., Baumgarten K., "A case-based approach to tailoring software processes", in: *International Conference on Case-Based Reasoning (ICCBR 01), Vancouver, BC*, 2001, pp. 249–262.

[89] Henninger S., Lappala K., Raghavendran A., "An organizational learning approach to domain analysis", in: *17th International Conference on Software Engineering, Seattle, WA*, ACM Press, New York, 1995, pp. 95–104.
[90] Henninger S., Li Y., Modali S., Yu L., "Adaptive process tool support for the CeBASE method", *CrossTalk*. In preparation.
[91] Henninger S., Schlabach J., "A tool for managing software development knowledge", in: *3rd International Conference on Product Focused Software Process Improvement (PROFES 01), Kaiserslautern, FRG*, Springer, 2001, pp. 182–195.
[92] Hollenbach C., Frakes W., "Software process reuse in an industrial setting", in: *Fourth International Conference on Software Reuse, Orlando, FL*, IEEE Computer Society Press, Los Alamitos, CA, 1996, pp. 22–30.
[93] Holtzblatt K., Jones S. (Eds.), *Contextual Inquiry: A Participatory Technique for System Design*, Erlbaum, Hillsdale, NJ, 1993.
[94] Humphrey W.S., *Managing the Software Process*, Addison Wesley, Reading, MA, 1989.
[95] Humphrey W.S., Snyder T.R., Willis R.R., "Software process improvement at Hughes Aircraft", *IEEE Software* **8** (4) (1991) 11–23.
[96] Johnson R.E., "Frameworks = (components + patterns)", *Communications of the ACM* **40** (10) (1997) 39–42.
[97] Kaiser G.E., Feiler P.H., Popovich S.S., "Intelligent assistance for software development and maintenance", *IEEE Software* **5** (3) (1988) 40–49.
[98] Kaiser G.E., Popovich S.S., Ben-Shaul I.Z., "A bi-level language for software process modeling", in: *Proc. Fifteenth International Conference on Software Engineering, Baltimore, Maryland*, 1993.
[99] Kehoe R., Jarvis A., *ISO 9000–3: A Tool for Software Product and Process Improvement*, Springer, New York, 1996.
[100] Kling R., "Organizational analysis in computer science", *The Information Society* **9** (2) (1993).
[101] Kolodner J.L., "Improving human decision making through case-based decision aiding", *AI Magazine* **12** (1) (1991) 52–68.
[102] Kolodner J.L., *Case-Based Reasoning*, Morgan-Kaufman, San Mateo, CA, 1993.
[103] Konrad M.D., Paulk M.C., "An overview of SPICE's model for process management", in: *Proc. 5th International Conference on Software Quality, Austin, Texas*, 1995.
[104] Kuvaja P., Bicego A., "BOOTSTRAP—A European assessment methodology", *Software Quality Journal* **3** (1994) 117–127.
[105] Lee H., Osterweil L.J., "HI-PLAN and Little-JIL: A study of contrast between two process languages", in: *International Conference on Software Theory and Practice (ICS2000), Beijing, PRC*, 2000.
[106] Lee J., "Design Rationale capture and use", *AI Magazine* **14** (2) (1993) 24–26.
[107] Lim W.C., "Effects of reuse on quality, productivity, and economics", *IEEE Software* **11** (5) (1994) 23–30.
[108] Lindvall M., Rus I., "Process diversity in software development", *IEEE Software* **17** (4) (2000) 14–18.

[109] Maclean A., Bellotti V., Young R., Moran T., "Questions, options, and criteria: Elements of design space analysis", *Human–Computer Interaction* **6** (3–4) (1991) 201–251.
[110] March J.G., "Exploration and exploitation in organizational learning", *Organizational Science* **2** (1) (1991) 71–87.
[111] Mi P., Scacchi W., "Modeling articulation work in software engineering processes", in: *1st International Conference on the Software Process, Redondo Beach, CA*, 1991, pp. 188–201.
[112] Moran T., Carroll J. (Eds.), *Design Rationale: Concepts, Techniques and Use*, Lawrence Erlbaum Associates, Hillsdale, NJ, 1996.
[113] Muñoz-Avila H., Aha D.W., Breslow L.A., Nau D.S., Weber R., "Integrating conversational case retrieval with generative planning", in: *Proc. 5th European Workshop on Case Based Reasoning, Trento, Italy*, 2000, pp. 322–334.
[114] NASA GSFC, Recommended Approach to Software Development. Available at http://sel.gsfc.nasa.gov/website/documents/online-doc.htm, last update: June 1992, 1999, last accessed: August 2002.
[115] Nau D., Cao Y., Lotem A., Muñoz-Avila H., "SHOP: Simple Hierarchical Ordered Planner", in: *Proc. 16th International Conference on Case-Based Reasoning, Stockholm*, AAAI Press, 1999, pp. 968–973.
[116] Neighbors J., "The Draco approach to constructing software from reusable components", *IEEE Transactions on Software Engineering* **10** (1984) 564–573.
[117] Nick M., Althoff K.-D., Tautz C., "Systematic maintenance of corporate experience factories", *Computational Intelligence* **17** (2) (2001) 364–386.
[118] Nonaka I., Takeychi H., *The Knowledge-Creating Company: How Japanese Companies Create the Dynamics of Innovation*, Oxford Univ. Press, New York, 1995.
[119] Oivo M., Basili V.R., "Representing software engineering models: The TAME goal oriented approach", *IEEE Transactions on Software Engineering* **18** (10) (1992) 886–898.
[120] Osterweil L., "Software processes are software too", in: *Ninth International Conference on Software Engineering, Monterey, CA*, ACM, IEEE, Los Alamitos, CA, 1987, pp. 2–13.
[121] Paulk M.C., Curtis B., Chrissis M., Weber C.V., "Capability maturity model, version 1.1", *IEEE Software* **10** (4) (1993) 18–27.
[122] Pearce M., Goel A.K., Kolodner J.L., Zimring C., Sentosa L., Billington R., "Case-based design support: A case study in architectural design", *IEEE Expert* **7** (5) (1992) 14–20.
[123] Perry D.E., Staudenmayer N.A., Votta L.G., "People, organizations, and process improvement", *IEEE Software* **11** (4) (1994) 36–45.
[124] Poulin J.S., Caruso J.M., "A reuse metrics and return on investment model", in: *Advances in Software Reuse*, IEEE Computer Society Press, Los Alamitos, CA, 1993, pp. 152–166.
[125] Prieto-Díaz R., "Domain analysis: An introduction", *ACM SigSoft Software Engineering Notes* **15** (2) (1990) 47–54.

[126] Prieto-Díaz R., "Implementing faceted classification for software reuse", *Communications of the ACM* **35** (5) (1991).
[127] Prieto-Díaz R., Arango G., *Domain Analysis and Software Systems Modeling*, IEEE Computer Society Press, Los Alamos, CA, 1991.
[128] Prieto-Díaz R., Arango G., "Domain analysis concepts and research directions", in: Prieto-Díaz R., Arango G. (Eds.), *Domain Analysis and Software Systems Modeling*, IEEE Computer Society Press, Los Alamos, CA, 1991, pp. 9–33.
[129] Radice R., Roth N., O'Hara A., Ciarfella W., "A programming process architecture", *IBM Systems Journal* **24** (2) (1985).
[130] Rich C.H., Waters R.C., "Automatic programming: Myths and prospects", *Computer* **21** (8) (1988) 40–51.
[131] Scharff E., "Applying open source principles to collaborative learning environments", in: *Proc. Conference on Computer Supported Collaborative Learning (CSCL 2002), Boulder, CO*, 2002, pp. 499–500.
[132] Scharff E., "Open source: A conceptual framework for collaborative artifact and knowledge construction", in: *Computer Science*, Univ. of Colorado–Boulder, 2002, p. 198.
[133] Schneider K., Schwinn T., "Maturing experience base concepts and DaimerChrysler", *Software Process Improvement and Practice* **6** (2001) 85–96.
[134] Schön D.A., *The Reflective Practitioner: How Professionals Think in Action*, Basic Books, New York, 1983.
[135] Schwaber K., Beedle M., *Agile Software Development with Scrum*, Prentice-Hall, 2001.
[136] Shaw M., Garlan D., *Software Architecture: Perspectives on an Emerging Domain*, Prentice-Hall, Upper Saddle River, NJ, 1996.
[137] Shipman F., McCall R., "Supporting knowledge-base evolution with incremental formalization", in: *Proc. Human Factors in Computing Systems (CHI '94), Boston, MA*, ACM, New York, 1994, pp. 285–291.
[138] Simos M., "Organization domain modeling (ODM): Formalizing the core domain modeling lifecycle", in: *Proc. Symposium on Software Reusability SSR'95, Seattle, WA*, 1995, pp. 196–205.
[139] Simos M., Creps D., Klinger C., Levine L., *Organization Domain Modeling (ODM) Guidebook*, Unisys Corporation, Reston, VA, 1995.
[140] Simos M.A., "The growing of an Organon: A hybrid knowledge-based technology for software reuse", in: Prieto-Díaz R., Arango G. (Eds.), *Domain Analysis and Software Systems Modeling*, IEEE Computer Society Press, 1991, pp. 204–221.
[141] Stein E.W., Zwass V., "Actualizing organizational memory with information systems", *Information Systems Research* **6** (2) (1995) 85–117.
[142] Sutton S.M., Heimbinger D., Osterweil L.J., "APPL/A: A language for software process programming", *Transactions on Software Engineering and Methodology* **4** (3) (1995) 21–286.
[143] Tautz C., Althoff K.-D., "Using case-based reasoning for reusing software knowledge", in: *Proc. 2nd International Conference on Case-Based Reasoning (ICCBR'97)*, Springer-Verlag, 1997, pp. 156–165.

[144] Terveen L., Wroblewski D., "A collaborative interface for browsing and editing large knowledge bases", in: *National Conference of the American Association for AI, Boston, MA*, AAAI, 1990, pp. 491–496.
[145] Terveen L.G., Selfridge P.G., Long M.D., "Living design memory—framework, implementation, lessons learned", *Human–Computer Interaction* **10** (1) (1995) 1–37.
[146] Thomas M., McGarry F., "Top down vs. bottom up process improvement", *IEEE Software* **11** (4) (1994) 12–13.
[147] Tracz W., "International conference on software reuse summary", *ACM SIGSOFT Software Engineering Notes* **20** (2) (1995) 21–25.
[148] USC, Model-Based Architecting & Software Engineering. Available at http://sunset.usc.edu/research/MBASE/index.html, last update: 6/6/2002, 2002, last accessed: Nov. 2002.
[149] Vessey I., Glass R., "Strong vs. weak approaches to system development", *Communications of the ACM* **41** (4) (1998) 99–102.
[150] Walsh J.P., Ungson G.R., "Organizational memory", *Academy of Management Review* **16** (1) (1991) 57–91.
[151] Walz D.B., Elam J.J., Curtis B., "Inside a software design team: Knowledge acquisition, sharing, and integration", *Communications of the ACM* **36** (10) (1993) 62–77.
[152] Winn T., Calder P., "Is this a pattern?" *IEEE Software* **19** (1) (2002) 59–66.
[153] Winograd T., Flores F., *Understanding Computers and Cognition: A New Foundation for Design*, Addison-Wesley, Reading, MA, 1986.

Why New Software Processes Are Not Adopted

STAN RIFKIN

*Master Systems Inc.
2604B El Camino Real
Carlsbad, CA 92008
USA*

Abstract

Why do we often appear not to do what is best for us, at least what someone else thinks is? To what extent do the reasons have to do with what is being suggested vs. to how the implementation is planned and executed? Is there a way to accelerate the rate at which the implementation of process adoption can be achieved? These questions are addressed by reviewing the considerable literature on implementations of software engineering, information systems, and quality improvement.

```
1. Change Is Harder Than We Think . . . . . . . . . . . . . . . . . . . . . . .   84
2. The Answers . . . . . . . . . . . . . . . . . . . . . . . . . . . . . . . .   86
   2.1. The First Model . . . . . . . . . . . . . . . . . . . . . . . . . . . .   86
   2.2. Advantages of the First Model . . . . . . . . . . . . . . . . . . . . .   89
   2.3. The Second Model . . . . . . . . . . . . . . . . . . . . . . . . . . .   89
   2.4. Advantages of the Second Model . . . . . . . . . . . . . . . . . . . .   93
3. Beginning the Inquiry . . . . . . . . . . . . . . . . . . . . . . . . . . .   93
   3.1. Definition of Adoption . . . . . . . . . . . . . . . . . . . . . . . .   93
   3.2. Framework for Inquiry . . . . . . . . . . . . . . . . . . . . . . . .   93
   3.3. Fields Touched by Implementation Research . . . . . . . . . . . . . .   94
   3.4. Ambit of Software Processes . . . . . . . . . . . . . . . . . . . . .   95
4. Process Descriptions of Implementation . . . . . . . . . . . . . . . . . .   96
   4.1. Description of Stage or Phase Models . . . . . . . . . . . . . . . . .   96
   4.2. Duration of Stage or Phase Models . . . . . . . . . . . . . . . . . .   97
   4.3. Non-Linear (Messy) Models . . . . . . . . . . . . . . . . . . . . . .   98
5. Diffusion: The Most Popular Explanation . . . . . . . . . . . . . . . . . .  101
   5.1. Problems with Diffusion as an Explanation . . . . . . . . . . . . . .  103
6. Resistance . . . . . . . . . . . . . . . . . . . . . . . . . . . . . . . .  105
```

	6.1. Reluctance Because the Proposed Change is a Bad Idea. That Is, There Is Conflict!	105
	6.2. Reluctance Because We Are Inertial Beings and We Resist Change	106
	6.3. Institutional Forces Invite Us to Imitate, to Conform	107
	6.4. Latency Because There Is Gap between Knowing and Doing	108
7.	Path Dependence Theory	109
8.	Process Studies	110
9.	Factor Studies	110
	9.1. Characteristics of the Innovation	111
	9.2. Organizational Characteristics	113
	9.3. Environmental Factors	113
	9.4. Adopter Characteristics	114
	9.5. Leadership	114
	9.6. User Acceptance	115
10.	Case Studies	115
	10.1. Diffusion	115
	10.2. Other Case Studies	115
11.	Conclusion	115
	Acknowledgements	116
	References	116

In general, this chapter is a literature review of how to accelerate adoption of software engineering-related processes by software managers and engineers. It adds value by acting as a lens to help make sense of the numerous field studies on the subject (175 references are cited).

1. Change Is Harder Than We Think

"Not much has changed in a system that failed: The F.B.I. and C.I.A. missed signals a year ago. Now they do well in capital turf wars" [1]. So reads a recent headline related to change one year after the September 11th, 2001, attack on the World Trade Center. If ever there were motivation to change disaster has to be it.

Or does it? One way that the history of surgery is divided is pre- and post-Listerism.[1] Joseph Lister, also the namesake of Listerine-brand mouthwash, was the inventor of antiseptic surgery in the 1850s in Scotland. In the wars at the time there were more injuries from field surgery than from battle! Surgery then was considered a form of butchery because of the pain (there was no anesthesia) and the near certain death from infection. Lister missed many cues on his way to discover that cleaning the wound—and his hands, uniform, and instruments—before, during and

[1] I am indebted to Watts Humphrey for this example.

after surgery dramatically reduced mortality. But even after he demonstrated this dramatic decrease in mortality (from forty percent in one ward to two percent) antiseptic surgery was not adopted in England and the United States (it was adopted in Germany, where it saved many, many lives). An analysis of the diffusion of antiseptic surgery lists nine factors[2] that impeded its adoption [2]. Oddly, about the same time anesthesia during surgery was invented and it was promptly adopted in England and the U.S.

"Turf" referred to in the F.B.I. and C.I.A. headline, above, also was one of the factors in the impediments to adopting antiseptic surgery. As will be explored below, new processes often mean a change in power and a change in power can mean a change in the ability to pay the mortgage. What we ordinarily call resistance may be nothing more pernicious than protecting our ability to pay our mortgages.

> "This failure to sustain [improvement processes] recurs again and again despite substantial resources committed to the change effort (many are bankrolled by top management), talented and committed people 'driving the change,' and high stakes. [T]he sources of these problems cannot be remedied by more expert advice, better consultants, or more committed managers. The sources lie in our most basic ways of thinking." [3, p. 6]

In today's world of pressure to deliver software in a very short time, we barely have time to develop the software that is functionally required, so how would we have time to learn and become competent at a new process? This question is often produced when such "grand" improvements as the Software Engineering Institute's Capability Maturity Models are suggested or the Experience Factory or ISO 9000. Yet, when eXtreme programming or agile methods or the Rational Unified Process are suggested there appears to be a receptiveness absent to the grand processes. The explanation, suggested below (Section 9.1), is that the grand methods are not sufficiently divisible, even though they have a bunch of little moving parts. One has to adopt a totality of the processes in those grand methods in order to achieve certification or the promised benefits, but with the smaller methods the benefits appear to be incremental and closely follow the implementation of any one of the sub-practices (such as pair programming and refactoring in eXtreme programming).

We all adopt new practices for reasons, presumably rational ones. One observes that there is almost no empirical evidence for the most widely-adopted software engineering processes, which include structured programming, abstract data types, object-oriented design and programming, CASE tools, statistical process control, fourth-generation languages, and formal methods [4]. This applies as well to the

---

[2]Medical administration, social interpretation, professional tradition, national competition, theoretical orientation, experimental investigation, technical evaluation, surgical demonstration, and final assimilation.

more modern adaptations, such as eXtreme programming and agile methods (though there is some empirical evidence for pair programming [5]).[3]

Another observation would not be so flattering about the decision to adopt. In the most widely cited business journal article [6], the authors explain how they sought to understand how managers made decisions, which rational models did they apply to weigh the multiple factors that would need to be taken into account. Instead they found a garbage can: managers are presented solutions and problems asynchronously. Solutions are matched to problems when the presentation of the problem is proximate in time (especially just after) the presentation of the solution: they are taken out of the garbage can when a match is made with a problem.

Whether there is a good reason to change can be seen in either light (no empirical evidence or the garbage can), neither of which is potentially very compelling.

2. The Answers

Alas, our field is known for its impatience. In that spirit, I want to sum up the whole chapter with the best two descriptions of adoption. That is, I want to present The Answers. Each is more or less from a single reference; it is always dangerous to rely on a single source, and the justifications after the explanation of the models explore why that particular article is seminal.

The basis of selection for these two answers is over-simple: They elegantly explain a great deal of otherwise monolithic approaches, such as factor studies that try to identify and isolate the controlling influences on adoption. The two answers below are more dynamic and identify that certain factors are more influential during certain epochs or under certain conditions and not at other times/conditions. Such a contingency style ("What is critical for adoption?" "It depends!") reveals far more than any set of single factors that are linearly aligned in an inexorable (or unstated) time sequence. Also, both answers leave plenty of room for human forces, technical details, and organizational/environmental influences, all of which are part of the rich reality of implementing software engineering processes.

2.1 The First Model

The model is taken from Repenning [7]. The explanation of process adoption relies on Fig. 1. The grammar of the diagram was first popularized in Senge [8], where it is

---

[3] In all fairness, the journal *Empirical Software Engineering* (ISSN 1382-3256) has been created to fulfill the need for empirical evidence regarding software technologies. There is no evidence that the Journal is consulted by decision-makers, nor is there evidence that decision-makers consult any substantiation of advantage of the technology under consideration.

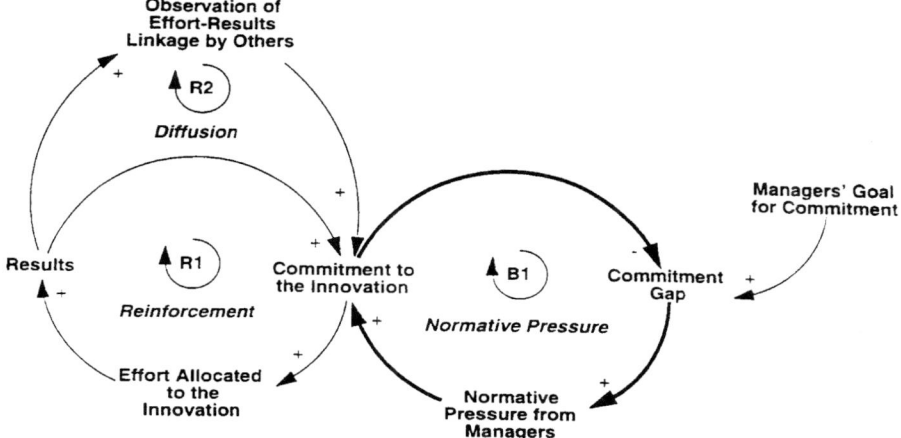

FIG. 1. Arrangement of the dynamic forces of implementation (from [7, pp. 109–127]. Reprinted by permission of the Institute for Operations Research and the Management Sciences (INFORMS)).

called a causal loop diagram. The intuition is that there are three forces that determine whether a new process will be used in practice: normative pressure, reinforcement, and diffusion.

- Normative pressure is that exerted by management to meet expectations, to achieve norms. Managers set goals for commitment to implement the innovation (in this case, process improvement). If the gap between the managers' goal and the current commitment is large enough, then the pressure on those affected is increased to raise their commitment to implement.
- Reinforcement is the process by which the pressure to increase commitment is translated into effort. In this model there is a direct relationship between effort and results, so as effort is increased then positive results are, too.
- Diffusion is something of the flywheel effect in which those affected observe improved results so they, in turn, increase their commitment to implement the improvement innovation.

The explanation—composed of the (necessarily) linear arrangement of words, sentences, and paragraphs—gives the appearance that managers' normative intentions might begin the whole process and then the flow proceeds in the manner described above for the first time through. After that, things can get interesting. For example, Repenning [7, p. 120] described an instance where the diffusion loop damps the commitment to implement when the results appear to be disproportionately low with respect to the effort allocated.

The simulation model in the title of Repenning's article illustrates the interaction among the three forces. Essentially, the two loops with the R1 and R2 labels tend to amplify effects, because there are + marks all the way around each loop; the one marked B1, where B stands for balancing, because it has an odd number of + marks [9], can reduce future commitment as the gap between actual commitment and the managers' goals closes.

Now we can see the ups and downs of implementation:

- When the managers' goals for commitment are not sufficiently different from the current commitment then there will be insufficient pressure to commit to going forward.
- Whenever the effort is (too) low, then the results will be low and the commitment will decrease in a vicious cycle.
- Whenever the effort-results linkage observed is (too) low, then others will not be inspired to commit and the effort allocated will be decreased, decreasing the results still more, in a vicious cycle.

Repenning was able to reproduce in his model the situation in which managers set appropriate goals, allocate sufficient effort and then underestimate the delay needed to achieve results, so the commitment is eroded and the results fall off because of the connections among the goal, commitment, effort, and results. With another set of values, Repenning showed that once the flywheel effect of diffusion is in place, due to the long-term positive relationship between effort and results, then normative pressure does not play such an important role, can be removed, and the implementation continues its virtuous cycle.

Repenning, at the end of the article gives advice to managers facing the task of implementation:

1. Do not prepare to implement something new until and unless "fully committed to the effort and patient in the months between adopting" and having the results motivate further deployment.
2. While seeking to have the results themselves stimulate the flywheel effect, do not do this at all costs. Such a Herculean effort would be seen by future adopters as an effort disproportionate to the results and therefore the virtuous cycle would not happen.

The first bit of advice is important because so many authors implore their readers to frame the process improvement implementation as a project, rather like a software project. This would miss the point that planning a software project is by and large a solved problem, while planning human changes, especially by engineers and engineering managers, is not. Accordingly, Repenning's advice can be seen as a case perhaps for *planning* a process improvement as a project, but then do not *implement* it as a project, as it is too difficult to estimate the relationships among the variables.[4]

2.2 Advantages of the First Model

There are several reasons that Repenning is a superior source on understanding why new processes are not adopted:

- It has face validity, that is, it tracks what we already know by personal, idiosyncratic experience, and by the experience of others (to be detailed below as part of the literature review).
- It pulls in the characteristics we customarily, perhaps cursorily, associate with implementation success, such as leadership (setting norms and sticking with them), managing change (how improvement is communicated, as in the effort-results link), allocating sufficient resources (effort in this case), rewards, and the need to begin improvement with sufficient energy.
- It takes into account many forces, not just a single one.
- Those forces are arranged in a simple structure that can have a complex, non-linear interaction. Causes may become effects, there can be competition among the forces or they can align, and, therefore, not only success can be explained but so can failure. And the model illustrates the possible ups and downs.
- It describes both a process and factors.
- It depends upon and sums up considerable theory. It is not just one person's bright idea.
- Without the insight gained by using the model we are unlikely to succeed on intuition alone.

We will visit and re-visit these desiderata in the course of reviewing the history of what is known about getting best software engineering practices into actual practice.

2.3 The Second Model

In her article, Markus [10] guides us through the "home grounds" of the two most prevalent arguments about why process innovations are not adopted: either the

---

[4] Mark Paulk frames it differently. Some software projects are planned as discovery activities, iteratively reducing equivocality in the problem, solution, and/or project spaces. Implementation can gainfully be planned and performed this way, in planned cycles that iteratively identify and reduce risk. (Personal communication.)

process (or system of processes) itself is flawed in some technical respect (e.g., hard to use) [11], or the intended targets of the improvement (we humans) have some inherent reason to resist the implementation [12]. That is, there is a system-determined answer and a people-determined answer; the result in both cases is resistance. It is, therefore, the role of the implementer to either restructure the technical aspects of the system or restructure the people aspects (rewards, incentives, span of control, new job titles).

Markus notes that we see this dichotomy in solutions: some solutions address purely technical aspects, such as user involvement in the requirements and design phases, and others address how humans change in response to new processes trying to be introduced. She proposes a third theory, interaction, which does not rely on the assumptions of the other two. There are two variants of interaction theory:

1. Sociotechnical: it's all one system, and every part interacts with the others [13–15].
2. Political: it's about power, who has it, and who loses and gains with the introduction of the new stuff.

Markus frames her insights in terms of resistance (see Table I).

Like any good theory, these three can be used to predict where to look for problems and solutions (see Table II).

What she finds, and asks us readers to look closely at our own situations for, is that (even) when people- and system-determined problems are addressed and solved, "resistance" remains, but when interaction with the organizational context or power distribution is addressed, then the "resistance" goes away. Accordingly, interaction theory is a better guide for implementation.

Looking at interaction instead of people or systems implies that a certain kind of information is used as evidence of implementation. That kind of information is not usually valued by us engineers or business people. The logic of using this kind of evidence begins with a worldview or ontology. Ontologies are basic beliefs about how the world works. One example is positivism, which believes that there is an enduring reality that exists independent of our sensing or perception of it. When we turn our backs on a mountain it is still there! Another example is that the world is socially-constructed, that we make sense of what we perceive based on what society instructs us to. Each of these two examples also implies epistemology and methodology, that is, what can be known for sure and what methods generate such knowledge. Positivism, sometimes called "normal science," believes in "hard" facts—that is, quantitative measurements—obtained in such a way that the measurements can be obtained by anyone else equipped with the instruments. Interpretivism, which corresponds to the social construction of reality, seeks to find the patterns that operate in social settings, the collections of phenomena that seem to fit together. In the interpre-

TABLE I
THEORIES OF RESISTANCE: UNDERLYING ASSUMPTIONS (FROM [10, PP. 430–444]. (C) 1983 ACM, INC. REPRINTED BY PERMISSION)

	People Determined	System-Determined	Interaction Theory
Cause of resistance	Factors internal to people and groups	System factors such as technical excellence and ergonomics	Interaction of system and context of use
	Cognitive style Personality traits Human nature	Lack of user-friendliness Poor human factors	*Sociotechnical variant:* Interaction of system with division of labor
		Inadequate technical design or implementation	*Political variant:* Interaction of system with distribution of intra-organizatonal power
Assumptions about purposes of information systems	Purposes of systems are consistent with Rational Theory of Management, can be excluded from further consideration	Purposes of systems are consistent with Rational Theory of Management, can be excluded from further consideration	*Sociotechnical variant*: Systems may have the purpose to change organizational culture, not just workflow *Political variant*: Systems may be intended to change the balance of power
Assumptions about organizations	Organizational goals shared by all participants	Organizational goals shared by all participants	*Sociotechnical variant*: Goals conditioned by history *Political variant*: Goals differ by organizational location; conflict is endemic
Assumptions about resistance	Resistance is attribute of the intended system user; undesirable behavior	Resistance is attribute of the intended system user; undesirable behavior	Resistance is a product of the setting, users, and designers; neither desirable nor undesirable

tivist paradigm it is acceptable that the search for those patterns is in a social setting that cannot be repeated, because the environment is not controlled or even controllable, as in a test tube laboratory. Objectivity in this paradigm cannot be obtained. The methods are generally called qualitative [16–20].

The interaction framework espoused by Markus means leaving the methods of normal science (and engineering and commerce) in favor of interpretation, a form

TABLE II
THEORIES OF RESISTANCE: PREDICTIONS (FROM [10, PP. 430–444]. (C) 1983 ACM, INC. REPRINTED BY PERMISSION)

	People-Determined	System-Determined	Interaction Theory (Political Variant)
Facts needed in real-world case for theory to be applicable	System is resisted, resistors differ from nonresistors on certain personal dimensions	System is resisted, system has technical problems	System is resisted, resistance occurs in the context of political struggles
Predictions derived from theories	Change the people involved, resistance will disappear	Fix technical problems, resistance will disappear	Changing individuals and/or fixing technical features will have little effect on resistance
	Job rotation among resistors and nonresistors	Improve system efficiency Improve data entry	Resistance will persist in spite of time, rotation, and technical improvements Interaction theory can explain other relevant organizational phenonema in addition to resistance

of subjective judgment. If we accept the invitation to take into account new kinds of information (namely subjective sources) then we may see things we did not before. But, it is a difficult habit to break by letting go what we think we can know for sure in exchange for learning more about the situation from less of an absolute perspective.

It is worth mentioning that one of the objections of normal science is that social scientists "make up" constructs, such as morale, intelligence, and power, that those constructs do not have an existence independent of their definitions. Abraham [21], a recovering physicist, has argued persuasively that the constructs of classical physics, such as distance, acceleration, and force, to mention but a few, are no less "made up" and do not exist independent of our thoughts about them. That we ascribe measurements to distance, acceleration, and force reify them precisely to the extent that measurements of morale, intelligence, and power do.

One of the popular ways to express that the social construction of reality acts as filter on what we see is the often-cited quip quoted by Karl Weick [22, p. 1]. It refers to American baseball, where a ball is thrown (pitched) towards a batter. If the batter does not swing, then a judge (an umpire) calls either "ball" if the trajectory was outside a mythical box between the shoulders of the batter and his knees, or "strike" if it was inside that box. Three umpires were talking. The first said, "I calls them as they is." The second said, "I calls them as I sees them." The third and cleverest umpire said, "They ain't nothin' till I calls them." Later Weick avers that when people say "I'll believe it when I see it," they more likely mean "I'll see it when I believe it." And, quoting another source, "man is an animal suspended in webs of significance he himself has spun" [22, pp. 134–135].

2.4 Advantages of the Second Model

Like the first model, this one incorporates other theories [23], so it is not (just) one person's bright idea. It also addresses competing theories that are likely the most prevalent in the implementation literature and practice, so the insights are novel and useful. It also predicts the problems and solutions better than the other two competing theories. In addition, "resistance" is redefined as natural and a part of any change, not something to be conquered and overcome. And last, it invites us to broaden our computer science-, software engineering-centric methods for observing and gathering information, something that many implementers feel is necessary to be successful, that somehow trying harder with what we already know how to do is not more effective [24].

3. Beginning the Inquiry

We begin by delimiting the scope of our inquiry. We examine definitions of adoption, phases of getting processes into practice, which fields might best contribute to our understanding, and what we mean by software processes. Then we examine the sources of insight one subject at a time. The conclusion is brief, as The Answers have already been presented above.

3.1 Definition of Adoption

There are many synonyms, such as technology transfer, technology transition, technology infusion, diffusion, dissemination, deployment, assimilation, and implementation. In the sense we use them we mean that some practice or process or procedure is in regular, normal use by those intended as targets of usage. The focus is on usage on the job, the actual practice of a process.

3.2 Framework for Inquiry

Lucas et al. [25] suggest a framework for reviewing what is known about implementation: theory, process, and factor; see also Kwon and Zmud [26]. To this we add the single category of case studies and personal (idiosyncratic) experiences. Essentially, theory represents the accumulation of empirical evidence of patterns. It is the highest form of knowledge because it sums so many observations. At the other end of the knowledge spectrum, case studies and personal experiences represent the least knowledge because they are points about which we must infer the salient factors for our own purposes.

In between theory and stories there are studies of the process or steps and the characteristics that imply success or failure, that is, the factors that bear on the outcome of implementation. There are naturally many studies that cross over, such as the theory of the process of implementation.

3.3 Fields Touched by Implementation Research

Why and how some implementations of processes are successful and others are not can be seen from many perspectives. Among those surveyed here, however briefly, are:

- Innovation—This is the creation of the new process. Many believe that taking implementation concerns into account during innovation increases the likelihood of adoption. Therefore, some scrutiny of the innovation process is common. In addition, there is belief that one of the important predictors of implementation success is an "innovative" atmosphere, one that is receptive to new ideas. This is also the place for path dependence, the notion that in order for certain innovations to be successful there must have been a path or trajectory of prerequisite occurrences.
- Managing human change and organizational culture—This is usually couched in terms of identifying and countering "resistance," though sometimes one can only infer that "resistance" is being addressed because it is not explicitly stated. There are many commercially available change management approaches and programs, all of which subscribe to the people-oriented theory in the Markus article, above. The notion is that some organizational cultures (for example, the unspoken rules) are more conducive to adoption than others. Qualitative organizational learning is in this category because it tries to leverage human change lessons learned (actually lessons observed).
- Leadership and management—It is received wisdom that change is accelerated when it is sponsored by the leader of the organization. Accordingly, this field is also based on the people-oriented theory, and can be part of the process description (that is, exactly what does leadership do) or part of the factors (strength of leader's support). Leadership is commonly the subject of idiosyncratic stories ("Here is how I led change"), perhaps because leadership is often thought to

be determinative of the outcome, and a common trait of failure: lack of upper management support (whatever that might mean) augurs for an unsuccessful outcome.

- Social construction of reality—All engineering takes place in a context, much of which is socially constructed. Therefore, it is useful to view adoption as an activity situated in a social system. Indeed, such a view is indispensable because it enables the planner of an implementation to take into account the human and collective aspects in addition to the technical or engineering aspects. The difference between this area and the one on managing human change is the unit of analysis. The unit in this area is a team, group, division, or other collective. The unit in the human change area is the individual, be it a leader, manager, champion, agent, or target.
- Social shaping of technology—Technology is not a value-free, neutral conduit through which new ideas flow. Rather, the technical aspects of innovations themselves are the results of choices, sometimes on a scale that is impacted by national policy, habits, culture, and economics. Sometimes, for example, the technology represents a dialectic between labor and management, as when it is applied to the de-skilling of workers.
- Mathematical modeling—This is normally applied to the view of adoption as diffusion, something like a contagion or bacterium spreading in a finite medium. This also includes quantitative learning curves, the steady improvement with practice.

3.4 Ambit of Software Processes

The scope of this chapter is software engineering processes and software development management processes. These processes include the type that are standardized by international standards organizations, such as ISO 9000, and standardized by governments, such as military standards, federal civilian agency standards (e.g., U.S. National Aeronautics and Space Administration, U.S. Federal Aviation Administration). They also include de facto standards, such as the Software Engineering Institute's Capability Maturity Model, Bootstrap, and other normative process standards. In addition, software engineering processes include computer-aided software engineering (CASE), about which much has been written with regard to implementation, adoption, deployment, and their many synonyms.

While we focus on software processes, we do not confine our inquiry solely to them. We borrow where appropriate from other engineering and business disciplines, including adopting new products. While products and processes have several important differences, primary among them the ability to observe adoption, we borrow from the understanding of product adoption when it helps us understand process adoption. See, for example, [27].

4. Process Descriptions of Implementation

4.1 Description of Stage or Phase Models

Adoption can be viewed as one phase or stage in a sequence of events. Here are several descriptions of the stream:

Redwine et al. [28] use:

1. Concept formulation, the emergence of the key idea.
2. Development and extension, usually via a seminal paper or demonstration system.
3. Enhancement and exploration (internal), in which usable capabilities are available.
4. Enhancement and exploration (external), which shifts usage outside of the development group.
5. Popularization, substantial evidence of value and application, such as 40–70% usage.

Maier [29], in Fig. 2, relying on Schumpeter [30], uses three stages:

1. Invention, when new products or processes are developed.
2. Innovation, when the products or processes are introduced in the market.
3. Imitation or diffusion, when they are spread.

The Software Engineering Institute has created the IDEAL model [31] to sequence the phases:

1. Initiating, a discovery activity, looking for motivation and alternatives.
2. Diagnosing, performing an appraisal of the baseline.
3. Establishing, setting goals and planning.
4. Acting, actually introducing the new process (in this case).
5. Leveraging, observing lessons and trying to feed them back into the next improvement cycle.

Caputo uses a framework that has grown through oral repetition [32,33]:

1. Contact with the new idea.
2. Awareness of the technical merits and its possible impact.
3. Understanding what it could mean in this organization.
4. Definition of the new process or how the new product will be used.

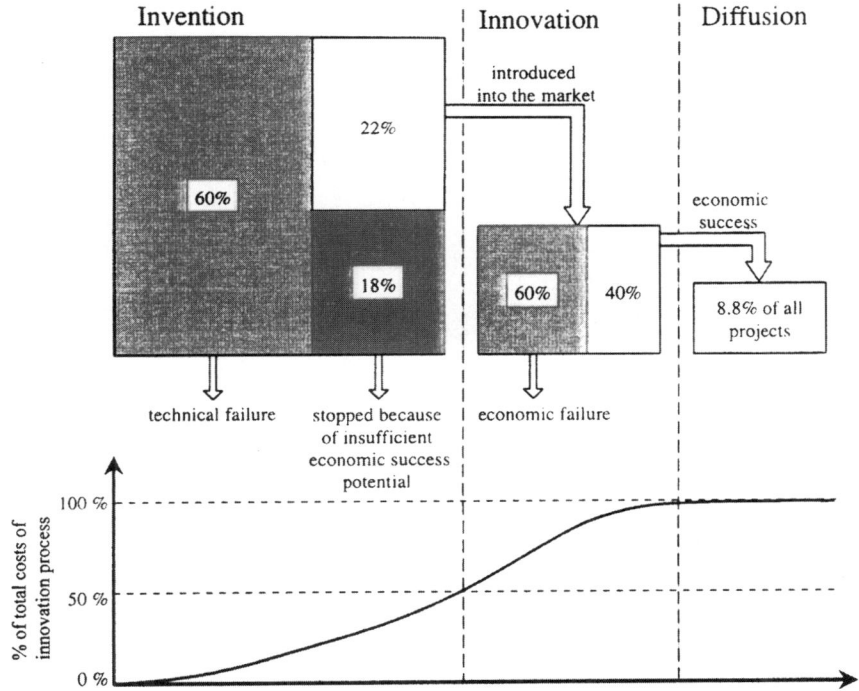

FIG. 2. Cascading outcome of innovation activity (from [29, p. 286]. © John Wiley & Sons Limited. Reproduced with permission).

5. Installation of the new product or process, evaluate first instances.
6. Adoption, requiring regular usage.
7. Institutionalization, during which the practice becomes the normal way.
8. Internalization, when one can no longer remember doing it any other way.

4.2 Duration of Stage or Phase Models

Two studies have measured the duration for software engineering process innovations to transit roughly from awareness to regular usage. Redwine and his colleagues found the duration to be 8 to 20 years across an industry [28], and Zelkowitz found it took four to five years within a given company [27]. One other study, of Hewlett Packard's adoption of the formal software inspection process, suggests it can take ten years to reach a 25% adoption level [34].

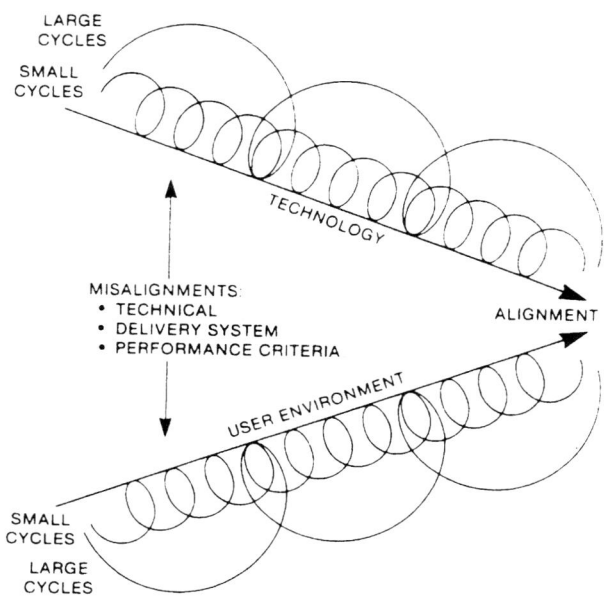

FIG. 3. Mutual adaptation of technology and organization. (Reprinted from [35]. © 1988, with permission from Elsevier Science.)

4.3 Non-Linear (Messy) Models

Leonard-Barton [35], in a model that augurs the future, proposes a messy process of mutual adaptation, where the technology to be adopted is modified as it is assimilated and the organization transforms, too, as the technology is assimilated. Each—the technology and the organization—accommodate to each other. Her Fig. 3 clearly indicates that this process is not algorithmic, not linear, not even predictable except at its highest level of granularity.

She also introduces the logic of "fit" by showing the potential for misalignments among the technical details of the technology, how success is measured, and how the technology is used in the user environment. Perhaps more than any other description of the process of adoption, this one tips away from normal engineering and towards a more liberal allowance for the evidence that will be admitted (translated) as knowledge. This view will argue against application of traditional project management for adoption because loops are not permitted in normal descriptions of projects and also because it will be difficult to estimate the transit time and resources needed to make forward progress. Rather, progress in this model is made by surfacing and addressing issues and bottlenecks, and it is difficult to anticipate what those might be and how

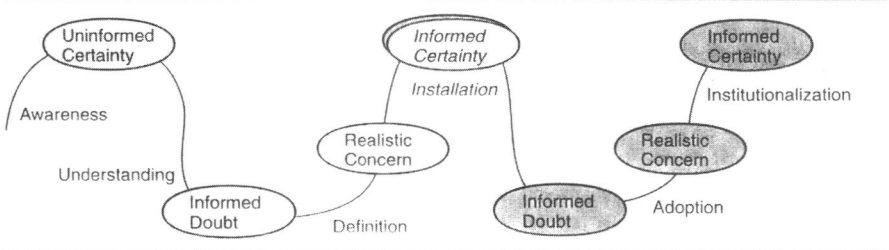

FIG. 4. Keep the rhythm going for two beats to make successful change (from [32, p. 61], fig. 4-12. © UNISYS Corp. Reprinted by permission of Pearson Education, Inc.).

long it might take to resolve each one. Accordingly, managing adoption *qua* learning has apparent appeal.

Inspired by Leonard-Barton, we can find additional evidence of the messiness of implementation. Caputo [32] offer a unique perspective, in which cycles of doubt, concern, and certainty are normal. She found that if two of these cycles could be completed then change, that is implementation, is successful (see Fig. 4).

Another view that supports the cyclic nature of change, and therefore the problem of predicting how many cycles an organization will transit in order to make change, comes from the addiction literature [36]. At the risk of conflating the unit of analysis by moving from organizational to individual, there is some value in seeing that in certain contexts it is normal that change is not a linear, step-by-step process, but rather an (*a priori*) unknown number of iterations, each of which consumes an unknown length of time (see Fig. 5).

In yet further support for the cyclic nature of adoption, Tyre and Orlikowski [37, 38] found that adoption and utilization of technology is not an incrementally adaptive pattern described by stage models. Instead they found that mutual adaptation à la Leonard-Barton occurs in a discontinuous pattern that frequently displays periods of routine use [39].

Perhaps the least "process" of the process models is due to Fowler and Rifkin [40], the so-called double-bubble (see Fig. 6); also shown without attribution in Rai [41, p. 99]. It differentiates between the push of technology attractiveness and the pull of market or technology needs [42]. The intuition is that technology producers create innovations that are advocated inside their own organizations, perhaps by staff members who have a marketing role. Those advocates communicate to a population containing potential adopters, sometimes using advertising or other public methods of communication. In organizations that are "eligible" to adopt there are other staff members who represent a "surface" of needs to the world. Those staff members have (many) contacts in the technology provider community so they are "connected" [43].

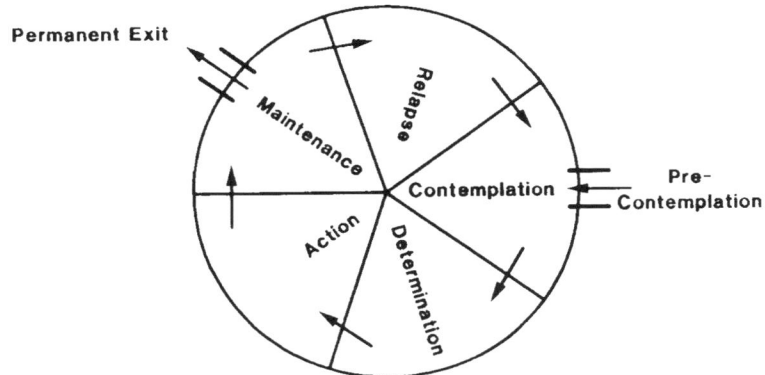

FIG. 5. Prochaska and DiClemente's six stages of change (from [36]).

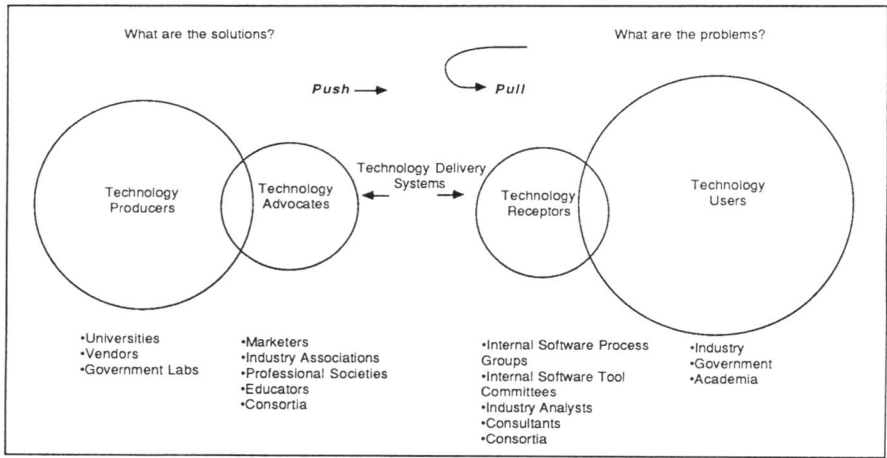

FIG. 6. "Double-bubble" process of technology adoption (from [40, p. 118], permission to reproduce © 1990 by Carnegie Mellon University is granted by the Software Engineering Institute).

When such a technology receptor locates what appears to be a solution to his/her organization's problems, then the diffusion process described by Rogers, below, begins.

Other process descriptions include Huff and Munro [44], and Lassila and Brancheau [39].

5. Diffusion: The Most Popular Explanation

"Diffusionism does not consist of a single idea." [45, p. 67]

Rogers has provided an encyclopedic description [46] of the diffusion of innovation from thought to implementation. He defines "diffusion is the process by which an innovation is communicated through certain channels over time among the members of social system" [46, pp. 5–6]. While Rogers takes pains to argue the contrary, most interpreters view diffusion as a linear, one-way process in which a small group of first adopters ("innovators" in Rogers' terminology) inform the next round of adopters, who in turn inform the next round, etc. And the usual growth of adoption is a pattern like the growth of bacteria in a finite medium, the familiar cumulative S-curve (see Fig. 7).

The first derivative of the S-curve can be the normal distribution, so many authors, including Rogers, use the symmetric bell curve to describe the population of adopters (see Fig. 8).

> Somebody develops an innovation. The innovation has (user) features that can be fairly exactly described and it is clearly separated from other physical objects or abstract phenomena. The innovation is in essence without modifications, spread to people who individually decide whether or not to adopt the innovation. Information about the innovation is initially spread through channels such as professional associations and journals. Next, the news about the innovation is communicated through a social network where the first adopters are key. From these prerequisites follows the division of adopters into the categories ... [47, p. 36]

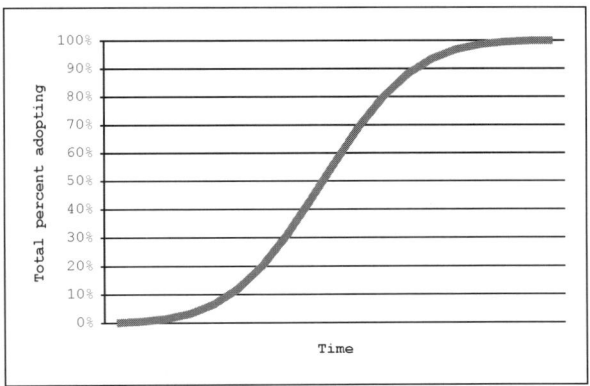

FIG. 7. Usual pattern of diffusion, according to [46, p. 106].

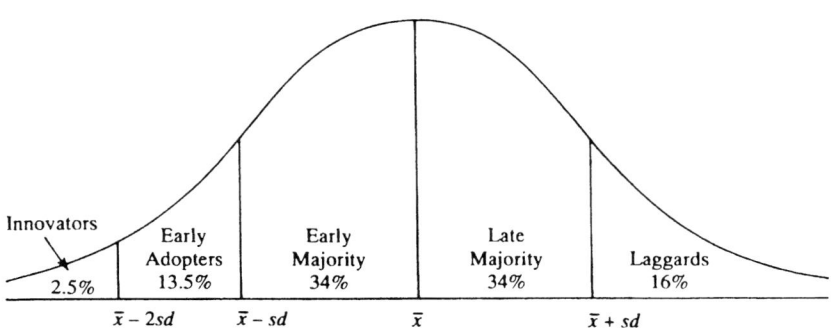

FIG. 8. Adopter categorization on the basis of innovativeness (from [46, p. 262]. Reprinted with the permission of The Free Press, an imprint of Simon & Schuster Adult Publishing Group. © 1995 by Everett M. Rogers. © 1962, 1971, 1983 by The Free Press.)

Since it is based on a mathematical formulation of a communication process, several authors [48–53] use diffusion to predict adoption. In particular they often use a formulation due to Bass [52] (q.v. for a diskette containing an Excel spreadsheet to compute the diffusion), in which additional forces are taken into account, namely the (internal) pressure to imitate and the (external) pressure to innovate.

The mathematical formulation of diffusion can be stated as:

$$\frac{dN(t)}{dt} = g(t)[\overline{N} - N(t)],$$

where $N(t)$ is the cumulative number of adopters at time t, $\overline{N}$ is the total number of potential adopters in the social system at time t (the ceiling or asymptote of the adoption curve), and $g(t)$ is the coefficient of diffusion. Then the general, mixed influence model is

$$\frac{dN(t)}{dt} = (a + bN(t))[\overline{N} - N(t)],$$

where everything is as before, and a is the coefficient of external influence and b is the coefficient of internal influence. As mentioned above, external influence refers to the pressure to innovate and internal influence refers to the pressure to imitate. With appropriate manipulation, the mixed influence equation can be solved for $N(t)$ for estimated values of a and b (which are usually estimated from history) [51].

The International Federation for Information Processing (IFIP) Working Group 8.6 was established by IFIP in 1994 to focus on diffusion, transfer and implementation of information technology. Working Group 8.6 conducts conferences and workshops, maintains a listserv, publishes books (usually workshop proceedings [54–57]) and a semi-annual newsletter (Eight.six at http://www.isi.salford.ac.uk/ifip/home.

html). In addition, the Diffusion Interest Group in Information Technology (DIGIT) usually holds an annual workshop in conjunction with the International Conference on Information Systems (http://www.icisnet.org/).

5.1 Problems with Diffusion as an Explanation

Despite its surface appeal there have been numerous objections. Perhaps the most striking one is "No theory of diffusion has been developed as yet. Hence, diffusion, at best, might is [sic] an umbrella for strategy, innovation, network theory, social structural theory, and a host of other approaches to understanding change in organizational settings" [47, p. 35]. Rogers himself has a section on "Criticisms of diffusion research" [46, Chapter 3] that addresses many of the arguments against diffusion as an explanation of adoption.

Perhaps two of the most unaddressed areas by Rogers are complexity and colonialization. Numerous authors [26,47,58–64] remark that Rogers' view of diffusion is too simple, too linear. It does not take into account price, substitutable alternatives, marketplace externalities (such as standardization or widespread adoption), network externalities (how many others are using it that I need to interconnect with) [65], the diversity of the adopter population, the complications of making the adoption decision (one part of the organization decides to adopt, another pays for it, and yet another is actually the target of change), simple vs. complex innovations, and radical vs. incremental innovation. Granstrand, for example, proposes a model where the diffusion is separable between buyers and sellers [66], Glaziev and Kaniovski propose a model that is stochastic, not just deterministic (as is Rogers) [67], Fichman and Kemerer study the situation in which the technology has been acquired but not deployed [59], Lyytinen takes into account transaction costs [68], Swanson and Ramiller note that innovation and diffusion are not separate and disconnected stages [69],[5] and Chaddha and Chitgopekar argue that Rogers explains successful diffusion but not its failure, in this case Picturephone [70].

One of the most popular of these views is Moore [61], a marketing specialist, who tried to apply Rogers' adopter categories and instead found gaps, chasms, between adjoining categories. Moore redrew Rogers' bell curve (see Fig. 9).

The speculation based on experience is that adoption is not a smooth process like a contagion, rather it is a difficult selling effort in which adopters of earlier categories do not and possibly cannot influence future adopters. Rather, it is up to marketing and sales forces to reframe the reasons for adoption and to act as the power behind the diffusion.

Similar to this view is that diffusion is a construct of reductionists who see the world as a set of problems to be solved, where the problems are defined in terms of a

---
[5] This is akin to the social structuring of technology.

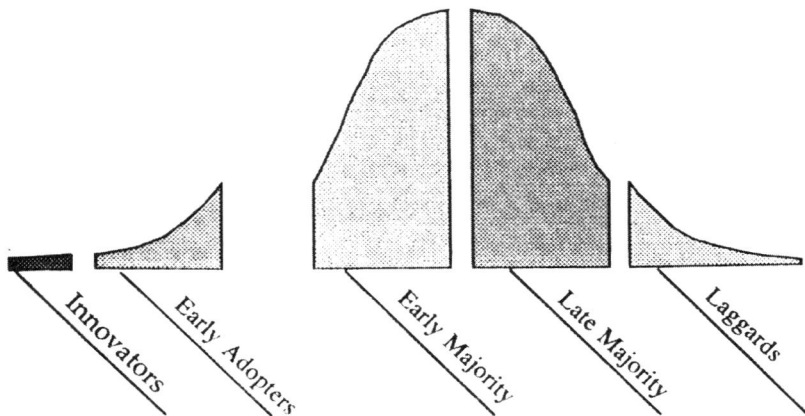

FIG. 9. The *revised* technology adoption life cycle (from [61, p. 17]. © 1991 by Goeffrey A. Moore. Reprinted by permission of HarperCollins Publishers Inc.).

(limited) number of variables that are usually related linearly. This ontological commitment relies on a persistent or observer-invariant truth, with time moving linearly at a universal rate with no consideration of different time perceptions [71].

The principal antidote applied to information systems is Soft Systems Methodology [72,73] and its cousin, Actor Network Theory [17]. These approaches are more qualitative than quantitative, see innovations not so much as waiting to be discovered but rather already in the landscape to be reframed (translated) into useful knowledge by any of the actors, not some specially-designated "inventors" or geniuses. There is a collective, holistic sense, not atomistic (that is, reductionist) sense, to these methods, so they tend to be rich with detail and a complexity that reflects the situation (that is, requisite complexity). In addition, these methods do not separate technology and the social system, rather technology is situated along with many other things in the social system. Another way of saying this is that adoption of technology is socially constructed [74].

The concept of the social construction of business events is illustrated by a business researcher [75], "Organizational change is stimulated not by *pressures* from the environment, resulting in a buildup of problems triggering an automatic response, but by *perceptions* of that environment and those pressures held by key actors" [75, p. 281] [italics in original]. Later she writes, "Organizational change consists in part of a series of emerging constructions of reality, including revision of the past, to correspond to the requisites of new players and new demands" [75, p. 287].

Perhaps the most intriguing critique is that diffusion à la Rogers is fundamentally imperialism, the standard model of Western colonialism [45]. Basically this view is that we view adopters as open vessels ready to accept (that is, adopt) our ideas because we are superior so then are our ideas. Traditional diffusion assumes evaluation of innovation on the basis of the transmitter, not necessarily of the receiver. "For example at a fundamental level, diffusionism takes 'facts' to be pre-existing (often hidden), waiting to be uncovered at some point by heroic discoverers and inventors" [45, p. 68].

6. Resistance

Markus [10] is not the first to observe that we often attribute our frustration with the rate of adoption to the individual personalities of the adopters. In particular, we typify them as "bad characters," resisters who eschew change, stuffy, viscous, and ossified. Certainly one of Rogers' contributions is that to the extent personalities enter into the adoption decision, there is a range of possibilities to consider, including those that easily, quickly, and readily adopt.

6.1 Reluctance Because the Proposed Change is a Bad Idea. That Is, There Is Conflict!

Sometimes conflict itself is the beacon that can serve to warns us that the change(s) we are proposing are bad ideas. It's not the actors, it's the technology being implemented: it does not fit in some significant way. This tension can be managed in a dialectic [76], or used as a barometer such that implementation is not attempted until and unless the tension has been resolved rationally.

One of the conflicts identified is a misfit with strategy [77,78]. Essentially, most process improvements are aimed at a particular organizational strategy or value proposition called operational excellence. This strategy is to be the lowest cost provider in a market by having the highest quality. Operationally excellent organizations have short menus of goods or services, and have a "formula" for addressing buyer needs. But that leaves two other strategies underserved by traditional process improvement. Those strategies are product innovativeness and customer intimacy.

Each of the three strategies requires a different set of software engineering process innovation in order to optimize the values it delivers to its clients. Therefore, one size cannot fit all, and therefore some of the organizations that attempt to adopt a particular innovation might find that it is ill suited for its purposes. Naturally, the members of that organization should be counted on to raise this possibility to those supporting adoption, not as resisters, but rather as protectors of the organization's unique value proposition.

Perhaps it is worth mentioning that sometimes hierarchical power is used to counter resistance. While in general beyond the scope of this chapter, there is at least one study [79] of software engineering innovation that indicates that when the power inherent in the hierarchy is imposed on those required to adopt we can expect a lack of adoption. The exercise of the power of the hierarchy is not an effective accelerator of innovation adoption.

In addition, exercise of the power of the hierarchy is coercive [80], something usually perceived and resented by software engineers. The most effective innovative organizations use influence instead of authority to stimulate change [81].

6.2 Reluctance Because We Are Inertial Beings and We Resist Change

Tushman and his colleagues [82,83] examined organizations that had made successful technological changes and compared them with organizations that had not successfully made such changes. They sought the critical difference that spelled success or failure.

They developed a construct, competency-enhancing and competency-destroying, to characterize technology and the way it is introduced for implementation. Competency-enhancing technology is that which performs functions we already perform another way. The standard examples are word processors and spreadsheet programs, as we have been writing and calculating for a long time before the advent of these computerized tools. We implement competency-enhancing technologies by executing the tutorials, reading the help screens, and asking central help desks.

Competency-destroying technologies, on the other hand, require that we learn something so new that everything we have learned to date may not help us understand this new technology. In the realm of software engineering, object orientation is a competency-destroying technology to a lifelong COBOL programmer. Nothing about COBOL or the years spent becoming competent would help prepare a COBOL programmer for object orientation. The authors in their study found that implementing a competency-destroying technology is different than implementing a competency-enhancing one. For competency-destroying, we are undermining the power relations in the organization, we are making people who have become competent and skilled look stupid and incompetent. We are threatening to move them from self-actualization down the Maslow hierarchy back to shelter and hygiene. That is, we are threatening them with losing their jobs.

In order to protect the ability to pay mortgages, people who have to adopt competency-destroying technologies have to be reassured that their competence will be gradually restored in a planning and managed way, that their power and ability to pay their mortgage are not at stake, and that they won't have their performance assessed for a long time as they learn this new technology. The method of implementation is more idiosyncratic, personal, one-to-one, adapted to the particular characteristics of the new learner.

There are other variations than competency-enhancing vs -destroying, e.g., evolution vs. revolution [84].

Many authors have suggested that "resistance" be dropped from our collective vocabularies [85–92] at least because by labeling a behavior we stop examining it, stop continuing to develop an understanding of it. One thing seems evident: we are *not* inertial beings, resistant to change. But it is natural that we do express doubts about changes that challenge either what we understand is the purpose of our organization or our long-earned power inside the organization.

6.3 Institutional Forces Invite Us to Imitate, to Conform

Institutionalization in sociology is the habit of an organization to repeat what it knows and to imitate others it admires.[6]

Just look at the title of the seminal article on the subject: *The Iron Cage Revisited: Institutional Isomorphism and Collective Rationality in Organizational Fields* [93]. The Iron Cage! Iron cage is the literary term for prison. Max Weber, one of the most famous sociologists, wrote: "... the care for external goods should only lie on the shoulders of the 'saint like a light cloak, which can be thrown aside at any moment.' But fate decreed that the cloak should become an iron cage." DiMaggio and Powell write that by this Weber warned that rationalism had ushered in an era in which capitalism and its offspring, bureaucracy, had become an iron cage for humanity [93, p. 147].

What accounts for the lack of diversity in organizational life when organizations themselves—from the standpoint of the diversity of the people in them and the diversity of their markets and market disciplines—seem so different? It's that organizations copy one another and there is great pressure to look and act alike, the authors show. The main point of the literature on institutionalization is what a strong, pervasive, and latent force it is. Organizations may not so much resist change; rather they conform to very large, powerful norms. One can see it in the number of organizations that try to imitate Microsoft's software development practices, but few try to imitate the Software Engineering Laboratory at NASA's Goddard Space Flight Center, a standard example of a measurement-centric high process maturity organization (http://sel.gsfc.nasa.gov/).

---

[6]Unfortunately the Software Engineering Institute has used the term to mean adoption, the way Rogers defined it as "regular usage."

6.4 Latency Because There Is Gap between Knowing and Doing

Authors Pfeffer and Sutton, in *The Knowing-Doing Gap* [94], explore a phenomenon that many of us see every day: we fail to do what we know we should. Their four-year in-depth study indicates that there are no simple answers, except, perhaps that more information is not needed (for example, ask a cigarette smoker if he/she needs more information in order to stop). They found eight guidelines for closing the gap between knowing what to do and actually doing it.

Why before how: Philosophy is important. Organizations that try to copy the processes of others often find those processes ineffective. The survey illustrates that processes are situated in organizations that have reasons for performing those processes and the borrowing organization might not have the "why," so the "how" does not work.

Knowing comes from doing and teaching others how. To some degree this is restatement of what Peters and Waterman [95] found long ago among some of the most successful organizations: a bias towards action. In a theme repeated often, we cannot know how to implement unless we try it because it's a messy process. And we should not mistake talk for action, we should not accept that deciding to implement is the same as implementing.

Action counts more than elegant plans and concepts. To some degree this is restatement of the principle above and borrows from Peters and Waterman's famous observation of "ready, fire, aim." There is such value in learning by doing that plans and concepts are no substitute.

There is no doing without mistakes. What is the company's response? In the world of action mistakes are inevitable. Organizations that have closed the knowing-doing gap treat mistakes as a natural part of doing and use the mistakes as occasions for learning. Surgeons call this "forgive and remember" [94, p. 132]!

Fear fosters knowing-doing gaps, so drive out fear. If we fear for our jobs then we are less likely to take the chances that are inherent in performing some new action, making the inevitable mistakes. We would fear that such mistakes would count against us and we may form a basis for poor performance and then we could lose our jobs.

Beware of false analogies: fight the competition, not each other.
In some organizations, particularly ones that are considered fiercely competitive, it is difficult to achieve teamwork because the external competitive spirit "leaks" into internal behavior and undermines cooperation. Therefore, internal competition defeats closing the knowing-doing gap.

Measure what matters and what can help turn knowledge into action. Those organizations that have closed the knowing-doing gap use (a) a few simple measures, and (b) have a clear implication of the impact of each person's performance on the goals of the organization. Some organizations use a balanced scorecard, but cut the number of measures way down from the number usually suggested for "completeness."

What leaders do, how they spend their time and how they allocate resources, matters. Time is a non-renewable resource. We all know that, so if our leader spends his or her time acting on knowledge then we all see that is valued and we begin to understand that is part of our job, too.

7. Path Dependence Theory

Path dependence is the observation that sometimes the trajectories of events leading to an innovation all pointed in the same direction. There was a path, more or less inexorable, along which our adoption travels. How could we fail to adopt microwave ovens and cellular phones? There were historical antecedents of what we thought is novel.

Sometimes this temporal process that underlies the construction of phenomena is called creative destruction [96]. If there is an inexorable path, then what about innovators and entrepreneurs? Garud and Karnøe [97] come to the rescue by proposing a relatively new construct, path creation. Stated most succinctly,

> For entrepreneurs attempting to create paths, the world is constantly in the making. Indeed, entrepreneurs creating new paths are more likely to embrace a logic of mindful deviation. Such logic involves spanning boundaries between structures of relevance. On one hand, entrepreneurs are insiders possessing knowledge of a technological field and an appreciation of what to deviate from and the value of pursuing such a strategy. On the other hand, they are outsiders evaluating how much they can deviate from existing relevance structures. And because many deviations are perceived as threatening, entrepreneurs have to buy time, with which and within which to protect and nurture new ideas and create provinces of meaning. From this perspective, ideas are carefully evaluated on an ongoing basis and even those that are abandoned may play a role in shaping ideas that survive over

time. Temporal elasticity is linked with intertemporal acumen. [97, p. 9, without notes and references]

This description is akin to Leonard-Barton's in Fig. 3, above. In this sense, we implementers are the entrepreneurs about which Garud and Karnøe speak because we are treading new ground as we try to weave technology and organization together.

8. Process Studies

Besides the process studies cited in Section 4, above, we add here a few of the details of the process of adoption from Rogers' explanation of diffusion [46]. He defines "the innovation-decision process as the process through which an individual (or other decision-making unit) passes from first knowledge of an innovation to forming an attitude toward the innovation, to a decision to adopt or reject, to implementation and use of the new idea, and to confirmation of this decision" (p. 20). The five main steps in time order, therefore, are (1) knowledge, (2) persuasion, (3) decision, (4) implementation, and (5) confirmation. For Rogers, the transit is a communication process, where individuals use communication channels to traverse the steps.

We can visualize the steps Rogers describes by thinking of a different kind of communication, that of a disease, the type that is, well, communicable. The progression of steps that Rogers describes is an epidemic, started in a particular locus and then transmitted to an ever-increasing radius of individuals by positive contact [98]. In this model, increased communication implies increased adoption. Increased speed of communication implies increased speed of adoption.

9. Factor Studies

Factor studies seek to identify and isolate the variables that correlate with outcomes. The usual criticism of factor studies most significant in our case is that factors represent some linear combination of influences, but offer little about the timing, interaction, and causal implications of the influences. Some studies cover a large number of factors [99–101] and others focus on a single factor or cluster of them that might be identified by a single term, such as "leadership."

Perhaps the best study for our purposes is Lopata's dissertation [102]. She examined a range of factors in four categories (see Fig. 10).

As the reader can see, Lopata attempts to predict what drives Leonard-Barton's model mutual adaptation between the organization and the technology [35]. Lopata's study is one of the very few that have any quantitative data, holding out the hope that one day we may be able to predict the duration, effort, and resources required to implement an information system.

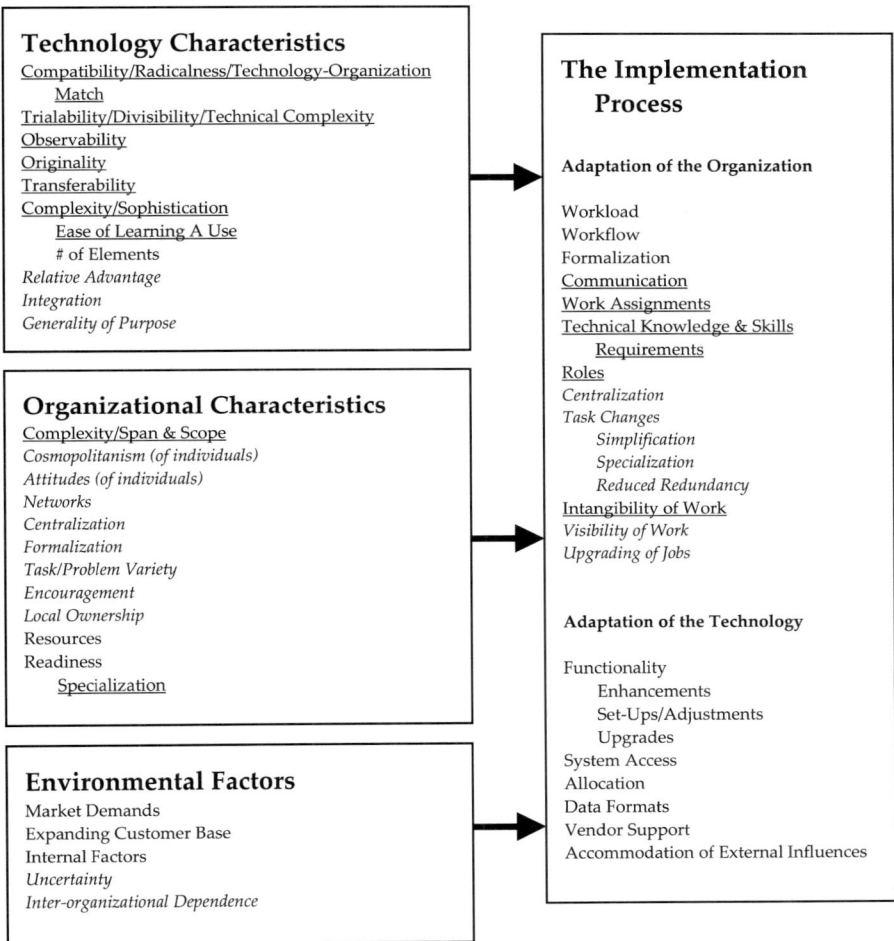

FIG. 10. Factor model of the information system implementation process. Adapted from [102, p. 95]. Legend: Plain = not predicted by the literature, yet found in the Lopata study, that is, a new factor; *italics* = predicted in the literature and not found in the study; underlined = predicted in the literature and found in the study.

9.1 Characteristics of the Innovation

Lopata uses five of Rogers' characteristics of innovations that predict adoption [46, pp. 15–16]:

1. Relative advantage is the degree to which an innovation is perceived to be better than the idea or product or process it supersedes.
2. Compatibility is the degree to which an innovation is perceived to be consistent with the existing culture and needs. See also Ramiller for a counterargument [103].
3. Complexity is the degree to which the innovation is difficult, or at least more difficult than its competitors.
4. Trialability and divisibility are measures of the degree to which an innovation may be taken apart and only a part tried. A thick, monolithic innovation has a lower trialability than one that has separable components, each of which adds some value.
5. Observability is the degree to which the results of the implementation will be visible.

Tornatzky and Klein [104], studying 75 reports of innovation characteristics, augment the list with:

6. Cost, presumably negatively related to adoption.
7. Profitability, presumably positively correlated with adoption.
8. Social approval is the degree to which one's status is improved by the innovation. In light of the "cost" and "profit" categories, this one refers to a nonfinancial reward.

Lopata found these factors to add:

9. Originality is the novelty of the innovation.
10. Transferability refers to the ability inherent in the innovation to transfer skill and knowledge about it to others.
11. Generality of purpose is the degree to which an innovation fills a large space of needs. Low generality would be a very specific innovation.

There is an important sense that in order to improve the chances of implementation, one must design into the technology (that is, product, services, or process) characteristics that make it possible to adopt a little at a time, factors such as trialability, divisibility, observability, and transferability. These all imply the "chopping" up of the technology so that it can be absorbed in small pieces, not as one whole, big chunk. This may be the reason for the popularity of the 12 eXtreme programming practices or the Rational Unified Process: one can select as much or as little as is needed in one application. And this may be part of the problem with grand improvement schemes, such as the SEI CMM or ISO 9000: they are a lot to swallow and you have to swallow the whole thing to earn the certification.

Swanson creates a typology of information systems innovations and notes that the pattern of adoption is different for different types of innovations [105].

9.2 Organizational Characteristics

The organization is the collective that is going to use the new product or process. There are factors in the target organization that can accelerate or impede implementation. Lopata [102] cites the following factors among many others:

1. Networks refers to the existence of communication channels via which information (buzz) about an innovation can travel.
2. Centralization is the degree to which decisions are made centrally, presumably taking into account factors from a wide perspective.
3. Formalization is the degree to which decisions are formally decided, with a written trail (see also [106]).
4. Task/problem variety is the degree to which the work that the innovation addresses is routine or varied.
5. Encouragement is the degree to which there is a climate of risk taking with respect to innovation.
6. Local ownership is the degree to which implementation is managed locally, independent of the decision to adopt (which would be centralization).
7. Resources is the degree to which the organization has the ability to adopt the innovation.

In addition, organization structure has been studied [107], the impact of information overload [108], task-technology fit, technology-strategy fit [109], product championship and top management support [110], and overall organizational context (a contingency approach) [111–115].

9.3 Environmental Factors

There are factors that surround the organization, adopters, and the innovation. They are large-scale forces that can impact the environment in which innovations are being created, introduced, and implemented.

1. Market demands is the degree to which this innovation is required by the market, reflects an imitation of a competitor organization, or is ahead of the market.
2. Uncertainty is the degree to which market conditions are unforeseen or unforeseeable.
3. Inter-organizational dependence is the degree to which an innovation will have a ripple effect among related organizations.

Slightly different lists can be found in other studies [116–119]. Also, there have been studies that focus on the relative strength of the pull of market needs vs. the push of technological advantages [120–122].

9.4 Adopter Characteristics

Rogers [46] lists the five categories that are in Figs. 8 and 9. He calls first adopters or innovators venturesome, early adopters respectful, the early majority deliberate, the late majority skeptical, and the laggards traditional. Moore [61] calls the first adopters deviant, early adopters visionaries, early majority needing a business case, late majority want the innovation shrink-wrapped, and laggards are, well, never going to adopt.

Lopata adds [102, p. 95]:

6. Span and scope, which refers to the reach of communications by an individual. This is sometimes called sphere of influence.
7. Cosmopolitanism, which implies that people who are more worldly adopt more easily.
8. Readiness is the degree to which an individual has the resources to attend to an innovation.
9. Specialization is the degree to which special knowledge is needed to implement the innovation or the benefits of the innovation. See also Fichman and Kemerer [58] and Marshall *et al.* [123].

Other authors offer additions, in particular voluntariness, management support, expectation realism, and the participation in the adoption decision by the targets [124], demographics [125], adoption beliefs [126], implementation history [127], characteristics of the external information sources and communication channel effectiveness [41,128], and job experience and persuasion strategy [129].

9.5 Leadership

Perhaps one of the most-cited characteristics of successful implementation efforts is executive sponsorship, that is, how people at the top of organizations express their leadership. Perhaps the most articulate and detailed advocate for the leadership effect on implementation is Rosabeth Moss Kanter [75,130–158].

Moss Kanter, through extensive and intensive case studies, has found a number of philosophies and behaviors that if leaders adopt them then there in markedly increased probability of implementation success. Her work straddles leadership, innovation, managing change, and implementation. Her mantra is "The imagination to innovate, the professionalism to perform, and the openness to collaborate, this is how to lead the change-adept organization" [155]. She is sanguine about providing The Answer [158]: "I also learned there are no easy answers. Indeed, I conceive of the task of 'managing change'—a task we perform in our personal lives as well as our business lives—as a series of perennial balancing acts. We must juggle contradictions, we must make tradeoffs between contrasting goals, and we must steer a course that does not go too far in any one direction lest events require an about-face. We are perched on a pendulum that is swinging back and forth faster and faster" [158, p. 13].

9.6 User Acceptance

A number of studies address the distinction among the factors of usage, perceived ease of use, and perceived usefulness [77,159]. Others have addressed user involvement in the systems development process, which, in our context would be akin to software engineers being involved in the design and development of their own management and engineering practices [160,161].

10. Case Studies

Case studies are perspectives or retrospectives that depend upon the observer's direct experience. While all case studies try to offer information that can be used generally, it is usually unclear how to generalize these personal observations.

10.1 Diffusion

As diffusion is a simple, easily-understood, and often-cited framework for adoption, there are many case studies that bear on software engineering processes [162–164]. See Zelkowitz for a particularly careful case study [27].

10.2 Other Case Studies

Swanson is a collection of case studies [165]. In addition there is a survey of software developers' perception of the value of software process improvement [166], expert systems adoption that does not appear to use an theoretical basis for data collection [167], evolution of CASE adoption in Finland [168], CASE adoption in Taiwan [169], the difference between user and non-users of CASE [170], the use of innovation characteristics to predict failure [171], phased adoption applied to reuse [172], and adoption patterns and attitudes about computer-supported meetings [173].

11. Conclusion

One observation is inescapable: we don't have models of adoption that we can use quantitatively to estimate the duration of adoption, the cost of adoption, or the impact of various accelerators and barriers on the rates and degree of penetration. Two studies give us hope:

- Lopata's in which she counted the number of meetings, hours, durations, documents, and other artifacts of adoption [102].
- Byrd and Marshall's model of the determinants of how information technology impacts organizational performance [174], which is what we seek for adoption. See also Cale and Curley [175].

A common theme is that there is not one single answer to why software engineering processes, or any other processes, are not implemented. Instead, implementation can be a messy, social process among humans and not have much in common with the expected practice of engineering. To illustrate this and give us hope that we can marshal the actions of implementation we might look at what Rosabeth Moss Kanter found as she chronicled the implementation of innovations in many organizations [75, pp. 284 ff]:

- Individuals disappear into collectives.
- Early events and people disappear into the background as later events and people come forward.
- Conflicts disappear into consensuses.
- Equally plausible alternatives disappear into obvious choices.
- Accidents, uncertainties, and muddle-headed confusions disappear into clear-sighted strategies.
- Multiple events disappear into single thematic events.
- The fragility of changes (that exist alongside the residues of the old system) disappear into images of solidarity and full actuality.

ACKNOWLEDGEMENTS

This chapter has benefited from improvements suggested by Ray Fleming, Robert Glass, Watts Humphrey, Philip Johnson, Steve Ornburn, Mark Paulk, Shari Lawrence Pfleeger, and John Tittle. I am especially grateful to the Series Editor, Marvin Zelkowitz, for letting me express some thoughts that had been brewing for a long time.

REFERENCES

[1] Risen J., Johnston D., "Not much has changed in a system that failed: The F.B.I. and C.I.A. missed signals a year ago. Now they do well in capital turf wars", *New York Times* (September 8, 2002), Section 4, p. 1.

[2] Gaw J.L., *'A Time to Heal': The Diffusion of Listerism in Victorian Britain*, American Philosophical Society, Philadelphia, PA, 1999.
[3] Senge P., et al., *The Dance of Change: The Challenges of Sustaining Momentum in Learning Organizations*, Currency Doubleday, New York, NY, 1999.
[4] Fenton N., Pfleeger S.L., Glass R.L., "Science and substance: A challenge to software engineers", *IEEE Software* **11** (4) (1994) 86–95.
[5] Williams L., Kessler R.R., Cunningham W., Jeffries R., "Strengthening the case for pair programming", *IEEE Software* **17** (4) (2000) 19–25.
[6] Cohen M.D., March J.G., Olsen J., "A garbage can model of organizational choice", *Administrative Science Quarterly* **17** (1) (1972) 1–25.
[7] Repenning N.P., "A simulation-based approach to understanding the dynamics of innovation implementation", *Organization Science* **13** (2) (2002) 109–127.
[8] Senge P.M., *The Fifth Discipline: The Art & Practice of the Learning Organization*, Currency Doubleday, New York, NY, 1990.
[9] Richardson G.P., *Feedback Thought in Social Science and Systems Theory*, University of Pennsylvania Press, Philadelphia, PA, 1991.
[10] Markus M.L., "Power, politics, and MIS implementation", *Communications of the ACM* **26** (8) (1983) 430–444.
[11] Fitzgerald B., "Formalized systems development methodologies: A critical perspective", *Information Systems Journal* **6** (1) (1996) 3–23.
[12] Roth G., Kleiner A., *Car Launch: The Human Side of Managing Change*, Oxford University Press, New York, NY, 2000.
[13] Bostrom R.P., Heinen J.S., "MIS problems and failures: A socio-technical perspective, part I: The causes", *MIS Quarterly* **1** (3) (1977) 17–32.
[14] Harris M., "Organizational politics, strategic change and the evaluation of CAD", *Journal of Information Technology* **11** (1) (1996) 51–58.
[15] Ryan T.F., Bock D.B., "A socio-technical systems viewpoint to CASE tool adoption", *Journal of Systems Management* **43** (11) (1992) 25–29.
[16] Burrell G., Morgan G., *Sociological Paradigms and Organizational Analysis*, Heinemann, Portsmouth, NH, 1979.
[17] McMaster T., Vidgen R.T., Wastell D.G., "Technology transfer: diffusion or translation?", in: McMaster T., Mumford E., Swanson E.B., Warboys B., Wastell D. (Eds.), *Facilitating Technology Transfer Through Partnership: Learning from Practice and Research, Proceedings of the IFIP TC8 WG8.6 International Working Conference on Diffusion Adoption and Implementation of Information Technology, Ambleside, Cumbria, UK*, Chapman & Hall, London, 1997, pp. 64–75.
[18] Meyerson D., Martin J., "Cultural change: An integration of three different views", *Journal of Management Studies* **24** (6) (1987) 623–647.
[19] Silva J., Backhouse J., "Becoming part of the furniture: The institutionalization of information systems", in: Lee A.S., Liebenau J., DeGross J.I. (Eds.), *Information Systems and Qualitative Research, Proceedings of the IFIP TC8 WG 8.2 International Conference on Information Systems and Qualitative Research, May 31–June 3, Philadelphia, PA, USA, 1997*, Chapman & Hall, London, 1997, pp. 389–414, Chapter 20.

[20] Orlikowski W.J., Baroudi J.J., "Studying information technology in organizations: Research approaches and assumptions", *Information Systems Research* **2** (1) (1991) 1–28.
[21] Kaplan A., *The Conduct of Inquiry: Methodology for Behavioral Science*, Chandler Pub. Co., San Francisco, 1964.
[22] Weick K., *The Social Psychology of Organizing*, 2nd ed., Wiley, New York, 1979.
[23] Markus M.L., Robey D., "Information technology and organizational change: Causal structure in theory and research", *Management Science* **34** (5) (1988) 583–598.
[24] Butler B., Gibbons D., "Power distribution as a catalyst and consequence of decentralized diffusion", in: Larsen T.J., McGuire E. (Eds.), *Information Systems Innovation and Diffusion: Issues and Directions*, Idea, Hershey, PA, 1998, pp. 3–28.
[25] Lucas Jr. H.C., Ginsberg M.J., Schultz R.L., *Information Systems Implementation: Testing a Structural Model*, Ablex, Norwood, NJ, 1990.
[26] Kwon T.H., Zmud R.W., "Unifying the fragmented models of information systems implementation", in: Boland Jr. R.J., Hirschheim R.A. (Eds.), *Critical Issues in Information Systems Research*, John Wiley, Chichester, England, 1987, pp. 227–251.
[27] Zelkowitz M.V., "Software engineering technology infusion within NASA", *IEEE Transactions on Engineering Management* **43** (3) (1996) 250–261.
[28] Redwine Jr. S.T., Becker L.G., Marmor-Squires A.B., Martin R.J., Nash S.H., Riddle W.E., *DoD Related Software Technology Requirements, Practices and Prospects for the Future*, Institute for Defense Analysis, Alexandria, VA, 1984 (P-1788).
[29] Maier F.H., "New product diffusion models in innovation management—a system dynamics perspective", *System Dynamics Review* **14** (4) (1998) 285–308.
[30] Schumpeter J.A., *Business Cycles: A Theoretical, Historical and Statistical Analysis of the Capitalist Process*, McGraw-Hill, New York, NY, 1939.
[31] McFeeley B., *IDEAL: A User's Guide for Software Process Improvement*, Software Engineering Institute, Pittsburgh, PA, 1996 (CMU/SEI-96-HB-001).
[32] Caputo K., *CMM Implementation Guide: Choreographing Software Process Improvement*, Addison-Wesley, Reading, MA, 1998.
[33] Conner D., *Managing at the Speed of Change: How Resilient Managers Succeed and Prosper Where Others Fail*, Villard Books, New York, NY, 1993.
[34] Grady R.B., Van Slack T., "Key lessons in achieving widespread inspection use", *IEEE Software* **11** (1994) 46–57.
[35] Leonard-Barton D., "Implementation as mutual adaptation of technology and organization", *Research Policy* **17** (5) (1988) 251–267.
[36] Miller W.R., Rollnick S., *Motivational Interviewing: Preparing People to Change Addictive Behavior*, Guilford Press, New York, NY, 1991.
[37] Tyre M.J., Orlikowski W.J., "The myth of continuous improvement", *Chemtech* **24** (1994) 12–19.
[38] Orlikowski W.J., "CASE tools as organizational change: Investigating incremental and radical changes in systems development", *MIS Quarterly* **17** (3) (1993) 309–340.
[39] Lassila K.S., Brancheau J.C., "Adoption and utilization of commercial software packages: Exploring utilization equilibria, transitions, triggers, and tracks", *Journal of Management Information Systems* **16** (2) (1999) 63–90.

[40] Fowler P., Rifkin S., *Software Engineering Process Group Guide*, Software Engineering Institute, Pittsburgh, PA, 1990 (CMU/SEI-90-TR-24).
[41] Rai A., "External information source and channel effectiveness and the diffusion of CASE innovations: An empirical study", *European Journal of Information Systems* **4** (2) (1995) 93–102.
[42] Zmud R.W., "An examination of "push-pull" theory applied to process innovation in knowledge work", *Management Science* **30** (6) (1984) 727–738.
[43] Spilka R., "Communicating across organizational boundaries: A challenge for workplace professionals", *Technical Communication* **42** (3) (1995) 436.
[44] Huff S.L., Munro M.C., "Information technology assessment and adoption: A field study", *MIS Quarterly* (1985) 327–339.
[45] McMaster T., "The illusion of diffusion in information systems research", in: Ardis M.A., Marcolin B.L. (Eds.), *Diffusing Software Product and Process Innovations, Proceedings of the IFIP TC8 WG8.6 Fourth Working Conference on Diffusing Software Product and Process Innovations, Banff, Canada*, Kluwer Academic Press, Boston, 2001, pp. 67–86.
[46] Rogers E.M., *Diffusion of Innovations*, 4th ed., The Free Press, New York, NY, 1995.
[47] Larsen T., "The phenomenon of diffusion: Red herrings and future promises", in: Ardis M.A., Marcolin B.L. (Eds.), *Diffusing Software Product and Process Innovations, Proceedings of the IFIP TC8 WG8.6 Fourth Working Conference on Diffusing Software Product and Process Innovations, Banff, Canada*, Kluwer Academic Press, Boston, 2001, pp. 35–50.
[48] Geroski P.A., "Models of technology diffusion", *Research Policy* **29** (2000) 603–625.
[49] Mahajan V., Muller E., Bass F.M., "New product diffusion models in marketing: A review and directions for research", *Journal of Marketing* **54** (1990) 1–26.
[50] Jaakkola H., "Comparison and analysis of diffusion models", in: Kautz K., Pries-Heje J. (Eds.), *Diffusion and Adoption of Information Technology, Proceedings of the First IFIP WG 8.6 Working Conference on the Diffusion and Adoption of Information Technology, Oslo, Norway*, Chapman & Hall, London, 1996, pp. 65–82.
[51] Mahajan V., Peterson R.A., *Models for Innovation Diffusion*, Sage, Beverly Hills, CA, 1985.
[52] Mahajan V., Muller E., Wind Y. (Eds.), *New-Product Diffusion Models*, Kluwer Academic, Boston, 2000.
[53] Larsen T.J., McGuire E. (Eds.), *Information Systems Innovation and Diffusion: Issues and Directions*, Idea, Hershey, PA, 1998.
[54] Levine L., in: *Diffusion, Transfer and Implementation of Information Technology, Proceedings of the IFIP TC8 Working Conference, Pittsburgh, PA*, North-Holland, Amsterdam, 1994.
[55] Kautz K., Pries-Heje J., in: *Diffusion and Adoption of Information Technology, Proceedings of the First IFIP WG 8.6 Working Conference on the Diffusion and Adoption of Information Technology, Oslo, Norway*, Chapman & Hall, London, 1996.
[56] McMaster T., Mumford E., Swanson E.B., Warboys B., Wastell D., in: *Facilitating Technology Transfer through Partnership: Learning from Practice and Research, Pro-*

ceedings of the IFIP TC8 WG8.6 International Working Conference on Diffusion, Adoption and Implementation of Information Technology, Ambleside, Cumbria, UK, Chapman & Hall, London, 1997.
[57] Ardis M.A., Marcolin B.L., in: *Diffusing Software Product and Process Innovations, Proceedings of the IFIP TC8 WG8.6 Fourth Working Conference on Diffusing Software Product and Process Innovations, Banff, Canada*, Kluwer Academic Press, Boston, 2001.
[58] Fichman R.G., Kemerer C.F., "The assimilation of software process innovations: An organizational learning perspective", *Management Science* **43** (10) (1997) 1345–1363.
[59] Fichman R.G., Kemerer C.F., "The illusory diffusion of innovation: An examination of assimilation gaps", *Information Systems Research* **10** (3) (1999) 255–275.
[60] Bayer J., Melone N., "A critique of diffusion theory as a managerial framework for understanding adoption of software engineering innovations", *Journal of Systems & Software* **9** (2) (1989) 161–166.
[61] Moore G.A., *Crossing the Chasm: Marketing and Selling Technology Products to Mainstream Customers*, HarperBusiness, New York, NY, 1991.
[62] Tornatzky L.G., Fleischer M., *The Processes of Technological Innovation*, Lexington Books, Lexington, MA, 1990.
[63] Lyytinen K., Damsgaard J., "What's wrong with the diffusion of innovation theory? A case of complex and networked technology", in: Ardis M.A., Marcolin B.L. (Eds.), *Diffusing Software Product and Process Innovations, Proceedings of the IFIP TC8 WG8.6 Fourth Working Conference on Diffusing Software Product and Process Innovations, Banff, Canada*, Kluwer Academic Press, Boston, 2001, pp. 173–189.
[64] Attewell P., "Technology diffusion and organizational learning: The case of business computing", *Organization Science* **3** (1) (1992) 1–19.
[65] Lange R., McDade S., Oliva T.A., "Technological choice and network externalities: A catastrophe model analysis of firm software adoption for competing operating systems", *Structural Change & Economic Dynamics* **12** (1) (2001) 29–57.
[66] Granstrand O., "Temporal diffusion and population dynamics: A systems model", in: Nakićenović N., Grübler A. (Eds.), *Diffusion of Technologies and Social Behavior*, Springer-Verlag, Berlin, 1991, pp. 247–263.
[67] Glaziev S.Yu., Kaniosvki Y.M., "Diffusion of innovations under conditions of uncertainty: A stochastic approach", in: Nakićenović N., Grübler A. (Eds.), *Diffusion of Technologies and Social Behavior*, Springer-Verlag, Berlin, 1991, pp. 231–246.
[68] Lyytinen K., "Penetration of information technology in organizations: A comparative study using stage models and transaction costs", *Scandinavian Journal of Information Systems* **3** (1991).
[69] Swanson E.B., Ramiller N.C., "The organizing vision in information systems innovation", *Organization Science* **8** (5) (1997) 458–474.
[70] Chaddha R.L., Chitgopekar S.S., "A "generalization" of the logistic curves and long-range forecasts (1966–1991) of residence telephones", *Bell Journal of Economics* **2** (2) (1971) 542–560.

[71] Linstone H.A., "Multiple perspectives on technological diffusion: Insights and lessons", in: Nakićenović N., Grübler A. (Eds.), *Diffusion of Technologies and Social Behavior*, Springer-Verlag, Berlin, 1991, pp. 53–92.
[72] Checkland P., Scholes J., *Soft Systems Methodology in Action*, John Wiley & Sons, West Sussex, England, 1999.
[73] Checkland P., *Systems Thinking, Systems Practice: Includes a 30-Year Retrospective*, John Wiley & Sons, West Sussex, England, 1999.
[74] Bijker W.E., Hughes T.P., Pinch T.J. (Eds.), *The Social Construction of Technological Systems: New Directions in the Sociology and History of Technology*, MIT Press, Cambridge, MA, 1987.
[75] Kanter R.M., *The Change Masters: Innovation & Entrepreneurship in the American Corporation*, Simon & Schuster, New York, NY, 1983.
[76] Easterbrook S. (Ed.), *CSCW: Cooperation or Conflict?* Springer-Verlag, London, 1992.
[77] Rifkin S., "What makes measuring software so hard?" *IEEE Software* **10** (3) (2001) 41–45.
[78] Rifkin S., "Why software process innovations are not adopted", *IEEE Software* **10** (4) (2001) 110–112.
[79] Bayer J., Melone N., *Adoption of Software Engineering Innovations in Organizations*, Software Engineering Institute, Pittsburgh, PA, 1988 (CMU/SEI-88-TR-27).
[80] Jermier J.M., Knight D., Nord W.R., "Resistance and power in organizations: Agency, subjectivity and the labour process", in: Jermier J.M., Knight D., Nord W.R. (Eds.), *Resistance and Power in Organizations*, Routledge, London, 1994.
[81] Lawrence P., Lorsch J., *Organization and Environment: Managing Differentiation and Integration*, Irwin, Homewood, IL, 1967.
[82] Tushman M.L., Anderson P., "Technological discontinuities and organizational environments", *Administrative Science Quarterly* **31** (1986) 439–465.
[83] Tushman M.L., Rosenkopf L., "Organizational determinants of technological change: Toward a sociology of technological evolution", *Organizational Behavior* **14** (1992) 311–347.
[84] Hardgrave B.C., "Adopting object-oriented technology: Evolution or revolution?" *Journal of Systems & Software* **37** (1) (1997) 19–25.
[85] Bartlem C.S., Locke E.A., "The Coch and French study: A critique and reinterpretation", *Human Relations* **34** (7) (1981) 555–566.
[86] Coch L., French J.R.P., "Overcoming resistance to change", *Human Relations* **1** (4) (1948) 512–532.
[87] Dent E.B., Goldberg S.G., "Challenging "resistance to change"", *Journal of Applied Behavioral Science* **35** (1) (1999) 25–41.
[88] Diamond M.A., "Resistance to change: A psychoanalytic critique of Argyris and Schon's contributions to organization theory and intervention", *Journal of Management Studies* **23** (5) (1986) 543–562.
[89] Hirschheim R., Newman M., "Information systems and user resistance: Theory and practice", *Computer Journal* **31** (5) (1988) 398–408.
[90] Krantz J., "Comment on "Challenging 'resistance to change'"", *Journal of Applied Behavioral Science* **35** (1) (1999) 42–44.

[91] Merron K., "Let's bury the term "resistance"", *Organization Development Journal* **11** (4) (1993) 77–86.
[92] Levine L., "An ecology of resistance", in: McMaster T., Mumford E., Swanson E.B., Warboys B., Wastell D. (Eds.), *Facilitating Technology Transfer through Partnership: Learning from Practice and Research, Proceedings of the IFIP TC8 WG8.6 International Working Conference on Diffusion, Adoption and Implementation of Information Technology, Ambleside, Cumbria, UK*, Chapman & Hall, London, 1997, pp. 163–174.
[93] DiMaggio P.J., Powell W.W., "The Iron Cage revisited: Institutional isomorphism and collective rationality in organizational fields", *American Sociological Review* **48** (2) (1983) 147–160.
[94] Pfeffer J., Sutton R.I., *The Knowing-Doing Gap: How Smart Companies Turn Knowledge into Action*, Harvard Business School Press, Boston, MA, 2000.
[95] Peters T., Waterman Jr. R.H., *In Search of Excellence: Lessons from America's Best-Run Companies*, Harper & Row, New York, NY, 1982.
[96] Schumpeter J.A., *Capitalism, Socialism, and Democracy*, Harper & Row, New York, NY, 1942.
[97] Garud R., Karnøe P., "Path creation as a process of mindful deviation", in: Garud R., Karnøe P. (Eds.), *Path Dependence and Creation*, Lawrence Erlbaum Associates, Mahwah, NJ, 2001, pp. 1–38.
[98] Ahire S.L., Ravichandran T., "An innovation diffusion model of TQM implementation", *IEEE Transactions on Engineering Management* **48** (4) (2001) 445–464.
[99] Roberts Jr. T.L., Gibson M.L., Fields K.T., Rainer Jr. R.K., "Factors that impact implementing a system development methodology", *IEEE Transactions on Software Engineering* **24** (8) (1998) 640–649.
[100] Yadav S.B., Shaw N.G., Webb L., Sutcu C., "Comments on 'Factors that impact implementing a system development methodology'", *IEEE Transactions on Software Engineering* **27** (3) (2001) 279–281.
[101] Roberts T.L., Gibson M.L., Rainer R.K., Fields K.T., "Response to 'Comments on factors that impact the implementation of a systems development methodology'", *IEEE Transactions on Software Engineering* **27** (3) (2001) 282–286.
[102] Lopata C.L., *The Cooperative Implementation of Information Technology: A Process of Mutual Adaptation*, Drexel University, Philadelphia, PA, 1993. Unpublished doctoral dissertation.
[103] Ramiller N.C., "Perceived compatibility of information technology innovations among secondary adopters: Toward a reassessment", *Journal of Engineering & Technology Management,* **11** (1) (1994) 1–23.
[104] Tornatzky L.G., Klein K.J., "Innovation characteristics and innovation-implementation: A meta-analysis of findings", *IEEE Transactions on Engineering Management* **EM-29** (1) (1982) 28–45.
[105] Swanson E.B., "Information systems innovation among organizations", *Management Science* **40** (9) (1994) 1069–1092.
[106] Zmud R.W., "Diffusion of modern software practices: Influence of centralization and formalization", *Management Science* **28** (12) (1982) 1421–1431.

[107] DeCanio S.J., Dibble C., Amir-Atefi K., "The importance of organizational structure for the adoption of innovations", *Management Science* **46** (10) (2000) 1285–1299.
[108] Edmunds A., Morris A., "The problem of information overload in business organisations: A review of the literature", *International Journal of Information Management* **20** (1) (2000) 17–28.
[109] Fan M., Stallaert J., Whinston A.B., "The adoption and design methodologies of component-based enterprise systems", *European Journal of Information Systems* **9** (1) (2000) 25–35.
[110] Premkumar G., Potter M., "Adoption of computer aided software engineering (CASE) technology: An innovation adoption perspective", *Data Base for Advances in Information Systems* **26** (2–3) (1995) 105–123.
[111] Rai A., Howard G.S., "Propagating CASE usage for software development: An empirical investigation of key organizational correlates", *Omega (Oxford)* **22** (2) (1994) 133–147.
[112] Rai A., Howard G.S., "An organizational context for CASE innovation", *Information Resources Management Journal* **6** (3) (1993) 21–34.
[113] Ravichandran T., "Swiftness and intensity of administrative innovation adoption: An empirical study of TQM in information systems", *Decision Sciences* **31** (3) (2000) 691–724.
[114] Ravichandran T., Rai A., "Quality management in systems development: An organizational system perspective", *MIS Quarterly* **24** (3) (2000) 381–386, 405–410.
[115] Wolfe R.A., "Organizational innovation: Review, critique and suggested research directions", *Journal of Management Studies* **31** (3) (1994) 405–431.
[116] Chau P.Y.K., Tam K.Y., "Factors affecting the adoption of open systems: An exploratory study", *MIS Quarterly,* **21** (1) (1997) 1–20.
[117] Chiasson M.W., Lovato C.Y., "Factors influencing the formation of a user's perceptions and use of a DSS software innovation", *Data Base for Advances in Information Systems* **32** (3) (2001) 16–35.
[118] Cooper R.B., Zmud R.W., "Information technology implementation research: A technological diffusion approach", *Management Science* **36** (2) (1990) 123–139.
[119] Fichman R.G., Kemerer C.F., "Adoption of software engineering process innovations: The case of object orientation", *Sloan Management Review* **34** (2) (1993) 7–22.
[120] Fowler P., Levine L., *Technology Transition Push: A Case Study of Rate Monotonic Analysis (Part 1)*, Software Engineering Institute, Pittsburgh, PA, 1993 (CMU/SEI-93-TR-29).
[121] Fowler P., Levine L., *Technology Transition Pull: A Case Study of Rate Monotonic Analysis (Part 2)*, Software Engineering Institute, Pittsburgh, PA, 1995 (CMU/SEI-93-TR-030. Note that the date from the edition ID is 1993).
[122] Rai A., Patnayakuni R., "A structural model for CASE adoption behavior", *Journal of Management Information Systems* **13** (2) (1996) 205–234.
[123] Marshall T.E., Byrd T.A., Gardiner L.R., Rainer Jr. R.K., "Technology acceptance and performance: An investigation into requisite knowledge", *Information Resources Management Journal* **13** (3) (2000) 33–45.

[124] Iivari J., "Why are CASE tools not used?" *Communications of the ACM* **39** (10) (1996) 94–103.
[125] Iivari J., "Factors affecting perceptions of CASE effectiveness", *European Journal of Information Systems* **4** (3) (1995) 143–158.
[126] Karahanna E., Straub D.W., Chervany N.L., "Information technology adoption across time: A cross-sectional comparison of pre-adoption and post-adoption beliefs", *MIS Quarterly* **23** (2) (1999) 183–213.
[127] Myers W., "Why software developers refuse to improve", *IEEE Computer* (1998) 110–112.
[128] Zmud R.W., "The effectiveness of external information channels in facilitating innovation within software development groups", *MIS Quarterly* **16** (1983) 43–58.
[129] Sagie A., Elizur D., Greenbaum C.W., "Job experience, persuasion strategy and resistance to change: An experimental study", *Journal of Occupational Behaviour* **6** (2) (1985) 157–162.
[130] Kanter R.M., Corn R.I., "Do cultural differences make a business difference? Contextual factors affecting cross-cultural relationship success", *Journal of Management Development* **13** (2) (1994) 5–23.
[131] Kanter R.M., "Swimming in newstreams: Mastering innovation dilemmas", *California Management Review* **31** (4) (1989) 45–69.
[132] Kanter R.M., North J., Richardson L., Ingols C., Zolner J., "Engines of progress: designing and running entrepreneurial vehicles in established companies: Raytheon's new product center, 1969–1989", *Journal of Business Venturing* **6** (2) (1991) 145–163.
[133] Kanter R.M., Fonvielle W.H., "When to persist and when to give up", *Management Review* **76** (1) (1987) 14–15.
[134] Kanter R.M., "Change masters vs. change stiflers", *Executive Excellence* **5** (3) (1988) 12–13.
[135] Kanter R.M., North J., Bernstein A.P., Williamson A., "Engines of progress: Designing and running entrepreneurial vehicles in established companies", *Journal of Business Venturing* **5** (6) (1990) 415–427.
[136] Kanter R.M., "Managing traumatic change: Avoiding the 'unlucky 13'", *Management Review* **76** (5) (1987) 23–24.
[137] Kanter R.M., "Championing change: An interview with Bell Atlantic's CEO Raymond Smith", *Harvard Business Review* **69** (1) (1991) 118–130.
[138] Kanter R.M., "Thinking across boundaries", *Harvard Business Review* **68** (6) (1990) 9.
[139] Kanter R.M., "Change masters: Playing a new game", *Executive Excellence* **5** (1) (1988) 8–9.
[140] Kanter R.M., "Transcending business boundaries: 12,000 world managers view change", *Harvard Business Review* **69** (3) (1991) 151–164.
[141] Kanter R.M., Richardson L., "Engines of progress: Designing and running entrepreneurial vehicles in established companies—the Enter-Prize Program at Ohio Bell, 1985–1990", *Journal of Business Venturing* **6** (3) (1991) 209–229.
[142] Kanter R.M., Richardson L., North J., Morgan E., "Engines of progress: Designing and running entrepreneurial vehicles in established companies; the new venture process at Eastman Kodak, 1983–1989", *Journal of Business Venturing* **6** (1) (1991) 63–82.

[143] Kanter R.M., Parkes C., "In search of a single culture", *Business (London)* (1991) 58–66.
[144] Kanter R.M., "Change: Where to begin", *Harvard Business Review* **69** (4) (1991) 8.
[145] Kanter R.M., "Discipline!" *Harvard Business Review* **70** (1) (1992) 7.
[146] Kanter R.M., "Six certainties for CEOs", *Harvard Business Review* **70** (2) (1992) 7.
[147] Kanter R.M., "Ourselves versus ourselves", *Harvard Business Review* **70** (3) (1992) 8.
[148] Stein B.A., Kanter R.M., "Leadership for change: The rest of the story", *Frontiers of Health Services Management* **10** (2) (1993) 28.
[149] Kanter R.M., Stein B.A., "New models, but where's the process?—Transforming Organizations edited by Thomas A. Kochan and Michael Useem", *Contemporary Sociology* **21** (6) (1992) 758.
[150] Kanter R.M., "Mastering change", *Executive Excellence* **10** (4) (1993) 11.
[151] Stein B.A., Kanter R.M., "Why good people do bad things: A retrospective on the Hubble fiasco", *The Academy of Management Executive* **7** (4) (1993) 58.
[152] Kanter R.M., "Can giants dance in cyberspace?" *Forbes (ASAP)* (1996) 247–248.
[153] Kanter R.M., "From spare change to real change", *Harvard Business Review* **77** (3) (1999) 122–132.
[154] Kanter R.M., "The enduring skills of change leaders", *Ivey Business Journal* **64** (5) (2000) 31–36.
[155] Kanter R.M., *Frontiers of Management*, Harvard Business School, Boston, MA, 1997.
[156] Kanter R.M., Stein B.A., Jick T.D. (Eds.), *The Challenge of Organizational Change: How Companies Experience it and Leaders Guide It*, Free Press, New York, NY, 1992.
[157] Kanter R.M., *Improving the Acceptance and Use of New Technology: Organizational and Inter-Organizational Challenges*, Division of Research, Harvard Business School, 1989 (Working Paper 90–043).
[158] Kanter R.M., *When Giants Learn to Dance*, Simon & Schuster, New York, NY, 1989.
[159] Venkatesh V., Smith R.H., Morris M.G., "Why don't men ever stop to ask for directions? Gender, social influence, and their role in technology acceptance and usage behavior", *MIS Quarterly* **24** (2) (2000) 115–118, 131–136.
[160] Ives B., Olson M.H., "User involvement and MIS success: A review of research", *Management Science* **30** (5) (1984) 586–603.
[161] Tait P., Vessey I., "The effect of use involvement on system success: A contingency approach", *MIS Quarterly* (1988) 91–108.
[162] Buxton J.N., Malcolm R., "Software technology transfer", *Software Engineering Journal* **6** (1) (1991) 17–23.
[163] Jurison J., "Perceived value and technology adoption across four end user groups", *Journal of End User Computing* **12** (4) (2000) 21–28.
[164] Williams L.R., Rao K., "Information technology adoption: Using classical adoption models to predict AEI software implementations", *Journal of Business Logistics* **18** (2) (1997) 43–54.
[165] Swanson E.B., *Information System Implementation: Bridging the Gap Between Design and Utilization*, Irwin, Homewood, IL, 1988.
[166] Kuilboer J.P., Ashrafi N., "Software process improvement deployment: An empirical perspective", *Journal of Information Technology Management* **10** (3–4) (1999) 35–47.

[167] Kunnathur A.S., Ahmed M.U., Charles R.J.S., "Expert systems adoption: An analytical study of managerial issues and concerns", *Information Management* **30** (1) (1996) 15–25.
[168] Maansaari J., Iivari J., "The evolution of CASE usage in Finland between 1993 and 1996", *Information & Management* **36** (1) (1999) 37–53.
[169] Yang H.-L., "Adoption and implementation of CASE tools in Taiwan", *Information & Management* **35** (2) (1999) 89–112.
[170] Nelson A.C., Rottman J., "Before and after CASE adoption", *Information & Management* **31** (1996) 193–202.
[171] Shim S.J., "Characteristics and adoption of generic financial expert systems: A case study of failure", *Journal of Information Technology Management* **9** (3) (1998) 43–51.
[172] Wartik S., Davis T., "A phased reuse adoption model", *Journal of Systems & Software* **46** (1) (1999) 13–23.
[173] Zigurs I., DeSanctis G., Billingsley J., "Adoption patterns and attitudinal development in computer-supported meetings: An exploratory study with SAMM", *Journal of Management Information Systems* **7** (4) (1991) 51–70.
[174] Byrd T.A., Marshall T.E., "Relating information technology investment to organizational performance: A causal model analysis", *Omega, International Journal of Management Science* **25** (1) (1997) 43–56.
[175] Cale E.G., Curely K.F., "Measuring implementation outcome: Beyond success and failure", *Information & Management* **13** (5) (1987) 245–253.

Impact Analysis in Software Evolution

MIKAEL LINDVALL

Fraunhofer Center for Experimental Software Engineering
Maryland, 4321 Hartwick Rd., Suite 500
College Park, MD 20742-3290
USA
mlindvall@fc-md.umd.edu

Abstract

Project planning relies on accurate estimates of the work at hand. In software development, the work at hand is represented by the requirements. In software evolution, when new requirements are added to an existing system in order to produce a new software release, it is important to base the project plan on how much the requirements will cause change in the software. Requirements-Driven Impact Analysis (RDIA) is a critical tool in the planning process as it identifies the set of software entities that need to be changed to implement a new requirement in an existing system. RDIA thus involves a transition from requirements to software entities or to a representative model of the implemented system. RDIA is performed during the release-planning phase. Input is a set of requirements and the existing system. Output is, for each requirement, a set of software entities that have to be changed. The output is used as input to many project-planning activities, for example cost estimation based on change volume.

The overall goal of this work has been to gather knowledge about RDIA and how to improve this crucial activity. The overall means has been an empirical study of RDIA in the industrial object-oriented PMR-project. RDIA has been carried out as a normal part of project developers' work. This in-depth case-study has been carried out over four years and in close contact with project developers.

Problems with underprediction have been identified and many more entities than predicted are changed. We have also found that project developers are unaware of their own positive and negative capabilities in predicting change. We have found patterns that indicate that certain characteristics among software entities, such as size, relations and inheritance, may be used together with complementary strategies for finding candidates for change. Techniques and methods for data collection and data analysis are provided as well as a thorough description of the context under which this research project was conducted. Simple and robust methods and tools such as SCCS, Cohen's kappa, median tests and graphical techniques facilitate future replications in other projects than PMR.

1. Introduction 130
   1.1. The PMR-Project 132
   1.2. Problem 133
   1.3. Research Issues and Research Questions 134
   1.4. Structure of This Chapter 135
2. Related Work 135
   2.1. Requirements-Driven Impact Analysis 135
   2.2. Other Impact Approaches 136
   2.3. A Software Change Process with Impact Analysis 137
   2.4. Ripple Effect Analysis and Dependency Analysis 138
   2.5. Traceability Approaches 140
   2.6. A Framework for Impact Analysis 141
   2.7. Evaluation of Impact Analysis Effectiveness 142
3. The PMR-Project and Its Context 143
   3.1. Ericsson Radio Systems 143
   3.2. The PMR-System 144
   3.3. The Structure of the System 144
   3.4. Design and Implementation of the System 146
   3.5. Software Development Process Model 146
   3.6. The Use of Objectory 147
   3.7. Input to Objectory 147
   3.8. Output from Objectory 148
   3.9. The Intentions Underlying Different Models 148
   3.10. The Use of Objectory during RDIA 149
   3.11. Objectory vs. Objectory SE 149
   3.12. Project Developers 150
4. Evaluation on the Class Level 151
   4.1. Questions on the Class Level 151
   4.2. Answering the Questions on Prediction I 153
   4.3. Discussion 154
   4.4. Answering the Questions on Prediction II 155
   4.5. Concluding Remarks on This Analysis 155
5. Evaluation of RDIA on the Member Function Level 156
   5.1. Questions on the Member Function Level 157
   5.2. Design 158
   5.3. Analysis on the Member Function Level 158
   5.4. Member Function Change Statistics 159
   5.5. Answering the Questions on Prediction 161
   5.6. Discussion 162
6. Summary of Statistics 162
7. Evaluation of RDIA per Requirement 163
   7.1. Questions on the per Requirement Level 163
   7.2. Analysis on the Requirements Level 163

- 7.3. Relative Rank-Order of Requirements 165
- 7.4. Concluding Remarks on This Analysis 169
- 8. Models vs. Actual Implementation 169
  - 8.1. Contents Analysis—Describing the Abstraction Level 169
  - 8.2. Questions Regarding the Design Model 171
  - 8.3. Preparation 171
  - 8.4. Analysis 172
  - 8.5. Discussion 173
  - 8.6. Describing Abstraction Using a Constant Set of Objects 174
  - 8.7. Inheritance Relations Change 174
  - 8.8. Inter-Object/Class Relations Change 175
  - 8.9. Discussion 176
  - 8.10. Answers to Questions Raised by the Design Model 176
  - 8.11. Concluding Remarks on This Analysis 177
- 9. Class Size 178
  - 9.1. Questions Regarding Class Size 178
  - 9.2. Size—Changed vs. Unchanged Classes 179
  - 9.3. Size—Predicted vs. Unpredicted Classes 179
  - 9.4. Size—Predicted vs. Changed Classes 180
  - 9.5. Answers to Questions Regarding Class Size 181
  - 9.6. Discussion 182
- 10. Relations between Classes 182
  - 10.1. Questions Regarding Relations 183
  - 10.2. Inter-class Relations—Changed vs. Unchanged 185
  - 10.3. Inter-Class Relations—Predicted vs. Non-Predicted 186
  - 10.4. Inheritance Relations—Changed vs. Unchanged 187
  - 10.5. Inheritance Relations—Predicted vs. Non-Predicted 188
  - 10.6. Answering the Questions 189
  - 10.7. Concluding Remarks on This Analysis 190
- 11. Discussion of Findings 190
  - 11.1. Qualitative and Quantitative Results 190
  - 11.2. Questionnaire Completed by Developers 190
- 12. Comments Regarding RDIA 193
  - 12.1. Summary of Quantitative Results 193
  - 12.2. Feeding Back the Results 194
  - 12.3. Comments about the Results and the Evaluation 195
  - 12.4. Explanation Building 196
  - 12.5. Suggested Improvements 197
  - 12.6. Complementary Release-to-Class View 198
  - 12.7. Complementary Conservative Prediction 199
  - 12.8. Using Historical Data to Support Prediction 200
  - 12.9. Tool Support 200
  - 12.10. Alternative Input to Cost Estimation 200

12.11. Discussion on Quantitative and Qualitative Results	201
12.12. RDIA Using Models and Traceability	202
12.13. Other Models for Identification of Change	202
12.14. Discussion on RDIA Using Models and Traceability	203
13. Summary and Conclusions	205
13.1. Summary	205
13.2. Conclusions	206
References	207

1. Introduction

The success of software is striking. Almost all technical products developed today are either based on software or partly implemented in software. This success leads to a dramatic increase in the economic importance of software, and software is now a major part of many firms' business. As such it will inevitably be subject to change due to changes of business prerequisites, as well as changes of expectations on software implied by technical development. To be able to change a software system in a controlled way, the implications of such a change must be fully understood. Full understanding is very difficult to achieve because of the complexity of the different parts of a software system, their characteristics and their dependencies of each other.

One way of dealing with this complexity is *release-oriented software development*, which results from an ever increasing demand for even more successful, faster and, in all possible ways, better software. The demand for better software is expressed in terms of new requirements stemming, for example, from the use of the system in that the users simply like it, get used to it and eventually want more from it. The effect is that the system has to evolve over time, where each step of evolution reaches the market as a new release of the system. Further success of the system, therefore, depends to a large extent on the ability to meet users' constant stream of new expectations within a reasonable time frame, within the time and cost budget and without destroying the possibility of adding future functionality to the system. The risk is that the new release of the previously successful system reaches the market too late, costs too much, or has reached a point beyond which further evolution is no longer feasible. The system manager of a successful software system can therefore never rest, but must continue to seek new ways for product and process improvement so that new releases of the software product can be smoothly developed and successfully delivered to and accepted on the market.

This section is focused on *Requirements-Driven Impact Analysis* (RDIA), which constitutes analyzing how new requirements generate change in an existing system. RDIA is new in a sense and distinguishes itself as being part of Impact Analysis (IA) as described by Bohner [6]. RDIA is conducted very early in the release-planning phase, while in Bohner's broader model IA can be conducted at every stage in the software development life cycle. Relevant work in the area, as, for example, collected by Bohner and Arnold [7] is mostly focused on change propagation as an effect of alteration of source code during the coding phase. RDIA deals with changes as an effect of new requirements proposed during the planning phase. Because of its early application, the constraints on RDIA are to be conducted fast and produce an accurate result to a low cost without performing detailed design or altering source code. Practitioners have conducted RDIA for a long time, but to the best of our knowledge there are few, if any, empirical investigations of RDIA before.

RDIA is the foundation for many activities related to maintenance, such as cost estimation, requirements selection, resource allocation, project planning, work distribution and detailed design of new functionality. While the input to RDIA is a set of new requirements together with the system to be altered, it is important to recognize that the different maintenance activities need different outputs from RDIA. Cost estimation requires knowledge of the *number* of software entities to be changed; initial design of the new functionality requires knowledge of exactly *which* software entities are changed and *how*. Performing RDIA correctly is hard and depends to a large extent on earlier experience with the task and the system.

The overall goal of this work is to build well-grounded knowledge about RDIA, understand it as a phenomenon, and discuss ways to improve this crucial activity. The overall means is an empirical study of RDIA in the context of a commercial software development project.

This work results from a long-term case study of the successful industrial object-oriented PMR-project performed at Ericsson Radio Systems (ERA) in Linköping, Sweden, as a part of the operation and support system of a cellular telecom system. The project and its resulting software system have been extensively studied since its inception in 1992 to the completion of the development of the sixth release of the system in early 1996. This analysis covers release R4 in which RDIA was conducted.

Conducting a case study is one way to empirically investigate RDIA and to gain knowledge about the phenomenon. The case study was a natural step as we studied and documented the development of the first release in order to acquire a deeper understanding of development of object models and relations in terms of traceability between them [27]. As the PMR-project turned out to be long-lived and a relevant study object, we seized the research opportunity to further study, document, and analyze the evolution of the system in terms of RDIA.

The result is a thorough description of a commercial object-oriented project in an industrial setting and its evolution. The process for RDIA as conducted in the project is documented, and the result in terms of how well change is predicted by experienced developers is presented. Characteristics of the main building blocks in object-oriented systems are used in order to explain discrepancies between predicted and actual change. We believe that these results together with our methods for data collection and analysis are useful for both researchers and practitioners, especially for understanding RDIA and for its improvement.

This case study relies largely on quantitative data, but a software development project such as PMR, which is a human activity, can never be fully characterized quantitatively. Consequently we gathered much qualitative and quantitative data during these years to

- formulate research questions,
- describe context,
- analyze and interpret the results, and
- suggest improvements.

1.1 The PMR-Project

The PMR-project was a successful project. Before getting into the detailed analyses it is important to note the following characteristics and circumstances.

The releases were delivered with the intended functionality, on time and within budget.[1]

- While some developers left the project and others joined it, the leading core of developers has been with the project since its inception. Thus the project team by large was familiar with initial requirements, design, and implementation as well as with the subsequent releases.
- All types of documentation of the system and the project were continually updated and inspected as a normal and well-established part of the development process.
- Requirements that had been subject for RDIA were stable during the development process, meaning that the customer did not change his mind regarding them.
- Neither the source code, nor any other system material were available to anyone other than the developers in the PMR-project, hence all changes were in the control of the project developers.
- The RDIA activity was conducted by developers together with requirements' analysts thus enabling both correct interpretation of requirements as well as correct information about the structure of the system.

[1] R4 was a little late and little more expensive than expected.

IMPACT ANALYSIS IN SOFTWARE EVOLUTION 133

- The RDIA activity was conducted over a considerably long time and the predicted changes of the system were documented on a detailed level, the member function level, as well as the class level.
- System development and maintenance have used object-oriented analysis, object-oriented design, and object-oriented implementation techniques.
- The Objectory method [23,38] and tool [40] have been used since the inception of the project, providing a maintained set of object and use-case models where inter-model relationships were documented with traceability links.

These circumstances form an impression of the PMR-project as an example of best-of-practice, consisting of preferable software engineering principles and a good environment. There are many projects and systems described in the literature where this is not the case. Instead requirements are commonly highly volatile, the system is not well understood by the developers or frequent changes occur among personnel, which lead to change of other developers' code. Often documentation, models or traceability are not included. We therefore have reason to believe that the RDIA approach in use in the PMR-project and the accuracy of its outcome are at least as good as other contemporary object-oriented software development projects.

1.2 Problem

Project planning is in general a hard problem, and there are many witnesses among software practitioners and their customers who are familiar with the effects of large deviations between planned time for delivery and the actual one.

Planning of software evolution, where RDIA is a part, is no exception and is therefore selected as the main problem for investigation in this work. While the output from the RDIA activity, the prediction, serves as input to many different activities related to planning of software evolution we have chosen to primarily limit and simplify our model of the planning process as follows:

1. To determine the size of the work to be done.
2. To calculate cost.

The size of the work to be performed is predicted during RDIA, whereas calculation of cost, a rough term for estimation of man-hours of which the cost is known, is based on the output from RDIA. Hence, there is a dependency between these two tasks.

The potential problems with this approach, which are likely to be the common case in contemporary planning of software evolution, are:

- the actual impact is different from that expected, or

- the cost model is not appropriate, or
- a combination of both of these.

A deviation between predicted impact and the actual results implies that the size of the work to be performed is greater (most likely) than expected. Bad input to the cost model results in the cost model, even if correct, producing bad output. Example: if the size of work is predicted in terms of 4 changed software items but 10 are actually changed, then the effect is that too few man-hours are planned for.

If the output from the RDIA is correct, but the cost model is not appropriate, then there is a problem in any case. Example: if the size of work is correctly predicted and is expected to require 40 man-hours, but instead requires 100 man-hours, the effect is the same as above: too few man-hours are planned for.

A combination of the two situations can, of course, also arise. In the fortunate case, the size of work would be underpredicted, while the cost for each size unit would be overestimated. In the unfortunate case, the situation would be the opposite.

At the time of planning the research project we knew from project developers that project planning was a problem, but as no evaluation of the accuracy of the prediction earlier had been made there were no facts regarding this issue. At the time it was unknown whether RDIA was a problem or not. Actually, project developers stated, at the time for conducting RDIA for R4, that the main problem was not determining the changes (conducting RDIA accurately), but to correctly estimate the amount of hours (cost estimation) required [29]. Together with our interest for RDIA the following circumstances strengthened our decision to focus on the subject:

- Well-known cost models have been published for a long time, for example, COCOMO [5] while work done on impact analysis is almost limited to the papers collected by Bohner and Arnold [7].
- Cost models are logically connected to RDIA and rely on accurate results from the RDIA activity.
- The effort involved is very hard to measure on a reasonably detailed level, and even worse, Ericsson would not, at the time, allow publication of time- or productivity-oriented measures for this kind of projects whose resulting products compete on the commercial market.

1.3 Research Issues and Research Questions

In this work we have tried to identify a space of research issues and questions related to RDIA. This has been done in order to set up an investigation as completely as possible. Not surprisingly, the space turns out to be very large. Our intention is not to answer all the questions, but a careful selection of them. To quote my mentor and good friend Al Goerner:

"A good question is often more interesting than the answer".

The space of research questions, so far identified as regarding RDIA, is largely based on the main building blocks provided in object-oriented software technology, which are:

- the objects/classes,
- their characteristics:
  - inter-relations,
  - size,
  - attributes,
  - methods,
  - predicted and actual reason for change.

The research questions concern and compare

- the set of objects/classes *predicted* to be changed, their characteristics, and predicted reason for change,
- the set of objects/classes actually *changed*, their characteristics, and actual reason for change.

1.4 Structure of This Chapter

This is a case study and as such hard to separate from its context. In order to let the reader interpret our results we provide an extensive set of context material. The aim is to separate background and context material from research issues. Following this introduction, each section deals with one research issue which is broken down into research questions; thus it consists of a set of chapters of the form: issues/questions, statistics and analysis, answers to the questions, interpretation and discussion. The section concludes with qualitative reflections and interpretations connecting quantitative and qualitative data and discusses the major points of the work in summary and conclusion.

2. Related Work

2.1 Requirements-Driven Impact Analysis

Requirements-driven impact analysis identifies the set of software entities that need to be changed to implement a new requirement in an existing system. RDIA thus involves a transition from requirements to software entities or to a representative model of the implemented system. RDIA is performed during the release planning phase. Input is a set of requirements and the existing system. Output is, for each requirement, a set of software entities that need to be changed. The output is used as input to many project-planning activities, for example, cost estimation based on change volume. Cost estimation is further used for requirements selection based on a cost-benefit analysis of each requirement, as described by Karlsson [24], for example. Requirements with the highest value are selected for implementation. RDIA is thus performed at an early stage in the project when little is known; the set of candidate requirements is known, but not which requirements should be implemented. This constrains the RDIA:

- RDIA must be performed as accurately as possible; cost estimation and requirements selection are conducted on the basis of its result.
- RDIA must be performed at a relatively low cost; it is desirable that the cost for analyzing the cost of a requirement is lower than the cost of implementing it. As not all requirements will be implemented, the cost for RDIA for unselected requirements must be kept low.
- RDIA must be performed without altering any source code; RDIA is conducted at the planning stage when it is not decided which source code changes actually should be implemented.
- RDIA must be documented so the result can be used in subsequent phases.
- RDIA must be evaluated; in order to improve RDIA and its dependent activities, for example, cost estimation, it is important to evaluate, in different aspects of how well the prediction corresponds to the actual outcome.

2.2 Other Impact Approaches

RDIA is a concept coined in [32]. The intention of this section is to describe some of the common concepts found in the literature. Related work is often found under *impact analysis* or *software change impact analysis*, but also in work on *ripple effects*, *dependency analysis* and *traceability*. The impact analysis literature is, however, limited. An excellent contemporary overview is provided by Bohner and Arnold [7] as a collection of some of the relevant papers in the area. Bohner is also one of the main authors in impact analysis and we have chosen to start by relating our work with his model for software change process.

2.3 A Software Change Process with Impact Analysis

In Bohner's detailed *software change process model* [6] IA is applied at every stage and phase during the maintenance life-cycle, including the release-planning phase. The model is built upon the following activities:

Manage software change. This activity manages the software change activities by establishing software quality goals, determining risks, producing estimates, tracking software change activities, and assigning resources.

Understand software change and determine impact. This activity regulates all other activities and its results are refined during the whole process. Its main subactivities are: review software documentation, clarify change request, identify change impacts, record software change impacts, and determine software stability.

Identify software change impacts. This activity supports all other activities and constantly adds newly identified impacts to the set of already known impacts. This is carried out by examining requirements traceability, determining requirements impacts, identifying software design impacts, analyzing source program impacts, classifying and exploring similar changes, and determining regression test candidates.

Specify and design software change. During this activity the clarified change requests are used as input to the generation of requirements and design. Subactivities are: analyze change requirements, examine software architecture changes, derive related change requirements, and design program changes.

Implement software change. During this activity the changes are determined on the module and statement level and implemented. Subactivities: Determine modules to be changed, identify statement level changes, apply program level changes, test modified software units.

Retest affected software. The system is tested to ensure that it meets both new requirements and old requirements. The subactivities are: generate test cases for new/added functionality, update test suites, perform integration tests, conduct system testing, and conduct acceptance testing.

Bohner's model uses different approaches for impact analysis to identify change in different work products. The approaches for impact analysis are: *traceability analysis* for dependencies between work-products, *ripple-effect analysis* for dependencies within work-products, and *change history analysis* for knowledge about similar changes made earlier. The work-products that can be impacted are *requirements* and *design specifications*, the *program*, and *test documents*.

Our work is focused on how requirements impact software entities (C++ classes and member functions) using a design object model and traceability as documentation aid. Bohner mentions the use of change history data, which is a way to learn from past experience, but says nothing explicitly about the importance of evaluating the impact analysis results. We propose an improvement of Bohner's model by adding an *Evaluate Impact Analysis*-activity after *Retest affected software*. We also propose the insertion of a *Select Requirements*-activity as an explicit subactivity of *Manage software change*.

2.4 Ripple Effect Analysis and Dependency Analysis

Impact analysis can be characterized as *detecting consequences of change* using some kind of *dependency analysis*. Haney's [17] model for module connection analysis is an early and typical example of this. It uses a probability connection matrix which subjectively models the dependencies between modules in order to determine how change in one module necessitates change in other modules. Haney's model is *probabilistic*, meaning that it is probable, but not necessarily true, that change will propagate as the model forecasts. *Mechanical approaches*, as described by for example, Queille and colleagues [42] are instead based on a model of the system in terms of the static dependencies between entities together with change propagation rules. Using a change propagation mechanism it is then possible to pinpoint changes that must be made, for example, as a consequence of a changed public interface.

Queille and colleagues [42] aim at analyzing how change propagates in order to identify *secondary change* as a consequence of planned or conducted *primary change*. *Change candidates* are entities in the source code that are likely to change and each candidate must be analyzed in order to determine whether it must be changed or not. *Secondary change candidates* can be found using change propagation techniques, while *primary change candidates* are found during the analysis of how the implementation of a new requirement generates change of source code.

It is also desirable to analyze which entities are *affected* by a change (ripple effects). An entity might be affected by a change, but it might not be necessary to change it. It is, however, necessary to retest the affected entity as it might *behave* differently though still producing a correct result. An example of this is given by Arango and colleagues [2] who present a technique for explaining how changes in data representation translate into performance changes. How these concepts are related is shown in Figs. 1 and 2.

A common motivation for impact analysis during the testing phase is to limit the need for regression testing—if it is known exactly which entities are affected by a change, the unaffected ones need no regression testing [25]. Examples of such analysis techniques, which are all based on static dependencies, are described in [53, 25], and [26].

A totally different approach aiming at the same problem is *slicing* [15]. The program is sliced into a *decomposition slice*, which contains the place of the change,

IMPACT ANALYSIS IN SOFTWARE EVOLUTION

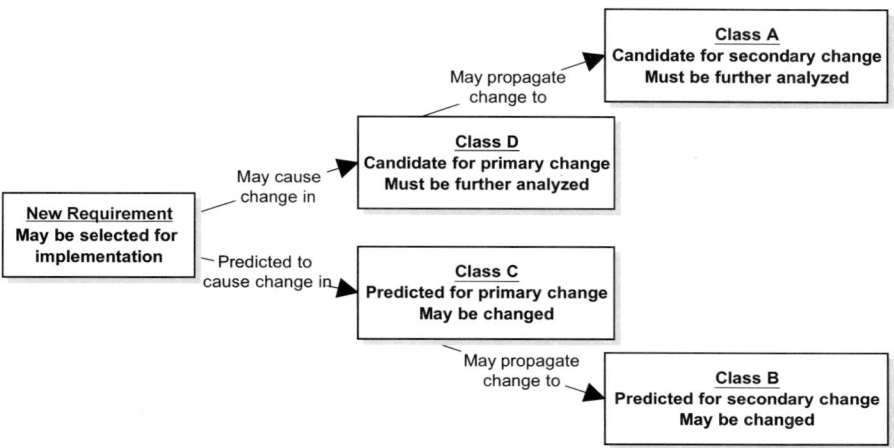

FIG. 1. Impact from a new requirement *not yet selected* for implementation.

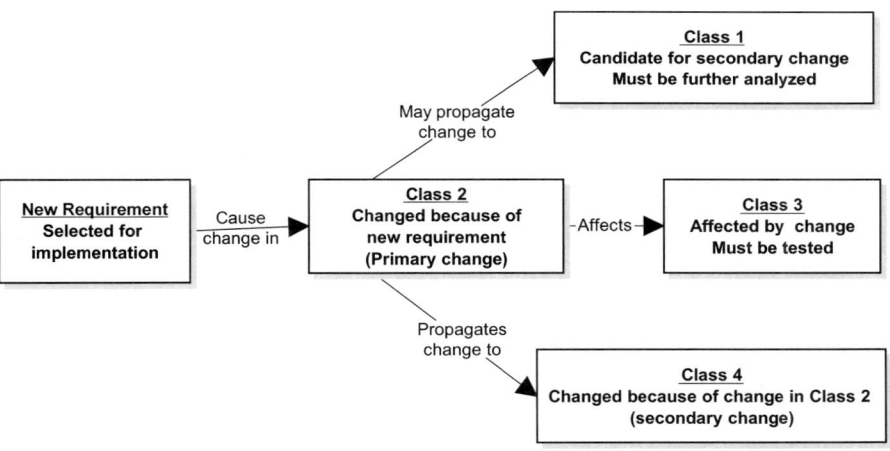

FIG. 2. Impact from a new requirement *selected* for implementation.

and the rest of the program, a *complement slice*. Slicing is based on data and control dependencies in the program. Changes made to the decomposition slice are guaranteed not to affect the complement if a certain set of rules is obeyed. Slicing limits the scope for propagation of change and make that scope explicit. The technique is, for example, used in [51] for slicing of documents in order to account for ripple effects as a part of impact analysis. Shahmehri and colleagues [45] apply the technique to debugging and testing. Pointer-based languages like C++ have not been supported, but this is changing as Tip and colleagues now present slicing techniques for C++ [50]. Slicing tools have long relied on character-based presentation techniques, but visual presentation of slices is now available and applied to impact analysis in Gallagher [15].

Comments

None of the above approaches for finding change candidates or affected software entities were used during the PMR project. There are, however, reasons to experiment with a selected set of them in order to improve the accuracy of the prediction.

2.5 Traceability Approaches

Traceability is germane to life-cycle meta-models such as Basili's iterative reuse model [4]. In this model, software includes not only the resulting source code, but also up-front documents such as requirements- and design specifications, which are regarded as models at various abstraction levels of the software in service [23].

Maintenance in Basili's perspective initially performs and documents changes of requirements that are subsequently propagated through the analysis and design models to the source code. Proponents of this approach, such as [41], assume a high level of traceability, which in practice implies that:

- all models of the software are consistently updated;
- it is possible to trace dependent items within a model (vertical traceability or intra-model traceability); and
- it is possible to trace correspondent items between different models (horizontal traceability or inter-model traceability).

Traceability can be graphically represented, where the software items are nodes and the traceable dependencies are edges forming a traceability web. A node denotes each requirement, each design component and each part of code and every link of dependence is denoted by an edge [41]. It is assumed that if tracing dependencies in the web is easy, the effort required to understand the software and assess the impact of a proposed change is decreased.

Traceability links are often provided as a feature in many life-cycle oriented tools (e.g., Objectory SE [40], SODOS [18]), but to our knowledge little has been published about how to actually use them [31]. One impact analysis experiment based on traceability is, however, provided by Abbattsista and colleagues [1]. It is seemingly a paradox that even though it is well known that the problem of understanding the relationship between requirements and code consumes much time and money [47], practitioners of today are not at all convinced of the usefulness of traceability.

Traceability is required by the Department of Defense [10] and recommended in many software engineering quality standards [19–22] and other Software Engineering related documents [11,44,46].

As a reaction to the fact that traceability between requirements and code is unlikely to be found in a real project, a test-case-based method for finding a starting place (finding primary changes) for further investigations prior to changing the system was proposed by Wilde and colleagues [52].

Comments

Traceability was used during RDIA in the PMR-project, but primarily as an aid for documentation of how new requirements were related to the C++ classes (design objects). In this research project traceability has been extensively used to establish a clear connection between new requirements, the set of classes predicted to change, and the set of classes actually changed. Our initial assumption was that models and traceability should be useful for finding change candidates. The models and the existing traceability proved, however, to be on a level not obviously useful for RDIA and project developers were reluctant to use this kind of information rather than the information provided by other developers and the source code.

2.6 A Framework for Impact Analysis

For the purpose of comparing different impact analysis approaches, Arnold and Bohner [3] defined a framework for impact analysis. It should be noted that the impact analysis approaches the framework aims at are change propagation approaches. This means that the primary changes are already determined and the goal is to analyze secondary changes or which entities can be affected by the changes. The approaches covered by the framework are, for example, determination by incremental compilers of which parts to recompile as well as changes induced by a maintainer and their potential effects. The framework is useful as it reveals the underlying mechanisms in most impact analysis approaches available.

The following parts of an impact analysis approach are identified:

- a change,
- the artifact object model (the system),
- the interface object model (a model of the system—its interface),
- the internal object model (a model of the system—its internals),
- the impact model (knowledge about change propagation).

We will now describe how the effects of a proposed *change* on the *artifact object model* are determined by using an impact analysis approach.

The impact analysis approach is based on a model of the system which describes dependencies between entities in the system. Communication with the impact analysis approach is carried out via the *interface object model* (interface for short). The interface is used to describe the change to be analyzed. The *internal object model* contains information about the objects in the system and the dependencies between them. The difference between the interface and the internal model is analogous to the difference between a database and the different views of it. The database constitutes the underlying representation of the structure and is populated with data. The database is manipulated via views (for example, a selected set of entities, their relations, and tools for manipulating them) which constitute the interface to the database.

While the internal object model captures information about the objects and their dependencies, the *impact model* captures knowledge about how change propagate from object to object via dependencies. The knowledge can be expressed in terms of rules or algorithms.

When the user orders an analysis of the change, the impact analysis approach uses the definition of the change, as defined using the interface, translates it to the internal object model, and uses the knowledge in the impact model to propagate the initial change throughout the internal object model. The result, in terms of a set of affected interface objects, is presented to the user via the interface. In totally automated environments (e.g., incremental compilers), some of the steps are automated and not visible to the user, while in less automated, or even manual environments (e.g., case tools with some support for dependency analysis, but without knowledge and routines for change propagation) much of the initial analysis work has to be done by the user. In the latter case, the user must also be prepared to spend time on the result from the impact analysis as objects presented as affected might be false positives and thus not needing to change.

2.7 Evaluation of Impact Analysis Effectiveness

The next part of the work by Arnold and Bohner [3] concerns evaluation of impact analysis effectiveness. Bearing parts of an impact analysis approach in mind, a number of concepts are defined based on the notion of sets.

The System Set represents the set of all objects in the system.
The Starting Impact Set (SIS) represents the set of objects that are initially changed. The SIS is defined by the user in some way and fed into the impact analysis approach by using the interface object model.
The Estimated Impact Set (EIS) is the result delivered by the impact analysis approach. The EIS always includes the SIS and can therefore be seen as an expansion

of the SIS. The expansion is the result from applying the change propagation rules to the internal object model over and over again until all objects that may be affected are discovered.

The Actual Impact Set (AIS) is the set of objects that actually were changed during the implementation. It is important to note that the AIS is not unique as there are many different ways to implement a solution.

Although these three sets are necessary, they are not sufficient. There are at least two[2] different models where these sets can occur:

- in the artifact object model, and
- in the interface object model.

The evaluation is conducted by comparing these different sets for different methods. Arnold and Bohner's underlying assumption is that the EIS should be safe (conservative) and thus greater than AIS.

3. The PMR-Project and Its Context

This section provides a context to our work and facilitates an understanding of the analyses presented in the following sections. We introduce the PMR-project, in which we participated, and the resulting system and its requirements and models, which we investigated. The intention is to allow the reader to judge the generality of our results. It starts with a short description of the company, an introduction to the system that was developed, an overview of the various development and implementation techniques used in the project, and a description of the process model used. As object models were used in the project and as object models constitute a central part of this work, their use in the PMR-project is extensively discussed. The section concludes with a description of the project developers.

3.1 Ericsson Radio Systems

Ericsson is a Swedish company that develops, produces and markets telecommunication equipment worldwide. One of the fastest growing markets is mobile telecommunication, and Ericsson dominates this market. Ericsson Radio Systems (ERA), the owner of the project under study, is involved in the development of all software products that make a mobile system. The department at ERA studied in this research is

---

[2]The internal object model is not treated in the paper by Arnold and Bohner, but may also be used to characterize the three sets.

responsible for the development of one particular system, namely Performance Management Traffic Recording (PMR).

3.2 The PMR-System

The operator of the *Network* needs to record traffic events during the communication between the *Network* and *Mobile Stations* for several reasons. PMR supports this by providing, among other features, a function for the recording of how the traffic is managed to keep connections established. The system has been developed in certain steps of evolution and packaged and delivered in various releases. This work starts with the result (object models and source code) from the third release (R3) and use it as a baseline for analyses of the fourth 4th release (R4). PMR offered, to begin with (in R1 to R4), two different ways of recording depending on the operator's need of data. It was possible to order the system to set a particular *Mobile Station* in focus and to record its interactions with different *Cells* (*Mobile Related Recording*). The other alternative was to set a particular *Cell* in focus and record the *Mobile Stations* communicating with it (*Cell Related Recording*). The operator initiates the recording process. The result of the recording is collected, parsed and stored in a database. The operator is able to select from several predefined reports showing the recording result from different viewpoints. By using this information, the operator is able to trace the events that occurred in the system.

3.3 The Structure of the System

The system can be divided into three main functions:

- initiation of a recording,
- collecting, parsing and storing the results from the recording process, and
- analyzing and presenting the recording results.

The system has three main parts, mapping to the functionality described above:

- a user interface,
- a parser-based part which collects, parses, and stores files, and
- a database with attached reports.

The system is configurable to support two different markets—the Japan market and the European market. Each release of the product is aimed towards one of the two markets. The two different markets have much in common, but also differences. The commonalities are placed together in common objects/classes, while differences have been placed in objects/classes whose name indicates which market it is designed for. The inheritance structure is used to explain these differences and commonalties. This conforms to how a family of products can be structured [16].

An analysis of the system shows that the objects/classes can be divided into domain-oriented classes and others. A domain-oriented class is a class that as part of its name has a domain-oriented concept, for example, *Cell*. Examples of domain-oriented classes are: *Cell.C, ActionCell.C*, and *CellTranslationTable.C*. Classes that are not domain-oriented are classes that do not have a domain-oriented name, but names that are common among software systems of all kinds of domains. Examples are: *PrintPopup.C, Menu.C, TextPane.C*. Classes with such names can with great likelihood be found in any window-based software system and are thus not specific to the PMR-system.

Of the 136 classes in release R4 of the PMR-system, 37 (27,2%) classes are domain-specific and the remaining 99 (72,8%) are not. The 37 domain-specific classes are built upon 14 important concepts, such as Network, Cell, MTR (Mobile Traffic Recording) and CTR (Cell Traffic Recording). These domain-specific classes were compared with the 13 basic domain objects in the initial domain object model developed during the first release. The comparison showed that 22 of the domain-specific classes could be name traced to domain objects, 12 could not be traced to domain objects, but could instead be traced to domain-related concepts used in the textual descriptions of the domain object model. Only three classes with domain-related names were unable to trace to the domain object model, which shows that the concepts central to the system were identified at the inception of the project.

The evolution of the domain object model also mirrors the development of the system. Releases R1, R2, and R3 were all analyzed and designed during R1, but incrementally implemented during R1, R2, and R3. Thus the domain object model was not changed at all during the first three releases. Release R4 was characterized as a common improvement of the system as well as porting it to a new operating system. These common improvements and the porting, did not require new concepts, thus the domain object model also remained unchanged during R4. Release R4 of the PMR-system is characterized as an overall improvement of usability-related functionality. There were 21 requirements in R4 divided into 14 functionality-related requirements, 3 performance-related requirements and 4 trouble-report-related requirements. The dominating requirement was "Porting to Solaris" because of its impact on the system. This requirement affected 44 of the 136 classes in the system (32.4%). "Porting to Solaris" allows the system to be executed under the newest operating system, which is of course a customer requirement, or rather it is a necessity to evolve together with the system's environment. The requirement was expensive in terms of changed classes, but no new functionality was added. In order to fulfill the set of new requirements, very few new classes had to be added to the system.

3.4 Design and Implementation of the System

The system is modeled with object-oriented modeling techniques. Some parts are implemented using C++ [48]. Some parts are implemented using a relational database (RDB) [8]. There are also many other implementation tools and techniques used for implementing the system. A large commercial system consists of a number of different parts developed using different implementation techniques. In this work we are investigating object-oriented techniques. Therefore we have included the models of the parts that were implemented in C++ in our discussions, but excluded the other parts described in the list above.

3.5 Software Development Process Model

The project process at ERA (PROPS) consists of two parts: one administrative part (the general project model) and a technical model. The administrative part is common to all types of projects, whereas the technical model depends on the project type [13]. The common technical model is called SDPM (software development process model) [12], and a significant amount of work has been performed to adapt SDPM to the Objectory process model that can be used to carry out some of the phases and activities described by SDPM. This implies that Objectory is used for some, but not all technical activities and phases during the project, but not at all for administrative issues.

Objectory can be configured to suit the type of project, i.e., appropriate phases and activities can be selected. The configuration used in this project conforms to the most comprehensive configuration—*Premium Analysis & Design*—described in the Objectory handbook [38].

The PROPS model itself has characteristics conforming to a rather strict waterfall model [43] as it prescribes the use of a number of tollgates (TG). Each tollgate serves as a decision point and due to the status of the project at the time of the tollgate, management decides on how the project should proceed, change its goals or whether it should be stopped. At the tollgate meeting all prescribed documents are reviewed. The project is not allowed to continue until the exit/entry criteria are fulfilled. A common and wrong interpretation of the waterfall model is that is not possible to go back to earlier activities if needed. It is, of course, possible to change a document completed earlier in the process. The analysis object model was, for example, updated with respect to traceability as changes were discovered during design.

The process used at ERA for software development is well defined and generally followed by both project managers and project developers. The process constitutes a common language between project members both within and between projects. Impact analysis has a clear role in the process and is conducted as a release planning activity in order to provide facts for decision support regarding planning and requirements selection.

3.6   The Use of Objectory

The tool as well as the methodology was used rather strictly, but in a practical way. Strictly in the sense that all modeling activities were performed according to the methodology and documented using the tool. Practical in the sense that the models did not have to be formally correct, but understandable. The Objectory methodology was almost used as is without mixing the methodology with features from other methodologies. This seems not to be the common case. Many reports from the use of object-oriented technology in large projects presented as experience reports at, for example, OOPSLA 1994 [28], indicate a need for mixing different object-oriented methodologies to form a sufficient resulting methodology. We noted, however, an emphasis on object modeling compared to use-case modeling in the development of the first release (R1) of the system and we base this statement on the fact that all object models seemed to be further elaborated, while the different use-case models were not. During the development of the subsequent releases the use-case models have been left as is, while the design object model has both been used and updated. The explanation by project developers as to why the use-case model has not been updated is that the use-cases actually were so broad that they not only covered the initial requirements but also all new requirements. New use-cases were simply not needed, and the existing use-cases did not need to be changed to reflect the new functionality, according to project developers.

3.7   Input to Objectory

Input to Objectory consisted of the *requirements specification*, which comprised functional as well as non-functional requirements, but only the functional requirements were explicitly modeled with Objectory.

Requirements analysis in this context means analysis of existing requirements. In other contexts requirements analysis is used to denote elicitation, definition and documentation of requirements.

A rough description of requirements analysis according to Objectory is to find the functional requirements and to map them onto use-cases. In this project, the developers responsible for writing the initial requirements specification (R1), knew the analysts were going to use Objectory. As a consequence they structured the requirements in such a way that it was easy to do the mapping. They even used the word use-case in the requirements specification to denote a major functional requirement.

At the same time they strove to keep the names of main requirements as the names of requirements. This resulted in quite an easy mapping from requirements to use-cases.

Over time it turned out that the new requirements fitted into the existing use-cases, which resulted in that the kind of requirements analysis described above was only carried out during R1. Instead requirements-driven impact analysis was used.

3.8 Output from Objectory

The output from Objectory consists mainly of detailed design descriptions, comprising a design object model, a designed use-case model and interaction diagrams. Some interactions between objects, particularly complex parts, were modeled in detail by using interaction diagrams. Hence, the output from the process that was used as input for programmers was an extensive design object model showing the structure of the system, an overall use-case description and interaction diagrams showing the complex parts of the system. A rudimentary skeleton for C++ was also generated during R1. Over time it turned out that it was the design object model that was used, especially for documentation of impact analysis.

3.9 The Intentions Underlying Different Models

During the project, the object models have been kept and maintained as much as *the time pressure has allowed*. Interviews with developers regarding this topic show that the intention has always been to keep and maintain models to make future enhancements easier. From interviews with developers in the PMR-project regarding the roles of the different models we learn the following:

The *domain object model* is intended to serve as a model of the real world entities important for this particular system. The intention is to refine the model over time adding more domain knowledge to it, to make the model more complete. The domain model provides a common terminology and description of the important parts of the problem domain.

The *analysis object model* shows commonalities and differences between the two different products within the family of products.

The *design object model* is an abstraction, a high level representation, of the actual implementation. This implies that if we examine a design object with associations to other design objects, we should be able to find the corresponding object[3] and its associations in the source code as a class.

---

[3] Actually, what we find in the source code are classes. The transformation from objects to classes may seem strange, due to the fact that Objectory does not distinguish between object diagram and class diagrams, but is quite straightforward. Each object in the *design object model* becomes a class in the implementation according to the approach used here.

The different *use-case models* mirror the requirements for the systems and all models are intended to serve to help for developers, especially newcomers, when they maintain and enhance the system in the future.

3.10 The Use of Objectory during RDIA

The development of a new release in the PMR-project can be generally described using Basili's *iterative reuse model* [4]. In Basili's model, software includes not only the resulting source code, but also up-front documents such as requirements- and design specifications, which are regarded as *models* at various abstraction levels of the software in service [23]. Maintenance in Basili's perspective initially performs and documents changes of requirements that are subsequently propagated through the analysis and design models to the source code. In the PMR-project, the effect of a new requirement is first analyzed and documented in terms of the design object model, and then the change is actually carried out in the code. The effects of a new requirement, which resulted from RDIA, was documented in the following way using Objectory:

- Each requirement was defined as a requirement in Objectory.
- Between each requirement and the design objects (classes) that were predicted to be changed as an effect of the requirement a traceability link was established.
- If a new design object/class was needed, it was defined in Objectory.
- For each requirement it was also documented how many, and sometimes which, member functions had to be changed or added in the particular object/class.

The linked requirements and design objects were used to answer questions about requirements and the amount of change that was predicted for them. It was also used to distribute work among the project developers and to inform them about which requirements were linked to the set of objects/classes they were about to change.

The *dependent objects* function was used, but in a limited way. *Dependent objects* is a function that is nearly ideal for impact analysis as it answers the question: "What other objects are dependent on a particular object?" There may be many reasons why this function was not extensively used during impact analysis. One of the reasons is that relatively few project developers were aware of it.

3.11 Objectory vs. Objectory SE

Objectory (the methodology) was never considered to be used without the use of Objectory SE (the accompanying CASE tool) in the PMR-project, which the following citation shows.

"A methodology is not worth more than its accompanying case tool".

The citation is from an interview with a former practitioner and now manager at ERA with experience from the use of methodologies and case tools. It clearly indicates that in the practical world there is a tight relation between a methodology and its tool.

3.12 Project Developers

The PMR-project was staffed with developers who were mainly not used to object-oriented modeling techniques from the beginning. An extensive series of courses was organized by ERA to teach the project developers system development using Objectory: [36,39], and [37]. Instructors from Objectory AB taught the courses. To make the transition to the new technology easier, the technical manager for the project was employed directly from Objectory AB.

C++ was familiar to some of the programmers, while others were not used to it. Hence, the staff represented a broad spectrum of developers with large differences in experience in object-oriented modeling and implementation. Over the years the group of project developers has become experienced with both object-oriented modeling using Objectory and with implementation using C++.

The composition of developers in the project group has changed over the years, but in a controlled way. Developers have left the project group and others have joined it, but the leading core of developers has been with the project since its inception. Thus within the project team there were always knowledgeable developers familiar with initial requirements, design, and implementation as well as with the subsequent releases. The need of teaching newcomers the system, its requirements, its design, and its source-code was, however, a major problem. Requirements-driven impact analysis was one way of dealing with this problem as it let developers exercise new requirements prior to implementing them. According to developers this led to an increased understanding of the system and its requirements.

Previously all documents were produced using FrameMaker, while in this project the Objectory SE was used. Most of the developers were eager to start learning the new technology and had high expectations on it. During the development of R1, project management performed evaluations of the methodology and the tool twice. These evaluations were used to collect and assess the developers' experience and to improve their use of the methodology and the tool. Among the experiences we note that many developers appreciated the methodology and the tool, but that several improvements regarding the tool were suggested, for example features for version management. Lack of version management also turned out to be one of the main problems for analyses of the content and evolution of the object models.

4. Evaluation on the Class Level

The goal of this section, is twofold. The first goal is to provide an introduction to the evaluation of impact analysis results when using both qualitative and quantitative data about the system and the project. The second goal is to investigate whether there is a deviation between predicted and actual changes and to use this result as a vehicle of motivation for further investigations of the problem. This section was published in [30].

The predicted changes, resulting from the project developers' impact analysis and which they had carefully documented with object models, have been compared with the actual changes in the source code. This comparative analysis has been conducted at several levels of detail, which are presented in forthcoming sections. In the analyses, a *release level view* is first taken: the predicted impact of all new requirements is compared with the actual impact on the system. Then the analysis is discussed and further refined in a number of steps until a level suitable for evaluating impact analysis is reached. Qualitative data is used to explain some of the discrepancies between the prediction and the actual outcome in order to adjust and refine the quantitative data. Project managers can analyze potential discrepancies between the estimated change volume and the actual using the results.

4.1 Questions on the Class Level

The questions we sought answers for are the following:

Q1 How good was the prediction on the class level?

One way of answering this question is by using Cohen's Kappa value, which measures the agreement between two groups ranging from -1.0 to 1.0. The -1.0 figure means total discompliance between the two groups, 1.0 means total compliance and 0.0 means that the result is no better than pure chance [9].

> Q1.1 How good was the prediction according to the kappa value?

The Q1-question can also be broken down into two subquestions (Q1.2 and Q1.3):

> Q1.2 How good was the prediction when it comes to predicting the *number* of classes to be changed?

The question can be broken down into two subquestions:

>> Q1.2.1 What is the percentage of correct predictions (p_0)?
>> Q1.2.2 Was the number of classes to be changed correctly predicted ($1/UF$)?
> Q1.3 How good was the prediction when it comes to predicting *which* classes should be changed?

This question can also be broken down into two subquestions:

> Q1.3.1 Were changed classes predicted (*CP*)?

and

> Q1.3.2 Were the predicted classes changed (*PC*)?

There is a total of 136 classes in the system. Of these 30 were predicted to be changed. Our analysis of the source code edits showed that 94 classes were actually changed, see Table I. This answers question Q1.2: In terms of the number of classes only 31.0% (30/94) of the number of changed classes were predicted.

Let us now go further and compare the prediction with the actual changes in more detail. We use a 2 × 2 contingency table (see Table II) which first separates the classes into two groups: *Predictive group* and *Actual group*. Each group has two subgroups: *Unchanged* and *Changed*. This gives us four groups and the 136 classes are distributed among these groups as follows.

Cell A represents the 42 classes that were not predicted to change and that also remained unchanged. Classes in this cell are correctly predicted, however, implicitly. They are correct as these classes were predicted to remain unchanged, which also turned out to be true. The prediction is implicit as these classes were indirectly identified—they resulted as a side effect as complement of predicting changed classes.

TABLE I
PREDICTED VS. ACTUAL CHANGES

No. Classes in System	Classes Predicted to Change	Classes Actually Changed
136 (100.0%)	30 (22.1%)	94 (69.1%)

TABLE II
PREDICTED VS. ACTUAL CHANGES. ALL CHANGED CLASSES INCLUDED

		Predictive group		
		Unchanged	Changed	
Actual group	Unchanged	A: 42 (30.9%)	B: 0 (0.0%)	A+B: 42 (30.9%)
	Changed	C: 64 (47.1%)	D: 30 (22.1%)	C+D: 94 (69.1%)
		A+C: 106 (77.9%)	B+D: 30 (22.1%)	N: 136 (100.0%)

Cell B represents the zero classes that were predicted to change, but actually remained unchanged. A large number here would indicate a large deviation from the prediction.

Cell C represents the 64 classes that were not predicted to change, but turned out to be changed after all. As with cell B, a large number in this cell indicates a large deviation from the prediction.

Cell D, finally, represents the 30 classes that were predicted to be changed and were, in fact, changed. This is a correct prediction. A large number in this cell indicates a good prediction.

On the basis of the values in the cells the answers to the questions can be calculated. p_0 = the proportion of units in which there is an agreement:

$$p_0 = \frac{A+D}{N} = \frac{42+30}{136} = 0.529;$$

p_c = the proportion of units for which agreement is expected by chance:

$$p_c = \frac{A+B}{N} \times \frac{A+C}{N} + \frac{B+D}{N} \times \frac{C+D}{N}.$$

The kappa value is finally calculated:

$$\kappa = \frac{p_0 - p_c}{1 - p_c} = \frac{0.529 - 0.393}{1 - 0.393} = 0.224.$$

The Underprediction Factor, UF, is calculated:

$$UF = \frac{C+D}{B+D} = \frac{94}{30} = 3.1.$$

The percentage of Predicted classes that were also Changed, PC:

$$PC = \frac{D}{B+D} \times 100 = \frac{30}{30} \times 100 = 100.0\%.$$

The percentage of Changed classes that were also Predicted, CP:

$$CP = \frac{D}{C+D} \times 100 = \frac{30}{94} \times 100 = 31.9\%.$$

4.2 Answering the Questions on Prediction I

On the basis of calculations we can now answer the questions.

A1.1 The kappa value is 0.22.
    A1.2.1 The percentage of correct predictions, p_0, is $(42+30)/136 = 52.9\%$.

A1.2.2 The number of classes predicted to be changed compared with the number of actually changed classes, is 30 and 94, respectively; the underprediction factor, UF, $94/30 = 3.1$.

A1.3.1 The ratio of changed classes that were predicted, CP, is $30/94 = 31.9\%$.

A1.3.2 The ratio of classes that were predicted to be changed and changed, PC, was $30/(30+0) = 100\%$.

From the answers we can see the following:

- The kappa value indicates a *fair* prediction.
- The prediction was correct in about half of the cases.
- The number of classes predicted to be changed is largely underpredicted.
- Only about one third of the set of changed classes were identified.
- All of the classes that were predicted to be changed were in fact changed.

4.3 Discussion

While this information might be sufficient for the project manager to be able to explain the difference between the expected workload and the actual one, more information is needed to explain the discrepancy between the prediction and the actual outcome. Questions such as "Is it the prediction approach in use to be blamed or do other circumstances impede an accurate prediction?" cannot be answered without more data, both quantitative and qualitative. Quantitative data on a more detailed level involves, in this case, data about each implemented requirement: what was the predicted impact and what was the actual impact? Qualitative data regards knowledge about the project and its context, which in this case means non-quantifiable information such as additional work required, i.e., work not known about at the time for Impact Analysis, but which was performed during the project.

An analysis per requirement shows that one requirement in particular is extraordinary in this case: *Porting to another operating system*. This requirement is extraordinary both in its nature and in that it was predicted to affect only six C++ classes, while it turned out to affect as many as 44. The changes for the port were, in other words, scattered around the system affecting as many as 32.4% of the classes in the system.

Knowledge about the project shows that some additional work was carried out during the project. The additional work arose, for example, from trouble reports from earlier releases that also affected the current release. These trouble reports were not known at the time for impact analysis; they were reported during the project. Analysis of the data shows that 13 C++ classes were changed for this reason alone.

IMPACT ANALYSIS IN SOFTWARE EVOLUTION 155

TABLE III
ACTUAL VS. PREDICTED CHANGES. ONLY CHANGES CAUSED BY "NORMAL" REQUIREMENTS INCLUDED

		Predictive group		
		Unchanged	Changed	
Actual group	Unchanged	80 (58.8%)	1 (0.7%)	81 (59.6%)
	Changed	31 (22.8%)	24 (17.6%)	55 (40.4%)
		111 (81.6%)	25 (18.4%)	136 (100.0%)

Adjusting the figures in Table II results in a new set of figures saying more about the Impact Analysis approach in use (Table III). In the new table the requirement "Porting to Solaris" and additionals are not considered as changes. Still there is a high potential for improvement, especially in finding the 31 classes that were predicted to remain unchanged but turned out to be changed—a challenging task.

4.4 Answering the Questions on Prediction II

The new answers are as follows.

A1.1 The new kappa value is 0.46.
    A1.2.1 The percentage of correct predictions, p_0, is $(80 + 24)/136 = 76.5\%$.
    A1.2.2 The underprediction factor, UC, is $55/25 = 2.2$.
    A1.3.1 CP, changed classes that were predicted, is $24/55 = 43.6\%$.
    A1.3.2 PC, predicted classes that were changed, is $24/25 = 96.0\%$.

These new values are interpreted as follows:

- The new kappa value now indicates a moderate prediction.
- The prediction was correct in three cases out of four.
- The number of classes predicted to be changed is still underpredicted.
- Less than half of the classes that were changed were predicted.
- Nearly all of the classes that were predicted to be changed were, in fact, changed.

4.5 Concluding Remarks on This Analysis

The RDIA approach used in the development of release R4 of the PMR-system was evaluated on the release level, meaning that all of the requirements were analyzed together, while the source code was analyzed on the C++ class level. It was demonstrated that to be able to refine the analysis, it is important to be able to separate new requirements and their impact from additional ones and their impact. The separation of each requirement's impact on the system was also important. To achieve this, both quantitative and qualitative data were necessary.

The results from the evaluation when considering all changes conducted during the project were that the prediction was fair according to the kappa value, which is the effect of a large underprediction in the total numbers of changed classes, but a correct prediction of classes that had to be changed. When the data was adjusted by filtering out the effects caused by an extraordinary requirement and all additional changes, the result was a moderate prediction according to the kappa value, but otherwise the same patterns as earlier. In the last analysis 24 of 25 predicted classes were changed, thus evaluation on the requirements level resulted in a worse prediction than on the release level regarding the *PC* value. The reason is that the 25th class was predicted to be changed because of one of the new requirements, but was actually changed because of an additional trouble report or requirement. Separating the causes for change from each other is necessary in order to discover this fact. The general pattern is, however, that the large majority of the predicted classes are actually changed, but the total number of changed classes is largely underpredicted.

With these patterns in mind a series of new pattern-related questions arises:

1. Is there a problem of underprediction in other releases and for all requirements?
2. If so, what is the variation of the underprediction factor?
3. Is it always the case that classes predicted to be changed are changed?

These questions will be examined in forthcoming sections.

5. Evaluation of RDIA on the Member Function Level

The previous analysis was concerned with evaluation of impact analysis as conducted on the class level. The question is, however, what a reasonable level of RDIA would be? Is the class level the optimum level, or would some other level be more appropriate? Should the number of changed member functions be predicted as a complement to classes? Or should the prediction be conducted on an even more detailed level, for example, in terms of how many statements or lines of code that will be changed? Cost estimation models, for example, COCOMO [5], often base the calculation of cost on very detailed measures, for example, on the number of lines of code that should be produced or altered. So it seems that lines of code is an accepted level for estimation of size, at least among COCOMO users.

IMPACT ANALYSIS IN SOFTWARE EVOLUTION

During RDIA, project developers specified which classes they predicted to be changed by a certain requirement and how many member functions for each class had to be added or changed to implement the requirement. This made it possible in this study to evaluate the prediction on two levels—the class level and the member function level. We can compare the prediction conducted at the class level with the prediction conducted at the member function level, which will be done mainly in terms of the number of predicted and changed member functions. The reason for this is that member functions was generally predicted and documented as the *number* of member functions that would be changed for each new requirement. This means that an analysis of whether the *right* member functions were predicted or not is impossible to perform.

5.1 Questions on the Member Function Level

The following questions are answered:

Q2 How good was the prediction on the member function level?

The question is usually broken down into subquestions, but only question Q2.2 is used in this analysis as often only the number of member functions to be changed was predicted, not which ones.

> Q2.1 How good was the prediction according to the kappa value? (not applicable)
>
> Q2.2 How good was the prediction when it comes to predicting the right number of member functions to be changed?

The question is usually broken down into the two subquestions.

>> Q2.2.1 What was the percentage of correct predictions (p_0)? (not applicable)

This subquestion is, however, *not applicable* for the same reason as above. The only subquestion possible to deal with when it is not known which member functions were predicted is thus:

>> Q2.2.2 Was the number of member functions to be changed correctly predicted ($1/UF$)?
>
> Q2.3 How good was the prediction when it comes to predicting which member functions should be changed? (not applicable)

Finally we want to compare the result with previous results:

Q3 How good was the prediction compared with previous analyses?

5.2 Design

For the evaluation of predicted vs. changed member functions, the classes were divided into two sets: classes changed because of new requirements and classes not changed because of any of these requirements. This implies that the second set of classes includes both classes that remained totally unchanged and classes being changed for some other reason than a new requirement. The analysis on the class level is presented in previous section, but a class level analysis will also be presented here for the reader's convenience. The analysis regards changes caused by new requirements (requirements level analysis) and have not been presented earlier (see Table IV). The classes in the first set (changed classes) were then analyzed regarding member functions, which were divided into two sets: changed member functions and unchanged. The number of changed member functions was then compared with the number of predicted member functions in calculating the underprediction factor. This was then compared with the results from analyses on the class level.

The number of classes predicted to be changed compared with the number of actually changed classes are 30 and 81, respectively; $30/81 = 37.0\%$. This is an underprediction factor of 2.7. The kappa value is 0.32 (Fair).

5.3 Analysis on the Member Function Level

The analysis on the member function level required much more work to be conducted than the analysis on the class level, we refer to the section on preparation for data analysis in [32] for details. The prediction was stored in Objectory SE as a traceability link between the requirement and the predicted design objects together with the number of predicted member functions.

DEFINITION 1. The number of member functions predicted for a class is represented by the number documented in Objectory SE.

TABLE IV
R4 CHANGED CLASSES—PREDICTED VS. ACTUAL. ONLY CHANGES CAUSED BY A REQUIREMENT ARE INCLUDED. 81 CLASSES CHANGED

		Predictive group		
		Unchanged	Changed	
Actual group	Unchanged	55 (40.4%)	0 (0.0%)	55 (40.4%)
	Changed	51 (37.5%)	30 (22.1%)	81 (59.6%)
		106 (77.9%)	30 (22.1%)	136 (100.0%)

30 of 136 (22.1%) classes were predicted to be changed as a consequence of implementing the new requirements and 98 member functions out of 1179 (8.3%). In this analysis we are interested in member functions that are changed in any way and therefore we use the following definition.

DEFINITION 2. A member function is considered changed if it is either reused from the previous release and edited, or added.

5.4 Member Function Change Statistics

The number of member functions is presented in Table V. The statistics of member function change based on source code edits during the release-project has been collected as described earlier and is summarized in Table VI. The three columns represent the different ways to classify the cause of change. The first column (Total) represents all changes on the member function level that were conducted during the release-project (release level). The second column (Cause: Req. Class) represents the changes that were caused by requirements, additionals have been filtered out. The third column (Cause: Req. Edits) results when every edit is examined to filter out irrelevant edits (requirements level).

The figures in Table VI are now inserted into Tables VII, VIII, and IX. As this analysis does not concern *which* member function were predicted to be changed, the resulting table based on the statistics can only be partially filled.

According to the definition of a changed member function (reused and edited + added) we get $262 + 338$ changed member functions, i.e., 600.

TABLE V
MEMBER FUNCTION INCREASE STATISTICS

Measure	Prior to R4	R4
No. of member functions	1046	1179 To Table VII–IX

TABLE VI
R4 MEMBER FUNCTION CHANGE STATISTICS

Measure	Total	Cause:Req. Class	Cause:Req. Edit
No. of added mfs	262	237	175
No. of edited mfs	338	320	268
Total of changed mfs	600 Table VII	557 Table VIII	443 Table IX

TABLE VII
R4 CHANGED MEMBER FUNCTIONS—PREDICTED VS. ACTUAL. ALL CHANGES (TOTAL) INCLUDED

		Predictive group		
		Unchanged	Changed	
Actual group	Unchanged	x	x	579 (49.1%)
	Changed	x	x	600 (50.9%)
		1081 (91.7%)	98 (8.3%)	1179 (100.0%)

TABLE VIII
R4 CHANGED MEMBER FUNCTIONS—PREDICTED VS. ACTUAL. ONLY MFS IN CLASSES CHANGED BECAUSE OF NEW REQUIREMENTS INCLUDED

		Predictive group		
		Unchanged	Changed	
Actual group	Unchanged	x	x	622 (52.8%)
	Changed	x	x	557 (47.2%)
		1081 (91.7%)	98 (8.3%)	1179 (100.0%)

TABLE IX
R4 CHANGED MEMBER FUNCTIONS—PREDICTED VS. ACTUAL. ONLY MEMBER FUNCTIONS CHANGED BECAUSE OF NEW REQUIREMENTS INCLUDED

		Predictive group		
		Unchanged	Changed	
Actual group	Unchanged	x	x	736 (62.4%)
	Changed	x	x	443 (37.6%)
		1081 (91.7%)	98 (8.3%)	1179 (100.0%)

An analysis of the table regarding the accuracy of the number of predicted shows that $98/600 = 16.3\%$ or, calculated as a ratio, it says that the number of predicted member functions is underpredicted with a factor 6.1.

While this factor is important as it shows the ratio between the number of member functions that were changed during the release-project and the predicted number, it is still not an evaluation of the impact analysis approach. The first step towards such an evaluation is to exclude all member functions belonging to changed classes that were altered for other reasons than new requirements. The list of such classes resulted from the analysis conducted on the class level presented in Table IV. The new table is shown in Table VIII.

The table shows that 17.6% (98/557) of the actual number of changed member functions were predicted, which is underprediction by a factor of 5.7.

While this investigation might be appropriate in the normal case, that is when data about causes is not available on the member function level, we intend to continue and refine the results even more. The problem with the previous analyses is that they are based on the division of classes into classes changed because of new requirements, and unchanged classes or classes changed for some other reason than new requirements. This division might result in edits of a particular class conducted because of new requirements, which is correct, while not all of the member functions in that class were changed each time. Hence, to be fair, we need to identify not only member functions defined in those classes that are changed because of new requirements, but also member functions that are truly changed because of new requirements.

An analysis of Table IX regarding the accuracy in number of predicted shows that $98/443 = 22.1\%$ or, calculated as a ratio, it says that the number of predicted member functions is underpredicted by a factor 4.5.

5.5 Answering the Questions on Prediction

Q2 How good was the prediction on the member function level?

The only applicable subquestion is:

> Q2.2.2 Was the number of member functions to be changed correctly predicted ($1/UF$)?
>
> A2.2.2 The underprediction on the member function level ranges between 4.5 and 6.1 depending on the level of change analysis.

Q3 How good was the prediction compared with previous analyses?

A3 The underprediction factor on the class level is 3.1. The factor in the example given in this section is 2.7 (Table IV). The answer is that a comparison between the class level and the member function level results in lower underprediction factors for the class level.

5.6 Discussion

We have calculated the accuracy in predicting the number of changed member functions and the predicted number of changed classes. The prediction on the two levels was compared with the actual changes on the two levels respectively. The result is that there is an underprediction also on the member function level. The other results is that the underprediction factor for classes was lower than for member functions. This is important and largely influences the cost estimation process following RDIA, which is based on the number of changed member functions, not changed classes. The conclusion based on these analyses is that it is not necessarily better to perform RDIA on as detailed level as possible because of the large deviations between predicted and actual number of member functions.

6. Summary of Statistics

The underprediction factor has now been calculated on the release level as well as on the evaluation of the requirements level on both class and member function level. As a conclusion for the evaluation part of the work, Table X summarizes the results.

TABLE X
SUMMARY OF UNDERPREDICTION FACTORS

Level	Category	Release 4
Class level	Release level	**3.1** *Max on class level* 94 changed classes
Class level	Selected requirements level	**2.2** 81 changed classes
Class level	Requirements level	**2.7** 55 changed classes
Member Function level	Release level	**6.1** *Max over all levels* 600 changed mfs
Member Function level	Requirements level based on changes of member functions in changed classes	**5.7** 557 changed mfs
Member Function level	Requirements level	**4.5** 443 changed mfs

IMPACT ANALYSIS IN SOFTWARE EVOLUTION   163

7. Evaluation of RDIA per Requirement

We have seen that change was underpredicted on the release level, the requirements level and on the selected requirements level, for example, in terms of the predicted number of changed classes compared with the actual number of changed classes. In this analysis we move to a finer granularity level as regards cause for change and examine single requirements. We do this by comparing, *for each requirement*, the prediction with the actual outcome.

7.1 Questions on the per Requirement Level

The questions we sought answers for are the following:

Q4 How good was the prediction on the requirements level?
    Q4.1 How good was the prediction according to the kappa value? (not applicable)
    Q4.2 How good was the prediction when it comes to predicting the number of classes to be changed?
        Q4.2.1 What was the percentage of correct predictions? (not applicable)
        Q4.2.2 Was the number of classes to be changed correctly predicted?
    Q4.3 How good was the prediction when it comes to predicting which classes should be changed?
        Q4.3.1 Were changed classes predicted (CP)?
        Q4.3.2 Were the predicted classes changed (PC)?
Q5 Was the rank-order among requirements the same when it comes to the predicted and actual change volumes?

7.2 Analysis on the Requirements Level

The requirements are presented in Table XI. The first row represents the set of classes predicted to be changed per requirement. The first row should be compared with the last row where the set of changed classes for each requirement is presented. In between the first and the last row, the data that is normally presented in contingency tables are presented. In the middle row, for example, the intersection between the two sets, classes that were both predicted and changed, is presented.

EXAMPLE 1. Requirement 1.01 was predicted to cause change in three classes, but four were actually changed. The question is: were the three predicted classes also changed? The middle row in the table reveals that two of the three classes were both

TABLE XI
PREDICTED VS. CHANGED CLASSES PER REQUIREMENT[a]

Reqs./ Status	1.01	1.02	1.03	1.04	1.05	1.06	1.07	1.08	1.09	1.10	1.12	1.14	2.01	2.02	2.03	3.01	3.03	3.04
Total Predicted	3	6	10	1	5	4	4	1	5	4	1	1	0	0	0	0	0	0
Predicted not Changed	1	1	3	0	2	0	1	0	2	0	1	0	0	0	0	0	0	0
Predicted and Changed	2	5	7	1	3	4	3	1	3	4	0	1	0	0	0	0	0	0
Changed not Predicted	2	37	6	2	8	6	5	3	2	1	0	0	8	3	3	1	3	3
Total Changed	4	42	13	3	11	10	8	4	5	5	0	1	8	3	3	1	3	3

[a]Requirements 1.11, 1.13, and 3.02 are removed as they had no values but zeros. Zeros occur, for example, when non-C++ related parts were subject for change.

predicted and changed. Thus one class was predicted but not changed, while two classes were not predicted but changed.

The table shows that in almost all cases, there is an underprediction in terms of number of classes, for example, Requirement 1.01 where three classes were predicted and four actually changed. The exceptions to the rule are Requirement 1.09 (five predicted, five changed) and 1.12 (one predicted, zero changed).

For six of the requirements one to three classes were predicted, but not changed, see Example 1. It should be noted that such a class (predicted but not changed) very well might have been changed in order to implement some other requirement. The analysis on the release level (all requirements analyzed together) is not sensitive to that kind of error, while this analysis is.

For the calculations of PC, CP, and UF, Table XI is divided into three tables in the following way: Tables XII to XIV.

From Table XII we can see that the number of predicted classes that were also changed divided by the number of predicted classes ranges from 60% to 100%.

Table XIII tells that the number of predicted classes that were also changed divided by the number of changed classes ranges from 11.9% to 100%.

The underprediction factor, the number of changed classes divided by the number of predicted classes (Table XIV), ranges from 1.0 to 7.0.

TABLE XII
PC, PREDICTED CLASSES THAT WERE ALSO CHANGED

Reqs./Status	1.01	1.02	1.03	1.04	1.05	1.06	1.07	1.08	1.09	1.10	1.12	1.14	2.01	2.02	2.03	3.01	3.03	3.04
Predicted and Changed	2	5	7	1	3	4	3	1	3	4	0	1	0	0	0	0	0	0
Total Predicted	3	6	10	1	5	4	4	1	5	4	1	1	0	0	0	0	0	0
Ratio (%)	67	83	70	100	60	100	75	100	60	100	0	100	-	-	-	-	-	-

TABLE XIII
CP, CHANGED CLASSES THAT WERE ALSO PREDICTED

Reqs./Status	1.01	1.02	1.03	1.04	1.05	1.06	1.07	1.08	1.09	1.10	1.12	1.14	2.01	2.02	2.03	3.01	3.03	3.04
Predicted and Changed	2	5	7	1	3	4	3	1	3	4	0	1	0	0	0	0	0	0
Total Changed	4	42	13	3	11	10	8	4	5	5	0	1	8	3	3	1	3	3
Ratio (%)	50	12	54	33	27	40	38	25	60	80	-	100	0	0	0	0	0	0

TABLE XIV
UF, UNDERPREDICTION FACTOR

Reqs./Status	1.01	1.02	1.03	1.04	1.05	1.06	1.07	1.08	1.09	1.10	1.12	1.14	2.01	2.02	2.03	3.01	3.03	3.04
Total Changed	4	42	13	3	11	10	8	4	5	5	0	1	8	3	3	1	1	3
Total Predicted	3	6	10	1	5	4	4	1	5	4	1	1	0	0	0	0	0	0
Factor	1.3	7.0	1.3	3	2.2	2.5	2.0	4.0	1.0	1.2	0	1.0	-	-	-	-	-	-

7.3 Relative Rank-Order of Requirements

Estimating cost in requirements selection is often based on the prediction, which means that requirements predicted to cause change in few entities are regarded cheap, while requirements predicted to cause change in many entities are regarded expensive. This makes the rank-order of requirements selection equal to a requirements list

TABLE XV
ORDERING OF REQUIREMENTS. ORDERING: PREDICTED TO BE CHEAPEST REQUIREMENT FIRST

Data set	2.01	2.02	2.03	3.01	3.03	3.04	1.04	1.08	1.12	1.14	1.01	1.06	1.07	1.10	1.05	1.09	1.02	1.03
Number of classes predicted	0	0	0	0	0	0	1	1	1	1	3	4	4	4	5	5	6	10
Order	1	1	1	1	1	1	7	7	7	7	11	12	12	12	15	15	17	18

sorted by the number of items predicted. The way of analyzing whether the requirements kept their order used here is to compare the relative order based on the number of predicted classes with the relative order based on the number of actually changed classes. In Table XV the requirements in R4 are ordered in terms of the number of classes that were predicted for each requirement. Note that requirements that predict the same number of classes are not distinguished from each other, but given the same ordering number.

EXAMPLE 2. Requirement 1.02 was predicted to cause change in six classes, see the right part of Table XV. Requirement 1.03 was predicted to cause change in ten classes. We can say that Requirement 1.02 is predicted to be cheaper than Requirement 1.03 in terms of the predicted number of changed classes. The requirements are rank-ordered as number 17 and number 18 respectively.

The next step is to order the requirements according to the number of classes that were actually changed per requirement, which is done in Table XVI. The row showing the previous order (from Table XV) for the requirements indicates any re-ordering.

TABLE XVI
ORDERING OF REQUIREMENTS; THE ACTUALLY CHEAPEST REQUIREMENT FIRST

Data set	1.12	1.14	3.01	1.04	2.02	2.03	3.03	3.04	1.01	1.08	1.09	1.10	1.07	2.01	1.06	1.05	1.03	1.02
Number of classes changed	0	1	1	3	3	3	3	3	4	4	5	5	8	8	10	11	13	42
Prev. Order (Table XV)	7	7	1	7	1	1	1	1	11	7	15	12	12	1	12	15	18	17

EXAMPLE 3. The requirements 1.02 and 1.03 ordered as 17 and 18 according to the prediction (Table XV) are now reversed based on the number of classes actually changed, see right part of Table XVI. This means that Requirement 1.02, which was predicted to be cheaper than Requirement 1.03, is actually more expensive in terms of the number of changed classes.

Many (6) of the requirements were predicted to cause change in zero classes (see Table XV) and therefore are regarded cheapest, zeros are however doubtful and the analysis is therefore conducted once more, with these requirements excluded, see Tables XVII and XVIII.

The two tables are illustrated in Fig. 3, which is used for a comparison of the predicted order with the actual order. The diagram shows the following:

Three requirements were correctly predicted.

Six requirements were relatively more expensive than predicted.

Three requirements were relatively cheaper than predicted.

The maximum difference in order (predicted order–actual order) is three.

The conclusion drawn from this is that even if the predicted order is correct in only three cases and that in six cases the requirements were relatively more expensive

TABLE XVII
ORDERING OF REQUIREMENTS; REQUIREMENT PREDICTED TO BE CHEAPEST FIRST

Data set	1.04	1.08	1.12	1.14	1.01	1.06	1.07	1.10	1.05	1.09	1.02	1.03
Number of classes predicted	1	1	1	1	3	4	4	4	5	5	6	10
Order	2	2	2	2	6	7	7	7	10	10	11	12

TABLE XVIII
ORDERING OF REQUIREMENTS; THE ACTUALLY CHEAPEST REQUIREMENT FIRST

Data set	1.12	1.14	1.04	1.01	1.08	1.09	1.10	1.07	1.06	1.05	1.03	1.02
Number of classes changed	0	1	3	4	4	5	5	8	10	11	13	42
Prev. Order (Table XVII)	2	2	2	6	2	10	7	7	7	10	12	11

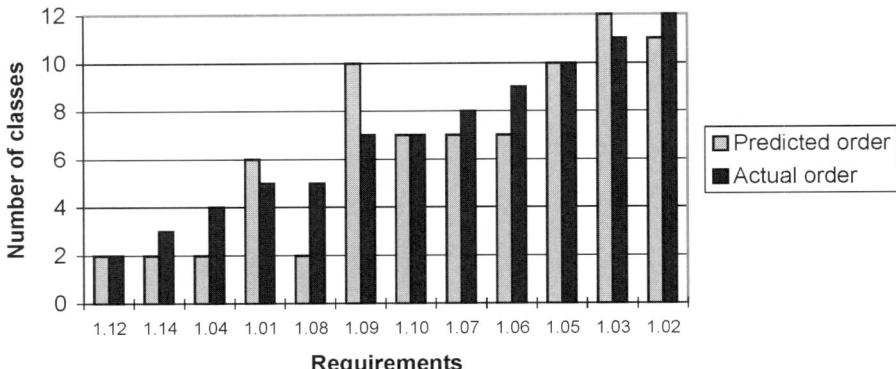

FIG. 3. Predicted vs. actual order of requirements.

than predicted, in general the prediction is reliable as the maximum disorder is three. This means that requirements predicted to be cheap are also relatively cheap. It must be noted, though, that the range of the number of predicted classes is small (1–6 and 10), while the range of the number of changed classes is greater (0–13 and 42), which confirms earlier analyses that there is an underprediction. However, the number of requirements is too small to base a hard conclusion on. Instead the phenomenon should be observed over time, in this and in other projects.

Answering the Questions on Prediction

Q4.2.2 Was the number of classes to be changed correctly predicted?

A4.2.2 The underprediction factor ranges from 1.0 to 7.0.

Q4.3.1 Were changed classes predicted (CP)?

A4.3.1 The ratio of changed classes that were predicted ranges from 11.9% to 100%.

Q4.3.2 Were the predicted classes changed (PC)?

A4.3.2 The ratio of predicted classes that were also changed ranges from 60% to 100%.

Q5 Was the rank-order among requirements the same when it comes to the predicted and actual change volumes?

A5 The ordering based on predicted number of classes compared to the actual number of classes should not be literally interpreted. This means that the ordering of requirements is not entirely intact, but the disorder is limited. The requirements are, however, too few for drawing any hard conclusions.

7.4 Concluding Remarks on This Analysis

The analysis on the requirements level shows that a majority of the requirements are underpredicted. It is also clear that it is relatively common that classes predicted for one requirement are not changed because of this particular requirement, but because of some other requirement. The analysis of the ordering among requirements based on number of predicted classes shows that the ordering is not kept intact, but are in general good. Small requirements seem to be small, and vice versa.

8. Models vs. Actual Implementation

Object models and object modeling techniques are often used as design aids, helping designers to identify objects and to structure the system during the development of the first release. In the PMR-project the design object model was not only developed during the first release, it was also kept, updated and further used to develop a set of subsequent releases. During RDIA for these releases the most obvious sign of this use is that the design object model was used for documentation of the predicted impact. The result of RDIA was documented using the Objectory case-tool—the set of new requirements was defined, and traceability links were established between each new requirement and the predicted set of design objects.

In the first set of analyses in this work, the extent to how well the prediction matched the actual outcome was investigated. This was done by comparing the set of predicted classes (documented as a set of design objects) with the set of changed classes. In the current analysis (the third research issue) we will take a broader approach comparing the main structural elements of the model with the main structural elements of the system. The motivation for this analysis is that, as with all sorts of documentation, the common intuition among practitioners would be that the design object model would have deteriorated after so long a time after its creation. A deterioration of the object model would make it a inadequate basis for impact analysis. A related study is also published in [34].

8.1 Contents Analysis—Describing the Abstraction Level

A model is an abstract representation of an object [14]. The design object model was always intended to serve as an abstract model of the actual system, but how

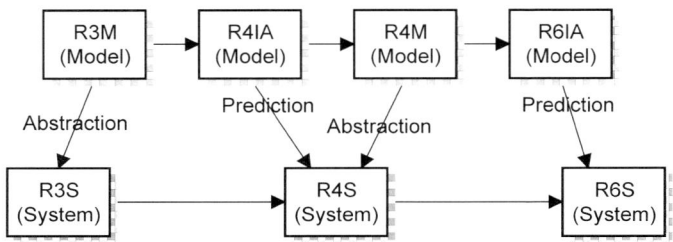

FIG. 4. The relationship between models and code for R3 to R6.

abstract? Abstract means emphasizing important entities, while suppressing details and less important entities. The intention of this analysis is to describe the abstraction level of the design object model. We do this done by comparing the content of the model with the actual system in two ways. First we compare the part of the design object model corresponding to C++ classes with the whole C++ implementation. As the first analysis shows that there is almost a one-to-one relationship between objects and classes and their inheritance relationships, we proceed with a second analysis. In the second analysis we select a subset of objects and corresponding classes and examine these. By doing this we are able to investigate how the inheritance structure, the relations and the operations/member functions change over time for a well-defined and constant set of objects and classes.

The analysis covers four object models and three releases of source code, Fig. 4.

The first model, R3M, played the role as an abstract model of the third release of the system, R3S. R3M together with the system R3S served as input to the impact analysis conducted prior to release R4S. When the impact analysis was done, the R3M model had been updated and now described (predicted) the system to be, namely R4S. The new model is called R4IA. When R4S was developed, R4IA was updated to adjust for the changes that were not anticipated. R4IA then became R4M, which is an abstract model of the system.

The main structural elements in use in the design object model that we have selected as elements for analysis are

- objects,
- operations,
- inheritance relations, and
- inter-object relations.

The corresponding structural elements in object-oriented source code are

- classes,

IMPACT ANALYSIS IN SOFTWARE EVOLUTION   171

- member functions,
- inheritance relations, and
- inter-class relations.

Hereafter we refer to design objects as "objects" or "design objects" and to C++ classes as "classes" or "source code classes". Thus "object" never refers to the source code. "Class" never refers to the design object model.

8.2 Questions Regarding the Design Model

We will now investigate how well the content of the design object model describes the system, which generates the following questions:

Q6 Is the object model a good abstraction of the system?
    Q6.1 On the object level?
        Q6.1.1 How many objects are there in the object model?
        Q6.1.2 How many classes are there in the source code?
    Q6.2 On the method level?
        Q6.2.1 How many operations are there in the model?
        Q6.2.2 How many member functions are there in the source code?
    Q6.3 On the inheritance level?
        Q6.3.1 How many inheritance relations are there in the model?
        Q6.3.2 How many inheritance relations are there in the source code?
    Q6.4 On the inter-object/class relations level?
        Q6.4.1 How many inter-object relations are there in the source code?
        Q6.4.2 How many inter-class relations are there in the model?
    Q6.5 Will the answers be the same for a constant set of classes?

8.3 Preparation

In this analysis the C++-related part of the system and its corresponding design object model is analyzed to describe the level of abstraction. The analysis of the design object model was conducted by first identifying all the design objects directly corresponding to C++ classes.[4] When the set of design objects was identified, all operations (corresponding to member functions) associated with these design objects were identified. Last, all relations between any two design objects in the set were identified. The result of the analysis of the design object model, i.e., a count of the number of items in each set, is presented in the first row of Table XIX. The

---
[4]Design objects not included are, for example, database tables.

analysis of the C++ source code was conducted in a similar way. The C++ classes were identified, all member functions associated with these classes were identified, and eventually, all relations between the classes were identified. While a relation between two design objects is well-defined, it is not the common case with relations between C++ classes. Our definition of an inter-class relation is as follows.

DEFINITION 3. A relation between class A and B occurs if class A references class B by mentioning its name in a source code statement, which is not a file name.

The implication of this definition is that the relation between C++ classes is unidirectional, which corresponds to the definition of relations between design objects. The problem with the definition is that it also includes inheritance relations, which therefore must be compensated for. To compensate for this fact we have included the inheritance relations in the set of object-relations.

It is important to note that member functions are counted using a different technique than was used in previous sections. The technique used here is based on an analysis of the assembly files, thus after the compilation, rather than analysis of the C++ source code itself. The result is a larger number of member functions, which corresponds to a conservative measure of the number of member functions. Counting member functions in C++ source code corresponds to an optimistic measure.

8.4 Analysis

The analysis results in a table representing the object models (Table XIX), a table representing the source code releases (Table XX), and a table with the calculated abstraction factors (Table XXI). The factors are calculated as the value for the source code divided by the corresponding value for the model.

TABLE XIX
THE FOUR DESIGN OBJECT MODELS AND THEIR CONTENT

Entity/Model	R3M	R4IA	R4M
Objects	125	142	142
Operations	727	980	997
Object-inheritance	22	51	51
Inter-object relations[a]	107	232	228

[a] Inter-object relations include inheritance relations

IMPACT ANALYSIS IN SOFTWARE EVOLUTION   173

TABLE XX
THE THREE RELEASES AND THEIR CONTENT

Entity/System	R3S	R4S
Classes	129	136
Member Functions	1590	1789
Inheritance relations	64	66
Inter-class relations[a]	572	610
Member Function calls[b]	18382	21102

[a] Inter-class relations includes inheritance relations
[b] This statistic is inserted for comparison only

TABLE XXI
FACTORS OF ABSTRACTION, MODEL VS. SYSTEM SOURCE CODE

Entity Factor	R3M vs. R3S	R4IA vs. R4S	R4M vs. R4S
No. Classes / No. Objects	1.0	1.0	1.0
No. Member Functions / No. Operations	2.2	1.8	1.8
No. Class Inheritance / No. Object Inheritance	2.9	1.3	1.3
No. Inter-Class Relations / No. Inter-Object relations	5.3	2.6	2.7

8.5 Discussion

The comparison between the various models and the corresponding system source code in the various releases shows that both the models and the source code grew in all of the four aspects that we have analyzed. This is a sign of the evolution of the system and also verifies the assumption that time is spent on the design object model with the intention of keeping it alive and up-to-date with the source code.

It is interesting to note the one-to-one correspondence on the object/class level, which is almost true on the inheritance level as well, with R3M as an exception. The more detailed levels, inter-object/class relations and operations/member functions, deviate more.

Knowing that the skeleton of source code of the first release of the system was generated directly from the design object model, it is clear that over the years the number of member functions has increased in a way that is not reflected in the model. The number of object/classes, on the other hand, has not changed much in comparison with the number of member functions. The great difference in the number of relations tells us that the actual interaction between C++ classes is much more complex than is shown in the model.

8.6 Describing Abstraction Using a Constant Set of Objects

Now when the abstraction level considering objects/classes is quantified to be one-to-one (one design object maps to one class), we will investigate how a well-defined subset of the C++ source classes change over time and how that change is reflected by change in the corresponding models. Let us call this subset a baseline to be used for comparisons, not only between model and system, but also between releases. While the model and the system grow in many directions, the purpose of this baseline is to provide a constant set of objects/classes to investigate how relations change in more detail. The analysis resembles in much the kind of analysis we conducted in Section 8.4, with the difference that 96 classes that existed in all three releases and were possible to trace by name to their 96 corresponding design objects were selected for analysis. Thus these 96 objects can be found in all models (R3M, R4IA, and R4M) and the corresponding 96 classes (object name = class name) can be found in the source code of all releases (R3S and R4S).

All relations between the design objects and the classes, respectively, were identified. Of the 96 classes, 70 (72.9%) were changed in the transition between R3S and R4S. Thus a major part of the changed system is represented by this set of classes.

8.7 Inheritance Relations Change

The data showing how inheritance relations in the models correspond to the source code is presented in Table XXII. *Total no. relations in model* represents all inheritance relations in the model that are defined between any of the investigated design objects. *No. relations only in model* represents the inheritance relations that could not be traced to corresponding inheritance relations in the source code. *No. relations in both model and system* represents the inheritance relations in the model that could be traced to corresponding inheritance relations in the source code. *No. relations only in system* represents the inheritance relations in the system source code that could not be traced to corresponding inheritance relations in the design object model. *Total no. relations in system*, finally, represents the total number of inheritance relations in the system source code.

The table and the diagram show that there was a great discrepancy between the model R3M and the source code R3S, which was adjusted in the subsequent model

IMPACT ANALYSIS IN SOFTWARE EVOLUTION   175

TABLE XXII
INHERITANCE RELATIONS AND THE MODEL'S REPRESENTATION OF THE SYSTEM

Model/Inheritance relations	R3M	R4IA	R4M
Total no. relations in model	19	40	40
No. relations only in model	3	4	4
No. relations in both model and system	16	36	36
No. relations only in system	25	5	5
Total no. relations in system	41	41	41
System/Inheritance relations	**R3S**	**R4S**	**R4S**

R4IA and then stabilized. It should be noted that the inheritance hierarchy was unchanged as regards this set of 96 classes. Thus the 41 inheritance relations between classes in the source code remained completely unchanged in the three releases. What we see in the table and in the diagram is thus an effort to seek conformance of the model to the source code, i.e., the model has changed, but not the source code.

8.8 Inter-Object/Class Relations Change

While the inheritance hierarchy was stable and remained unchanged as regards these three releases, this was not the case as regards inter-class relations. How inter-class relations were changed over time is shown in Table XXII. The value in each cell represents the number of inter-class relations present. The set of unchanged relations represents a large part of all relations: 90.9% (450/495).

Analysis shows that 6 relations were deleted and 28 were added for the creation of R4. The change of inter-class relations is thus relatively small. The interesting part, though, is that in a constant set of classes which represent a major part of the changes in the system where the inheritance hierarchy is stable, there still is a need of removing and adding inter-class relations.

Let us now see how the models mirror this change, which is presented in Table XXIII. The cells in the table are first explained. *Total no. relations in model* represents all relations in the model that are defined between any of the investigated design objects. *No. relations only in model* represents the relations that could not be traced to corresponding relations in the source code. *No. relations in both model and system* represents the inter-object relations in the model that could be traced to corresponding inter-class relations in the source code. *No. relations only in system* represents the inter-class relations in the system source code that could not be traced to corresponding inter-object relations in the design object model. *Total no. relations*

TABLE XXIII
INTER-OBJECT/CLASS RELATIONS FOR MODELS AND SOURCE CODE

Model/inter-object relations	R3M	R4IA	R4M
Total no. relations in model	81	176	176
No. relations only in model	8	13	13
No. relations in both model and system	73	163	163
No. relations only in system	399	332	332
Total no. relations in system	472	495	495
System/inter-class relations	**R3S**	**R4S**	**R4S**

in system represents the total number of inter-class relations in the system source code.

The same pattern as was found for the inheritance hierarchy can be seen here as well. The model R3M diverges relatively largely from the system, but is adjusted in the model R4IA. The number of inter-object relations has increased dramatically, which not only accounts for the deletions (6) and additions (28), but must be seen as a common improvement of the model. There is, however, a great discrepancy between the model and the source code as regards inter-class relations. The discrepancy varies over time, but is stabilized with a discrepancy factor of 2.8 $((163+13)/(163+323))$.

8.9 Discussion

This detailed analysis of the design object model compared with the source code confirms the earlier results showing that the actual relations between classes are much more complex than the model indicates.

8.10 Answers to Questions Raised by the Design Model

Q6 Is the object model a good abstraction of the system?

Q6.1 On the object level?

A6.1 There is a very high correspondence between the model and the system on the Object/Class level, the abstraction level is 1.0 in all cases.

Q6.2 On the method level?

A6.2 There is a lower correspondence on the operations/member function level starting with a factor of 2.2 later stabilizing at 1.8.

Q6.3   On the inheritance level?

A6.3   The deviation between model and system on the inheritance level starts with a high factor (2.9), but the model becomes adjusted along the way and stabilizes at 1.3.

Q6.4   On the inter-object/class relations level?

A6.4   The deviation on the inter-object/class level is high in the first model (5.3), but decreases to 2.8.

Q6.5   Will the answers be the same for a constant set of classes?

A6.5   The inheritance relations in the *source code* were constant over the three releases, but not in the model. This is interpreted as an effort to seek conformance of the model to the source code. The inter-class relations changed some, but not much during the transition from release R3S to release R4S. The model R3M diverges relatively largely from the system as regards inter-object/class relations, but is slightly adjusted in the model R4IA. The number of inter-object relations has increased significantly, which must be seen as a common improvement of the model. The final discrepancy factor regarding inter-object/class relations is 2.8.

8.11   Concluding Remarks on This Analysis

We have compared the three design object models with the corresponding source code in order to characterize the models' level of abstraction and how they reflect changes that occur in the source code.

The abstraction level can be characterized as a one-to-one mapping between design objects and classes, and almost the same regarding the inheritance hierarchy. There is an abstraction regarding operations/member functions, which is about 1.8. The greatest abstraction is about 3, regarding inter-object/class relations.

In a situation where a constant set of classes are selected, where the inheritance hierarchy is also constant, we have seen that the previous results are confirmed. We have also seen that changes as regards inter-class relations, which are relatively few even though many of the classes changed (70 of 96), are not clearly captured by the model.

The results confirm the common belief among analysts that the model is a good abstraction of the system and the common belief among designers/programmers that the model is not a good abstraction of the system. In fact, both groups are right. It serves as a good abstraction—on the object/class level and regarding the inheritance hierarchy, but it certainly lacks information (which is a consequence of abstraction) on more detailed levels.

The implication of this lack of information is that it is doubtful whether to use the model for dependency analysis as a part of RDIA. The real world is simply more complex than the model indicates. The model can still be useful for documenting impact analyses, provided that it is kept up-to-date, at least as regards objects/classes.

9. Class Size

In the source code of an object-oriented system, the most prominent entity is the class. The class has many different characteristics which can affect its likelihood to change, and in this section, which deals with the fourth research issue, we will search for patterns regarding one of these characteristics: the size of the class. We will investigate whether large classes were changed or not. We will also investigate whether it is likely that developers conducting RDIA base their prediction, consciously or not, on such a factor as size. Size is a factor that is likely to explain why a class is changed. Let us use an extreme example for illustration. Assume that we have a system of 1001 classes of varying sizes. One class contains about 10 000 lines of source code, the other 1000 contain only 10 lines each. If a developer had to choose ten classes as candidates for change, no doubt that the 10 000-lines class would be one of the classes selected. This is an extreme example, but intuition tells us that such a relationship is possible. In this section we will see if the reasoning holds for the PMR-project. We will also calculate how large a part of the system, in terms of uncommented lines of source code, was covered by the changed set of classes and the predicted set of classes, respectively. This section was also published in [33].

9.1 Questions Regarding Class Size

The size is measured in terms of number of uncommented lines of source code, and the source code is counted in the C++ files in the system release. In each analysis, the classes are divided into two categories: changed or unchanged, and predicted or non-predicted. For each analysis the distribution of the sizes of the changed/predicted classes is presented in one box plot and compared with the distribution of the size of the unchanged/non-predicted classes.

The three questions:

Q7 Were large classes changed?
Q8 Were large classes predicted?
Q9 Were large classes predicted compared to changed classes?

9.2 Size—Changed vs. Unchanged Classes

The distribution of the size of unchanged classes is compared with the distribution of the size for changed classes (see Table XXIV). The changed classes are measured in terms of their size in R3. The distribution of the unchanged classes is kept fairly tight with a median of 47.0. The distribution of the changed classes, on the other hand, is skewed to the left and much wider with a median of 175.0. The median differs by a factor of 3.9 (175.0/47.0). The observation is that unchanged classes are smaller than changed classes, but a few large classes also remained unchanged.

To test whether the difference in the median value is statistically significant the median test is conducted.

The statistics used for the median test are presented in Table XXV. It shows how the classes in the two groups discriminate above and below the combined median of 108.5. The χ-test is calculated from the data in the table, resulting in $\chi = 14.35$ which is larger than the critical value of 6.64. The conclusion is that the 0-hypothesis that the median values for the two groups are not different is *rejected* on the 0.01 level. The conclusion is that the median of the size of changed classes is larger than unchanged classes.

9.3 Size—Predicted vs. Unpredicted Classes

An analysis of non-predicted classes vs. predicted classes was also carried out (see Table XXIV). The distribution shows a median for non-predicted classes of 80.0 to

TABLE XXIV
STATISTICS FOR UNCHANGED CLASSES VS. CHANGED CLASSES

Statistics	Unchanged classes	Changed classes
Median	47.0 LOC	175.0 LOC
First & Third quarter	13.0 and 106.0	80.5 and 348.0
Graphical Outliers	0	5: 1724,1138,905,891,755

TABLE XXV
SIZE DISTRIBUTIONS FOR CLASSES

	Unchanged	Changed	
Size GT 108.5 LOC	10	54	64
Size LE 108.5 LOC	31	33	64
	41	87	128

TABLE XXVI
STATISTICS FOR NON-PREDICTED CLASSES VS. PREDICTED CLASSES

Statistics	Unpredicted classes	Predicted classes
Median	80.0 LOC	315.5 LOC
First & Third quarter	32 and 138	233.5 and 423.3
Graphical Outliers	12: 1724,891,617,606,504, 453,416,405,353,343, 328,308	4: 1138,905,755,734

TABLE XXVII
SIZE DISTRIBUTIONS FOR CLASSES, RELATED TO COMBINED MEDIAN: 108.5

	Unpredicted	Predicted	
Size GT 108.5 LOC	37	27	64
Size LE 108.5 LOC	61	3	64
	98	30	128

be compared with non-predicted classes: 315.0. A factor of 3.9 (315.0/80.0). The numbers indicate that the predicted classes are generally large, while the majority of the non-predicted classes are small.

The median test was also carried out for the predicted sets.

The statistics for the median test are presented in Table XXVII. The combined median is 108.5. The χ-test results in $\chi = 23.03$—the 0-hypothesis is *rejected* at the 0.01 level. The conclusion is that the median of the size of predicted classes is larger than non-predicted classes.

9.4 Size—Predicted vs. Changed Classes

We have seen that the median value of predicted classes is larger than the median value for unpredicted classes. The same is true for changed classes compared with unchanged classes. We will now compare predicted classes with changed classes as regards size. The median value for predicted classes is however greater than the median value for changed classes, see Table XXVIII.

To test whether the difference in the median value is statistically significant the median test is conducted.

The combined median is 230.0 (Table XXIX). The χ-test results in $\chi = 7.88$ which is larger than the critical value 6.64. The conclusion is that the 0-hypothesis that the median values for the two groups are not different is *rejected* on the 0.01

TABLE XXVIII
STATISTICS FOR BOX PLOT IN PREDICTED VS. CHANGED CLASSES IN R4

Statistics	Predicted classes	Changed classes
Median	315.5 LOC	175.0 LOC
First & Third quarter	233.5 and 423.3	80.5 and 348.0
Graphical Outliers	4: 1138,905,755,734	5: 1724,1138,905,891,755

TABLE XXIX
SIZE DISTRIBUTIONS FOR CLASSES, RELATED TO COMBINED MEDIAN: 230.0

	Predicted	Changed	
Size GT 230.0 LOC	22	36	58
Size LE 230.0 LOC	8	51	59
	30	87	128

level. Our conclusion is that the median of the size of predicted classes is larger than changed classes.

9.5 Answers to Questions Regarding Class Size

Q7 Were large classes changed?

A7 The median-based factor is 3.9 indicating that, in general, changed classes are large, while unchanged classes are small. The median test shows that the difference is significant on the 0.01 level.

Q8 Were large classes predicted?

A8 The median-based factor is 3.9 indicating that, in general, predicted classes are large, while non-predicted classes are small. The median test shows that the difference is significant on the 0.01 level.

Q9 Were large classes predicted compared to changed classes?

A9 The median-based factor is 1.8 indicating that, in general, predicted classes are larger than the changed classes. The median test shows that the difference is significant on the 0.01 level.

9.6 Discussion

The analyses indicate that large classes are changed, while small classes remain unchanged. They also indicate that large classes were predicted which leads to the conclusion that class size may be one of the ingredients used by developers, maybe unconsciously, when searching for candidates for change. A further investigation of the large outliers in R4 that were non-predicted shows that all 12 of the outliers (non-predicted) were actually changed. According to these results an investigation based on the largest classes should be an strategy to encourage. The comparison between the median value for predicted and changed classes results in that the median value for changed classes is greater. Thus large classes are predicted, while a set of large classes are non-predicted but changed.

10. Relations between Classes

In an object-oriented system there are classes, and relations tie classes together. Without the relations, the classes would be isolated chunks of data and code totally independent of other classes. Relations between classes make it possible for one class to take advantage, in different ways, of other classes. The object-oriented paradigm is perhaps most known because of the inheritance relation, which is one of the possible relations, but there are also others. While the inheritance relation makes it possible for one class to inherit (copy) the properties of another class, the communications relation makes it possible for one class (the sender) to send messages (invoke functions) to another class (the receiver). Relations can be seen in another perspective: as a concern of class visibility. To be able to send a message to a class the receiving class must be visible to the sending class. The inverse is not true: the sender of the message is not necessarily visible to the receiver of the message. Visibility means that the receiving class's name is, at least, mentioned (referenced) by the sending class, which in turn creates a unidirectional coupling between the two classes. Such a coupling is certainly a source for a ripple of change, i.e., that a change in one class causes changes to occur in other classes. The following two examples show what is meant. Assume that class A references class B, but the opposite is not true. Then

1. If the name of class B is changed, then all references in A to B must be changed to the new name.
2. If class B is removed from the system, then all references in A to B must be removed.

A strong factor here is the degree of coupling between classes. Think of a system with N classes which is completely coupled in that each class references all other

IMPACT ANALYSIS IN SOFTWARE EVOLUTION 183

classes. In such a system the examples above would generate changes, not only in class A, but in $N-1$ classes. The number of unidirectional relations in such a system would be $N(N-1)$.

Besides these obvious examples of ripple effects, there are other but more subtle situations where change in one class will cause change in other classes. For the RDIA, however, it is important to be aware of whether this is a real problem or not and a factor that should be regarded during the analysis process. Tools for impact analysis are often built upon the assumption that dependencies between entities are the source for change propagation. The analyses presented in this section investigate this assumption.

10.1 Questions Regarding Relations

The questions regarding relations are broken down in the following way:

Q10 Is there a pattern related to relations?

It is desirable to compare what was predicted to change with the actual changes, so the question is divided into the following subquestions:

> Q10.1 Can relations describe clusters of changed and unchanged classes?
> Q10.2 Can relations describe clusters of predicted and unpredicted classes?
> Q10.3 Can inheritance relations describe clusters of changed and unchanged classes?
> Q10.4 Can inheritance relations describe clusters of predicted and unpredicted classes?

Let us regard the system as a set of unique unidirectional binary relations between two different classes. Hence, each class can occur as a referencing class and/or ref-

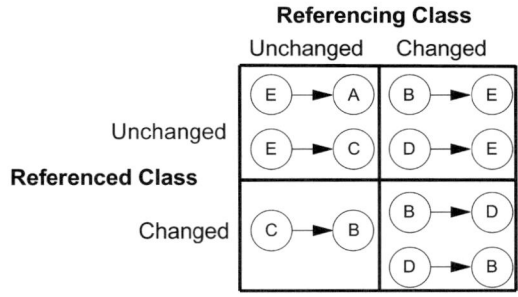

FIG. 5. Classification of relations in Fig. 6.

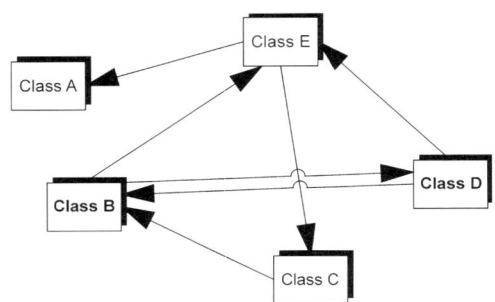

FIG. 6. Example of relationships between classes (see Fig. 5).

TABLE XXX
RELATIONS BETWEEN REFERENCING AND REFERENCED CLASSES

		Referencing Classes		
		Unchanged	Changed	
Referenced Classes	Unchanged	A: "U->U"	B: "C->U"	A+B
	Changed	C: "U->C"	D: "C->C"	C+D
		A+C	B+D	N (100.0%)

erenced class in many different relations, but there is only one unique occurrence of each relation. Classes are either changed (predicted) or unchanged (non-predicted). Let us divide the set into four disjunct subsets (Table XXX)

"U->U": Relations where both classes are *unchanged*.

"C->U": Referencing class is *changed*, referenced class is *unchanged*.

"U->C": Referencing class is *unchanged*, referenced class is *changed*.

"C->C": Relations where both classes are *changed*.

Clusters of changed/predicted classes and unchanged/non-predicted classes would occur if the changed/predicted classes had many relations with other changed/predicted classes and few relations with unchanged/non-predicted classes, and vice versa. Table XXX shows how the contingency table is used for analysis in this section.

Each of the questions is answered by identifying patterns according to how their relations distribute among the four subsets. In each analysis, the set of *predicted* or *changed* classes is compared with the set of relations as was extracted from the *previous release*, which was at hand during the impact analysis. This means that the prediction made for Release 4 is compared with the relations in the source code from Release 3. The consequence is that added or deleted relations are not regarded and the analysis of R4 examines the relations in R3, but not the relations added or deleted during the R4-project in order to develop release R4.

10.2 Inter-class Relations—Changed vs. Unchanged

As we mentioned above, relations can be of several types. In this analysis we will analyze all kinds of inter-class relations together including inheritance relations.

The data for the first analysis, all relations, was collected by extracting, for each class, all unique references to other classes. The number of relations according to this definition is 572. The number of references, for each class, to other classes ranges between 1 and 23 and the median number is 4. This should be compared with a situation where a system with 136 classes is completely coupled. The number of unidirectional binary relations would be $136(136 - 1) = 18360$. The system is thus far from being completely coupled.

The 572 relations and the four subsets are presented in Table XXXI. If it always were the case that a relation between two classes transferred change from one class to another then the two subsets "U->U" and "C->C" would together contain the main part of the relations, only leaving a few for "U->C" and "C->U". As a matter of fact, it would be possible to measure how well the four subsets conform to this pattern by using the kappa value. For R4 the kappa value is -0.02 (poor), which means that the described pattern does not occur here.

The relative number of relations in the "C->C" subset and the number of changed classes in this set indicate that a majority of the changed classes is related to other changed classes and not isolated as regards relations. As many as 59.8% of the relations are found in "C->C" together with 89.3% (84 of 94) of the changed classes.

TABLE XXXI
R4S 80. RELATIONS—ACTUAL. ALL CHANGES INCLUDED

		Referencing Classes		
		Unchanged	Changed	
Referenced Classes	Unchanged	151 (24.8%)	216 (35.4%)	367 (60.2%)
	Changed	80 (13.1%)	163 (26.7%)	243 (39.8%)
		231 (37.9%)	379 (62.1%)	610 (100.0%)

10.3 Inter-Class Relations—Predicted vs. Non-Predicted

In this analysis we will investigate whether inter-class relations could be used to describe the prediction as clusters of predicted and non-predicted classes. For this analysis the set of predicted classes are regarded "changed" and all other classes regarded "unchanged" which was the point of the prediction.

The result is the following. The kappa value for R4 is 0.09 (Table XXXII), which indicate a slight conformance to the pattern where "U->U" and "C->C" would dominate the table.

There is a relatively small number of relations in the sub set "C->C", 15.0% in Table XXXII and 7.9% in Table XXXIII. The last fact is important when we remind ourselves of the number of classes involved: 30 were predicted to be changed, but it must be remembered that we compare with the classes that existed already in the previous release. An adjustment of the figures shows that all 30 classes that were predicted in R4 also existed in R3. Let us also consider how *many* classes there are in the subset "C->C". In the case of R4, 29 of 30 predicted and existing classes reside in "C->C". This means that there are relations between the classes in the predicted set, the classes are not isolated from each other. The analysis shows that the classes predicted to be changed are related to each other in some way.

TABLE XXXII
R3S 30. ALL RELATIONS—PREDICTED SET OF CLASSES

		Referencing Classes		
		Unchanged	Changed	
Referenced Classes	Unchanged	234 (40.9%)	181 (31.6%)	415 (72.6%)
	Changed	71 (12.4%)	86 (15.0%)	157 (27.4%)
		305 (53.3%)	267 (46.7%)	572 (100.0%)

TABLE XXXIII
R4S 36. ALL RELATIONS—PREDICTED SET OF CLASSES

		Referencing Classes		
		Unchanged	Changed	
Referenced Classes	Unchanged	352 (57.7%)	176 (28.9%)	528 (86.6%)
	Changed	34 (5.6%)	48 (7.9%)	82 (13.4%)
		386 (63.3%)	224 (36.7%)	610 (100.0%)

10.4 Inheritance Relations—Changed vs. Unchanged

While the previous analysis included all kinds of relations, the following analyses only include inheritance relations. The inheritance relations were extracted from the derivation list for each class in the header files of the system. The inheritance relations follow the same patterns as other relations: the inheriting class, the subclass, references the class to inherit from, the superclass. The superclass does not reference the subclass, and the subclass is thus not visible to the superclass. The superclass does not know which subclasses inherit from it. We illustrate with two examples.

A changed name of a superclass, for example, requires that all references to the superclass in subclasses must be changed.

A removed superclass means that the subclass's references must be removed, but also that all other classes that use the inherited properties must be changed.

The set of inheritance relations is a much smaller subset of the set of all relations as discussed above. In R4S, for example, there were 66 inheritance relations involving 75 classes. Of these 75 classes the great majority (73) has a single inheritance and 2 have multiple inheritance from two super classes. Taking the viewpoint from superclasses, the median value of subclasses per superclass is 2 and the maximum value is 12.

The 64 relations between the 73 super- and subclasses in R3 are distributed among the four subsets as presented in Table XXXIV.

The same reasoning as above is applied here, too. The kappa value would indicate whether there is a pattern that relations gather in the subset "U->U" and "C->C". The kappa value for Table XXXIV is −0.24 (poor). The kappa values thus do not indicate a common pattern, even if a fair correspondence (0.21) is observed in the latter case.

TABLE XXXIV
R4S 94. INHERITANCE RELATIONS—ACTUAL. ALL CHANGES INCLUDED

		Referencing (Sub) Classes		
		Unchanged	Changed	
Referenced (Super) Classes	Unchanged	4 (6.3%)	27 (42.2%)	31 (48.4%)
	Changed	12 (18.8%)	21 (32.8%)	33 (51.6%)
		16 (25.0%)	48 (75.0%)	64 (100.0%)

10.5 Inheritance Relations—Predicted vs. Non-Predicted

In the analyses carried out above we have used the set of actually changed classes. We will now analyze the set of predicted classes and their relations in the same way, which can give an indication of whether relations were used as a vehicle for finding changed classes during the prediction.

The set of predicted classes are considered changed in this analysis, which was actually almost true in both cases, see previous sections for more information. The set is again compared with the set of relations which was extracted from the previous release. Thus, the prediction for Release R4 is compared with the relations from Release R3.

The kappa value is −0.19 (poor) for Table XXXV and 0.13 (slight) for Table XXXVI, which conforms to previous kappa values regarding associations.

The most striking fact is that there are very few relations between the classes in the predicted set: 0 (Table XXXV) and 2 (Table XXXVI). This is interpreted as inheritance not being considered as an indication of change during the impact analysis.

TABLE XXXV
R3S 30. INHERITANCE RELATIONS—PREDICTED

		Referencing (Sub) Classes		
		Unchanged	Changed	
Referenced (Super) Classes	Unchanged	41 (64.1%)	15 (23.4%)	56 (87.5%)
	Changed	8 (12.5%)	0 (0.0%)	8 (12.5%)
		49 (76.6%)	15 (23.4%)	64 (100.0%)

TABLE XXXVI
R4S 36. INHERITANCE RELATIONS—PREDICTED

		Referencing (Sub) Classes		
		Unpredicted	Predicted	
Referenced (Super) Classes	Unchanged	49 (74.2%)	13 (19.7%)	62 (93.9%)
	Predicted	2 (3.0%)	2 (3.0%)	4 (6.1%)
		51 (77.3%)	15 (22.7%)	66 (100.0%)

10.6 Answering the Questions

Based on the analyses above we will now return to the questions stated at the beginning of the section.

Q10 Is there a pattern related to relations?

A10 No pattern with a significant kappa value was found in any of the analyses. Analyses of the "C->C" subset showed that, in the case of all relations, a majority of the classes in the set are connected. This was true both for actual outcome and predicted, and for actual inheritance relations. In the case of predicted inheritance relations, this was not true.

Q10.1 Can relations describe clusters of changed and unchanged classes?

A10.1 No pattern with a significant kappa value was found even if the majority of relations and changed classes were found in "C->C". An investigation of the subset "C->C" shows that 61.0% of the relations and 84.0% of the changed classes reside in this subset. This indicates that a majority of the changed classes is related to other changed classes and not isolated as regards relations as defined here.

Q10.2 Can relations describe clusters of predicted and unpredicted classes?

A10.2 No pattern with a significant kappa value was found even if the majority of relations and predicted classes were found in "C->C". The kappa values were 0.09 and 0.14 which indicates a slight conformance to the kappa-pattern. As many as 29 of 30 predicted and existing classes reside in "C->C".

Q10.3 Can inheritance relations describe clusters of changed and unchanged classes?

A10.3 No pattern with a significant kappa value was found even if the majority of inheritance relations and changed classes were found in the subset "C->C". The kappa value is -0.24 and 0.21, respectively. The relative number of relations in the subset "C->C" and the relative number of classes in the subset, 34.8% and 60% for R4.

Q10.4 Can inheritance relations describe clusters of predicted and unpredicted classes?

A10.4 No pattern with a significant kappa value was found. Few inheritance relations between predicted classes were found in the subset "C->C". The kappa value is -0.19 for and 0.13. There are very few relations in the subset "C->C" 0 and 2.

10.7 Concluding Remarks on This Analysis

The following conclusions are drawn based on the results from the analyses:

- No pattern with a significant kappa value was found.
- There are reasons for using all kind of relations when looking for candidates of change during impact analysis.
- There are reasons to believe that inheritance relations were not used as an indicator of change during impact analysis.
- There are reasons to believe that other relations were used as indicators of change during impact analysis.

The relatively low kappa values indicate that relations do not describe changed/predicted and unchanged/unpredicted classes as clusters. This means that the assumption that dependencies in terms of relations between classes propagate change may be true, but not in a simple and obvious way. The implication is that when a changed class is encountered, the probability is relatively low that each related class is changed, too. Thus it is reasonable to believe that an impact analysis tool which propagates change based on relational-dependencies would generate too large a set of change candidates than would be useful.

11. Discussion of Findings

11.1 Qualitative and Quantitative Results

In this section we will connect the qualitative and quantitative results, which will be commented on and interpreted.

11.2 Questionnaire Completed by Developers

After that release R4 was implemented we asked participating developers to fill out a questionnaire on the RDIA, the information available and used, and finally how they assessed the prediction compared with the actual result. Here are some of the responses we got from the questionnaire.

Developers' perceived strengths with requirements-driven impact analysis are, for example:

> Developers have a chance to get to know the new requirements, the system, and the changes that have to be conducted in order to implement the requirements. It is a way of learning by doing in a structured way.

IMPACT ANALYSIS IN SOFTWARE EVOLUTION   191

The result from RDIA constitutes a basis for further estimation of effort and resources required. It is also useful for final design and implementation of the requirements as designers know exactly where to start.

Perceived weaknesses are:

To achieve an accurate result using RDIA requires deep insight into the system and its structure.

RDIA consumes much effort and takes much time to conduct.

It is easy to become optimistic and believe that the result from RDIA covers all necessary changes and all aspects of the requirements, which is not the case.

Developers were asked about what kind of information they used during the RDIA to identify software entities that would be changed:

The most common way to acquire information was to interview knowledgeable developers of what they believed would be the effect of implementing a new requirement. The explanation developers provided is that it is highly cost-effective to ask a knowledgeable person instead of searching in documents or other forms of information sources. Extensive communication between developers was also mentioned as a success factor for software development projects.

Analysis of source code was the second most common way of acquiring information.

While all developers said they interviewed other developers and consulted source code, about half of the developers answered that they also consulted the information stored in Objectory SE. On the question about the reason why information in Objectory SE was not used more extensively, developers answered that the information in Objectory SE was not detailed enough for RDIA, and that they did not believe that the information in the model was up-to-date. "Source code, on the other hand, is always up-to-date". Among some developers, especially newcomers, the attitude towards Objectory was almost negative. Objectory SE was, however, mentioned as a good tool for documenting RDIA and for answering questions about the relation between requirements and design objects.

On the question about what they believed about the result from RDIA immediately after RDIA had been conducted, developers gave the following answers.

About half of the developers doubted that they had found all the changed software entities, but believed that the result was accurate enough. One developer mentioned that he had conducted RDIA before and therefore knew that "some changes are always forgotten and the prediction has a tendency to be too optimistic".

The other developers said they believed that almost all changed software entities were found during RDIA.

On the question about how they considered the result from RDIA after completion of implementation, the following characteristic examples of answers were given:

- We were pretty close, one developer said.
- The result from RDIA was relatively good in that we found all software entities, but for each entity more work than expected was conducted, another developer stated.

There was a consensus among developers that the result from RDIA should be treated conservatively rather than optimistically, which means that it is better that too many software entities are predicted than too few.

Developers were asked to comment about what makes it easy and hard respectively, to conduct RDIA. Their answers are as follows.

- Well-defined requirements make it easier.
- "Small" requirements make it easier.
- Repetitious requirements, i.e., requirements of a certain kind that appear in nearly every release around which experience is built make it easier.
- Knowledge about the system makes it easier.
- Loose coupling between software entities makes it easier.
- Localized functionality makes it easier.
- Ill-defined requirements make it harder.
- Many subclasses (inheritance) make it harder.

All developers said they wanted to continue with RDIA in the future, but suggested improvements:

- To use the source code analysis tool, Sniff, more extensively in order to reveal dependencies between source code entities.
- To up-date the information in Objectory SE in a structured way, for example, by incorporating a reverse-engineering feature that generates object models from analyses of source code.
- To annotate each check-in in SCCS with explicit comments about member functions that were added, changed, or deleted.

12. Comments Regarding RDIA

Our comments regarding RDIA and developers' opinions:

1. RDIA seems to be a good exercise for team building and the way it is conducted in the PMR-project seems to be valuable alternating between individual investigations and group discussions. It allows the possibility to discuss the prediction and to identify potential forgotten aspects at the same time as it allows developers to work individually on the problem. It certainly gives developers a chance to get to know the system, the new requirements, and the changes they generate at a very early stage in the release-project.
2. We believe RDIA could be performed in a more structured way using the available information in terms of object models, source code, and text documents. We are surprised that developers are very good at writing documentation while at the same time being reluctant to read other developers' documents. Instead RDIA relies on interviews with knowledgeable developers in an informal way. A structured approach using available written information may result in better prediction.
3. We are surprised of the attitude towards Objectory SE among developers. After five years experience with it, developers are in general not too happy about the tool. The pattern is that new developers are more negative than developers who have been with the project for a longer time. This is surprising as the intention was to ease newcomers' understanding of the system by providing a set of abstract models of it. This has obviously not happened even though much effort has been spent on training and working with the models.
4. It was also notable that tools available at the work-place were not used in a coherent manner—some developers used the tools extensively, some were unaware of their existence. The basic tool set seemed to be based on very fundamental tools: EMACS, SCCS, make, a debugger, and a compiler and linker, while other tools such as the source code browser, SNIFF, were used by some developers, but not by others.

12.1 Summary of Quantitative Results

In brief, the results from the previous sections show that

- Change was underpredicted by a factor of 2.2–3.1 on the class level.
- Change was underpredicted by a factor of 4.5–6.1 on the method level.
- Change was underpredicted by a factor of 1.0–7.0 per requirement.
- Size seems to explain prediction: large classes are predicted.

Size seems to explain change: large classes are changed.

The design object model is a one-to-one abstraction of the source code on the object/class level. This is almost true as regards the inheritance hierarchy, too. There is a discrepancy between methods in the model and member functions in the code. The largest discrepancy is, however, on the relations level—there are about 3 times as many relations between classes than between design objects.

The design object model is changed over time—the conclusion drawn is that it is actively used and updated.

In a selected set of 96 design objects/classes that existed in all models and all releases of source code it was shown that the inheritance hierarchy in the source code was completely stable even though many of the classes were changed.

Relations do not seem to explain prediction: when a super-class is predicted to change, for example, it does not seem to lead to sub-classes are being predicted.

Relations seem not to explain change propagation, even if changed classes are connected via relations.

The number of relations seems to explain prediction: classes with many relations to other classes are predicted; classes that reference many other classes are predicted. Nothing can be said, however, about classes that are referenced by many classes.

The number of relations seems to explain change: classes with many relations to other classes are changed; classes that reference many other classes are changed. Nothing can be said, however, about classes that are referenced by many classes.

12.2 Feeding Back the Results

The result was fed back to developers in order to discuss it, but first we asked developers for their comments. The answers were mixed, but the common pattern is that

Developers believed that the prediction was much better than it proved to be.

Even the requirements that were mostly underpredicted were by some developers regarded as relatively well-predicted.

Some developers thought that the number of changed member functions was better predicted than the number of changed classes because reasoning on the member function level requires more detailed knowledge about the required change.

Some developers thought that the number of changed classes as better predicted than the number of changed member functions because classes represent larger chunks of code and are therefore easier to identify.

All developers were surprised by the large difference between the prediction and the actual outcome, but found no reason to believe that our analysis was anything but correct.

When asked about common characteristics among the changed classes developers mentioned the size: large classes are anticipated to change, while small ones are not. This was, however, an unspoken theory not used as a guide to find change candidates during RDIA.

Inheritance was not used as an indication of change propagation and developers did not believe that inheritance itself generates change.

Dependencies between member functions were used as an indication of change during RDIA as developers tried to determine which member functions were dependent on a predicted member function.

12.3 Comments about the Results and the Evaluation

Our comments regarding RDIA and the developers' opinions, and the actual results are:

1. At the inception of the research project we did not know whether prediction of changed software entities was a problem, or the dimensions of the possible problem. We are surprised that underprediction is of such a large magnitude despite the good conditions in the project. It is notable that the underprediction is so much greater regarding changed member functions than regarding changed classes. It is also surprising that the releases were delivered on time despite these facts. Our conclusion is that good marginal are built into the cost estimation model used in the project, which is also confirmed by interviews with the project leader—an optimist factor is used to compensate for prediction errors of this kind. We are also surprised that developers' knowledge of their own capability to predict is limited—that developers believe the prediction is much better than it actually is. Knowledge about the current capability is necessary in order to understand why the workload was worse than initially planned, for example. On the other hand, developers appreciate RDIA and want to continue with it. Developers have told us they feel comfortable after having conducted RDIA despite the underprediction and of which they knew nothing until we told them. We see this as a reason to believe that the RDIA process itself has a high value, perhaps a greater value than the result of the prediction.

2. Although we expected this research project to consume much effort, it has indeed consumed much more effort than expected. It was, for example, surprisingly hard to analyze C++ source code and to measure change over many versions of a C++ program. It was reasonably simple to analyze change on the class level, but due to features such as overloading, overriding, inheritance, and division of definition and declaration into a header and a text file made it hard and time-consuming to analyze change on the member function level.
3. Written information can be useful during RDIA, but also other information, such as the edit-history that has proven to be useful for evaluation, can be used to support RDIA. The edit-history provides data about which software entities have been changed, when the changes occur and why, together with information about what was changed. After working extensively with the edit-history, we have a strong belief that the data is also useful for conducting RDIA to achieve a better result. The data is, however, hard to use as is, which is why we needed to define procedures and build tools to make data more available.
4. Evaluation of RDIA was not conducted by the project developers but by us on our initiative and would not have been conducted if the release project had not been part of the research project. We believe that evaluation as such is necessary as a first step to improvement. The first evaluation describes the current situation and the subsequent evaluations can be used to measure the relative improvement that has been achieved. Evaluations set focus on the problem and we have seen that by conducting the evaluations and feeding the result back developers start thinking about how to improve.

12.4 Explanation Building

The quantitative and qualitative information led to the following hypothesis as an explanation of the RDIA process as conducted in the PMR-project:

> Developers were concerned with determining how each requirement would cause change in the source code.
>
> The changes in source code were mainly determined by finding 'starting' member functions to be changed, thus localizing *primary changes*. This was conducted first by interviewing knowledgeable developers, secondly by analyzing source code.
>
> *Secondary changes* were determined by examining how the member functions call each other and which other member functions needed to be changed.
>
> The results from this analysis were discussed with the group of developers in order to reveal change that had not yet been uncovered.

The procedure was repeated until the group decided that a substantial number of the changes had been determined.

The number of member functions was used to calculate the estimated cost in terms of man-hours required.

The selected requirements were implemented.

Evaluation was conducted: The actual number of man-hours spent on the project and the time for actual delivery was compared with the estimated number of man-hours and the planned time for delivery.

This RDIA procedure could be characterized as "determining how single requirements cause change in member functions". The evaluation was conducted on the release level considering the two different time estimates.

12.5 Suggested Improvements

In our analysis we have taken a different perspective which we also suggest as an improvement for conducting more accurate RDIA. Based on our experiences from evaluation of RDIA together with the quantitative and qualitative results, the following improvements for forthcoming PMR-projects conducting RDIA are suggested:

1. Evaluations of release projects should be conducted on the same granularity level as prediction are conducted.
2. The requirements-to-member-function-view used during RDIA should be complemented with a release-to-classes-view in order to use characteristics of classes to find candidates for change.
3. The optimistic prediction should be complemented with a conservative one.
4. The edit-history should be extended, made available and used to support RDIA and to evaluate the result.
5. Tools should be used to support RDIA.
6. An alternative to using the number of member functions as input to cost-estimation is to use the prediction on the class level, which historically has been more accurate.

In the remainder of this section we will explain these items in more detail.

Evaluations of Release Projects

Evaluation carried out as an ordinary task in the release project was conducted on a high level of abstraction, namely on the effort level. While this level is suitable for evaluation of the predicted effort compared with the actual one, it does not necessarily reveal underprediction on the software entity level, as is the result from our analysis. The prediction was conducted on the level of classes and member functions. Therefore it seems natural to suggest that to get proper feedback, evaluation of the accurateness of the prediction should be carried out on the same level as the prediction was conducted. In this case this means that if prediction is carried out on the member function level and the number of changed member functions is used to estimate cost, then the evaluation should be carried out beginning with counting the actual number of changed member functions.

The cost for conducting evaluation on this detailed level was relatively high for this research project, while it should be much less now when a set of data collection and analysis methods have been defined and validated. The benefits from conducting evaluations on this level are that it will be possible to detect problems with prediction, possible to determine whether improvements have occurred and achieve better predictions, and thus better cost estimations.

12.6 Complementary Release-to-Class View

As an addition to analyzing the prediction vs. the actual outcome on the member function level in the research project we also conducted the analysis on a more abstract level on the class level and for all requirements together.

Conducting the RDIA on the more concrete level makes the developer focus on questions of the kind: "How should member functions be changed in order to implement this requirement". Our suggestion is that a *complementary* view should also be adopted, namely the more abstract view. A more abstract reasoning about the changes would steer developers' reasoning to ask questions such as:

> "Which classes are changed in each release seemingly independently of the requirements? (change-prone classes)" and
>
> "What characteristics of classes lead to change in each release?"

The first question would lead to an investigation and identification of a set of change-prone classes that are changed in each release—such as central classes. All these classes should then be regarded as candidate classes in the future and inspected in order to exclude those classes that would not be changed in the current release.

The second question would lead developers to look for large and small classes, for example. All large classes would be regarded as change candidates and inspected in order to identify those large classes not needed to be changed during the release. Small classes would be inspected in order to find the relatively small set of these classes needed to be changed. The same reasoning could be applied to those classes with many, respectively few, relations to other classes.

We also have reason to believe that current reasoning about changes in the source code are not explicitly object-oriented. An indication of this is the focus on changed member functions instead of changed classes. The result is that inheritance relations are not investigated for change. Concretely this means that whenever a superclass is changed, its subclasses should be investigated for change as well and vice versa. This is not explicitly conducted today.

The cost of implementing the complementary view is low—it requires that developers think in another way. Using characteristics among software entities requires more work, though. It requires that someone analyses the classes in order to find change candidates, which would be best done with tool support. The benefit would be better prediction and thus a possibility to produce better plans.

12.7 Complementary Conservative Prediction

We would like to emphasize that the more abstract way of conducting RDIA should be a *complement* to the more concrete way as performed today. Obviously the developers are very accurate in their prediction of finding the classes that will change. Very few classes are predicted but not changed, on the release level. This is not true on the requirements level. This means that relatively often a class is predicted to change for one particular requirement, but is actually changed because of some other requirement. The knowledge that predicted classes will always be changed but also many others indicate that developers find 'the lowest level' or that the prediction is optimistic. Optimistic means that the predicted set of classes represents the least possible amount of work. It cannot be easier, only worse. As some developers mentioned, it would be preferable also to make a conservative prediction and 'the worst level' and the amount of work will with high probability be less than this level. Successively the actual outcome should lie somewhere between the predicted conservative and predicted optimistic level. The next goal would then be to decrease the variation as the process stabilizes.

The cost associated with producing a conservative prediction depends on its expected accuracy. The cheapest way to produce a worst prediction would be to predict all software entities in the system. A more useful prediction requires, however, an entirely different approach than the RDIA approach used today, which may be relatively expensive to incorporate. Such an approach could, for example, be based on change propagation techniques mentioned earlier. The risk associated with producing conservative predictions is that so large part of the system is predicted that developers have a hard time to believe it is realistic. The benefit from having a conservative prediction is that the actual result would be somewhere between the optimistic and the conservative prediction, and a most probable prediction could be determined.

12.8 Using Historical Data to Support Prediction

To be able to identify change-prone software entities the information in SCCS must be extended and be available. We suggest that each change be annotated with the reason behind the change and what was changed, for example, added, deleted and changed member functions of a changed class. Together with a tool that lets developer analyze the edit-history, the possibility to improve prediction would increase substantially.

The cost associated with finding change-prone software entities can be relatively low as the data is already available in terms of SCCS edit-histories. To develop a tool that makes data available for such analyses is also relatively inexpensive as a working program for internal use could be developed relatively quickly. Extending the information associated to each source code edit is very inexpensive, but requires that developers work in a different way—they have to add the information. This might be a problem as developers can have a hard time understanding why this would be necessary. The benefit, on the other hand, is that better prediction could be achieved and also better controls over the change activities, together with better system understanding. This is because it provides information about which parts are change-prone and which parts are not.

12.9 Tool Support

We suggest that source-code browsers like Sniff [49] or source code analysis tools like CIA++ be incorporated into the project in order to find change candidates based on dependencies between software entities. In these cases tools are already available and we have reason to suggest that developers are trained how to use them.

The cost for buying software tools is almost always less than the cost that developers spend on projects. The cost for convincing developers they should use tools can very well be higher. The risk is that tools are bought, but not used. To reduce this risk it is important that tools solve real problems in a convenient way. The benefit from having good tools that are used is better predictions.

12.10 Alternative Input to Cost Estimation

Prediction was carried out on two different levels: class and member function level. The prediction based on the number of changed member functions was used as an input to the cost estimation model while the prediction on the class level was more accurate. We suggest that a new cost estimation model be used which takes the number of changed classes as input while the prediction of changed member functions should still be used, but as input to detailed design and implementation.

The associated cost lies in correlating cost or effort to change on the class level. The benefit would be better input to the cost estimation model.

12.11 Discussion on Quantitative and Qualitative Results

Requirements-driven impact analysis is a crucial activity, many subsequent activities are dependent on its result. Achieving an accurate result from RDIA is hard. We have seen that experienced and knowledgeable software developers conducting RDIA in a stable environment still largely underpredict the number of classes and the number of member functions to be changed. This underprediction is compensated for during the cost estimation by project leaders who 'know' that underprediction is always the case. On the other hand, developers are not aware themselves of how good they are in predicting—they are surprised about the large discrepancies between the prediction and the actual outcome. This is true even after the implementation of the requirements, which means that developers do not remember how much work was actually spent on implementing the requirements and therefore believe that the prediction is much better than it actually is. Remembering that the developers studied were experienced and that the conditions were good, we have reason to believe that underprediction in other projects might very well be the same or even worse.

On the other hand, the potential for improvements is great. We believe that by combining the requirements-to-member-function view with a release-to-classes-view much could be gained. Developers should look for classes with certain characteristics that tend to change, such as large classes, and classes, which tend to change in every release. This is likely to be a good way to start with hunting down the classes that are not predicted, but changed. We also recommend to strive for establishing a conservative prediction and successively narrowing the gap between the optimistic and the conservative prediction, thus decreasing the variation.

Much time is spent on RDIA and the result is largely underpredicted. Should RDIA be discarded in the future to save time?

Developers like RDIA and appreciate that it gives them a possibility to review the requirements, the system, and understand the changes prior to design and implementation. We feel that RDIA becomes even more valuable when all the experienced developers have left the project and newcomers are to predict change. It will be even more important to discuss and analyze each requirement in order to produce a high quality system on time and within budget. RDIA will be even more important and we recommend that all available statistics from previous releases be used in order to support and improve prediction capability. It might even be the case that the process, actually conducting RDIA, is more important than the product, the prediction itself. The effect of the major discrepancy between the predicted number of member functions and the actual number of changed member functions could even be limited by treating the prediction on the member function level solely as an implementation proposal, not as a basis for cost estimation. As the prediction of the number of classes improves, this number should be used for cost estimation instead.

12.12 RDIA Using Models and Traceability

The design object model was used to document the RDIA and was appreciated by developers for this possibility. On the other hand, some developers distrusted the model because of lack of information. We will now discuss the possibilities of using the design object model more extensively in the light of the analyses conducted in this work. The main reason for this discussion is that we assumed that all models (the domain object model to the design object models, and the use-case model) and various forms of traceability could be extensively used during RDIA [27,31]. We found, however, that this was not practical as requirements stated for the first to the third release, R1–R3, were formulated on a much higher level of abstraction than the requirements in R4.

12.13 Other Models for Identification of Change

RDIA was documented by defining traceability links between requirements and design objects, both stored in Objectory SE. There were, however, also other models available: the domain object model, the analysis object model, and the use-case model.

The Use-Case Model

The use-case model has not been changed since the first release, R1, because "new requirements fitted into the existing set of use-cases". Our conclusion is that the use-cases are defined on a very high level of abstraction, as are the initial requirements. When new requirements, on a finer level of granularity, were added developers saw no reason for altering the use-cases. Used in this way the use-case model is an indicator of change only if a new requirement did not fit into the existing use-case model, thus generating entirely new use-cases, or causing change in existing use-cases. On the other hand, this would be an early warning of relatively large changes of the system as the use-case model shows the broad paths the system is designed for. As long as a new requirement resides inside these paths, changes are relatively small, while new requirements outside these paths indicate that new paths are needed.

The Domain Object Model

It was previously reported that the domain object model remained unchanged from the first release, R1, to the fourth release, R4. The domain object defines the vocabulary needed for building the system was still sufficient.

The Analysis Object Model

The analysis object model lies between the domain object model and the design object model. It was not changed during R4. The analysis object model is an ideal, or logical description of the system to be built, while the design object model is a real, or physical description. The analysts used this fact, as they knew how many physical files that were needed in order to implement, for example, a new report. For each new report a new analysis object was defined and between the new report analysis object and the set of new design objects generated by the report traceability links were defined. Each of these design objects represented a physical file needed and by using the traceability links it was possible to relate the logical report object to its physical implementation as represented by design objects.

Seriousness of Software Change

We have seen that the different models indicate change but on different levels. We propose a model based on the Software Architecture Analysis Method (SAAM) (1996) criterion for evaluation of the adaptability in terms of source code impact factors, see Table XXXVII. The higher the impact factor, the more severe the change.

Our model-related impact factors in Table XXXVIII complement the source code-related impact factors in Table XXXVII and should be used in combination with these. For example, an addition of a use-case not related to the existing use-cases should raise a warning flag that entirely new kinds of functionality of the system may now be required. Traceability between the different models should ease the localization of changed objects in related models, and the structure that traceability links constitute should make it easier to localize where new objects should be added.

12.14 Discussion on RDIA Using Models and Traceability

The use of models and traceability has been discussed and we conclude the following: Objectory SE supports analysis on the object level, thus supporting the more abstract analysis discussed here. It does not, however, support the more concrete level—the analysis on the member function level. To serve as good support, it must be up-dated so that it reflects the source code on a determined level. If the determined

TABLE XXXVII
SOURCE CODE-RELATED IMPACT FACTORS ACCORDING TO [35]

Impact Factor	Impact Description
S1	Change a configuration file or variable and restart. These changes require no coding.
S2	Modify data, data types or data structures within the code and recompile. These changes require only minor modifications within the existing code. The general structure and functionality of the code remain the same.
S3	Change the functionality of the source code for the modules. These changes impact large amounts of code in one or more modules. The programmer must have an understanding of the existing code and a plan for implementing the code.
S4	Change the software architecture. These changes require additions and deletions to the architecture's modules and connections. One or more modules must be written from scratch.

TABLE XXXVIII
MODEL-RELATED IMPACT FACTORS

Impact Factor	Impact Description
M1	Change of the design object model. These changes regards the real or physical description of the system and may generate change in the software architecture about the size of the change in the model.
M2	Change of the analysis object model. These changes regards the ideal or logical description of the system. A small change here may generate change in the software architecture larger than the change in this model.
M3	Change the domain object model. These changes regards the vocabulary needed in the system. A small change here may generate large change in the software architecture.
M4	Change the use-case model. These changes require additions and deletions to the use-case model. Small changes here may require large change in the software architecture.

level is, for example, classes, then relations between design objects should mirror the situation in the source code.

A new set of model related impact factors for using all available models defined in Objectory based on the indication of change observed in the PMR-project has been proposed.

13. Summary and Conclusions

13.1 Summary

The overall goal of this work has been to gather knowledge about RDIA and how to improve this crucial activity. The overall means has been an empirical study of RDIA in an industrial object-oriented project and the PMR-project. RDIA has been carried out as a normal part of project developers' work. The work on RDIA was preceded by observational research on traceability between various models during the development of the first release (R1) of PMR. In the licentiate thesis of this work [27] it was shown how traceability could be used to aid changing the system in general. What was lacking for continued research was a concrete real-life problem that could be treated both quantitatively and qualitatively. At the time of planning the research project we knew from project developers that project planning was a problem but not whether RDIA was a problem or not. Actually, project developers stated, at the time for conducting RDIA for R4, that the main problem was not determining the changes (conducting RDIA accurately), but to correctly estimate the number of hours (cost estimation) required [29]. Ericsson would not, however, at the time, allow publication of time- or productivity-oriented measures for this kind of project, which is why we decided to form the research project around RDIA viewing cost estimation as a consumer of the result from RDIA. As the evaluation of release projects at Ericsson was conducted on the project level—estimated time vs. actual time—finer granular evaluation techniques and entities predicted to change vs. entities actually changed— were not available. The first issue thus dealt with the development of such techniques and use them for evaluation of RDIA resulting in quantification of the accuracy of the result from RDIA. In the development of evaluation techniques we searched for simplicity and robustness so that the techniques could be used in a broader context. The deep knowledge about the project was used to ensure a fair evaluation, for instance by removing changes not due to requirements known at the time of prediction.

After having conducted evaluation of RDIA on several different levels, we concluded that the number of entities predicted to change was largely underpredicted. After having quantified the magnitude of the underprediction and concluded that the underprediction was a problem with great impact on subsequent activities, such as cost estimation, work distribution, and initial design, we continued with investigations of how characteristics of software entities, for example size, were related to change. We did this in order to find factors and patterns that could explain the situation. This comparative analysis approach, which is used in all analyses conducted in this work, compares the prediction with the actual changes made. We compared, for example, the number of predicted classes with the number of actually changed classes, and the size of predicted classes with the size of changed classes.

We also compared the size of predicted classes with the size of unpredicted classes. Other characteristics we examined were the number of relations between classes and whether relations between classes could describe clusters of changed/predicted and unchanged/unpredicted classes. We also examined the abstract models that were used for documenting the predicted change in terms of traceability between new requirements and design objects. The level of abstraction of the models and how change in the source code was reflected in models were investigated. This was performed in order to find differences and similarities between prediction and actual result, and the use of abstract models. As reported in [32] this was done for two releases (R4 and R6). When we found the same results in the two releases, we regarded it as a pattern that could be used as decision support in future RDIA activities, primarily in the PMR-project, but also in other related projects.

The result is thus well-grounded knowledge about RDIA as a phenomenon and its context, defined and used methods for quantification of RDIA on various dimensions together with the evaluation results, and patterns various characteristics. The quantitative results were connected to qualitative results from interviews with, and questionnaires completed by, project developers and also commented on by us as observers. The results were then discussed in terms of suggestions for future improvements.

13.2 Conclusions

We can scientifically conclude that we have gathered knowledge about the RDIA phenomenon in two releases of the PMR-project owned by ERA. The result from RDIA was quantified by using evaluation techniques defined and used during the research project. Qualitative data was used to support the quantitative results. The context, the procedures, the data collection, the analyses, the results and the reflections have been thoroughly documented.

We have identified a problem in terms of underprediction of the number of changed entities and also identified problems with using object models and traceability for detailed RDIA. We have found that project developers are unaware of their own capability in predicting change. We have also found that certain characteristics of software entities can indicate change-prone classes. We have proposed improvements based on the findings in order to improve the accuracy of future RDIA.

In retrospect, the work can be viewed as an experiment investigating whether the methods for data collection capture the RDIA process so faithfully that evaluation and analysis lead to process improvement. The documented methods together with the existing database provide enough information for replication in other contexts, such as subsequent PMR-releases, and other similar projects. To support this we have initiated a research project with the goal of the automation of data collection and data analysis as described in this work. The tool provides project developers with the possibility of actively using the edit-history of source code both for complementing on the requirements-to-member-function-view with a release-to-classes-view and to evaluate the prediction. The tool is intended to be used in object-oriented projects using SCCS as a version management system where RDIA is conducted and edits are annotated with the cause of the change.

The status of the research project is that the complete data set (i.e., the set of new requirements, the set of causes for change, the three releases of source code, the edit-history, the four versions of design object models, and traceability between all these entities) is stored in relational database tables using Microsoft Access together with a large set of queries used for analyses of the data. The data and the queries are connected to Microsoft Excel for further analysis and generation of diagrams of various kinds. This arrangement makes it possible to conveniently conduct analyses of the data in different ways. New data sets from new releases can be inserted smoothly into the existing structure and analyzed using the existing queries. New kinds of analyses can be defined in terms of new queries on existing data.

The status of the PMR-project has reached a point where the development of 13th release (R13) has now started. All of the original developers are now busy with other products and thus the development group is entirely different than was the case for R4. We look forward to comparing the result of conducting RDIA under these new circumstances. The PMR-project will, however, be moved to a design office in India in the near future which generates entirely new possibilities for research based on cultural differences.

REFERENCES

[1] Abbattsista F., Lanubile F., Mastelloni G., Vissaggio G., "An experiment on the effect of design recording on impact analysis", in: *International Conference on Software Maintenance 1994*, IEEE Computer Society Press, Los Alamitos, CA, USA, 1994, pp. 253–259.

[2] Arango G., Schoen E., Pettengill R., "A process for consolidating and reusing design knowledge", in: *Software Change Impact Analysis*, IEEE Computer Society Press, Los Alamitos, CA, USA, 1996, pp. 237–248.

[3] Arnold R.S., Bohner S.A., "Impact analysis—towards a framework for comparison", in: *International Conference on Software Maintenance 1993*, IEEE, 1993, pp. 292–301.

[4] Basili V., "Viewing maintenance as reuse-oriented software development", *IEEE Software* **7** (1) (1990) 19–25.
[5] Boehm B.W., *Software Engineering Economics*, Prentice-Hall International, Inc., Englewood Cliffs, NJ, USA, 1981.
[6] Bohner S., "Impact analysis in the software change process: A year 2000 perspective", in: *International Conference on Software Maintenance 1996*, IEEE Computer Society Press, Los Alamitos, CA, USA, 1996, pp. 42–51.
[7] Bohner S.A., Arnold R.S. (Eds.), *Software Change Impact Analysis*, IEEE Computer Society Press, Los Alamitos CA, USA, 1996.
[8] Codd E.F., "A relational model for large shared databanks", *Communications of the ACM* **13** (6) (1970) 377–387.
[9] Cohen J., "A coefficient of agreement for nominal scales", *Educational and Psychological Measurement* **20** (1) (1960) 37–46.
[10] DOD-STD-2167A, *Military Standard. Defense Systems Software Development*, Department of Defense, Washington, D.C. 20301, USA, 1988.
[11] EEA, *Guide to Software Quality Audit*, Electronic Engineering Association, 1988.
[12] Ericsson, *System Development Process Model, Design Rules & Guidelines*, Ericsson, Sweden, 1993.
[13] Ericsson Telecom AB, *Your Guide to PROPS*, Ericsson Telecom AB, Sweden, 1990.
[14] Fenton N.E., *Software Metrics A Rigorous Approach*, Chapman & Hall, New York, USA, 1991.
[15] Gallagher K.B., Lyle J.R., "Using program slicing in software maintenance", *IEEE Transactions on Software Engineering* **17** (8) (1991) 751–761.
[16] Gomaa H., "Reusable software requirements and architectures for families of systems", *The Journal of Systems and Software* **28** (3) (1995) 189–202.
[17] Haney F.M., "Module connection analysis—a tool for scheduling software debugging activities", in: *AFIPS Joint Computer Conference*, 1972, pp. 173–179.
[18] Horowitz E., Williamson R., "SODOS: A Software Documentation Support Environment—its definition", *IEEE Transactions on Software Engineering* **12** (8) (1986) 849–859.
[19] IEEE Std. 1219, *IEEE Standard for Software Maintenance*, Institute of Electrical and Electronic Engineers, New York, USA, 1992.
[20] IEEE Std. 830, *IEEE Guide to Software Requirements Specifications*, Institute of Electrical and Electronic Engineers, New York, USA, 1984.
[21] IEEE Std. 982.1, *IEEE Standard Dictionary of Measures to Produce Reliable Software*, Institute of Electrical and Electronic Engineers, New York, USA, 1989.
[22] ISO9000-3, *Quality Management and Quality Assurance Standards*, International Organization for Standardization, Geneve, Switzerland, 1991.
[23] Jacobson I., Christersson M., Jonsson P., Overgaard G., *Object-Oriented Software Engineering*, Addison-Wesley, Menlo Park, CA, USA, 1992.
[24] Karlsson J., "Software requirements prioritizing", in: *2nd IEEE International Conference on Requirements Engineering*, 1996, pp. 100–116.

[25] Kung D., Gao J., Hsia P., Wen F., Toyoshima Y., Chen C., "Change impact identification in object-oriented software maintenance", in: *International Conference on Software Maintenance 1994*, 1994, pp. 202–211.
[26] Li W., Henry S., "Object-oriented metrics that predict maintainability", *The Journal of Systems and Software* **23** (1993) 111–122.
[27] Lindvall M., *A Study of Traceability in Object-Oriented Systems Development*. Licentiate thesis, Linköping Studies in Science and Technology No. 462, Linköping University, Institute of Technology, Sweden, 1994.
[28] Lindvall M., "Report from OOPSLA'95", *The Software Practitioner* **5** (3) (1995).
[29] Lindvall M., *Traceability Aspects of Impact Analysis in the Fourth Release of an Industrial Object-Oriented System*. Memo 95-03, ASLAB, Linköping University, Linköping, Sweden, 1995.
[30] Lindvall M., "Evaluating impact analysis—a case study", in: *International Workshop on Empirical Studies of Software Maintenance*, 1996.
[31] Lindvall M., Sandahl K., "Practical implications of traceability", *Journal of Software Practice and Experience* **26** (10) (1996) 116–1180.
[32] Lindvall M., *An Empirical Study of Requirements-Driven Impact Analysis in Object-Oriented Systems Evolution*. PhD thesis No 480, Linköping University, Institute of Technology, Sweden, 1997.
[33] Lindvall M., "Are large C++ classes change-prone? An empirical investigation", *Software Practice and Experience* **28** (15) (1998) 1551–1558.
[34] Lindvall M., Runeson M., "The visibility of maintenance in object models: An empirical study", in: *International Conference on Software Maintenance*, IEEE, Los Alamitos, CA, 1998, pp. 54–62.
[35] McCrickard D.S., Abowd G.D., "Assessing the impact of changes at the architectural level: A case study on graphical debuggers", in: *International Conference on Software Maintenance 1996*, 1996, pp. 59–67.
[36] Object-Oriented Software Engineering, *Course Material: Object-Oriented Software Engineering*, Objective Systems SF AB, Kista, Sweden, 1993.
[37] Objectory Design, *Course Material: Objectory Design*, Objective Systems SF AB, Kista, Sweden, 1993.
[38] Objectory Process, *Objectory Analysis and Design 3.3 Process*, Objective Systems SF AB, Kista, Sweden, 1993.
[39] Objectory Requirements Analysis and Robustness Analysis, *Course Material: Objectory Requirements Analysis and Robustness Analysis*, Objective Systems SF AB, Kista, Sweden, 1993.
[40] Objectory Tool, *Objectory Analysis and Design 3.3 Tool*, Objective Systems SF AB, Kista, Sweden, 1993.
[41] Pfleeger S.L., Bohner S.A., "A framework for software maintenance metrics", in: *Conference on Software Maintenance*, IEEE Computer Society Press, Los Alamitos, CA, USA, 1990, pp. 320–327.
[42] Queille J., Voidrot J., Wilde N., Munro M., "The impact analysis task in software maintenance: A model and a case study", in: *International Conference on Software Maintenance 1994*, IEEE Computer Society Press, Los Alamitos, CA, USA, 1994, pp. 234–242.

[43] Royce W.W., "Managing the development of large software systems: Concepts and techniques", in: *Proceedings IEEE WESCON*, 1970, pp. 1–9.
[44] SEI, *Software Process Maturity Questionnaire, Capability Maturity Model, Version 1.1*, Software Engineering Institute, Carnegie Mellon University, Pittsburgh, PA, USA, 1994.
[45] Shahmehri N., Kamkar M., Fritzson P., "Semi-automatic bug localization in software maintenance", in: *International Conference on Software Maintenance 1990*, 1990, pp. 30–36.
[46] Singer C.A., "Software quality program, generic requirements", Technical Report TR-TSY-000179 issue 1, Navesink Research and Engineering Center, Bellcore NJ, USA, 1989.
[47] Soloway E., Pinto J., Letovsky S., Littman D., Lampert R., "Designing documentation to compensate for delocalized plans", *Communications of the ACM* **31** (11) (1988) 1259–1267.
[48] Stroustrup B., "Classes: An abstract data type facility for the C language", *SIGPLAN Notices* **17** (1) (1982) 42–51.
[49] TakeFive Software, I., *Sniff+ Release 2.0*, sniff-gst-002 Edition, 1995.
[50] Tip F., Jong D.C., Field J., Ramlingam G., "Slicing class hierarchies in C++", in: *Conference on Object-Oriented Programming, Systems, Languages & Applications 1996*, 1996, pp. 179–197.
[51] Turver R.J., Munro M., "An early impact analysis technique for software maintenance", *Journal of Software Maintenance Research and Practice* **6** (1) (1994) 35–52.
[52] Wilde N., Gomez J.A., Gust T., Strasburg D., "Locating user functionality in old code", in: *Conference on Software Maintenance 1992*, IEEE Computer Society Press, Los Alamitos, CA, USA, 1992, pp. 200–205.
[53] Yau S., Collofello J.S., "Some stability measurements for software maintenance", *IEEE Transactions on Software Engineering* **6** (6) (1980).

Coherence Protocols for Bus-Based and Scalable Multiprocessors, Internet, and Wireless Distributed Computing Environments: A Survey

JOHN SUSTERSIC AND ALI HURSON

The Department of Computer Science and Engineering
Pennsylvania State University
202 Pond Laboratory
University Park, PA 16802
USA

Abstract

Caching has been widely used in many diverse computer applications to improve performance. Although these applications often utilize diverse platforms due to their inherent natures and scope of applicability, there are elements of the caching scheme and the coherence protocol operations that are common to all implementations, regardless of the differences in implementation. This paper attempts to take a wide survey of caching applications to illustrate both the common and the differing elements of caching implementations. Widely researched, traditional caching applications using snoopy (bus-based) and directory protocols will be reviewed, then the relatively newer problems of web caching and the unique implementation issues of wireless networking will be considered. This analysis will be utilized to build a characterization of the various caching implementations, specifically considering the order of complexity in memory requirements, message complexity, message size, and synchronization delay. These parameters will be used to suggest that the underlying network topology, the sharing characteristics and the granularity of the data items being cached strongly affect the performance of coherence protocols.

1. Introduction and Background 212
   1.1. Introduction 212
   1.2. Motivation 214
   1.3. Major Parameters of Survey 214
   1.4. Road Map 215

2. Broadcast (Bus-Based) Protocols 216
   2.1. Background 216
   2.2. The Update Based Coherence Protocols 217
   2.3. The Invalidation Based Coherence Protocols 219
   2.4. The Hybrid Protocols 220
   2.5. The Adaptive Hybrid Protocols 221
   2.6. The Selective Protocol 223
   2.7. Summary of Broadcast Protocols 224
3. Message-Passing (Directory Based) Protocols 227
   3.1. Introduction 227
   3.2. CC-NUMA Architecture 228
   3.3. Directory-Based Organizations—Principal 230
   3.4. Directory-Based Organizations—Implementation 234
   3.5. Summary of Message-Passing Protocols 246
4. Coherence on the World Wide Web 246
   4.1. Introduction 246
   4.2. Hierarchical Web Caching Schemes 250
   4.3. Distributed Web Caching Schemes 251
   4.4. Hybrid Web Caching Schemes 252
   4.5. Coherence in Web Caching Schemes 253
   4.6. Summary of Web Coherence 258
5. Wireless Protocols 259
   5.1. Introduction 259
   5.2. Cache Coherence Design Requirements in the Wireless Network Environment 261
   5.3. Analysis of Basic Wireless Coherence Protocols 263
   5.4. Summary of Wireless Protocols 266
6. Summary and Conclusions 267
   6.1. Introduction 267
   6.2. Summary of Bus-Based Coherence Protocols 269
   6.3. Summary of Message-Passing (Directory) Coherence Protocols . . . 269
   6.4. Summary of Caching Coherence on the World Wide Web 270
   6.5. Summary of Wireless Cache Coherence 271
   6.6. Conclusions and Recommendations 271
   Acknowledgements 273
   References 273

1. Introduction and Background

1.1 Introduction

Data duplication has long been used as a performance-enhancing technique in reducing access latency in computer systems. The basic concept is simple: make a copy of frequently-used data in a higher performance storage device that is logically, physically, and temporally closer to the processing unit than the primary storage location of the data. This reduces the latency of accessing frequently used data and, consequently, increases the process's performance. However, this performance improvement does not come without a cost. Specifically, there are now two copies of the same data in the system. What happens if one of the copies of the data is modified? The problem becomes increasingly complicated as more copies of the data are created. This process, known as caching, has become a staple of modern computer architecture. To deal with the complexity of managing these cached copies of data, cache coherence protocols were developed [1–43,83].

Formally, a distributed memory (storage) system is said to be coherent if, for each shared memory location in the system, there exists some total serial order of the operations on those storage locations that is consistent and that satisfy the following conditions [44]:

- Operations issued by any process are applied to the storage location in the order in which they were issued by that process.
- Each read operation returns the value written by the last write operation to that storage location in the total serial order.

It is the responsibility of the coherence protocol to manage all copies of data throughout the system, keep track of which copy or copies are valid, and enforce the aforementioned conditions on the memory system. Most importantly, the coherence protocols define what actions are necessary when some process modifies a cached copy of the shared data.

At first, caching was utilized in uniprocessor systems to improve system performance. Later, these techniques were adapted for use in multiprocessor and distributed systems for similar purposes. More recently disk caching is employed in modern computer systems to provide lower-latency access to frequently used disk blocks (storage locations) and web browsers cache Internet documents to provide lower-latency access to those files (remote storage locations).

As one might expect, the great variety of caching applications has led to a similar diversity in coherence protocols that have been developed for those applications. The evolution of cache coherence protocols also illustrates some of the underlying rationale for the diversity exhibited by these protocols.

This chapter will examine the protocols developed for several of these applications and analyze the protocol operation in terms of several key parameters. The goal of these analyses is simple: to compare and contrast coherence protocol operation of a wide variety of protocols from different points of view. This will provide a useful perspective in applying the concepts and techniques developed for coherence operations to new applications in arbitrary distributed systems and in web-based systems.

1.2 Motivation

Caching has been employed for decades in computer architecture to improve system performance; consequently, a tremendous amount of research has been expended in this area over the past twenty-five years. The concept of caching is universal. However, the application of caching varies considerably, even among different solutions for similar caching problems.

This work analyses coherence protocols for various applications from bus-based, directory-based, and wireless domains in a common, generalized context. This analysis compares and contrasts the operation of these protocols in terms of global messaging of coherence protocol traffic and protocol behavior in the event of a modification to shared data. A generalized set of metrics is introduced to facilitate the analysis of these heterogeneous coherence protocols. The analysis developed in this paper is then used to identify key elements of effective coherence protocols and to make some recommendations on the development of coherence protocols particularly well-suited for internet and wireless internet applications.

1.3 Major Parameters of Survey

To properly compare the heterogeneous coherence protocols employed in the variety of applications considered by this paper, it is first necessary to identify and define a generalized set of metrics. These parameters may then be used in a quantitative analysis of these sundry protocols.

In the following discussion, N and M stand for the number of nodes in the system, and the number of global memory blocks, respectively. The parameters employed in this survey may be categorized into two well-defined groups: *Message Parameters* and *Memory Requirements*.

1.3.1 Message Parameters

Message Parameters are necessary to quantitatively compare and contrast the communication requirements of the various coherence protocols. The specific metrics used to quantify the message complexity are:

- Transaction Size—This metric quantifies the size of each transaction defined in the protocol operation. Unless otherwise noted, the transaction size is specified in units of bits per transaction.
- Messaging Complexity—The message complexity of the coherence protocol is specified in $O(\ )$ notation and is defined as the number of messages required for protocol operation. This complexity is a function of the number of processes in the distributed system.

- Synchronization Delay—The synchronization delay of the coherence protocol is also specified in O( ) notation. This delay is defined as the time (in terms of global clock cycles) required for protocol operation. As with the message complexity, the synchronization delay is a function of the number of processes in the distributed system.

1.3.2 Memory Requirements

A single memory metric is employed to quantify the storage requirements of the coherence protocol for each node in the distributed system. The memory requirements of the protocol are specified in bits per node unless otherwise noted. The complexity of the memory requirement is also given in O( ) notation.

1.4   Road Map

Abstract has expressed the background, motivation, and approach used in this chapter. The remainder of this document is organized in the following manner.

First, selected coherence protocols are divided into several broad categories:

- *The bus-based, or broadcast protocols*—As these protocols were the first developed in the evolution of coherence protocols, they provide a logical start point for this survey. Furthermore, they provide valuable illustration to the basic operation of the various types of coherence protocols. Broadcast protocols are discussed in Section 1.

- *The directory-based protocols*—These protocols are the natural evolution of the broadcast, bus-based protocols. Specifically, directory-based protocols are designed for the large-scale interconnected network of symmetric multiprocessor machines. Directory-based coherence protocols are also suitable for non-uniform multiprocessor systems and arbitrary distributed systems. These protocols are discussed in Section 2.

- *The wireless protocols*—The wireless network environment has proven to be the most challenging for several reasons. Most notably, wireless protocols must deal with frequent disconnections, lower bandwidth, and limited resources. Section 3 discusses wireless coherence protocols.

Section 4 considers coherence issues on the World Wide Web from a high-level perspective, then drills down to evaluate the low-level protocol requirements of this exceptionally diverse arrangement.

Finally, Section 5 summarizes the key points of this paper and provides an outline of key components of coherence protocols for internet and wireless internet applications.

2. Broadcast (Bus-Based) Protocols

2.1 Background

The issue of coherence protocols within the scope of memory hierarchy has evolved considerably over the past decades. Originally, coherence protocols were used to maintain the consistency of a local cache in a uniprocessor environment. In this role, coherence protocols supported the cache memory abstraction—a low latency, high-speed memory that mirrored an exclusive main memory to improve performance. Later, multiprocessor systems forced coherence protocols to evolve and support the more complicated abstraction of shared global and/or private memory. Recently, the explosive growth of the world wide web has forced computer system engineers to use the more literal interpretation of 'global' in the global memory abstractions required for pure applications of the distributed computing paradigm. However, the technical requirements of implementing such a memory abstraction are not trivial. Indeed, only specific applications can justify the cost of such an implementation.

Central to any of these aforementioned computing paradigms are the coherence protocols that maintain the consistency between the different levels of memory abstractions. In this section, the traditional coherence protocols will be summarized and analyzed in terms of coherence operation, transaction size, messaging complexity, memory requirements, and synchronization delay for an N node system.

The basic problem of maintaining consistency is straightforward. A process wishes to access a memory block B that resides at address A in the global address space. With no other processes involved, the requesting process need only load a copy of the memory block into its cache. That process is free to use the block as necessary, either reading or writing to the block, with the restriction that any changes made in the block are somehow updated in the global memory. The problem complicates considerably when multiple processes access the same memory block. Consider the case when J processes require access to the memory block B. If all J processes require only read-access to the block B and stores that block in their respective local caches, then there exists $J + 1$ copies of memory block B. The difficulty occurs when a process modifies one of those $J + 1$ copies—how does the system efficiently communicate this change, or at least that a change has occurred, to the other processes that hold a copy of block B is the principle challenge faced by coherence protocol developers.

The coherence protocols first developed took advantage of the broadcast nature of the busses on which they operated. In these systems, the full bandwidth of the bus was available to every node in a time-division multiplexed manner. As will be discussed later, the broadcast coherence protocols are the most efficient ones in terms of both hardware requirements and synchronization delays.

By returning to the simple example introduced previously, one can see the great advantage the broadcast medium offers in maintaining coherence. Recall that J processes have each a copy of memory block B. Consider that process k ($1 \leqslant k \leqslant J$) now modifies block B. The broadcast medium permits all remaining memory modules holding that block to be aware of the change concurrently. The various broadcast protocols differ in handling of those additional copies as described in the following sections. For perspective, it should be noted that the machines that employ bus-based protocols typically have between 2 and 32 processors, an address space on the order of gigabytes, and cache block sizes on the order of tens or hundreds of bytes.

It should be noted that, by no means, the following discussion is comprehensive. While the literature is abandon with many coherence protocols, due to the space limitations, only a generalization of the concept, illustrated with a few examples with be covered in this paper.

2.2 The Update Based Coherence Protocols

Update coherence protocols attempt to modify replicated memory blocks immediately, updating the remote copies. All remote nodes listen to (snoop) all bus transactions: when a node indicates that it is writing to a block that is cached on a remote node, the remote node simply reads the updated data and stores it in its cache. If the update protocol were used in the example above, after a process updated memory block B, there would be J processes that each had an updated copy of that block. Update-based protocols developed include the Dragon [15], Firefly [35], and Reduced State Transition (RST) [36]. Of these, the Dragon protocol has been more widely used and will be used as a representative of update protocol in this paper.

The Dragon protocol implementation is quite straightforward. Each block can be in one of the following four possible configurations:

- VALID-EXCLUSIVE: Cached copy is valid, not different from main memory, and no other copy exists in other caches.
- SHARED-DIRTY: Copy in cache is valid, is different from main memory (hence write-back is required when cache line is replaced) and other copies exist in other caches.
- SHARED-CLEAN: Copy in cache is valid, not different from main memory, and other copies exist in other caches.
- DIRTY: Copy in cache is valid, different from main memory (write-back required) and no other copies exist in other caches.

These four states dictate how the protocol will respond to any possible read or write access in the multiprocessor environment. To aid in the understanding of the operation of this and the other protocols discussed in this chapter, a very basic discussion of the operation of the Dragon protocol is discussed here (please see the literature for more information [15]). Consider a multiprocessor system with all caches initially empty. Some processor P1 requests a read access to a particular block of memory B. Processor P1's cache will load a copy of B from main memory, and mark the block VALID-EXCLUSIVE, since no other cache has block B stored. If another processor P2 requests a read request to block B, P1's cache observes the request and signals that it has a copy of B. Both P1 and P2 caches change their states for B to SHARED-CLEAN, indicating now that multiple caches have the block, and that the cached copies are identical to main memory. If additional processors request block B for read access, that processor's cache will load the block as SHARED-CLEAN as well. Now consider a write request for block B made by processor P3. The caches of P1, P2, and any other processor that may have previously read block B will indicate that the block is shared. P3 will then provide the updated data block to the system bus, and the caches that hold an old copy of block B will update their copies. All caches now change the state of block B to SHARED-DIRTY to reflect the fact that the copies held in the caches differ from main memory. A block may enter the DIRTY state when a write access for an uncached block is executed, or when a write access is requested by a processor whose cache contains the block in VALID-EXCLUSIVE state. In either case, the writing processor will contain the single cached copy of a data block—a block that differs from main memory.

Three types of transactions are allowable, the Read Block (RB), Write (W), and Update (UP) transactions. The RB transaction is used when a block is to be read from memory. The W transaction stores a block in memory. The UP transaction is used when a block loaded by a prior transaction is modified. Remote caches use the UP transaction to update their copies. Note that the data block is transferred during each of the three transactions in the Dragon protocol. Each transaction therefore requires a size sufficient large to hold the entire data block, the address of that block, and the status (control) bits.

The memory overhead of the Dragon protocol is small. Only two bits are required for each block to indicate its state. Additionally, tag bits are required to match addresses. The number of tag bits varies depending on cache size and degree of associativity. The maximum size of the tag bits is the number of bits of address used. In caches, this would correspond to a fully associative cache of any size. For the purposes of this paper, the maximum size is used.

Since update protocols operate in a broadcast medium, both the complexity of the messaging and the delay in synchronizing the caches is independent of the number of nodes in the system. Therefore, both these metrics are $O(1)$. Table I summarizes the physical characteristics of this protocol.

TABLE I
THE DRAGON PROTOCOL

Transaction Size	RB: number bits (A) + number bits (B) + 2 status bits
	W: number bits (A) + number bits (B) + 2 status bits
	UP: number bits (A) + number bits (B) + 2 status bits
Messaging Complexity	$O(1)$
Memory Requirements	2 bits state + number bits (A) per block
	$O(N)$
Synchronization Delay	$O(1)$

Where: A is the Address, B is the Data Block.

2.3 The Invalidation Based Coherence Protocols

While there is a certain aesthetic appeal in update protocols, the update transactions are expensive. More importantly, many applications exhibit a sharing pattern that makes many of those update transactions unnecessary [39,40,43–45]. Invalidation coherence protocols maintain consistency by simply broadcasting that a change has occurred in a block.

An invalidation protocol would handle our running example as follows: When process k modifies block B, instead of broadcasting an update transaction that includes block B, the process simply broadcasts an *upgrade transaction* containing the address A of the block and the appropriate status information. Remote processes listen for these upgrade transactions, and when a block that is stored locally is upgraded, the cache simply marks that block as Invalid. Of the many invalidation protocols developed, the Illinois–MESI protocol [14] has by far been the most widely used protocol; this protocol will be discussed in this work.

The complexity of the MESI protocol is quite similar to that of the Dragon protocol. The MESI protocol is also a four-state protocol (Modified, Exclusive, Shared, and Invalid–MESI). It also uses three transactions: Read Block (RB), Write (W), and Upgrade (UP). The RB and W transactions are identical in both Dragon and MESI; the Upgrade transaction differs from Dragon's Update transaction primarily in size, as the Upgrade transaction does not include the memory block. The Upgrade transaction's primary purpose is to invalidate stale copies of a block in remote caches.

As the RB and W transactions are identical in both Dragon and MESI, so are the sizes of those transactions. The principle benefit of the MESI protocol is the smaller size of the UP transaction and the corresponding reduction in traffic from that of the Dragon protocol. The messaging complexity, memory requirements, and synchronization delay of the MESI protocol are identical to their Dragon counterparts as depicted in Table II.

TABLE II
THE ILLINOIS–MESI PROTOCOL

Transaction Size	RB: number bits (A) + number bits (B) + status bits
	W: number bits (A) + number bits (B) + status bits
	UP: number bits (A) + status bits
Messaging Complexity	$O(1)$
Memory Requirements	2 bits state + number bits (A) per block $O(N)$
Synchronization Delay	$O(1)$

Where: A is the Address, B is the Data Block.

2.4 The Hybrid Protocols

In the study of the access patterns of applications, two metrics [39,40] were introduced to characterize access patterns to shared data. The first, "write-run length" (*WRL*), is defined as the number of write operations issued by a process before a shared memory block is accessed by another process. The second, "external rereads" (*XRR*), is defined as the number of external processes that access a memory block between two consecutive write runs. An application that exhibits a high *WRL* metric and a low *XRR* metric would benefit most from an invalidation-based protocol; the update protocol traffic of an update protocol is largely unnecessary and a waste of communication bandwidth. Conversely, applications exhibiting high *XRR* and low *WRL* would benefit from that coherence traffic, as external processes would have the updated block available in cache on demand. More seriously, if a large number of external processes require a modified block, each request would be satisfied by a separate *RB* transaction in an invalidation scheme. An update scheme would satisfy all these requests (assume the block was previously loaded) with a single *UP* transaction. Analyzing application access patterns revealed a large variation in both these metrics.

As individual access patterns determine if an update or an invalidation protocol would be more efficient in a given application, clearly neither can be optimal for all cases [37]. Hybrid protocols switch between update and invalidation behaviors based on some defined transitions threshold; the aim is to provide more efficient coherence protocol operation.

The literature has addressed several coherence protocols that fall into this class. One of the first coherence protocols to exhibit a hybrid behavior was the Read Write Broadcast (RWB) [41]. This protocol switches to an invalidation scheme after one update on a shared memory block.

The 'competitive snooping' algorithm was introduced that dynamically switches between update and invalidation modes when the cumulative costs of executing the updates equals the cost of reading the blocks [42].

Similar to competitive snooping, Efficient Distributed Write Protocol (EDWP) [43] uses an invalidation threshold of three and an additional signal to indicate a

TABLE III
THE UPDATE-ONCE PROTOCOL

Transaction Size	RB: number bits (A) + number bits (B) + status bits
	W: number bits (A) + number bits (B) + status bits
	UP: number bits (A) + status $\{$+ number bits $(B)\}$[a]
Messaging Complexity	$O(1)$
Memory Requirements	3 bits state + number bits (A) per block $O(N)$
Synchronization Delay	$O(1)$

Where: A is the Address, B is the Data Block.
[a] When updating remote caching.

consensus among processes holding a copy of a shared memory block to switch from update behavior to invalidation behavior.

The "Update-Once" [44] protocol is a variant of the EDWP algorithm. Update-Once uses an invalidation threshold of one and was shown to have the highest average performance over a wide range of traces and architectural parameters when compared with several coherence protocols including; Write-Once, Illinois–MESI, Dragon, and EDWP.

The complexity of the Update-Once protocol is not significantly greater than that of Dragon or MESI. Requiring six states, Update-Once needs three bits per block to record state. However, the messaging complexity and synchronization delay are $O(1)$.

Update-Once uses only three transactions. Two (RB and W) are identical in Dragon and MESI. The third, UP, behaves either like Dragon's Update transaction or MESI's Upgrade transaction, depending on a block's current state. The first write on a shared block issues an UP transaction that includes the updated memory block. Second or later writes to that block result in an UP transaction that does not include the data block that signals external caches holding a copy of that block to invalidate them (Table III).

2.5 The Adaptive Hybrid Protocols

The hybrid protocols discussed thus far have been static in that the threshold between the update and invalidate modes was predetermined and fixed. However, the large variations in *XRR* and *WRL* metrics—not only between applications, but also between different blocks of the same applications, indicate that a dynamic coherence protocol may provide additional benefits. Adaptive Hybrid protocols dynamically modify their behavior to adjust to varying application access patterns.

An adaptive hybrid protocol was introduced specifically to detect migratory sharing (AHDMS) [45]. Migratory data is defined as data used exclusively by a single process for an extended period before moving to another process. A six-state protocol, AHDMS uses an additional bus signal to indicate data blocks identified as migratory, and adapts its coherence operation on this basis. The six states utilized in the protocol are defined as follows:

- EE—Exclusive state: Cache has only copy, and the copy is valid.
- D—Dirty: Cache has valid copy, and the copy in memory is invalid.
- S2—Shared 2: Block is stored in exactly two cache memories, and both are consistent with main memory.
- S—Shared: Block is stored in more than two cache memories, and all are consistent with main memory.
- MC—Migratory Clean: Block is identified as Migratory, and as such may exist in exactly one cache at a time. Block is consistent with main memory.
- MD—Migratory Dirty: Block is identified as Migratory and may exist in exactly
- One cache at a time. Memory copy is invalid.

AHDMS has a complexity similar to the Update-Once hybrid protocol. Using six states, 3 bits per block are required to store this information. Furthermore, three coherence transactions are required. The first, Read Block (*RB*) is identical to the other transactions employed by the aforementioned coherence protocols discussed.

The second, invalidate (*I*) is analogous to the upgrade transactions used in the invalidation-based protocols and is used as an explicit directive for remote caches to invalidate the cached memory block specified by address. The third transaction, Update (*UP*) is identical to the *UP* transaction used in the Dragon's update protocol. Unlike the other protocols discussed herein, an explicit write transaction is not used in the AHDMS protocol—it is assumed that memory also snoops the protocol transactions and updates itself on *UP* transactions. Finally, AHDMS has identical metrics of messaging complexity, memory requirements, and synchronization delay, as does the Update-Once protocol (see Table IV).

TABLE IV
THE ADAPTIVE HYBRID PROTOCOL TO DETECT MIGRATORY SHARING

Transaction Size	*RB*: number bits (*A*) + number bits (*B*) + status bits
	I: number bits (*A*) + status bits
	UP: number bits (*A*) + status + number bits (*B*)
Messaging Complexity	O(1)
Memory Requirements	3 bits state + number bits (*A*) per block O(*N*)
Synchronization Delay	O(1)

Where: *A* is the Address, *B* is the Data Block.

2.6 The Selective Protocol

The coherence protocols studied so far assumed no a-priori knowledge about the nature of the data block. In lieu of foreknowledge about a block's sharing characteristics, the best these coherence protocols can do is to employ some heuristic to approximate an optimal coherence behavior. A-priori knowledge about a data block's sharing status could prove useful in developing a concurrency protocol. For example, an application's private data blocks need never be updated across multiple caches—the block will only be needed by the owner process. However, as processes may not always be scheduled in the same processors, a static coherence protocol may generate useless coherence traffic, unaware that a particular block is private. This is known as passive sharing [46].

Modern compilers and operating systems normally distinguish between private and shared data. Therefore, it is a simple matter to use this information by the coherence protocol to adjust its behavior accordingly. The Passive Shared Copy Removal (PSCR) [13] protocol does just this.

PSCR utilizes an additional bit on the bus to communicate the shared/private information for a given data block. Three states are legal for private (P) blocks—Invalid, Private Clean, and Private Dirty. For shared (S) blocks, there are four valid states (two of which are common with P blocks)—Private Clean, Private Dirty, Shared Clean, and Shared Dirty. With five distinct states, three bits are required to store the state information. For P blocks, the protocol behaves similarly to an invalidation protocol with two significant exceptions. First, there is no shared state (private data should not be shared). Second, the block is invalidated by any remote action on the block. For S blocks, the protocol behaves like a standard static update protocol.

PSCR has a complexity similar to AHDMS and Update-Once. Three transactions are required: Read Block (RB), Write (W), and Update (U). These transactions are identical to the Dragon protocol's transactions. PSCR initiates invalidation based on RB transactions to a private data block, eliminating the necessity of an explicit invalidation transaction. The Message Complexity and the Synchronization Delays

TABLE V
THE PSCR PROTOCOL

Transaction Size	RB: number bits (A) + number bits (B) + status bits
	W: number bits (A) + number bits (B) + status bits
	UP: number bits (A) + status + number bits (B)
Messaging Complexity	$O(1)$
Memory Requirements	3 bits state + number bits (A) + 1 bit (P/S) per block and 1 bit per block in global memory. $O(N + M)$
Synchronization Delay	$O(1)$

Where: A is the Address, B is the Data Block.

are identical to the other broadcast protocols. The memory requirements for PSCR differ from AHDMS and Update-Once by only one additional bit (P/S) for each block in the cache memory. In addition, a single bit per block is required to store the Private/Shared flag. Table V summarizes the physical characteristics of this protocol.

2.7 Summary of Broadcast Protocols

Broadcast protocols have made coherence operation on bus-based multiprocessors fast and (relatively) efficient. Early broadcast protocols required no knowledge of the actual use of a data block. Later protocols found that using some readily-available knowledge about the sharing status of a data block was useful in optimizing a protocol's behavior. Finally, an application's unique access patterns to shared data largely determine these algorithms' efficiencies.

Researchers in [13] compared several broadcast cache coherence protocols against each other. Figure 1 illustrates the bus utilization results for a sample application mix for the five coherence protocols outlined in this survey. While most of the protocols have similar performance in terms of bus utilization, two exhibit significantly different performance. The Dragon protocol saturates the bus for a much smaller number of processors (~16) than the other protocols for the same application mix (~30). This is significant in that it implies that the fixed update characteristic of the Dragon protocol generates considerably more bus traffic than other coherence protocols for the same set of applications. Additionally, the selective PSCR protocol

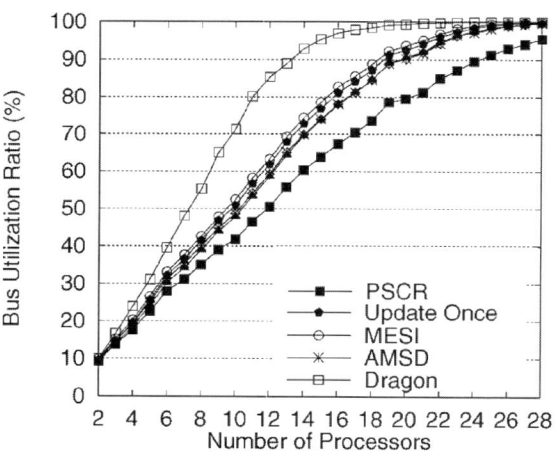

FIG. 1. Bus utilization for an application mix [13].

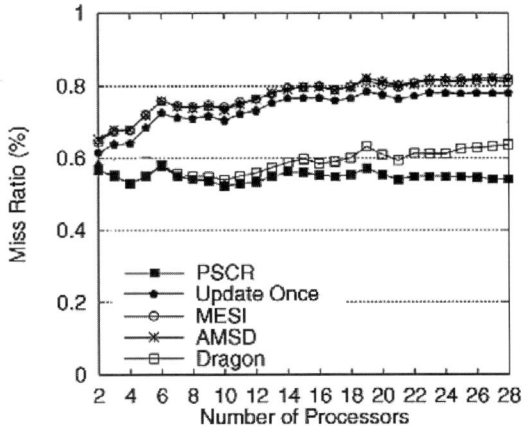

FIG. 2. Cache miss ratio for an application mix [13].

exhibits lower bus utilization for a given number of processors. This implies that the additional knowledge of the sharing characteristics of the cached data blocks enable the protocol to more effectively perform coherence operations.

Figure 2 illustrates the cache miss ratio vs. number of processors [13]. These data indicate that, as in the case of Fig. 1, Update Once, MESI, and AHMSD protocols are similar in performance, while Dragon and PSCR show quite different miss ratios. As one might expect, the update-based Dragon protocol exhibits lower miss ratios than average; this is reasonable as the update transactions make frequently-accessed shared data available in all caches when one process updates the block. However, the PSCR protocol outperforms even the Dragon protocol in terms of miss ratio. The implied conclusion is significant—not only does the additional knowledge of a block's sharing characteristics improves the bus utilization for a given number of processors, that knowledge also reduces the cache miss rate. This indicates that the a prior knowledge of sharing characteristics enable the selective protocol to provide a lower miss ratio (and, consequently, lower latency and higher performance) while using significantly less bus bandwidth for a given application load and number of processors.

The summary of the major parameters of each of the five broadcast protocols discussed in this section is displayed in Table VI. All five protocols have identical Message Complexity and Synchronization Delays. This may be attributed to the broadcast nature of the system bus—a single message simultaneously directs the specified coherence activity in all elements of the memory hierarchy. Clearly, the message complexity is therefore independent of the number of nodes in the system. By simi-

TABLE VI
SUMMARY OF BROADCAST PROTOCOLS

	Dragon (Update)	Illinois–MESI (Invalidate)	Update Once (Hybrid)	AHDMS (Adaptive)	PSCR (Selective)
Transaction Size	RB: number bits (A) + number bits (B) + status W: number bits (A) + number bits (B) + status UP: number bits (A) + number bits (B) + status	RB: number bits (A) + number bits (B) + status W: number bits (A) + number bits (B) + status UP: number bits (A) + status	RB: number bits (A) + number bits (B) + status W: number bits (A) + number bits (B) + status UP: number bits (A) + status {+ number bits (B)}[a]	RB: number bits (A) + number bits (B) + status I: number bits (A) + status UP: number bits (A) + status + number bits (B)	RB: number bits (A) + number bits (B) + status W: number bits (A) + number bits (B) + status UP: number bits (A) + status + number bits (B)
Message Complexity	$O(1)$	$O(1)$	$O(1)$	$O(1)$	$O(1)$
Memory Requirements	2 bits state + number bits (A) per block $O(N)$	2 bits state + number bits (A) per block $O(N)$	3 bits state + number bits (A) per block $O(N)$	3 bits state + number bits (A) per block $O(N)$	3 bits state + number bits (A) + 1 bit (P/S) per block and 1 bit per block in global memory $O(N + M)$
Synchronization Delay	$O(1)$	$O(1)$	$O(1)$	$O(1)$	$O(1)$

[a] When updating remote caching.

lar argument, the synchronization delay is also independent of the number of nodes in the system. Table VI also illustrates that each protocol requires three transactions. Furthermore, these required transactions are very similar in size and complexity.

The principle difference in the quantitative parameters of these five coherence protocols is in their memory requirements. Each protocol requires a certain number of bits for each data block. Each protocol requires a number of bits equal to the number of address bits employed in the system. Additional bits are dependent on the specifics of the protocol. The simplest of the protocols—Dragon and MESI—require only two bits to store the status (state) of the corresponding block. The hybrid Update-Once protocol and the adaptive AHDMS protocol require three bits per block for this purpose. For an implementation that utilizes a sixty-four-bit address space, this additional memory requirement is a modest 1.5% increase over the simpler protocols. For the PSCR protocol, the memory cost is significantly higher. In addition to the three bits per block to hold the status of the block, two additional bits per block are required—one in the cache tag and one for each data block in the main memory. For the sixty-four bit address space implementation, the additional cache tag bit requires 3.0% more memory than the simple Dragon and MESI protocols and 1.5% more memory than the hybrid and adaptive protocols. Each of these percentages of memory requirements refers to the per-cache block storage for each cache memory in the system. For the PSCR protocol, the additional bit required per block in main memory adds to the memory requirement. This additional bit is required for all memory blocks; consequently, the total memory required for this protocol is dependent on the total storage capacity of the main memory. As a result, the affect on the memory requirements of the protocol cannot be directly included in quantitative comparisons with the other protocols that have no such main memory storage requirements. Qualitatively, since the ratio of main memory to cache memory is generally two orders of magnitude, one may safely conclude that the additional bit required in main memory is quite significant in terms of total memory cost.

3. Message-Passing (Directory Based) Protocols

3.1 Introduction

As illustrated in Section 1, there are several effective and efficient methods of providing memory coherence in bus-based multiprocessor systems using broadcast coherence protocols. However, in bus-based organizations, since every transaction from every processor is visible globally, it seems reasonable to expect the system bus to become a performance bottleneck. This fact was evident in Fig. 1, where the bus utilization quickly approaches unity for systems composed of fourteen to twenty-eight processors. Once the bus utilization approaches one (i.e., saturation) the scalability of the system should be questioned since, any new processors added to the system will provide little performance gain as the processors' idle time increases. One should also note that the coherence protocol operation does account for some fraction of the observed bus utilization. Note that the update-based protocols, such as Dragon, saturate the system bus at a considerably lower number of processors. Conversely, the PSCR protocol does not completely saturate the system bus even for twenty-eight processor nodes. Nevertheless, there is a limit to the number of processors any of these protocols could effectively support. Consequently, for systems with a greater number of nodes, a different, more scalable approach to memory system coherence is required. As one will see, this approach extends beyond the coherence protocol to include the fundamental architecture of the underlying platform. While it is not the intention of this chapter to discuss the architecture of the multiprocessor systems, it is necessary, for the sake of clarity, to briefly discuss the similarities and the differences between these architectures.

3.2 CC-NUMA Architecture

Bus-based multiprocessor systems feature one or more processors, each of which may (and typically does) have a cache memory. These processors communicate with a centralized, global memory via the system bus. Figure 3 illustrates this basic organization. This organization is generally described as a Symmetric Multi-Processor (SMP) and is distinguished by the property that every process has uniform access to the shared system memory [46].

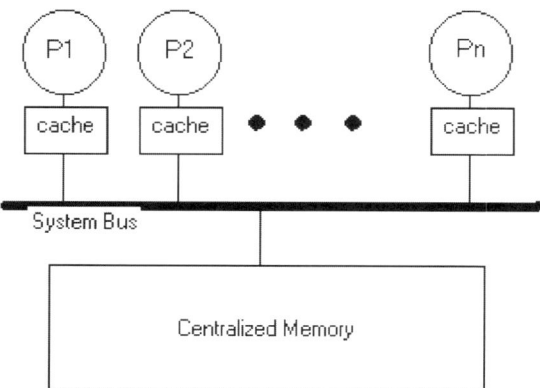

FIG. 3. Bus-based multiprocessor organization.

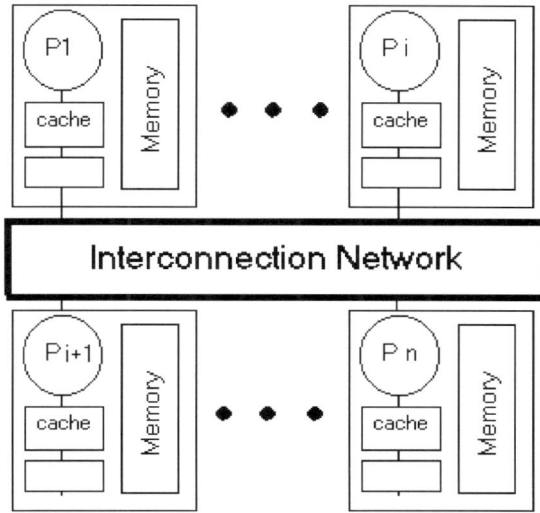

FIG. 4. General CC-NUMA architecture.

As discussed before, in such an organization all nodes, including processor nodes, the memory, and the bus, form a performance bottleneck. To alleviate this bottleneck, computer architects have devised alternative communication organizations to establish a higher bandwidth between processor and memory nodes. The term *bandwidth* refers to both the bandwidth of the communication medium and the available memory bandwidth.

Alternatively, the global memory is distributed among the processors of the system. In this way, each node in the system contains some fraction of the total global memory. To connect these nodes, an interconnection network is employed. Figure 4 illustrates the basic block diagram of such a system, generally described as a scalable multiprocessor. When such a multiprocessor employs some coherence protocol, the system is termed as Cache-Coherent, Non-Uniform Memory Access (CC-NUMA) system [46].

In scalable multiprocessor configurations, each processor node has a portion of the global shared memory that may be accessed directly. To access a memory block from other portions of the global memory, the coherence protocol must provide three important functions:

- determine the states of the block in other caches to know what actions to take,
- locate the other copies (if necessary, for example, to invalidate them), and

- communicate with the other copies—obtain the data, or invalidating/update them, as necessary.

By contrast, the bus-based protocols utilized the broadcast nature of the system bus to provide key features that support efficient coherence protocols. First, every bus operation (transaction) can be seen by every node in the system. Second, since the system bus is shared by all processes, its nature inherently enforces a serial order on the bus transactions. Recall from section one that the second condition is a necessary condition for a consistent memory, e.g., a read must return the value of the latest write operation in the hypothetical serial order. The message-passing protocols developed for CC-NUMA architectures must provide these functions directly.

There are two basic approaches to provide coherence for CC-NUMA architectures—hardware based and software based [46,56,58]. Software based approaches view the address space of each processing node as independent memories and provide global coherent memory via a software layer [46,58]. Typically, this software layer uses a lower network communication protocol to generate coherence traffic to remote nodes. Hardware-based approaches, as the name implies, require dedicated hardware support in processor caches, memories, and in their communication assists [46,56]. This additional hardware is used by the coherence protocol to generate coherence messages to remote nodes. Typically, the messages generated by the coherence protocol are managed by the communication assist, and as such, are transparent to the processors of the system and, consequently, the operating system. For these reasons, the hardware approach tend to provided better overall performance and are more commonly used in CC-NUMA applications [46]. Therefore, this paper will consider several variations of full hardware supported directory-based approaches to cache coherence. The machines that typically employ directory based cache coherence schemes have on the order of hundreds or thousands of processors, an address space on the order of terabytes, and cache block sizes on the order of kilobytes to tens of kilobytes.

3.3 Directory-Based Organizations—Principal

To manage the complexity of finding cached copies of memory blocks, determining the state of these copies, and communicating the appropriate information among the various copies when coherence activities are required, a directory-based approach is typically used in CC-NUMA organizations.

In discussing the operation of these directories, it is necessary to make a few key definitions:

- Home Node: System node in which the memory block is allocated.
- Dirty Node: System node whose cache holds a modified (dirty) block.

- Owner Node: System node that holds a valid copy of the block and that must supply the data when requested by another node. The Owner node is the Home node when no node has the block in the dirty (modified) state.
- Exclusive Node: System node that has a copy of a block in exclusive state (only existing copy). Exclusive states are either Dirty or Exclusive (i.e., Clean[1]).
- Local (requesting) Node: The node from which a processor has issued a request for a block.
- Local Blocks: Memory blocks for which the local node is the home node.
- Remote Blocks: Memory block for which the local node is not the home node.

There are two basic divisions in directory schemes, namely, the full mapped directory [46,54,56] and the partial mapped directory [46,56]. In full mapped directories, the precise location of every cached copy of a memory block is maintained by the system. In partial-mapped directories, a specific number of copies is permitted within the system. These systems may provide support for situations when this supported number of copies is exceeded in the system.

3.3.1 Fully-mapped Directory Organizations

Fully-mapped directory organizations can be categorized by the logical structure of the directory. There are three basic structures: centralized, flat, and hierarchical.

Centralized directories bring all of the directory information to a common location—the memory of the system is still distributed among the nodes of the system. Since this organization creates a bottleneck at the directory, centralized directories are not commonly used.

In flat organizations, the directory information for a memory block is immediately available to the requesting node, typically by decoding the address of the block. In flat schemes, the location of the directory is fixed.

In hierarchical directory organizations, the location of the directory information for a requested block is not known a priori. Hierarchical directories are organized as a logical tree where the leaves of the tree are the processing nodes and the internal nodes of the tree are directories of the memory blocks for the processing nodes of its children. When a request is made for a block whose directory information is not available directly for this node, the request simply traverses up the tree until a node is found that has the directory information. While hierarchical organizations have received some academic attention for their mathematical aesthetics, the additional latency of determining the home node of a memory block has prevented widespread utilization of this organization.

---

[1] Recall clean copies are consistent with main memory; dirty copies have been updated and, consequently, are valid, but differ from main memory. (The block has not yet been updated in main memory.)

Based on the physical location of the directory, the flat directory schemes may be classified into three groups:

1. Memory-based: The directory information is stored directly with the memory block on the home node.
2. Cache-based: Directory information is stored with a cached copy of the data block. The home node contains only a pointer to the node with the directory copy.
3. Hybrid: An intermediate approach that is partially memory-based and partially cache-based.

Fully-mapped directories typically use an N bit wide vector and additional bits to indicate the location and state of the cached copies for each block. In this scheme, the ith bit of the vector corresponds to the ith node of the system: if the bit is set, then the corresponding node holds a cached copy of the data block. For most of these directory schemes, the memory requirements will therefore grow as $O(N^2)$.[2] By comparison, the broadcast protocols discussed in Section 1 have memory complexities of $O(N)$. For this reason, alternative directory implementations were developed that will support only a limited number of cached copies [46,56].

3.3.2 Partially-Mapped Directory Organizations

Investigations into the sharing patterns of parallel programs have determined that the probability of a large number of processors accessing a particular data block is small [43]. It logically follows that a practical approach to reducing the large memory requirements of the fully-mapped directory would be to limit the number of cached copies the directory can maintain. In this way, the system will be able to handle most applications without difficulty. A performance penalty must be incurred only when the maximum number of directly supported copies is exceeded.

The most common approach to partially-mapped directories involves maintaining a certain number of pointers to nodes that contain a cached copy of a memory block. Recall that in the fully mapped bit vector, the state of a bit indicated whether or not a particular node currently holds a valid copy of that block; in partially-mapped directories this bit vector is replaced by multi-bit pointers, each of which is $\log_2(N)$ bits wide. For the directory to support ι copies of a data block, then the total storage requirements for a directory entry is $\iota \log_2(N)$; for small ι, this storage requirement is much less than the N bits required for the fully-mapped directory. When a limited number of pointers are used to indicate the location of cached data blocks, the directory scheme is called a dir_ι organization.

---
[2]This will be developed in detail later in this section.

By using a small number of pointers, partially-mapped directories reduce the large storage requirements of directory coherence protocols; however, what happens when the supported number of copies is exceeded (i.e., pointer overflow)? In practice, several approaches address this issue [46,47,49–58]. The simplest approach is to absolutely forbid more than the supported number of copies in the system. Under this implementation, when an application requests the $\iota + 1$ copy, a previously allocated copy is simply invalidated; therefore, there is never more than ι copies of any memory block in the system. This approach works fine when fewer than ι copies are required. However, when an application does frequently exceed the supported number of copies, then the repeated invalidations of active remote copies generates considerable excessive coherence traffic and seriously reduces the overall system performance. This type of partially-mapped directory is known as the dir_ι-NB directory organization.

The second approach to handling the pointer overflow problem is to broadcast coherence traffic to all nodes when more than ι copies of a data block are cached. To facilitate this, an additional bit, the overflow bit, is set whenever broadcasts must be used for coherence protocol operations. However, as the interconnection network is not a broadcast-based network, the network must propagate the message to all nodes of the network. This approach is effective in maintaining cache coherence; however, the high cost of propagating these messages introduces considerable performance penalties. As many of the messages are sent to nodes that do not have a valid copy of the data block, these additional messages are unnecessary. This approach is known as the dir_ι-B directory organization.

The third approach to solve the pointer overflow problem is known as the coarse vector. In this organization, the directory behaves as a simple dir_ι directory when the number of active copies of a data block is less than ι. However, when the number of active copies is greater than or equal to ι, the directory switches to a coarse vector. As a coarse vector, the directory bits used for the pointers are redefined as a bit vector. The coarse vector identifies not a single node, but rather a specific group of nodes. As a result, a bit indicates whether or not at least one copy of the data block is cached in a group of nodes. Therefore, coherence protocol messages are broadcast to all the nodes of a group whose corresponding bit in the coarse vector indicates the presence of a cached copy. This reduces the total network coherence protocol traffic generated when the number of cached copies exceeds ι without paying the higher storage costs of a fully-mapped directory. This scheme is known as the $\text{dir}_\iota\text{-CV}_\kappa$ directory organization, where κ is the number of nodes in the group. When $\kappa = 1$, the scheme is equivalent to a fully-mapped directory; when $\kappa = N$, the scheme reduces to the dir_ι-B directory organization. Figure 5 illustrates this hierarchy of directory organizations.

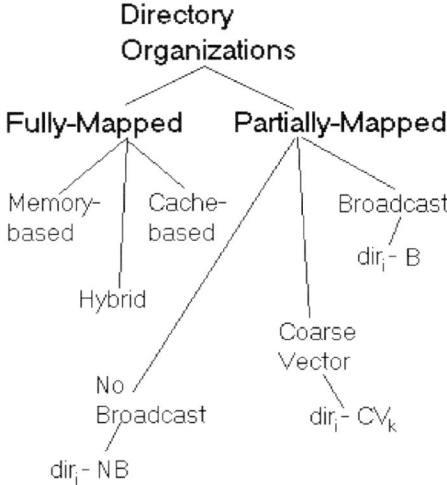

FIG. 5. Overview of directory organizations.

3.4 Directory-Based Organizations—Implementation

The variety of approaches outlined thus far supply the necessary information that allows a directory-based coherence protocol to operate properly. As yet, we have not addressed the actual implementation of any protocols. In general, coherence directories require multiple point-to-point messages; consequently, they load the interconnection network heavily. As illustrated in section two, update-based coherence approaches generate more traffic than do simple invalidation-based approaches. For this reason, directory-based systems tend to use some variant of the Illinois–MESI coherence protocol [46].

Due to the space constraints, this paper looks at a selected number of hardware-based protocols. Interested reader is further referred to [46–58]. Within the class of fully-mapped directory organization two implementations based on the SGI Origin [43] and the Scalable Coherence Interface (SCI) [55] is discussed. This discussion is further enhanced by a study a hybrid fully-mapped organization [50].

Within the class of partially-mapped directory organizations, three directory organizations are discussed as indicated below and illustrated in Fig. 5:

- dir_t-NB.
- dir_t-B.
- dir_t-CV_K.

It should be noted that the literature is abandon with significant research in software-based coherence schemes. Interested reader is referred to [46,58] for further study.

3.4.1 Fully-Mapped Directories

3.4.1.1 Flat, Memory-Based Directory.
In a flat directory scheme, the home node of any given memory block can be directly determined from the address of that block. In the Stanford Flash, the directory information for its distributed memory is maintained with the main memory at its home node. The full bit vector is provided for each memory block in its directory entry. An additional bit, the dirty bit, is maintained to indicate that a cached copy has been modified and that the main memory result differs from that cached copy. Since only one cache may hold a dirty copy at any one time, when a node must modify a copy, all other cached copies of the block must be invalidated. Consequently, when the dirty bit is set, the memory block must be cached at exactly one processor node. Additionally, a single bit is used to provide mutual exclusion of potentially simultaneous requests. These various combinations represent the three directory states of the Flash's directory:

- Shared (Unowned)—Main memory has a valid copy of the block. One or more valid cached copies may exist as indicated by the bit vector.
- Busy—A pending request to the block is in progress. SGI Origin replies with a NACK when a request is received for a block in this state.
- Exclusive—A single cache (as indicated by a single bit set in the vector and the dirty bit) is the owner of the block. The owner must provide the block to both the requesting node and to the home node since its state will change to shared upon completion.

Additionally, the state of each block in every cache must be maintained as was done for the bus-based protocols. Three states analogous to the MESI protocol's ESI states are used. The modified state cannot be represented by the directory structure (recall that a block in modified state is cached in multiple locations and the block is not consistent with main memory). In order to represent this state, the directory size must be increased to $2N$ instead of the $N + 1$. The Flash's directory (as well as most other flat organizations) eliminates the need for this additional state by requiring a write back when a request is made for a block in Exclusive state.

As one might expect, the messages generated by the coherence protocol operation are somewhat more complicated than the messages in the bus-based transactions. In addition to the status bits attached to every message, a network header must be included that specifies the source and destination nodes of the message, each of which consists of $\log_2 N$ bits.

The coherence protocol in the Flash's architecture is based on three categories of transactions:

- Read, Read Exclusive, Upgrade, and Intervention messages each requesting a data block.
- Shared Response, Exclusive Response, Revision, and Speculative Reply are generated in response to request messages. All include the data block.
- ACK, NACK, and Intervention messages are issued by the home node in response to request messages.

When read transactions are sent to the home node of a block, the status of that block is checked in the directory; if the block is not in the Exclusive state, the home node responds with a shared response or an exclusive response transaction that contains the requested data, as appropriate.

If the block is in an exclusive state, the home node responds with a speculative reply and sends an intervention request to the owner node: the owner node must then send the updated node to the requesting node and write back the block to the home node.

When Read Exclusive transactions are requested, the home node immediately sends invalidation requests to every node with a copy of the data block and supplies the data block in an Exclusive Response message. To maintain consistency, the Requesting node must block the requesting process until each node that had a valid copy of the block acknowledges the transaction. Similarly, Upgrade requests generate the same set of coherence activity and invalidation messages; the only difference is that the home node will simply acknowledge the request instead of supplying the data block in an exclusive response.

Lastly, when any request for a block is made to a memory block whose directory is in the busy state (i.e., there is a pending request) the home node replies with a NACK message that instructs the requesting node to try the transaction again later.

Table VII depicts physical characteristics of the SGI Origin's Directory and Coherence Protocol based on the performance parameters as discussed in section one. As the SGI Origin employs a switch-based interconnection network, the latency of transaction is independent of the number of nodes in the system.[3] Therefore, the Synchronization Delay is constant with respect to the number of nodes in the system ($O(1)$).

The message complexity of the protocol varies with the requests and the directory state. For exclusive or upgrade requests to a block in shared states, invalidation messages and acknowledgements must be sent to every node that holds a copy. Therefore, the complexity of these messages is $O(N_c)$. The other valid sets of transactions also

---

[3] Assuming that the network is scaled with the number of nodes in the system.

TABLE VII
STANFORD FLASH—FLAT, MEMORY-BASED DIRECTORY AND COHERENCE PROTOCOL

Transaction Size	Read, Read Exclusive, Invalidation, Upgrade: number bits (A) + number of bits header + number of status bits
	Shared Response, Exclusive Response, Revision, Speculative Reply: number bits (A) + number bits (B) + number of bits header + status
	ACK, NACK, Intervention: number bits (A) + number of bits header + status
Messaging Complexity	Read Exclusive, Upgrade Transactions to shared block: $O(N_c)$
	Other Transactions: $O(1)$
Memory Requirements	2 bits state + number bits (A) per node and $N + 2$ bits per block in global memory $O(N + NM + M)$
Synchronization Delay	$O(N_c)$

differ in the number of messages necessary; however, since the number of messages required for all of these transactions is independent of the number of nodes in the system, the complexity for these is O(1).

To support the memory requirements, two types of storage is needed—the directory itself and the cache tags of each node. Each cache tag is sized similarly to the MESI protocol, consisting of two bits to represent the state of the cached block and a field to represent an address. Remember that each node has one or more cache blocks; consequently, this component of the memory requirement is O(N). A directory entry requires the N bit vector and two additional bits—one to indicate a dirty status and one to provide mutual exclusion. Since there are M global memory blocks, each of which has a directory entry, the total storage requirement for the directory is $N(M + 2)$, or O($NM + N$). Therefore, the total storage requirement for both directory and cache tags is O($N + NM + M$). If one expresses the total number of memory blocks as the product of the average number of blocks per node times the number of nodes, or $M = \alpha N$, then the complexity reduces to O($N + N^2$)-typically, $N \ll M$.

3.4.1.2 Cache-Based Directory.
The memory-based directory organization discussed in the previous section is not scalable, and the storage requirements are quadratic in complexity—a directory entry is maintained for every global memory block (even unused blocks and blocks that are not cached). Cached-based directories reduce these memory requirements by storing the directory entry not based on the block in main memory, but rather with a cached copy of the block instead. Since the number of cache blocks available in a system is typically much less than the total number of memory blocks, a storage savings should be evident. To illustrate

this operation, the SCI protocol implementation used in the Sequent NUMA-Q will be discussed.

The NUMA-Q multiprocessor consists of a number of processing nodes, each of which consists of a four processor bus-based multiprocessor, a portion of the globally shared memory, a remote cache for non-local memory blocks, multiple cache levels for each of the four processors, and a communication controller. The Illinois–MESI protocol is used to maintain coherence within the multiprocessor node. The directory does not distinguish between the individual processors of these multiprocessor nodes, only tracking that at least one cache in a given node has a copy of the memory block.

In the NUMA-Q directory, the presence of a cached copy by a node is tracked using a doubly linked list. The home node of a block maintains a small directory entry that consists of a pointer to the head node (of size $\log_2 N$) and several bits that indicate the status of the memory block.

The linked list implementation consists of forward and backward pointers, each of which is also of size $\log_2 N$. The head node of the list generally has read and write access to the memory block, where other members of the list have read-only privilege.

Three directory states are provided in the NUMA-Q system, roughly analogous to their SGI Origin counterparts.

- Home—No remote cache contains a copy of the block. Analogous to the Unowned state in the Flash. Linked list is empty.
- Fresh—Similar to the shared state in the SGI Origin, one or more remote caches may have a read-only copy. Copy in memory is valid. Linked list has one or more elements.
- Gone—A remote cache contains an exclusive (dirty) copy of the memory block. Home node does not have a valid copy.

Since each node employs a four-state MESI bus-based protocol internally, the interactions between these directory states create a large number of possible states for each cached copy. Seven bits are used for each remote cache block to represent the 29 stable states and additional busy (pending) transient states.

Three primitive operations specified in the SCI standard are used to implement memory operations.

- Constructing the List—A new node (sharer) is added to the head of the list.
- Rollout—Removing a node from the list.
- Purge—Issued by the head node exclusively; used to invalidate all other copies by successive rollouts.

In the case of a read miss to a remote node, the list construction primitive is issued to the home node of the block. If the directory state is Home or Fresh, then the list is modified so that the requesting node is the new head, the directory state is updated as required, and the data is provided to the requestor. If the state is Gone, then the location of the valid copy is sent in the reply to the requesting node. The requesting node will then make a request directly to the current owner of the block, and the list is adjusted so that the requesting node is now the head. The previous head node supplies the data block to the requestor.

When a write miss to a remote node occurs, the list construction primitive again is issued to the block's home node. If the state is either Fresh or Gone, the purge primitive is issued to invalidate every cached copy, the state is set to Gone, and the list is set to consist of only the single requesting node. If the state is Home, then the state is simply sent to gone and the list is set as before.

Similar primitive transactions are issued when upgrade requests are made to a block. When a cache block in Fresh state or in Gone state is replaced and the request is not from the head, the rollout primitive is used to remove that node from the list. When a cache replacement is required by the head node, then the memory is updated, the directory state is changed to Fresh, and the list is updated appropriately.

Table VIII summarizes the key parameters of this protocol implementation. As in the Stanford Flash, the number of transactions used by the protocol is considerable: the basic transactions are listed for comparison. Furthermore, for the three primitive

TABLE VIII
SEQUENT NUMA-Q FLAT, CACHE-BASED DIRECTORY AND COHERENCE PROTOCOL

Transaction Size	List Construction Request: number bits (A) + number of bits header + number of status bits
	Response to read, Home or Fresh State: number bits (A) + number of bits header + number bits status + number bits (B)
	Response to write, or state Gone: number bits (A) + number of bits header + number bits status
	Rollout: number bits (A) + number of bits header + status bits
	Purge: number bits (A) + number of bits header + status bits
Messaging Complexity	Purge: $O(N_c)$
	Rollout: $O(1)$
	Constructing List: $O(1)$
Memory Requirement	7 bits state + number bits (A) + 2 $\log_2 N$ per node and 2 bits state + $\log_2 N$ per block in global memory. $O(N + (N + M) \log_2 N + M)$
Synchronization Delay	$O(N)$

operations used in the SCI standard, the messaging complexity is indicated. For the rollout and the construct list primitives, a constant number of messages is required for protocol operation; consequently the complexity for these primitives is O(1). The complexity of the purge primitive is dependent on the length of the list and is indicated as such in the summary.

The NUMA-Q multiprocessor utilizes a high-speed ring for its interconnection network; consequently, the latency of messages across the network scale linearly with the number of nodes in the system [46]. Therefore, the synchronization delay of this implementation is $O(N)$.

The principle difference found between the SGI Origin's flat memory-based directory organization and the NUMA-Q's flat, cache-based directory organization can be traced in their storage requirements. In the case of the NUMA-Q, main memory storage is required for the two directory state bits and the pointer to the head node (of size $\log_2 N$) for each memory block. Therefore, the storage complexity of this portion of the organization is $O(M + M \log_2 N)$. As outlined in the preceding discussion, the directory requires a forward and backward pointer for each directory entry and seven state bits per cache line. As each pointer is of size $\log_2 N$, then the storage complexity for the cache directory entries of the multiprocessor system is $O(N + N \log_2 N)$. Taken together, the total storage complexity is $O(N + (N + M) \log_2 N + M)$.

3.4.1.3 Hybrid Directory.
Design of a hybrid fully-mapped directory based has been reported in [50] It should be noted that, in some respects, the NUMA-Q is also a hybrid organization since both home node and a remote cache store directory information. The NUMA-Q directory, however, is a quite special cache of cache-based directories. Typically, cached-based directories use a bit vector, similar to the memory-based directory, which is just stored in the cache. NUMA-Q organization improves the storage complexity over traditional cache-based directory organizations (which are $O(N^2 + N)$). However, the implementation discussed in Section 3.4.1.2 entails significantly higher synchronization delays over the traditional hybrid approach. The hybrid approach improves the storage requirements over both the memory-based directory and the traditional cache-based directory while providing latencies of the order of traditional cache-based directories.

The hybrid directory is formed by first logically partitioning the N processor nodes into K clusters of N/K nodes. The memory-based component of the directory entry then consists of a K bit vector, the ith bit of which indicates the presence of a cached copy on one or more of the N/K nodes in the corresponding cluster. Additionally, K pointers, each of size $\log_2(N/K)$, are used to indicate which of the nodes in the cluster holds the cache portion of the directory entry; this node is known as the cluster owner.

TABLE IX
FLAT, HYBRID DIRECTORY AND COHERENCE PROTOCOL

Transaction Size	Read, Read Exclusive, Invalidation, Upgrade: number bits (A) + number of bits header + number of status bits
	Shared Response, Exclusive Response, Revision, Speculative Reply: number bits (A) + number bits (B) + number of bits header + status bits
	ACK, NACK, Intervention: number bits (A) + number of bits header + status bits
Messaging Complexity	Read Exclusive, Upgrade Transactions to shared block: $O(K_c N_c)$
	Other Transactions: $O(K_c)$
Memory Requirements	2 bits state + $(N/K) - 1$ bits + number bits (A) per node and $K + 2$ bits + $K \log_2(N/K)$ per block in global memory
	$O(N + (N^2/K) + MK(\log_2(N/K) + 1))$
Synchronization Delay	$O(K_c N_c)$

In this way, the precise location of every cached copy throughout the multiprocessor system can be determined by searching the main memory directory entry and the indicated cache directory entries for that block.

In fact, the protocol implementation, directory states, and message types are nearly identical to those used in the memory-based SGI Origin protocol.[4] Consequently, the transaction sizes are also identical to those of that protocol. However, there is a difference in messaging complexity. In the hybrid scheme, a cache directory must be consulted for every cluster that holds a copy of the memory block. Therefore, the complexity of even simple transactions is dependent of the number of clusters holding a block. As a result, the complexity of these transactions is $O(K_c)$, where K_c is the number of clusters with a valid copy. Similarly, the more complex transactions on shared blocks are $O(K_c N_c)$ complex.

The memory complexity of the aforementioned hybrid protocol may be described as follows.

- The main memory directory entry consists of $K + 2$ bits + $K \log_2(N/K)$ bits.
- Each cache entry consists of 2 bits state + $(N/K) - 1$ bits + number bits (A), where A is the address.

Therefore, the total storage complexity of this directory organization is $O(N + (N^2/K) + MK(\log_2(N/K) + 1))$.

Table IX summarizes the key parameters of this protocol.

3.4.2 Partially-Mapped Directories

The directory in fully-mapped implementation requires significant storage resources mainly due to the fact that a large number of processors may cache a block.

---
[4] The differences are found only in elements of the protocol not discussed directly in this chapter.

Research into the sharing characteristics of parallel programs has indicated that a large number of cached copies is not likely [40,56]. Limited directory schemes reduce the storage required for the directory by providing direct support for only a specific number of cached copies. These limited directory schemes are denoted as dir_i directories, where i is the number of cached copies that may be directly mapped in the scheme. The major difference among the many protocols that fall into this class is due to the manner in which the protocol handles requests for more than i copies.

3.4.2.1 No-Broadcast Limited Directories.

The simplest implementation of a limited directory is the no-broadcast directory, designated as dir_i-NB. This organization utilizes a directory entry that consists of i pointers, each of which indicates a node that has a valid cached copy of the data block corresponding to a directory entry. In this way, the coherence protocol maintains the precise location of up to i copies for each block in the multiprocessor system. While a memory block is cached in i or fewer locations, the protocol operates exactly as the fully-mapped directory organizations do. When an application makes a memory reference that would require $i + 1$ cached copies, the protocol simply invalidates one of the older cached copies [46].

Table X summarizes the parameters of the dir_i-NB directory coherence protocol. Though discussed extensively in the literature, no actual, full-scale implementation of this directory organization was found. Consequently, the metrics used to illustrate this organization have been developed from the descriptions described purely through the academic analyses of the literature [46,50–53,83,84]. The format, complexity, and size of transactions utilized in this scheme are identical to those used in the fully-mapped directory schemes.

The major improvement in this directory organization may be found in its memory complexity. Each cache requires 2 bits per block for each cache block and a number of bits equal to the number of address bits, the same as the other directories. The directory entry consists of $i \log_2 N$ bits per block for the i pointers. For small i, this quantity is much less than the N bits needed for fully-mapped directory schemes.

3.4.2.2 Broadcast Limited Directories.

The limited directory scheme dir_i-NB provides significant reduction in the storage requirements relative to fully-mapped directory protocols at the expense of poor performance when more than i copies of a memory block are actively shared. In these cases, the repeated invalidations and subsequent cache misses require considerable communication overhead—particularly when the cache block is read-shared only [46]. When a block is only being read by multiple processes, a fully-mapped directory would require no coherence communication traffic.[5] The same is true for limited directories when the number of

---
[5] After the initial read miss.

TABLE X
dir_i-NB LIMITED DIRECTORY

Transaction Size	Read, Read Exclusive, Invalidation, Upgrade: number bits (A) + number of bits header + number of status bits
	Shared Response, Exclusive Response, Revision, Speculative Reply: number bits (A) + number bits (B) + number of bits header + status bits
	ACK, NACK, Intervention: number bits (A) + number of bits header + status bits
Messaging Complexity	Read Exclusive, Upgrade Transactions to shared block: $O(N_c)$ Other Transactions: $O(1)$
Memory Requirements	2 bits state + number bits (A) per node and $i \log_2 N$ bits per block in global memory $O(N + M \log_2 N)$
Synchronization Delay	$O(N_c)$

cached copies is below that threshold limit. However, when the limit is exceeded, repeated read misses generate remote invalidations and consequent coherence protocol traffic.

One proposed approach to this limitation is the dir_i-B limited directory organization. This coherence protocol is identical in structure to the dir_i-NB directory. However, instead of forcing invalidation when the number of cached copies exceeds the limit, the protocol simply abandons the precise locations of the cached copies and proceeds under the assumption that *ALL* nodes of the multiprocessor have a cached copy of that block. Consequently, coherence operations that generate messages to remote caches must broadcast those messages to all nodes. This is significant in that the interconnection network is not a broadcast medium. As such, the broadcast is accomplished by propagating individual messages to every node in the system. In this way, the system provides for an arbitrary number of allowed caches to hold a copy of any memory block [46].

As was the case for the dir_i-NB directory organization, no actual, full-scale implementation of this directory organization was found in the literature. Consequently, the metrics used to illustrate this organization have been developed from the descriptions described purely through the academic analyses of the literature [46,50–53,83, 84].

The transactions and their respective sizes utilized in a dir_i-B limited directory are identical to those used in the dir_i-NB directory organization. Furthermore, the memory requirements are nearly identical, with the dir_i-B directory organization requiring a single additional bit per directory entry to indicate the overflow state of the directory when broadcast messages are required.

The messaging complexity, and consequently, the synchronization delay, is also identical to the previous limited directory organization when the number of cached

TABLE XI
dir_i-B LIMITED DIRECTORY

Transaction Size	Read, Read Exclusive, Invalidation, Upgrade: number bits (A) + number of bits header + number of status bits
	Shared Response, Exclusive Response, Revision, Speculative Reply: number bits (A) + number bits (B) + number of bits header + status bits
	ACK, NACK, Intervention: number bits (A) + number of bits header + status bits
Messaging Complexity	Read Exclusive, Upgrade Transactions to shared block: $c < \iota\, O(N_c)$ else $O(N)$ Other Transactions: $O(1)$
Memory Requirements	2 bits state + number bits (A) per node and $\iota \log_2 N + 1$ bits per block in global memory $O(N + M \log_2 N)$
Synchronization Delay	$c < \iota\, O(N_c)$ else $O(N)$

copies can be precisely represented in the directory entry. However, when an overflow condition is encountered, the messaging complexity increases to $O(N)$, regardless if a particular node is currently caching that block. Similarly, the synchronization delay is also $O(N)$ under an overflow condition. Table XI summarizes these parameters.

3.4.2.3 Coarse-Vector Limited Directories.

The broadcast approach utilized in the dir_i-B directory organization eliminates unnecessary coherence messages when a larger number of processors are actively read-sharing a given data block. However, the solution introduces significant overhead when only $\iota + 1$ copies are active in the system.

To address this limitation, researchers in [57] introduced the coarse-vector limited directory. When the number of cached copies is less than ι, the directory organization is the same as both limited directories discussed previously. However, when an overflow condition exists, the bits of the directory entry are reorganized as a 'coarse-vector', where a bit indicates the presence of a cached copy in at least one node of the well-defined cluster of nodes represented by the bit. In this way, coherence messages need not be sent to ever node in the system, only to the nodes of those clusters whose directory bit indicates the presence of a cached copy. While this approach does not offer optimal performance in terms of the number of messages sent, it does significantly reduce the total messaging load generated by the coherence protocol.

This directory organization was designated as a dir_i-CV_κ limited directory organization, where κ is the number of nodes in the cluster. It should be noted that when

COHERENCE PROTOCOLS

TABLE XII
SGI ORIGIN 2000—$\text{dir}_\iota\text{-CV}_K$ LIMITED DIRECTORY

Transaction Size	Read, Read Exclusive, Invalidation, Upgrade: number bits (A) + number of bits header + number of status bits
	Shared Response, Exclusive Response, Revision, Speculative Reply: number bits (A) + number bits (B) + number of bits header + status bits
	ACK, NACK, Intervention: number bits (A) + number of bits header + status bits
Messaging Complexity	Read Exclusive, Upgrade Transactions to shared block: $c < \iota\ O(N_c)$ else $O(N_K)$ Other Transactions: $O(1)$
Memory Requirements	2 bits state + number bits (A) per node and $\iota \log_2 N + 1$ bits per block in global memory $O(N + M \log_2 N)$
Synchronization Delay	$c < \iota\ O(N_c)$ else $O(N_K)$

$\kappa = \iota$, the organization becomes a full-broadcast limited directory (dir_ι-B). When $\kappa = 1$, then the directory becomes a fully-mapped directory.

Table XII indicates the study parameters for the $\text{dir}_\iota\text{-CV}_\kappa$ directory organization as employed in the SGI Origin 2000.[6] The SGI Origin 2002 uses two different sized vectors, either 16 or 64 bits. To enhance the scalability of the directory organization, the Origin utilizes different interpretations of each directory entry, as well. Of concern to this discussion is when a directory entry indicates that a block is in the shared state. In this case, the bit vectors (either 16 or 64 bit variants) are coarse vectors that divide the 1024 processor nodes into 64 node octants. When one or more nodes of a particular octant hold a copy of the shared block, the corresponding bit in the directory is set; when an invalidation message is generated for the block, invalidation messages are sent to all 64 nodes of the octant indicated by the coarse vector. The transaction types and sizes are identical to those utilized in the other limited directory organizations. The memory requirements are identical to the dir_ι-B directory organization, as on the definition of the bits change in the overflow condition, not the number of bits.

The principle improvement in the coarse-vector directory organization is found in the messaging complexity and synchronization delays. When the number of cached copies of a given data block is less than or equal to ι, the directory operates as before. When a directory overflows and the directory entry is restructured as a coarse vector, the messaging complexity is reduced from $O(N)$ of the broadcast-based limited

---

[6]The operation of the SGI Origin's directory changes as the number of processors is changed; for simplicity, this analysis considers only the basic directory operation.

directory to $O(N_\kappa)$, where N_κ is the number of clusters that contain at least once cached copy of a block.

3.5 Summary of Message-Passing Protocols

The fully-mapped memory-based directory organization was outlined and shown to maintain the precise location of each remotely cached copy with quadratic complexity in storage requirements. To reduce the overall storage requirement of the memory-based fully-mapped directory the cache-based fully-mapped directory was then developed. In comparison with memory-based fully-mapped directory, cache-based fully-mapped directory still offers quadratic memory complexity at a significant cost in messaging complexity and latency. Finally, a hybrid fully-mapped approach was discussed that provides an intermediate cost in terms of storage requirements at a performance comparable to that of the fully-mapped memory-based directory.

Organizations and limitations of partially mapped directory organizations were addressed. The three approaches summarized identify the trade-offs between storage requirements and performance (i.e., synchronization delay and messaging complexity). Table XIII summarizes the three significant parameters of these six directory based organizations. The details of the transactions are omitted, as they are constant over all the directories.

4. Coherence on the World Wide Web

4.1 Introduction

The preceding sections have described caching and cache coherence schemes for small and medium-scaled parallel computer systems. Bus-based coherence solutions are appropriate for small-scale parallel systems utilizing a broadcast interconnect medium—the system bus. As these systems grew, the system bus became a limiting factor in the scalability; thus, a different approach to interprocessor communication was developed and consequently, the directory-based coherence approaches were proposed. As shown in previous section, directory-based coherence protocols scale up well regardless of the interconnection network employed. The exponential growth in the world's largest parallel and distributed system, the world wide web [59], has forced evolutionary changes in the caching techniques and the coherence protocols employed in its operation. This section is intended to survey the caching schemes and the coherence methods employed in this environment.

Caching on the World Wide Web has found three principle applications:

COHERENCE PROTOCOLS

TABLE XIII
SUMMARY OF SELECTED SURVEY PARAMETERS OF THE MESSAGE-PASSING COHERENCE PROTOCOLS

	Messaging Complexity	Memory Requirements	Synchronization Delay
SGI Origin—Flat, Memory-Based Directory	Read Exclusive, Upgrade Transactions to shared block: $O(N_C)$ Other Transactions: $O(1)$	2 bits state + number bits (A) per node and $N + 2$ bits per block in global memory $O(N + NM + M)$	$O(N_C)$
Sequent NUMA-Q Flat, Cache-Based Directory	Purge: $O(N_C)$ Rollout: $O(1)$ Constructing List: $O(1)$	7 bits state + number bits (A) + $2\log_2 N$ per node and 2 bits state + $\log_2 N$ per block in global memory $O(N + (N + M)\log_2 N + M)$	$O(N)$
Flat, Hybrid Directory	Read Exclusive, Upgrade Transactions to shared block: $O(K_C N_C)$ Other Transactions: $O(K_C)$	2 bits state + $(N/K) - 1$ bits + number bits (A) per node and $K + 2$ bits + $K\log_2(N/K)$ per block in global memory $O(N + (N^2/K) + MK(\log_2(N/K) + 1))$	$O(K_C N_C)$
$\text{dir}_i\text{-NB}$	Read Exclusive, Upgrade Transactions to shared block: $O(N_C)$ Other Transactions: $O(1)$	2 bits state + number bits (A) per node and $\iota \log_2 N$ bits per block in global memory $O(N + M\log_2 N)$	$O(N_C)$
$\text{dir}_i\text{-B}$	Read Exclusive, Upgrade Transactions to shared block: $c < \iota\ O(N_C)$ else $O(N)$ Other Transactions: $O(1)$	2 bits state + number bits (A) per node and $\iota \log_2 N + 1$ bits per block in global memory $O(N + M\log_2 N)$	$c < \iota\ O(N_C)$ else $O(N)$
$\text{dir}_i\text{-CV}_K$	Read Exclusive, Upgrade Transactions to shared block: $c < \iota\ O(N_C)$ else $O(N_K)$ Other Transactions: $O(1)$	2 bits state + number bits (A) per node and $\iota \log_2 N + 1$ bits per block in global memory $O(N + M\log_2 N)$	$c < \iota\ O(N_C)$ else $O(N_K)$

1. Server Caches—Cache memories employed at WWW server to reduce access latency of the pages it serves.
2. Client Caches—Cache memories employed at WWW clients to reduce the access latency of the requested pages.
3. Proxy Caches—Cache memories placed intermediate to the server and the client at a proxy server (often a network firewall) to reduce the access latency of commonly accessed documents within the proxy server's domain.

A significant volume of research has shown that there are several considerable advantages in using web caching [59–62]:

- Web caching reduces network traffic, and hence reducing congestion.
- Web caching reduces *average* access latency due to the reduced network traffic and by providing a copy of requested document from a lower latency location.
- Web server workload is reduced by cache hits in client and proxy server caches.
- Improved system robustness in allowing a cache to provide a document whose server is temporarily unavailable.

As with previous cache applications studied thus far, the advantages are found at the expense of some disadvantages. Primarily, the use of caching can result in incoherence between the cached copies throughout the system. Secondarily, cache misses will experience slightly longer access times due to the additional processing required by the cache implementation. However, the focus of web caching implementations remains on ensuring coherence among the shared documents.

In general, the web caching applications indicate the basic client-server abstraction employed in WWW operations. The client-server computational paradigm is a significant departure from the large-scale parallel computer systems that employ directory-based cache coherence protocols, where the system organization is one of a peer-to-peer configuration. Figure 6 illustrates the basic elements of this hierarchy with web caching [59].

While Fig. 6 indicates the hierarchy of the WWW, it cannot accurately impress upon the reader the scale of the hierarchy. The ratio of clients for any particular server may vary widely from server to server over several orders of magnitude. Additionally, these ratios may change over time.

Figure 6 also indicates the possibility of some degree of cooperation among the proxy servers of the web hierarchy. As a result, certain proxy servers may operate independently of others, while some may work with a trusted set of proxy servers as configured by their administrators.

There are several specific approaches to web caching identified in the literature [59]. Three general approaches are defined as:

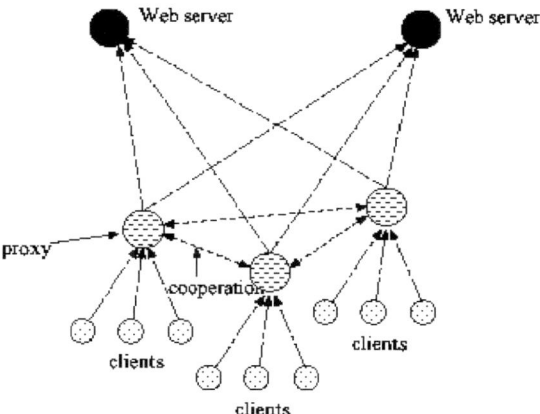

FIG. 6. Basic Web hierarchy [59].

1. Hierarchical web caching conventionally utilizes a four-level cache hierarchy superimposed on the typical hierarchy of Internet Service Providers (ISPs) [63]; hierarchical web cache architectures are discussed in Section 3.2.
2. Distributed web caching approaches do not deepen the client-server hierarchy of the World Wide Web with additional cache levels. Instead, improved client caching is facilitated by cooperation between client caches. Distributed web caching is discussed in Section 3.3.
3. Hybrid web caching approaches blend elements of both hierarchical and distributed web caching in varying proportions to improve the caching performance while reducing some of the undesirable side effects introduces by the basic cache configurations. Hybrid web caching is discussed in Section 3.4.

Additionally, a highly simplified, specialized form of web caching—web site mirroring—has been used extensively to achieve some of the benefits of caching without fully implementing a traditional caching system. Typically, a high-traffic web site is replicated on one or more separate web servers, each with its own unique IP address. These additional web servers contain an exact duplicate, or 'mirror image' of the original web server; consequently, accessing a page from one of the mirror sites is equivalent to accessing the original host. Mirror sites are typically located in geographically separate networks (e.g., a site based in the UK frequently accessed in North America might establish a mirror site in the United States, potentially eliminating trans-continental routing expenses and delays, etc.) This arrangement permits many of the advantages of caching discussed previously. In effect, a mirror site is similar to a proxy cache that is constantly synchronized to the original host. However, there are some distinct differences between web caching and site mirroring. Most significantly, a mirror site copies the entire contents of the original web site, regardless of the access frequency of individual data items within that site. Additionally, the mirror site—as a replica of one particular web server—does nothing to improve the performance of any other web server; a proxy server, for comparison, copies frequently-used data items from multiple web servers. In some cases, load balancing between the primary server and its mirror sites may be automatic and, therefore, transparent to the user; more often, the user might simply select a mirror site when unhappy with the performance of the primary site. In these cases, mirroring is not transparent to the user. In general, mirror sites are most effective when dealing with heavily-accessed, globally read-only data, where changes are only made at the host server and reflected at the mirror sites. However, since mirroring is a limited, specialized application of web caching, it will not be discussed in detail in this paper. Please refer to the literature for more information [59–72].

It should be noted that, due to the space limitations of this paper, the web caching organizations discussed herein are by no means meant to be comprehensive. One should refer to the literature for further information [59–72].

4.2 Hierarchical Web Caching Schemes

Hierarchical web cache organizations employ proxy server caching at network-level gateways or firewall along the general structure of the World Wide Web [63–66]. At the lowest level, client machines are serviced by an institutional (i.e., local) level network. These institutional-level networks are serviced by regional-level networks, which in turn are serviced by national-level networks. Figure 7 illustrates this basic hierarchy [63].

In hierarchical web cache organizations, client requests propagate up the hierarchy until the request can be satisfied. Client requests that cannot be satisfied by the client's cache are sent to the institutional level. The institutional-level cache is then examined for the requested document; if the document does not currently exist in the institutional cache, the request is then resolved to the host server if the server resides in the institutional domain. Cache misses to host that do not remain in the institutional domain are transmitted to the regional level network. In this way, cache misses propagate up the hierarchy tree. The same algorithm described for the institutional level request processing is used at the regional level. At the national level, cache misses are resolved to the particular national network where the server containing the requested document resides. When a document request is satisfied at any level, the document is transmitted back along the hierarchy to the requesting client, with a copy left at the caches of each level of the hierarchy.

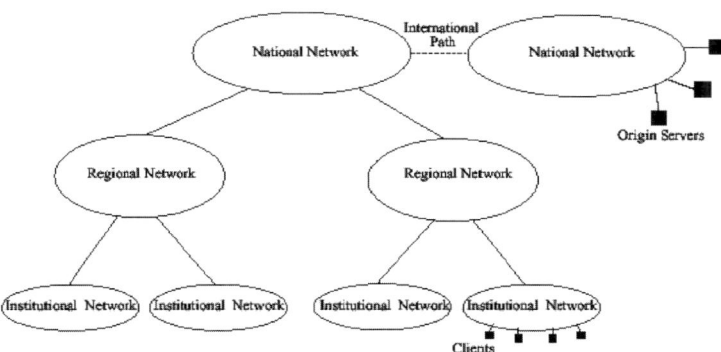

FIG. 7. Basic hierarchical cache organization.

While hierarchical caching architectures offer certain advantages—most notably simple basic implementations into the pre-existing network hierarchy, there are several significant disadvantages to this web caching organization [59,61,63].

- Since the cache server must be placed at key access points in the networks, significant coordination may be required among participating cache servers.
- Hierarchical levels may introduce additional delays.
- Higher-level caches may have long queuing delays, producing a bottleneck.
- Multiple copies of the same document may be stored in multiple caches at each level.

Most significant among these disadvantages is in having multiple copies of the same document at different levels of the hierarchy. This is particularly troublesome in that the ratio of lower-level caches to the regional and national-level caches is quite large; consequently, it is not possible to guarantee inclusion in the cache hierarchy—that is every document contained in a lower-level cache is also contained in every higher-level cache. This effect must be considered in attempting to maintain coherence of the caches.

4.3 Distributed Web Caching Schemes

In distributed web caching, only the institutional level caches are employed to cache web documents, and cooperating groups of these institutional caches attempt to serve each other's cache misses [59,63,65,67]. In this organization, each proxy cache at the institutional level keeps meta-data information on the contents of every cooperating proxy cache. This meta-data information is used to allow the cooperating cache that contains a requested document to serve that document, presumably at a cost lower than that incurred by retrieving the requested document from the server. The meta-data used in the caching schema may be organized as a hierarchy similar to that employed in a hierarchical web caching organizations. The principle difference between these distributed caching organizations and hierarchical caching schemes is that only meta-data, not the actual documents, is distributed by a hierarchy.

In general, the distributed web caching approaches generate more network traffic at the lower levels while reducing network traffic at the higher levels which tend to become bottlenecks to the overall distributed system performance [59]. The various distributed web caching organizations proposed in the literature, however, differ in how they achieve distributed caching [59].

- Internet Cache Protocol—Provides a mechanism to locate cached copies throughout the network.
- Cache Array Routing Protocol—URL-space is hashed to a set of cooperating proxy caches; only cache to which a document URL is hashed may store a copy of that document.
- Distributed Internet Cache [67]—Higher-level caches of hierarchical cache organizations are enhanced by directory servers that point to the location of cached copies of requested documents.
- Fully distributed internet Cache [65]—Is similar to the Distributed Internet Cache scheme, except that replicated location information is maintained at each cache instead of using a meta-data hierarchy.
- Central Directory Approach (CRISP) [69]—A central mapping service is employed to provide location information of a set of cooperating proxy cache servers.
- Cachemesh [70]—A group of cooperative proxy caches jointly generate routing tables to indicate the location of cached copies of requested documents. A particular cache server will service only a subset of the requested documents.
- Summary Cache [72], Cache Digest [71]—Cooperating caches exchange information regarding contents of their caches; maintain directories of local document copies.

4.4 Hybrid Web Caching Schemes

Hybrid web caching schemes feature characteristics of both hierarchical and distributed web caching architectures [59,63,68,69,72]. As in hierarchical web caching, proxy caches are implemented for multiple network levels; as in distributed web caching, proxy caches are permitted to interoperate with other proxy caches at the same or higher cache levels. This arrangement is designed to take advantage of the desirable characteristics of hierarchical and distributed web caching while mitigating some of the undesirable characteristics of each. Hierarchical web caching potentially may increase access latency due to the increased cache processing at each level of the hierarchy. Additionally, hierarchical web caching may result in multiple copies of a document at various cache level—this increases the complexity of the coherence problem. Distributed caching attempts to leverage spatial locality of cooperating caches at a considerable cost of both the memory and the processing overhead required to maintain the meta-data information stored at every cache. By design, distributed cache organizations tend to reduce the number of cached copies of a document by maintaining limited numbers of copies in strategic locations. Hybrid web caching offers an intermediate configuration between these two, reducing the number of cached copies at various levels of the caching hierarchy by enabling interoperation between caches at multiple levels.

4.5 Coherence in Web Caching Schemes

The previous sections have outlined the basic approaches described in the literature to implement web caching [59–72]. To be complete, however, some discussion of potential coherence mechanisms must be provided. In principle, this problem is no different from maintaining coherence among the various caches of parallel processors as discussed in sections two and three. Each block of memory has some set of zero or more caches that are storing a copy of that block; some mechanism must be provided to locate each copy so that a change to any copy may be properly reflected in all copies in a timely manner. Section 2 outlined several directory-based approaches reported in the literature that were scalable for a large number of shared copies. Several important factors make a straight implementation of one of these directories impractical in the WWW environment.

1. Scale of shared memory space—Clearly, the total memory available over the World Wide Web is by orders of magnitudes greater than the largest distributed shared memory multiprocessor organization. Additionally, the number of potential caches that might share a particular block of memory is similarly as large. As noted in Section 2, the memory requirements of the directory schemes where at best $O(N + M \log_2 N)$, scaling both N and M by any factor reasonable for the internet environment results in an impractical complexity in memory requirements.
2. Access Latencies and Communication Link Bandwidths—The parallel systems for which bus-based and directory based protocols were designed for featured high-bandwidth, tightly coupled intercommunication networks. The World

Wide Web is a collection of heterogeneous networks and network topologies, each of which has varying bandwidths and latencies. To hide this complexity, the Internet Protocol (IP) was developed to allow communication across these heterogeneous topologies. However, the cost of implementing IP includes additional latencies for such functions as Domain Name Service (DNS) and connection delays. These delays have been found to dominate the latency of WWW transactions, particularly on the initial access to a web resource [63].

3. Message Complexities—The communication overhead associated with scalable directory-based coherence organizations are significant; Section 2 showed that the best-case complexity was of the order of the number of cache blocks in the total system. Similar to the memory requirement outlined above, a scale in the system at the level of the WWW environment increases communication complexity, drastically. Additionally, the access latency issues outlined previously further increases the expense of these increasingly complex messages.

These factors have combined to affect the way in which web designers structure their websites and online applications. The World Wide Web has exhibited exponential growth over its lifetime [59], and this explosive growth in the Internet has further complicated the cache coherence issue.

Initial web caching organizations offered no inherent coherence mechanism; consequently, there was a finite chance that a cached copy was delivered stale. Hyper-Text Transfer Protocol (HTTP) incorporates several directives to help manage proxy caches. These directives may be used by the web designer to customize proxy response to requests for that page, in an attempt to provide best coherence and performance. The directives provided by HTTP are outlined as follows:

1. GET—Retrieve a document from the specified Uniform Resource Locator (URL).
2. Conditional GET—Used in conjunction with an *if-modified-since* header to retrieve a page only if the page was changed since a specified time stamp.
3. Pragma No-cache—A header directive that forces all caches along a request path to retrieve the requested page directly from the server.
4. Last modified Time stamp—Returned with every accessed web document to indicate the last time resource was updated.
5. Date—A time stamp indicating when last the document was considered fresh.[7]

Cache coherence has been researched and implemented in two basic forms: *strongly consistent cache coherence* and *weakly consistent cache coherence* [59]. These basic coherence schemes and several broad implementation approaches for each scheme will be discussed in the following sections.

---

[7] One of the most popular web browsers, Netscape, provides no mechanism for accessing this data [59].

TABLE XIV
STRONGLY CONSISTENT WEB COHERENCE, CLIENT VALIDATION

Transaction Size	Conditional GET: Size of (TCP/IP Header + request URL)
	Server Reply, cached page valid: Size of (TCP/IP Header + request URL)
	Server Reply, cached page valid: Size of (TCP/IP Header + request URL + requested page)
Messaging Complexity	$O(1)$
Memory Requirements	$O(N + M)$
Synchronization Delay	$O(1)$

4.5.1 Strongly Consistent Web Caching

Strongly consistent cache coherence provides each requested document to the client with perfect consistency—that is, each read request returns the document with all previous writes and updates. Strongly consistent coherence has been implemented as client validation and server invalidation.

4.5.1.1 Client Validation.
Client validation is implemented by appending a conditional get HTTP directive to each request for an Internet document. If the document has not been changed since the last request, the server responds with a simple acknowledgement and the cached document may be used with confidence; otherwise, the server returns the updated document. This document is provided to the client and is used to update the cache(s).

Table XIV outlines the performance metrics for strongly consistent, client validation based web cache coherence.

4.5.1.2 Server Invalidation.
Server invalidation requires each server to maintain a list of every client that has requested a particular document. When a document is modified, the server will send an invalidation message to every client that had previously requested that document. As one might imagine, the overhead in maintaining these lists can be considerable. Additionally, the lists themselves may become stale. Table XV outlines the performance metrics for strongly consistent, server invalidation based web cache coherence.

4.5.2 Weakly Consistent Web Caching

Weakly consistent web caching allows for the possibility of retrieving a stale copy of a web document in exchange for an improvement in overall performance. Two approaches to weakly consistent caching will be discussed here—Adaptive Time-To-Live (TTL) and Piggyback Invalidation.

TABLE XV
STRONGLY CONSISTENT WEB COHERENCE, SERVER INVALIDATION

Transaction Size	GET: Size of (TCP/IP Header + request URL) Server Reply, cached page valid: Size of (TCP/IP Header + request URL + requested page) Server Invalidation: Size of (TCP/IP Header + request URL)
Messaging Complexity	Request: $O(1)$ Invalidation: $O(N_c)$
Memory Requirements	$O(N + M)$
Synchronization Delay	Request: $O(1)$ Invalidation: $O(N_c)$

4.5.2.1 Adaptive Time-To-Live (TTL) [73].

Adaptive TTL is a weakly consistent approach to web cache coherence. Adaptive TTL takes advantage of bi-modal nature of update patterns to web documents—either web documents are updated frequently, or they are not likely to be updated for a long time. In adaptive TTL, the cache will fetch a requested page that it currently holds only when a heuristic based on the document's time-to-live so indicates. Researchers have shown that this approach will provide stale data only in approximately 5% of the requests.

Table XVI outlines the performance metrics for weakly consistent, adaptive TTL based web cache coherence. A close comparison of Tables XVI and XIV illustrates the similarity in these performance metrics; while the transactions used and performance metrics are identical, the primary differences in the performance of the two protocols is determined by the frequency with which the various transactions are used. In client validation, every client request generates a conditional request to the server. In adaptive TTL, only requests indicated by the heuristic algorithm generate this request.

TABLE XVI
WEAKLY CONSISTENT WEB COHERENCE, ADAPTIVE TTL

Transaction Size	Conditional GET: Size of (TCP/IP Header + request URL) Server Reply, cached page valid: Size of (TCP/IP Header + request URL) Server Reply, cached page valid: Size of (TCP/IP Header + request URL + requested page)
Messaging Complexity	$O(1)$
Memory Requirements	$O(N + M)$
Synchronization Delay	$O(1)$

4.5.2.2 Piggyback Coherence Techniques.
The literature has outlined several implementations to piggyback coherence traffic on requests messages. The general philosophy behind these approaches is to incorporate (or piggyback) relatively small-sized coherence information with any messages to the same server, when needed. This eliminates additional connection time costs for coherence traffic and hence reduces communication overhead costs. The first proposed approach, Piggyback Cache Validation (PCV) [74], appends proxy cache validation messages to a particular server to *htt:get* requests sent to that server. The second approach utilizes piggybacked invalidation messages from a server to mark cache entries as dirty. This approach is called Piggyback Server Invalidation (PSI) [75] in the literature.

Coherence achieved through PCV appends coherence validation requests to requests made to a particular server. A cache maintains a history of a document's source and the last time that document was out of date; at an interval determined by the coherence heuristic, the cache will attempt to obtain a validation from the server to ensure that the document is still valid. Therefore, PCV is most effective when there are many requests to a particular server on which to piggyback these validations. By contrast, PSI sends explicit invalidations to documents sent to a requesting cache. In addition to the added complexity of having to maintain a list of every cache that has requested every document served, PSI has the additional complexity of dealing with cache page replacements—in effect, the coherence of the lists of the requested cache documents must be maintained. However, as with the invalidation approaches discussed in previous sections, invalidation schemes have the advantage of reducing overall communication requirements. PSI sends a list of the documents that have changed since the last access by a given proxy cache. The proxy cache may then invalidate those documents that have changed since the last access. The lifetimes of cached documents not invalidated may also be extended. Therefore, PSI approaches are most effective when documents are frequently retrieved from a server, providing more opportunities for piggybacked coherence messages.

A third hybrid approach was proposed in the literature to help provide more optimal performance by switching between PSI and PCV modes [76]. As outlined previously, the PSI approach is more efficient when requests are frequently made from a server—therefore, the list of changed documents is small and the time a document may sit stale in a cache is consequently small as well. When the time between requests is longer, then it is prudent to explicitly perform a PCV validation to ensure that the documents have not changed. The hybrid approach maintains the time since a server was last accessed, and selects which of the two coherence protocols would most efficiently handle each request. Table XVII displays the performance metrics of the general hybrid weakly consistent web coherence protocols.

TABLE XVII
WEAKLY CONSISTENT WEB COHERENCE, PIGGYBACK CACHE TECHNIQUES

Transaction Size	Conditional GET: Size of (TCP/IP Header + request URL)
	Server Reply, cached page valid: Size of (TCP/IP Header + request URL)
	Server Reply, cached page valid: Size of (TCP/IP Header + request URL + requested page)
Messaging Complexity	$O(N)$
Memory Requirements	$O(N + M)$
Synchronization Delay	$O(1)$

4.6 Summary of Web Coherence

This section has attempted to outline the basic approaches utilized in implementing caching and cache coherence in the challenging heterogeneous environment of the World Wide Web. Table XVIII compares the performance characteristics of the various approaches discussed, and illustrates the similarity in these metrics. The biggest difference may be found between the strongly consistent and the weakly consistent approaches. However, these differences are small and heavily dependent on the sharing characteristics and access patterns of not only a particular document, but also on the access patterns of other documents from the same servers and the set of documents cached at a particular proxy. The analysis of these interactions is complex and beyond the scope of this paper; however the existence of these interactions must be kept in mind while considering the various coherence approaches—and in planning new ones.

TABLE XVIII
SUMMARY OF SELECTED SURVEY PARAMETERS OF THE WEB COHERENCE PROTOCOLS

	Messaging Complexity	Memory Requirements	Synchronization Delay
Strongly Consistent Web Coherence, Client Validation	$O(1)$	$O(N + M)$	$O(1)$
Strongly Consistent Web Coherence, Server Invalidation	Request: $O(1)$ Invalidation: $O(N_c)$	$O(N + M)$	$O(1)$
Weakly Consistent Web Coherence, Adaptive TTL	$O(1)$	$O(N + M)$	$O(1)$
Weakly Consistent Web Coherence, Piggyback Cache Techniques	$O(N)$	$O(N + M)$	$O(1)$

5. Wireless Protocols

5.1 Introduction

Through the evolution of the coherence protocols outlined in this paper, the complexity of the problem has increased exponentially. Bus-based systems utilize broadcast coherence messages, permitting each node to track every transaction to analyze how the transactions might affect the contents of that node's cache. Directory-based protocols were developed to accommodate the point-to-point communication networks used in scalable multiprocessor architectures. In the next step in this evolution trend, the heterogeneous distributed computing environment of the World Wide Web forced further adaptations not only in the coherence mechanisms but also in the access patterns and sizes of shared documents. The final step outlined in this evolution will involve the adaptations of cache coherence techniques to wireless networking environments [28–30]. This environment has all the complexity of the heterogeneous World Wide Web environment and additional complexity as well [77–82]. These additional technical difficulties include three principle components:

- Mobility—Mobile computing devices potentially change location; this introduces considerable complexity in tracking that device to and, consequently, in routing coherence traffic (as well as other internet communications).
- Limitation of Wireless Bandwidth—While the World Wide Web generally has a lower throughput than the tightly integrated, high bandwidth intercommunication networks found in large-scale multiprocessor architectures, wireless networking introduces even tighter restrictions on bandwidth. Furthermore, the available bandwidth costs are considerably higher for the available wireless networks.
- Frequent Disconnection—Wireless network resources are subject to frequent disconnection from the network. Consequently, network protocols (including coherence protocols) must account for this characteristic of the wireless network and provide mechanisms to handle the likely occurrences of requiring communication with a resource that is not available from time to time.

These three factors introduce significant difficulties, particularly when attempting to implement a strongly consistent cache coherence protocol. For example, consider the following scenario: a wireless device accesses a WWW document and stores that document in a local cache. After disconnecting from the network, the document is again accessed—without access to the network, there is no mechanism for the local cache to determine the status of the stored copy. Validation schemes cannot query the server to learn if the document had changed, and any invalidation sent from the server has no way of reaching the disconnected node. Clearly, this is a difficult problem to handle efficiently. Is it necessary to block accesses to the document? Are there cases where it is most likely safe to use the cached copy, even if it cannot be validated? These are some of the questions that the wireless coherence protocols must address in order to be effective and practical.

The limited bandwidth of a wireless network poses the most serious restriction to the environment. Internet applications have taken full advantage of the growing bandwidth of the wired network, further straining the already tight bandwidth availability of the wireless networks. Caching is an important architectural feature of computer environments that can be quite useful in reducing network traffic. As we have seen throughout the evolution of coherence protocols, however, maintaining the coherence of these caches imposes additional applied load to the network. Consequently, coherence protocols for wireless networking have strict design requirements that strongly emphasis the efficiency of its operation.

5.1.1 The Mobile Computing Network Environment

The mobile computing network environment consists of a series of contiguous wireless cells, each of which contains a fixed, central server. The servers are interconnected by a conventional, wired network. Within each cell is some number of mobile computing devices; the exact number of mobile computers within a cell may change with time, and a mobile computer is free to move between cells in any pattern and at any time. Figure 8 illustrates the basic configuration of the mobile network environment.

Duplex communications between the server and the mobile computing nodes are provided via radio communications. The server communicates with all nodes within the cell using broadcast communications: this is the downlink, or server-to-client channel. Every node within the cell receives all communications from the server.

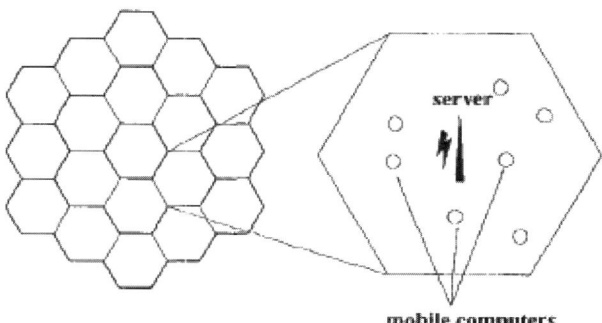

FIG. 8. The mobile computing network environment.

Mobile computing nodes communicate with the server using point-to-point communication: this is the uplink, or client-to-server channel. Thus, the wireless network environment is a hybrid between the broadcast intercommunication network used in bus-based multiprocessors and the point-to-point intercommunication network used in the scalable multiprocessor architectures for which the directory class protocols were developed. However, it must remain clear that the broadcast transmissions within a given cell are broadcast only within that cell.

5.2 Cache Coherence Design Requirements in the Wireless Network Environment

The basic cache coherence mechanism in wireless networks operates in a periodic update mode. Each server maintains a list of data blocks (or records) that have been updated recently; this list is then periodically broadcast to all nodes within the cell Client caches may then utilize these reports to make informed decisions on the status of its cached data blocks. This approach solves the problem of disconnection from the network, for a node that misses an update while disconnected will be able to receive a future update. As long as the disconnection period is smaller than the time the server will broadcast an update, the client will receive at least one—more likely several—update reports that indicate the change.

One must be careful to differentiate the term 'update report' from the update-based protocols discussed previously in this paper. While the update report implies an update-based coherence operation, in fact the update report may be configured to operate in either an update mode or an invalidation mode. In invalidation mode, the update report contains only the identifier of the data blocks that have changed; consequently, client caches may only note that a particular data block has changed by invalidating its copy. This mode of operation has been called 'update invalidation' (UI) in the literature [29]. Similarly, the update report may include the modified data; in this case, the update report is utilized in an update mode to modify the cached data. This scheme is referred to as 'update propagation' (UP) in the literature [29].

With the update record as a basic mechanism for cache coherence, it is necessary to consider when the update report is to be broadcast. The most direct approach is to broadcast the report immediately upon a data block change. Under this approach, clients are notified immediately upon an update; this operating mode is referred to as asynchronous in the literature [29]. This operating mode is simplistic in operation, but since no regular times are defined for transmission of the update broadcast a disconnected client has no way to determine if a relevant update report was missed. Therefore, an alternate operating mode, called synchronous [29] establishes a fixed interval for the update reports. This interval provides an upper bound for the transmission of the update report. This bound allows a disconnected client to know precisely how long it must wait to ensure receiving a current update report. Furthermore, with a defined duration that an update record will be maintained, a disconnected client has both upper and lower bounds within which the update report itself will be sufficient to maintain coherence. Disconnections that last longer than this upper bound will require explicit validation messages from the client upon reconnection.

The demanding requirements of maintaining coherence between caches within the wireless network environment are driven by the limitations of the environment itself—the limited bandwidth of the environment is the most serious of these restrictions. Consider the implication of this limitation on the operation of the basic coherence protocol operations—update and invalidate. In broadcast invalidations, a changed data block that may be cached by multiple nodes is indicated by an explicit invalidation of that block; the receipt of this invalidation message instructs caches holding a dirty copy not to use their copy, and instead reload the data if it is needed by a future access. Similarly, in broadcast updates, a changed data block that is cached by at least one other node is broadcast, in its entirety, so that a snooping cache that holds a replica may update its copy to reflect the change. These protocols are employed regardless of the nature or the magnitude of the change, regardless if a single bit changes or if every bit of the block changes. For the bus-based applications, there is no advantage in distinguishing between these types of changes as bus-based multiprocessors typically utilize data blocks of 32, 64, 128, or 256 bytes. However, there is a cost in these approaches. Consider the case where an invalidation protocol is used to maintain coherence of 10 cached copies of a data block consisting of 128 bytes (1024 bits). Let one node change a single bit of that block; the invalidation protocol indicates this to the other caches of the system. Next, let the remaining 9 nodes access some data within that block. Since the block was invalidated, the entire block will have to be loaded by each of the 9 nodes, requiring the transmission of 9×1024 bits. Therefore, the change of a single bit resulted in a total bandwidth cost of about 10,000 bits. Most telling is the fact that, due to false sharing, the changed bit may not have even been relevant to the operation of the system—an access to any part of a data block must be treated the same, regardless of the part of the block that is accessed. A similar argument is valid for the update protocols. Clearly, in an environment with severe restrictions on communication bandwidth, these unnecessary transfers must be eliminated, particularly since the granularity of the data blocks (files, documents, records, or objects, depending on the particular application) is considerably coarser, with sizes varying between kilobytes and megabytes.

The limitations placed on bandwidth and its associated high cost has driven coherence protocol researchers to develop the class of incremental coherence protocol [29]. Incremental update protocols broadcast only the parts of a cached data object that have changed; this saves the expense of retransmitting those parts of the data that have not changed and are thus redundant.

5.3 Analysis of Basic Wireless Coherence Protocols

5.3.1 Definitions

The analysis of basic wireless coherence protocols requires the definition of a parameter to quantify the rate at which the update broadcasts occur.

- Let Φ_υ be defined as the frequency with which the update broadcasts occur. For asynchronous implementations, Φ_υ is the average frequency of the update broadcasts.
- Let $T_\upsilon = 1/\Phi_\upsilon$. Therefore, T_υ is the period of the update report broadcasts. For asynchronous implementations, T_υ is the average period of the update broadcasts.
- Let T_Δ be defined as the time duration a change report is maintained in the update report broadcast.
- Let N_υ be defined as the number of items, on average, contained in the update report.
- Let A be defined as the average percentage of the data item that changes.
- Let α_i be defined as the percentage of the ith data item that changes.

5.3.2 Update Invalidation Coherence

In update invalidation coherence operation, the periodic update report contains the identifiers of the data items that have changed within the interval T_Δ immediately preceding the broadcast. Clients receive the update report and invalidate cached data items indicated by the report. Consequently, those clients that then access the invalidated data item must retrieve the item again from the server. Therefore, the messaging complexity is $O(\Phi_\upsilon + N_c)$.

The synchronization time of the system, after a change, is proportional to the period of the update report broadcasts. To maintain a strongly consistent system, the node that changes a data item should be blocked until the next update report is delivered, thereby guaranteeing that the clients have been notified of the change before the new data is used. In the worst case, all caches may require access to the changed data item; since the clients may only re-access the data item serially, at most N_c transactions will be required at the upper bound. Consequently, the synchronization delay is $O(T_\upsilon + N_c) = O(1/\Phi_\upsilon + N_c)$. Interestingly, both synchronization delay and messaging complexity are dependent on the frequency of the update broadcasts but in opposite senses—synchronization delay decreases while messaging complexity increases with increasing broadcast frequency. Clearly, a trade-off must be reached between these conflicting design performance metrics. Table XIX tabulates the per-

TABLE XIX
GENERALIZED UPDATE INVALIDATION COHERENCE PROTOCOL FOR WIRELESS NETWORKS

Transaction Size	Conditional GET: Size of (TCP/IP Header + request URL)
	Server Reply, cached page valid: Size of (TCP/IP Header + request URL)
	Server Reply, cached page valid: Size of (TCP/IP Header + request URL + requested page)
	Update Report: Size of [Report Header + N_υ (request URL)]
Messaging Complexity	$O(\Phi_\upsilon + N_c)$
Memory Requirements	$O(N + M)$
Synchronization Delay	$O(T_\upsilon + N_c)$

formance metrics for a generalized update invalidation coherence protocol for wireless networks.

5.3.3 Update Propagation Coherence

Update propagation coherence protocol utilizes update reports that include not only the identifiers of the data items changed, but also the changed data items themselves. As with the update invalidation methodology, the update report includes entries for those data items changed within the interval T_Δ immediately preceding the broadcast. Clients receive the update report and update cached data items indicated by the report. Since the update report itself contains the updated data items, the clients need not retrieve the data item. Therefore, the messaging complexity is $O(\Phi_\upsilon)$.

As with the update invalidation approach to wireless coherence, the time required for system synchronization is proportional to the period of the update report broadcasts. However, since the update report contains the updated data items themselves, the clients need not re-access the data items directly. Consequently, the synchronization delay is $O(T_\upsilon) = O(1/\Phi_\upsilon)$.

Update propagation offers significant reduction in complexity of both synchronization delay and messaging complexity over update invalidation; the cost of these reductions may be found in the size of the update report itself. The update report includes not only the identifiers of the changed data items, but also the data item. Consequently, the update reports for update propagation coherence protocols are significantly larger than those for update invalidation coherence protocols. Specifically, the size of the update report is equal to the size of [Report Header + N_υ (request URL)] + $\sum_\upsilon$ sizeof(dataItem$_i$). Table XX contains the performance metrics for the generalized update propagation coherence protocol for wireless networks.

TABLE XX
GENERALIZED UPDATE PROPAGATION COHERENCE PROTOCOL FOR WIRELESS NETWORKS

Transaction Size	Conditional GET: Size of (TCP/IP Header + request URL)
	Server Reply, cached page valid: Size of (TCP/IP Header + request URL)
	Server Reply, cached page valid: Size of (TCP/IP Header + request URL + requested page)
	Update Report: Size of [Report Header + N_U (request URL)] + $\sum_U$ sizeof(dataItem$_i$)
Messaging Complexity	$O(\Phi_U)$
Memory Requirements	$O(N+M)$
Synchronization Delay	$O(T_U)$

5.3.4 Incremental Update Invalidation

As outlined earlier, incremental coherence strategies were devised to reduce the bandwidth requirements of the coherence protocol by removing the retransmission of redundant data—particularly the unchanged portions of the data items. Since providing incremental update of the changed data items does not affect the messaging requirements, the analyses of messaging complexity and synchronization delay are identical to that of the standard update invalidation protocol (see Table XIX).

Incremental update invalidation coherence protocol differs in performance from the standard update invalidation protocol primarily in the size of the server replies to a request for a modified data item. For standard update invalidation, the server will reply with the entire page; this message has the size of (TCP/IP Header + request URL + requested page). In incremental update invalidation, the reply message contains only a portion of the changed data item. The reply must also contain some additional header information to indicate which portion of the data item is contained in the reply. Therefore, the reply message for incremental update invalidation has the size of [TCP/IP Header + request URL + α(requested page) + incremental header], where α is the percentage of the data item contained in the server reply. Table XXI contains the performance metrics for the generalized incremental update invalidation coherence protocol for wireless networks.

5.3.5 Incremental Update Propagation

The incremental coherence approach may be applied to the standard update propagation coherence strategy. Using a similar argument to the one used in applying incremental updates to the update invalidation strategy, one may show that the messaging complexity and the synchronization delays for incremental and for standard update propagation are of the same order (see Table XX).

TABLE XXI
GENERALIZED INCREMENTAL UPDATE INVALIDATION COHERENCE PROTOCOL FOR WIRELESS NETWORKS

Transaction Size	Conditional GET: Size of (TCP/IP Header + request URL)
	Server Reply, cached page valid: Size of (TCP/IP Header + request URL)
	Server Reply, cached page valid: Size of [TCP/IP Header + request URL + α(requested page) + incremental header]
	Update Report: Size of [Report Header + N_υ (request URL)]
Messaging Complexity	$O(\Phi_\upsilon + N_c)$
Memory Requirements	$O(N + M)$
Synchronization Delay	$O(T_\upsilon + N_c)$

In update propagation, the modified data items are themselves included in the update report; therefore, the size of the update report must differ when using either the standard or the incremental update propagation strategies. For standard update propagation, the update report has the size of [Report Header + N_υ (request URL)] + $\sum_\upsilon$ sizeof(dataItem$_i$). For incremental updates, only a portion of the data item is included in the update record. Therefore, the report header for incremental update propagation has the size of [Report Header + N_υ (request URL)] + $\sum_\upsilon$ sizeof(α_i · dataItem$_i$ + incHeader$_i$). Table XXII contains the performance metrics for the generalized incremental update propagation coherence protocol for wireless networks.

5.4 Summary of Wireless Protocols

The preceding sections have outlined the basic, generalized operation and performance of both invalidation and update modes utilized for the update reports of co-

TABLE XXII
GENERALIZED INCREMENTAL UPDATE PROPAGATION COHERENCE PROTOCOL FOR WIRELESS NETWORKS

Transaction Size	Conditional GET: Size of (TCP/IP Header + request URL)
	Server Reply, cached page valid: Size of (TCP/IP Header + request URL)
	Server Reply, cached page valid: Size of (TCP/IP Header + request URL + requested page)
	Update Report: Size of [Report Header + N_υ (request URL)] + $\sum_\upsilon$ sizeof(α_i · dataItem$_i$ + incHeader$_i$)
Messaging Complexity	$O(\Phi_\upsilon)$
Memory Requirements	$O(N + M)$
Synchronization Delay	$O(T_\upsilon)$

herence protocols employed in wireless network environments. As one may clearly determine from these metrics as summarized in Table XXIII, there are inherent trade-offs in the two operating modes. Most significant is the trade-off between messaging complexity and synchronization delay with the sizes of the transactions employed in the two coherence strategies. Clearly, update propagation reduces both messaging complexity and synchronization delay while significantly increasing the size of the update report. It is not quite as easy to see the total bandwidth requirements of the two protocols. Update invalidation generates in the worst case N_c client request/server response pairs in addition to each data item invalidation, where each server response contains a copy of the data item. In update propagation, all N_c cached copies are updated by encapsulating the updated data item within the update report. Clearly, update invalidation increases bandwidth requirements linearly with N_c while the bandwidth requirements of update report are independent of N_c. Both, however, are linearly dependent on the size of the data items themselves. This result was also evident in the discussion of update-based and invalidation-based snoopy protocols included in Section 1. Clearly, when N_c is small or zero, the update invalidation coherence strategy will perform better and, more importantly, utilize a smaller portion of the available bandwidth, than the update propagation strategies. Similarly, when N_c is larger, the update propagation approach will prove advantageous over update invalidations.

Both update invalidation and update propagation coherence strategies may benefit from incremental update organizations. While incremental updates do not affect the messaging complexity or the synchronization delay, however, incremental updates do reduce wireless network bandwidth by reducing the sizes of at least one class of transactions—either the server reply in update invalidation or the update report in update propagation. Since the capability to make incremental updates require additional header information to indicate which part of the data item has changed, the reduction in the sizes of these transactions is lower bounded by the ratio A, which was defined previously as the average percentage of change with all data items. Therefore, methods of accommodating extremely small A—for example, a few bytes in a data item several megabytes in size—offers considerable performance improvements, particularly in terms of bandwidth requirements.

6. Summary and Conclusions

6.1 Introduction

Caching is an effective performance-enhancing technique that has proven its advantages on many levels of the parallel and distributed computing abstractions. However, caching introduces additional complexities into the system architecture—i.e.,

TABLE XXIII
SUMMARY OF COHERENCE PROTOCOLS FOR WIRELESS NETWORKS

	Update Invalidation	Update Propagation	Incremental Update Invalidation	Incremental Update Propagation
Transaction Size	Conditional GET: Size of (TCP/IP Header + request URL)	Conditional GET: Size of (TCP/IP Header + request URL)	Conditional GET: Size of (TCP/IP Header + request URL)	Conditional GET: Size of (TCP/IP Header + request URL)
	Server Reply, cached page valid: Size of (TCP/IP Header + request URL)	Server Reply, cached page valid: Size of (TCP/IP Header + request URL)	Server Reply, cached page valid: Size of (TCP/IP Header + request URL)	Server Reply, cached page valid: Size of (TCP/IP Header + request URL)
	Server Reply, cached page valid: Size of (TCP/IP Header + request URL + requested page)	Server Reply, cached page valid: Size of (TCP/IP Header + request URL + requested page)	Server Reply, cached page valid: Size of [TCP/IP Header + request URL + α (requested page) + incremental header]	Server Reply, cached page valid: Size of (TCP/IP Header + request URL + requested page)
	Update Report: Size of [Report Header + N_v (request URL)]	Update Report: Size of [Report Header + N_v (request URL)] + $\sum_v$ sizeof($\alpha_i \cdot$ dataItem$_i$ + incHeader$_i$)	Update Report: Size of [Report Header + N_v (request URL)]	Update Report: Size of [Report Header + N_v (request URL)] + $\sum_v$ sizeof($\alpha_i \cdot$ dataItem$_i$ + incHeader$_i$)
Messaging Complexity	$O(\Phi_v + N_c)$	$O(\Phi_v)$	$O(\Phi_v + N_c)$	$O(\Phi_v)$
Memory Requirements	$O(N + M)$	$O(N + M)$	$O(N + M)$	$O(N + M)$
Synchronization Delay	$O(T_v + N_c)$	$O(T_v)$	$O(T_v + N_c)$	$O(T_v)$

cache coherence issue that was the main theme of this chapter. This paper is an attempt to outline some of the basic approaches developed to maintain cache coherence, discussing the architectural issues that drive these coherence protocols, and illustrating the significant protocol advantages and limitations. Furthermore, the coherence protocols discussed in this paper have been presented in a generalized view; it was intended to highlight the similarities and differences of these coherence protocols. Exploiting the commonality between coherence protocols used for different network environments.

6.2 Summary of Bus-Based Coherence Protocols

The bus-based coherence protocols discussed in section two, as the name implies, are used in bus-based multiprocessor applications. The system bus permits all nodes in the system to 'snoop', or monitor all bus activities to detect any bus transaction that may affect cache content. Consequently, coherence may be maintained simply by monitoring all broadcasts over the system bus and update the status of the cache based on those broadcasts. Within this framework, two basic modes of operation were employed—invalidation and update modes. Since neither mode is optimal for all access patterns, hybrid and adaptive approaches were developed that switch between the two behavior modes. This trend of evolution resulted in a hybrid approach (PSCR) that attempted to make educated decisions about which update mode would be most effective given some knowledge about a data block's access expectations.

6.3 Summary of Message-Passing (Directory) Coherence Protocols

The message-passing, or directory-based, coherence protocols were developed to accommodate the evolving architecture of parallel processing systems. While the broadcast nature of the system bus simplified the design of coherence protocols, the system bus proved to be a bottleneck as the number of processing nodes was increased. Consequently, system architects turned to more scalable interconnection network topologies to permit even larger parallel systems. These general interconnection networks provide high-bandwidth, tightly integrated message-passing capabilities at the expense of more complicated cache coherence as explicit coherence messages must be used to communicate a change in status of shared memory. To support these explicit messages, it is necessary to know which nodes are caching which data blocks, or at least one node of a group of nodes is caching a particular data block (limited directory organizations). Within this framework, two issues motivated the employment of various invalidation based protocols:

TABLE XXIV
OVERVIEW OF FOUR CLASSES OF COHERENCE PROTOCOLS

	Bus-based	Directory-based	Coherence on the WWW	Coherence in Wireless Networks
Network Configuration	Bus	High-performance general interconnection network	Heterogeneous	Wireless Broadcast
Network Organization	Peer-to-peer	Peer-to-peer	Client-server	Client-server
Uplink channel	Broadcast	Unicast	Unicast	Unicast
Downlink channel	Broadcast	Unicast	Unicast	Broadcast
Coherence Modes Employed	Invalidation, Update, Hybrid, Adaptive, Selective	Invalidation	Invalidation, Update	Invalidation, Update
Coherence Organization	Snoop broadcast channels	Directory	Client-based validations, server-maintained directory	Update Report with client management of cache

- The explicit message-passing operations do not adapt well to update-based coherence, and
- The significant memory requirements of maintaining the directories drive most of the research in this area into developing directory organizations that provide effective coherence operation in a more memory-efficient manner.

Table XXIV contains the four classes of cache coherence organizations discussed in this paper and some of their key characteristics.

6.4 Summary of Caching Coherence on the World Wide Web

The World Wide Web has grown exponentially in the previous decades, not only in size, but also in average network bandwidth and traffic. Caching has been employed within this context to improve WWW performance. However, the cache coherence approaches thus employed have evolved along somewhat different lines, driven by the different sharing characteristics, network organization, and consistency requirements. The World Wide Web is typically viewed as a client-server model; as such the clients are not likely to make changes to a shared document—these changes are typically made at the server only. Furthermore, the sharing characteristics of World Wide Web document are generally bi-modal; either a document will change frequently, or it will not change for a long time. Finally, most Internet applications are only loosely coupled for most applications. As a result, a weaker consistency model is sufficient. In this environment, similar to the discussion in section three, the expense of implementing traditional update-based coherence protocols offsets their potential advantages; consequently, invalidation approaches are the focus. In addition, the large number of potential clients that may be caching a particular document led to the implementation of client-initiated validations on demand. Finally, researchers have investigated 'piggy-back' techniques that incorporate coherence messages into incoming or outgoing messages to the server. These piggyback techniques have included both invalidation-based and update-based organizations; later techniques have included some hybrid approaches similar to the hybrid approaches employed in bus-based multiprocessors.

6.5 Summary of Wireless Cache Coherence

Wireless networks introduce significant complications into the cache coherence problem. These problems include limited wireless bandwidth, mobility, and frequent disconnections. The limited bandwidth of wireless networks places a strong motivation to limit the bandwidth requirements of the coherence protocol. Mobility of network resources introduces serious difficulties with directory-based approaches to cache coherence. Finally, frequent disconnection from the network imposes the most serious difficulty in the cache coherence problem; if a node holding a cached copy is disconnected from the network when an invalidation is sent, the disconnected node will not receive the invalidation. More seriously, the server that sends the invalidation may not safely assume that the invalidation was received by all the mobile units. Therefore, wireless cache coherence strategies resort to the periodic broadcast of update reports. These update reports maintain a list of changed data items for a period of time; these well-defined periods permit upper and lower bounds on client disconnection times within which a client may safely be able to salvage some contents of its cache.

One additional network feature of the wireless network environment requires attention—the hybrid nature of the duplex communication channels from client to server and from server to client. The server-to-client channel of wireless networks is a broadcast channel, whereas the client-to-server channel is a point-to-point channel. Consequently, the periodic broadcast of the coherence protocol's update report is practical and well suited to this environment. Furthermore, the update report may be configured practically in either an update-based configuration or an invalidation-based configuration.

6.6 Conclusions and Recommendations

Considering these four distinct classes of cache coherence protocols, several key factors present themselves.

- The underlying network topology strongly influences the implementation of the cache coherence protocol.
- Invalidation-based and update-based coherence may offer advantages in particular applications or for particular shared data items, but are not optimal in general.
- Knowledge of the sharing characteristics of a particular data item may be used to help optimize coherence protocol operations; however, this optimization typically increases the costs in terms of memory requirements (and processor bandwidth).
- The granularity of shared data items significantly affects required network bandwidth requirements of the coherence protocol. Large granularity increases the negative effects of passive and false sharing, while smaller granularity mitigates these effects at the cost of increased complexity in memory and coherence protocol operation.

These observations imply several recommendations in continuing the development of coherence protocols.

First, there have been demonstrated consistent benefits in leveraging the underlying network topology to help perform coherence operations. To this end, an efficient *multicast* mechanism in network topologies would prove most effective in implementing coherence functionality.

Second, hybrid and adaptive coherence organizations have proven effective in improving coherence protocol performance in bus-based multiprocessors. These organizations should find effective applications in wireless network applications. It would be particularly interesting if these hybrid behaviors could be applied on a fine, even incremental, granularity; research into the subject in the context of bus-based coherence protocol analysis has shown that the sharing characteristics may vary even within a particular application.

Finally, the selective coherence protocol developed for bus-based multiprocessors has demonstrated that there is considerable data for which there is no reason to implement coherence. Furthermore, the analyses of web-based cache coherence for Internet applications have demonstrated that some applications may tolerate some degree of inconsistency; for these applications, a weaker consistency model is sufficient. However, some applications, in particular e-business and e-banking, require strongly consistent implementations. Since the level of consistency varies between classes of applications, it seems logical to provide only strong consistency where it is needed and allow weaker consistency where appropriate. To this end, a quality-of-service organization that may specify the required level of consistency should prove effective in reducing network traffic while guaranteeing that those applications that require strong consistency will enjoy it.

In conclusion, the coherence protocols discussed in this paper have proven effective in implementing cache coherence for their particular applications. The cache coherence problem is not exclusive to a particular application; therefore there are distinct advantages to considering the problem from different perspectives to learn what the problems in the different applications have in common, where their differences lie, and what techniques were used to overcome their particular obstacles. This paper has attempted to provide a small step towards this larger perspective, to illustrate a few of these commonalities and disparities, and to suggest a few possible courses to follow in the continuing development of cache coherence protocols.

ACKNOWLEDGEMENTS

This work in part has been supported by the Office of the Naval Support under the contract N00014-02-1-0282.

REFERENCES

[1] Theel O.E., Fleisch B.D., "A dynamic coherence protocol for distributed shared memory enforcing high data availability at low costs", *IEEE Transactions on Parallel and Distributed Systems* **7** (9) (1996) 915–930.

[2] Pong F., Dubois M., "A new approach for the verification of cache coherence protocols", *IEEE Transactions on Parallel and Distributed Systems* **67** (8) (1995) 773–787.

[3] Liu Y.A., "CACHET: An interactive, incremental-attribution-based program transformation system for deriving incremental programs", in: *Proceedings of the Tenth Knowledge-Based Software Engineering Conference*, 1995, pp. 19–26.

[4] Milutinovic V., "Caching in distributed systems", *IEEE Concurrency* **8** (3) (2000) 14–15.

[5] Yang Q., Thangadurai G., Bhuyan L.N., "Design of an adaptive cache coherence protocol for large scale multiprocessors", *IEEE Transactions on Parallel and Distributed Systems* **3** (3) (1992) 281–293.

[6] Won-Kee Hong, Nam-Hee Kim, Shin-Dug Kim, "Design and performance evaluation of an adaptive cache coherence protocol", in: *Proceedings of the International Conference on Parallel and Distributed Systems*, 1998, pp. 33–40.

[7] Bilir E.E., Dickson R.M., Ying H., Plakal M., Sorin D.J., Hill M.D., Wood D.A., "Multicast snooping: A new coherence method using a multicast address network", in: *Proceedings of the 26th International Symposium on Computer Architecture*, 1999, pp. 294–304.

[8] Cano J.-C., Pont A., Sahuquillo J., Gil J.-A., "The differences between distributed shared memory caching and proxy caching", *IEEE Concurrency* **8** (3) (2000) 45–47.

[9] Pérez C.E., Román A.G., Ruíz B.H., "Using CSP to derive a sequentially consistent DSM system", in: *Proceedings of the Eighteenth Annual ACM Symposium on Principles of Distributed Computing*, 1999, p. 280.

[10] Park S., Dill D.L., "Verification of FLASH cache coherence protocol by aggregation of distributed transactions", in: *Proceedings of the 8th Annual ACM Symposium on Parallel Algorithms and Architectures*, 1996, pp. 288–296.
[11] Williams C., Reynolds Jr. P.F., de Supinski B.R., "Delta coherence protocols", *IEEE Concurrency* **8** (3) (2000) 23–29.
[12] Lebeck A.R., Wood D.A., "Dynamic self-invalidation: Reducing coherence overhead in shared-memory multiprocessors", in: *Proceedings of the 22nd Annual International Symposium on Computer Architecture*, 1995, pp. 48–59.
[13] Giorgi R., Prete C.A., "PSCR: A coherence protocol for eliminating passive sharing in shared-bus shared-memory multiprocessors", *IEEE Transactions on Parallel and Distributed Systems* **10** (7) (1999) 742–762.
[14] Papamarcos M., Patel J., "A low overhead coherence solution for multiprocessors with private cache memories", in: *Proc. 11th Int'l Symposium Computer Architecture*, 1994, pp. 348–354.
[15] McCreight E.M., "The dragon computer system an early overview", *NATO Advanced Study Institute on Microarchitecture of VLSI Computers*, 1984.
[16] Kerhong C., Bunt R.B., Eager D.L., "Write caching in distributed file systems", in: *Proceedings of the 15th International Conference on Distributed Computing Systems*, 1995, pp. 457–466.
[17] Chenjie L., Pei C., "Maintaining strong cache consistency in the World-Wide Web", in: *Proceedings of the 17th International Conference on Distributed Computing Systems*, 1997, pp. 12–21.
[18] Adya A., Castro M., Liskov B., Maheshwari U., Shrira L., "Fragment reconstruction: Providing global cache coherence in a transactional storage system", in: *Proceedings of the 17th International Conference on Distributed Computing Systems*, 1997, pp. 2–11.
[19] Zaharioudakis M., Carey M.J., "Hierarchical, adaptive cache consistency in a page server OODBMS", in: *Proceedings of the 17th International Conference on Distributed Computing Systems*, 1997, pp. 22–31.
[20] Qing Y., Thangadurai G., Bhuyan L.N., "An adaptive cache coherence scheme for hierarchical shared-memory multiprocessors", in: *Proceedings of the Second IEEE Symposium on Parallel and Distributed Processing*, 1990, pp. 318–325.
[21] Krishnamurthy B., Wills C.E., "Proxy cache coherency and replacement-towards a more complete picture", in: *Proceedings 19th IEEE International Conference on Distributed Computing Systems*, 1999, pp. 332–339.
[22] Choi L., Pen-Chung Yew, "Hardware and compiler-directed cache coherence in large-scale multiprocessors: Design considerations and performance study", *IEEE Transactions on Parallel and Distributed Systems* **11** (4) (2000) 375–394.
[23] Tewari R., Dahlin M., Vin H.M., Kay J.S., "Design considerations for distributed caching on the internet", in: *Proceedings of the 19th IEEE International Conference on Distributed Computing Systems*, 1999, pp. 273–284.
[24] Rabinovich M., Rabinovich I., Rajaraman R., Aggarwal A., "A dynamic object replication and migration protocol for an internet hosting service", in: *Proceedings of the 19th IEEE International Conference on Distributed Computing Systems*, 1999, pp. 101–113.

[25] Makpangou M., Pierre G., Khoury C., Dorta N., "Replicated directory service for weakly consistent distributed caches", in: *Proceedings of the 19th IEEE International Conference on Distributed Computing Systems*, 1999, pp. 92–100.
[26] Asaka T., Miwa H., Tanaka Y., "Distributed web caching using hash-based query caching method", in: *Proceedings of the IEEE International Conference on Control Applications*, Vol. 2, 1999, pp. 1620–1625.
[27] Sinnwell M., Weikum G., "A cost-model-based online method for distributed caching", in: *Proceedings of the 13th International Conference on Data Engineering*, 1997, pp. 532–541.
[28] Fong C.C.F., Lui J.C.S., Man Hon Wong, "Quantifying complexity and performance gains of distributed caching in a wireless network environment", in: *Proceedings of the 13th International Conference on Data Engineering*, 1997, pp. 104–113.
[29] Jun Cai, Kian-Lee Tan, Beng Chin Ooi, "On incremental cache coherency schemes in mobile computing environments", in: *Proceedings of the 13th International Conference on Data Engineering*, 1997, pp. 114–123.
[30] Kung-Lung Wu, Yu P.S., Ming-Syan Chen, "Energy-efficient caching for wireless mobile computing", in: *Proceedings of the Twelfth International Conference on Data Engineering*, 1996, pp. 336–343.
[31] Degenaro L., Iyengar A., Lipkind I., Rouvellou I., "A middleware system which intelligently caches query results", in: *IFIP/ACM International Conference on Distributed Systems Platforms*, 2000, pp. 24–44.
[32] Menaud J.-M., Issarny V., Banatre M., "A scalable and efficient cooperative system for web caches", *IEEE Concurrency* **8** (3) (2000) 56–62.
[33] Tari Z., Hamidjaja H., Qi Tang Lin, "Cache management in CORBA distributed object systems", *IEEE Concurrency* **8** (3) (2000) 48–55.
[34] Graham P., Yahong Sui, "LOTEC: A simple DSM consistency protocol for nested object transactions", in: *Proceedings of the Eighteenth Annual ACM Symposium on Principles of Distributed Computing*, 1999, pp. 153–162.
[35] Thacker C., Stewart L., Satterthwaite E., "Firefly: A multiprocessor workstation", *IEEE Transactions on Computers* **37** (8) (1988) 909–920.
[36] Prete C.A., "RST: Cache memory design for a tightly coupled multiprocessor system", *IEEE Micro* **11** (2) (1991) 16–19, 40–52.
[37] Veenstra J.R., Fowler R.J., "A performance evaluation of optimal hybrid cache coherency protocols", in: *Proceedings of the Fifth International Conference Architectural Support for Programming Languages and Operating Systems*, 1992, pp. 149–160.
[38] Culler D.E., Jaswinder Pal Singh, Gupta A., *Parallel Computer Architecture*, Morgan Kaufmann Publishers, Inc. San Francisco, CA, 1999.
[39] Eggers S.J., Katz R.H., "A characterization of sharing in parallel programs and its application to coherency protocol evaluation", in: *Proceedings of the 15th International Symposium on Computer Architecture*, 1988, pp. 373–382.
[40] Eggers S.J., Simulation Analysis of Data Sharing in Shared Memory Multiprocessors. Ph.D. thesis UCB/CSD 89/501, University of California, Berkeley, 1989.

[41] Sleator D., "Dynamic decentralized cache schemes for MIMD parallel processors", in: *Proceedings of the 11th International Symposium on Computer Architecture*, 1984, pp. 244–254.
[42] Archibald J.K., "A cache coherence approach for large multiprocessor systems", in: *Proceedings of the International Symposium on Supercomputing*, 1988, pp. 337–345.
[43] Gee J.G., Smith A.J., Absolute and Comparative Performance of Cache Consistency Algorithms. Technical Report UCB/CSD-93-753, EECS Computer Science Division, University of California, Berkeley, 1993.
[44] Cox A.L., Fowler R.J., "Adaptive cache coherency for detecting migratory shared data", in: *Proceedings of the 20th International Symposium on Computer Architecture*, 1993, pp. 98–108.
[45] Prete C.A., Prina G., Giorgi R., Ricciardi L., "Some considerations about passive sharing in shared-memory multiprocessors", in: *IEEE TCCA Newsletter*, 1997, pp. 34–40.
[46] Culler D.E., Singh J.P., *Parallel Computer Architecture: A Hardware/Software Approach*, Morgan Kaufmann Publishers, Inc. San Francisco, California, 1999.
[47] Aggarwal A., Simoni R., Hennessy J., Horowitz M., "An evaluation of directory schemes for cache coherence", in: *Proceedings of the 15th Annual International Symposium on Computer Architecture*, 1988, pp. 280–289.
[48] Hao Che, Zhijung Wang, Ye Tung, "Analysis and design of hierarchical web caching systems", in: *Proceedings IEEE INFOCOM*, Vol. 3, 2001, pp. 1416–1424.
[49] Jong Hyuk Choi, Kyu Ho Park, "Segment directory enhancing the limited directory cache coherence schemes", in: *Proceedings of the 13th International and 10th Symposium on Parallel and Distributed Processing*, 1999, pp. 258–267.
[50] Jong Hyuk Choi, Kyu Ho Park, "Hybrid full map directory scheme for distributed shared memory multiprocessors", in: *High Performance Computing on the Information Superhighway*, 1997, pp. 30–34.
[51] Thapar M., Delagi B., "Distributed-directory scheme: Stanford distributed-directory protocol", *Computer* **23** (6) (1990) 78–80.
[52] Ashwini K., Nanda, Hong Jiang, "Analysis of directory based cache coherence schemes with multistage networks", in: *Proceedings of the ACM Annual Conference on Communications*, 1992, pp. 485–492.
[53] Hennessy J., "Retrospective: Evaluation of directory schemes for cache coherence", in: *25 years of the International Symposia on Computer Architecture (selected papers)*, 1998, pp. 61–62.
[54] Censier L.M., Feautrier P., "A new solution to coherence problems in multicache systems", *IEEE Transactions on Computers* **C-27** (12) (1978) 1112–1118.
[55] Gustavson D., "The scalable coherence interface and related standards project", *IEEE Micro* **12** (1) (1992) 10–22.
[56] Tomasevic M., Milutinovic V., *The Cache Coherence Problem in Shared-Memory Multiprocessors: Hardware Solutions*, IEEE Computer Society Press, Los Alamitos, California, 1993.
[57] Gupta A., Weber W.-D., Mowry T., "Reducing memory and traffic requirements for scalable directory-based cache coherence schemes", in: *Proceedings of the International*

Conference on Parallel Processing, The Pennsylvania State University Press, 1990, pp. I312–I321.
[58] Tartalja I., Milutinovic V., *The Cache-Coherence Problem in Shared-Memory Multiprocessors: Software Solutions*, IEEE Computer Society Press, Los Alamitos, California, 1996.
[59] Wang J., "A survey of web caching schemes for the internet", *ACM Computer Communication Review* **29** (10) (1999) 36–46.
[60] Caceres R., Douglis F., Feldmann A., Glass G., Rabinovich M., "Web proxy caching: The devil is in the details", *ACM Performance Evaluation Review* **26** (3) (1998) 11–15.
[61] Duska B.M., Marwood D., Feelay M.J., "The measured access characteristics of World Wide Web client proxy caches", in: *Proceedings of USENIX Symposium on Internet Technologies and Systems*, 1997. Available at http://cd.ubc.ca/spider/feeley/wwwap/wwwap.html.
[62] Kroeger T.M., Long D.D.E., Mogul J.C., "Exploring the bounds of web latency reduction from caching and prefetching", in: *Proceedings of the USENIX Symposium on Internet Technologies and Systems, Monterey, CA*, 1997.
[63] Rodriguez P., Spanner C., Biersack E.W., "Web caching architectures: Hierarchical and distributed caching", in: *Proceedings of WCW*, 1999.
[64] Michel S., Nguyen K., Rosenstein A., Zhang L., Floyd S., Jacobson V., "Adaptive web caching: Towards a new caching architecture", *Computer Network and ISDN Systems* (1998).
[65] Tewari R., Dahlin M., Vin H., Kay J., Beyond Hierarchies: Design Considerations for Distributed Caching on the Internet. Technical Report TR98-04, Department of Computer Science, University of Texas at Austin, 1998.
[66] Yang J., Want W., Muntz R., Wang J., Access Driven Web Caching. UCLA Technical Report #990007, 1999.
[67] Povey D., Harrison J., "A distributed internet cache", in: *Proceedings of the 20th Australian Computer Science Conference, Sydney, Australia*, 1997.
[68] Rabinovich M., Chase J., Gadde S., "Not all hits are created equal: Cooperative proxy caching over a wide-area network", *Computer Networks and ISDN Systems* **30** (1998) 2253–2259.
[69] Gadde S., Rabinovich M., Chase J., "Reduce, reuse, recycle: An approach to building large internet caches", in: *Proceedings of the HotOS'97 Workshop*, 1997. Available at http://www.cs.duke.edu/ari/cisi/crisp-recycle/crisp-recycle.htm.
[70] Wang Z., "Cachemesh: A distributed cache system for World Wide Web", in: *Web Cache Workshop*, 1997.
[71] Ewing D., Hall R., Schwartz M., A Measurement Study of Internet File Transfer Traffic. Technical Report CU-CS-571-92. University of Colorado, Department of Computer Science, Boulder, Colorado, 1992.
[72] Fan L., Cao P., Almeida J., Broder A.Z., "Summary cache: A scalable wide-area web cache sharing protocol", in: *Proceedings of SIGCOMM*, 1998.
[73] Cate A.V., "A global file system", in: *Proceedings of the USENIX File System Workshop*, 1992, pp. 1–12.

[74] Krishnamurthy B., Wills C.E., "Study of piggyback cache validation for proxy caches in the World Wide Web", in: *Proceedings of the USENIX Symposium on Internet Technology and Systems*, 1997, pp. 1–12.
[75] Krishnamurthy B., Wills C.E., "Piggyback server invalidations for proxy cache coherency", in: *Proceedings of the WWW-7 Conference*, 1998, pp. 185–194.
[76] Krishnamurthy B., Wills C.E., "Proxy cache coherency and replacement—towards a more complete picture", in: *ICDC99*, 1999.
[77] Alonso R., Korth H.F., "Database systems issues in nomadic computing", in: *ACM SIGMOD International Conference on Management of Data, Sigmod Record*, Vol. 22, 1993.
[78] Barbara D., Imielinski T., "Sleepers and workaholics: Caching strategies in mobile environments", in: *ACM SIGMOD International Conference on Management of Data*, 1994.
[79] Huang Y., Sista P., Wolfson O., "Data replication for mobile computers", in: *ACM SIGMOD International Conference on Management of Data*, 1994.
[80] Huang Y., Wolfson O., "Object allocation in distributed databases and mobile computers", in: *Proceedings of the 10th International Conference on Data Engineering*, 1994.
[81] Imielinski T., Badrinath B.R., "Data management for mobile computing", in: *ACM SIGMOD International Conference on Management of Data, ACM SIGMOD Record*, Vol. 22, 1993.
[82] Chung H., Cho H., "Data caching with incremental update propagation in mobile computing environments", in: *Proceedings Australian Workshop on Mobile Computing and Databases and Applications*, 1996.
[83] Kavi K., Kim H.S., Lee B., Hurson A.R., "Shared memory and distributed shared memory systems: A survey", in: *Advances in Computers*, Vol. 53, 2000.
[84] Archibald J., Baer J.L., "Cache coherence protocols: Evaluation using a multiprocessor simulation model", *ACM Transactions on Computer Systems (TOCS)* **4** (4) (1986).

Author Index

Numbers in *italics* indicate the pages on which complete references are given.

A

Aamodt, A., 39, *73*
Abbattsista, F., 140, *207*
Abowd, G.D., 204, *209*
Adya, A., 213, *274*
Aggarwal, A., 213, 233, 234, *274, 276*
Agile Alliance, 65, *73*
Aha, D.W., 34, 71, *73, 80*
Ahire, S.L., 110, *122*
Ahmed, M.U., 115, *126*
Almeida, J., 250, 252, 253, *277*
Alonso, R., 259, *278*
Althoff, K.D., 31, 34, 39, 41, 43, *73, 74, 76, 80, 81*
Ambriola, V., 66, *74*
Amir-Atefi, K., 113, *123*
Anderson, K.M., 38, *74*
Anderson, P., 106, *121*
Ante, S., 9, *27*
Applehans, W., 69, *74*
Arango, G., 32, 37, 39, *74, 81*, 138, *207*
Archibald, J.K., 213, 220, 242, 243, *276, 278*
Ardis, M.A., 102, *120*
Arnold, R.S., 131, 134, 136, 141, 142, *207, 208*
Asaka, T., 213, *275*
Ashrafi, N., 115, *125*
Ashwini, K., 233, 234, 242, 243, *276*
Attewell, P., 103, *120*

B

Backhouse, J., 91, *117*
Badrinath, B.R., 259, *278*
Baer, J.L., 242, 243, *278*

Ballard, B.W., 43, *76*
Banatre, M., 213, *275*
Bandinelli, S.C., 56, 66, 67, *74*
Barbara, D., 259, *278*
Barnes, B.H., 38, *74*
Baroudi, J.J., 91, *118*
Bartlem, C.S., 107, *121*
Basili, V.R., 31, 33, 34, 37, 38, 41, 43, 45, 61, 64–66, 71, *74, 75, 80*, 140, 149, *208*
Bass, F.M., 102, *119*
Batory, D., 40, *75*
Baumgarten, K., 39, *78*
Bayer, J., 103, 106, *120, 121*
Beach, B., 67, *77*
Becker, L.G., 96, 97, *118*
Beedle, M., 65, *81*
Belkhatir, N., 67, *75*
Belkin, N.J., 43, *75*
Bellotti, V., 68, *80*
Ben-Shaul, I.Z., 66, 67, *75, 79*
Beng Chin Ooi, 213, 259, 261, 262, *275*
Bernstein, A.P., 114, *124*
Bhuyan, L.N., 213, *273, 274*
Bicego, A., 66, *79*
Biersack, E.W., 249–254, *277*
Biggerstaff, T.J., 39, *75*
Bijker, W.E., 104, *121*
Bilir, E.E., 213, *273*
Billingsley, J., 115, *126*
Billington, R., 39, *80*
Birk, A., 31, 34, 41, 42, 62, *73–75*
Bock, D.B., 90, *117*
Boehm, B.W., 45, 49, 50, 63, 64, 66, 71, 75, 134, 156, *208*
Bohner, S.A., 131, 134, 136, 137, 140–142, *207–209*

Bohrer, K., 40, *75*
Bolcer, G.A., 67, *75*
Bollinger, T.B., 38, *74*
Bostrom, R.P., 90, *117*
Brachman, R.J., 43, *76*
Brancheau, J.C., 99, 100, *118*
Breslow, L.A., 71, *80*
Broder, A.Z., 250, 252, 253, *277*
Brooks, F.P., 30, *75*
Brooks, H.M., 43, *75*
Brown, A.W., 31, *75*
Brown, J.S., 42, *75*, *76*
Bunt, R.B., 213, *274*
Burrell, G., 91, *117*
Butler, B., 93, *118*
Buxton, J.N., 115, *125*
Byrd, T.A., 114, 116, *123*, *126*

C

Caceres, R., 248, 250, 253, *277*
Calder, P., 37, *82*
Caldiera, G., 31, 33, 34, 37, 38, 61, 71, *74*
Cale, E.G., 116, *126*
Cano, J.-C., 213, *273*
Cantone, G., 31, 33, 34, 37, 38, 61, 71, *74*
Cao, P., 250, 252, 253, *277*
Cao, Y., 71, *80*
Caputo, K., 96, 99, *118*
Carey, J., 40, *76*
Carey, M.J., 213, *274*
Carlson, B., 40, *76*
Carroll, J., 68, *80*
Caruso, J.M., 42, *80*
Castro, M., 213, *274*
Cate, A.V., 256, *277*
Cefriel, 38, *77*
Censier, L.M., 231, 233, 234, *276*
Chaddha, R.L., 103, *120*
Charles, R.J.S., 115, *126*
Chase, J., 250, 252, 253, *277*
Chau, P.Y.K., 113, *123*
Checkland, P., 104, *121*
Chen, C., 138, *209*
Chen, G., 40, *75*
Chenjie, L., 213, *274*
Chervany, N.L., 114, *124*

Chiasson, M.W., 113, *123*
Chitgopekar, S.S., 103, *120*
Cho, H., 259, *278*
Choi, L., 213, *274*
Chrissis, M., 66, *80*
Christersson, M., 133, 140, 149, *208*
Chung, H., 259, *278*
Ciarfella, W., 67, *81*
Cinti, S., 38, *77*
Coch, L., 107, *121*
Codd, E.F., 146, *208*
Cohen, J., 151, *208*
Cohen, M.D., 86, *117*
Collier, B., 42, *76*
Collofello, J.S., 138, *210*
Conklin, E.J., 68, 69, *76*
Conner, D., 96, *118*
Conradi, R., 46, 66, 67, *74*, *76*
Constantine, L., 6, *27*
Cooper, R.B., 113, *123*
Corn, R.I., 114, *124*
Costa, P., 31, 34, 41, 43, 65, *74*
Cox, A.L., 213, 219, 221, *276*
Creps, D., 37–39, *81*
CSTB, 39, 40, *76*
Cugola, G., 44, *76*
Culler, D.E., 213, 223, 228–235, 240, 242, 243, *275*, *276*
Cunningham, W., 86, *117*
Curely, K.F., 116, *126*
Curtis, B., 38, 61, 66, 67, *76*, *80*, *82*

D

Dahlin, M., 213, 250–253, *274*, *277*
Damsgaard, J., 103, *120*
Daskalantonakis, M.K., 38, *74*
Davis, T., 115, *126*
de Supinski, B.R., 213, *274*
DeCanio, S.J., 113, *123*
Decker, B., 31, 34, 39, 41, *76*
Degenaro, L., 213, *275*
Delagi, B., 233, 234, 242, 243, *276*
DeMarco, T., 6, *27*, 42, *76*
Dent, E.B., 107, *121*
DeSanctis, G., 115, *126*
Deshpande, A., 67, *77*

AUTHOR INDEX

Devanbu, P., 43, *76*
Diamond, M.A., 107, *121*
Dibble, C., 113, *123*
Dickson, R.M., 213, *273*
Dieters, W., 67, *76*
Dill, D.L., 213, *274*
DiMaggio, P.J., 107, *122*
Dingsøyr, T., 42, 62, *75*
DiNitto, E., 66, *74*
DOD-STD-2167A, 141, *208*
Dorta, N., 213, *275*
Douglis, F., 248, 250, 253, *277*
Drouin, J.N., 66, *76*
Dubois, M., 213, *273*
Duguid, P., 42, *75, 76*
Duska, B.M., 248, 250, 251, 253, *277*
Dybå, T., 44, 72, *76*

E

Eager, D.L., 213, *274*
Easterbrook, S., 105, *121*
Edmunds, A., 113, *123*
EEA, 141, *208*
Eggers, S.J., 213, 219, 220, 242, *275*
Elam, J.J., 38, *82*
Elizur, D., 114, *124*
Emam, K.E., 66, *76*
Ericsson Telecom AB, 146, *208*
Estublier, J., 67, *75*
Ewing, D., 250, 252, 253, *277*

F

Fan, L., 250, 252, 253, *277*
Fan, M., 113, *123*
Fearey, P., 42, *76*
Feautrier, P., 231, 233, 234, *276*
Feelay, M.J., 248, 250, 251, 253, *277*
Feiler, P.H., 46, 66, *76, 79*
Feldmann, A., 248, 250, 253, *277*
Feldmann, R., 34, 41, *76*
Fenton, N.E., 85, *117*, 169, *208*
Fernström, C., 67, *77*
Fichman, R.G., 103, 113, 114, *120, 123*
Field, J., 140, *210*

Fields, K.T., 110, *122*
Fischer, G., 32, 37, 38, 40, 42–44, 68, *77*
Fitzgerald, B., 90, *117*
Fleisch, B.D., 213, *273*
Fleischer, M., 103, *120*
Flores, F., 42, 58, *82*
Floyd, S., 250, 253, *277*
Fong, C.C.F., 213, 259, *275*
Fong, W., 67, *77*
Fonvielle, W.H., 114, *124*
Fournier, R., 21, *27*
Fowler, P., 99, 100, 113, *119, 123*
Fowler, R.J., 213, 219–221, *275, 276*
Frakes, W., 67, *79*
French, J.R.P., 107, *121*
Frey, M., 34, *76*
Fritzson, P., 140, *210*
Fuggetta, A., 38, 56, 66, 67, *74, 77*

G

Gadde, S., 250, 252, 253, *277*
Gallagher, K.B., 138, 140, *208*
Gamma, E., 37, 46, *77*
Gao, J., 138, *209*
Gardiner, L.R., 114, *123*
Garg, P.K., 56, 66, 67, *77*
Garlan, D., 31, *81*
Garud, R., 109, 110, *122*
Gaw, J.L., 85, *117*
Gee, J.G., 213, 219, 220, 232, 234, *276*
Geroski, P.A., 102, *119*
Ghezzi, C., 56, 66, 67, *74*
Gibbons, D., 93, *118*
Gibson, M.L., 110, *122*
Gil, J.-A., 213, *273*
Ginsberg, M.J., 93, *118*
Giorgi, R., 213, 219, 221, 223–225, *274, 276*
Girgensohn, A., 40, *77*
Glass, G., 248, 250, 253, *277*
Glass, R.L., 35, 37, 40, *82*, 85, *117*
Glaziev, S.Yu., 103, *120*
Globe, A., 69, *74*
Goel, A.K., 39, *80*
Goldberg, A., 9, *27*
Goldberg, S.G., 107, *121*
Golding, A., 71, *77*

Gomaa, H., 145, *208*
Gomez, J.A., 141, *210*
Grady, R.B., 97, *118*
Graham, P., 213, *275*
Granstrand, O., 103, *120*
Greenbaum, C.W., 114, *124*
Griss, M.L., 34, 61, *77, 78*
Grudin, J., 31, 42, 68, *77, 78*
Gruhn, V., 67, *76*
Grundy, J.C., 66, *78*
Gupta, A., 213, 233, 234, 244, *275, 276*
Gust, T., 141, *210*
Gustavson, D., 233, 234, *276*

H

Hall, R., 250, 252, 253, *277*
Hamidjaja, H., 213, *275*
Haney, F.M., 138, *208*
Hao Che, 234, *276*
Hardgrave, B.C., 107, *121*
Harris, M., 90, *117*
Harrison, J., 250–253, *277*
Hartkopf, S., 34, *73*
Heimbinger, D., 56, *81*
Heinen, J.S., 90, *117*
Helm, R., 37, 46, *77*
Hennessy, J., 233, 234, 242, 243, *276*
Henninger, S., 31, 32, 34–36, 38–40, 43–45, 64–67, 69, 71, *78, 79*
Henry, S., 138, *209*
Hill, M.D., 213, *273*
Hirschheim, R., 107, *121*
Hollenbach, C., 67, *79*
Holtz, H., 19, *27*
Holtzblatt, K., 63, *79*
Hong Jiang, 233, 234, 242, 243, *276*
Horowitz, E., 140, *208*
Horowitz, M., 233, 234, *276*
Hosking, J.G., 66, *78*
Howard, G.S., 113, *123*
Hsia, P., 138, *209*
Huang, Y., 259, *278*
Huff, S.L., 100, *119*
Hughes, T.P., 104, *121*
Humphrey, W.S., 45, 46, 49, *76, 79*
Hurson, A.R., 213, 242, 243, *278*

I

IEEE Std. 1219, 141, *208*
IEEE Std. 830, 141, *208*
IEEE Std. 982.1, 141, *208*
Iivari, J., 114, 115, *124, 126*
Imielinski, T., 259, *278*
Ingols, C., 114, *124*
Iscoe, N., 61, *76*
Ishizaki, A., 67, *77*
ISO9000-3, 141, *208*
Issarny, V., 213, *275*
Ives, B., 115, *125*
Iyengar, A., 213, *275*

J

Jaakkola, H., 102, *119*
Jacobson, I., 133, 140, 149, *208*
Jacobson, V., 250, 253, *277*
Jain, A., 45, 64, 66, 71, *75*
Jarvis, A., 66, *79*
Jaswinder Pal Singh, 213, *275*
Jedlitschka, A., 34, *76*
Jeffries, R., 86, *117*
Jermier, J.M., 106, *121*
Jick, T.D., 114, *125*
Johnson, R.E., 31, 37, 40, 46, *77, 79*
Johnson, V., 40, *75*
Johnston, D., 84, *116*
Jones, S., 63, *79*
Jong, D.C., 140, *210*
Jong Hyuk Choi, 233, 234, 240, 242, 243, *276*
Jonsson, P., 133, 140, 149, *208*
Jun Cai, 213, 259, 261, 262, *275*
Jurison, J., 115, *125*

K

Kaiser, G.E., 66, 67, *75, 79*
Kamkar, M., 140, *210*
Kaniosvki, Y.M., 103, *120*
Kanter, R.M., 104, 114–116, *121, 124, 125*
Kaplan, A., 92, *118*
Karahanna, E., 114, *124*

Karlsson, J., 136, *208*
Karnøe, P., 109, 110, *122*
Katz, R.H., 213, 219, 220, *275*
Kautz, K., 102, *119*
Kavi, K., 213, 242, 243, *278*
Kay, J.S., 213, 250–253, *274*, *277*
Kehoe, R., 66, *79*
Kellner, M.I., 67, *76*
Kemerer, C.F., 103, 113, 114, *120*, *123*
Kerhong, C., 213, *274*
Kessler, R.R., 86, *117*
Khoury, C., 213, *275*
Kian-Lee Tan, 213, 259, 261, 262, *275*
Kim, H.S., 213, 242, 243, *278*
Klein, K.J., 112, *122*
Kleiner, A., 90, *117*
Kling, R., 41, *79*
Klinger, C., 37–39, *81*
Knight, D., 106, *121*
Kolodner, J.L., 39, 73, *79*, *80*
Konnecker, A., 19, *27*
Konrad, M.D., 66, *79*
Korth, H.F., 259, *278*
Krantz, J., 107, *121*
Krasner, H., 61, *76*
Krishnamurthy, B., 213, 257, *274*, *278*
Kroeger, T.M., 248, 250, 253, *277*
Kröschel, F., 31, 41, *75*
Kuilboer, J.P., 115, *125*
Kung, D., 138, *209*
Kung-Lung Wu, 213, 259, *275*
Kunnathur, A.S., 115, *126*
Kuvaja, P., 66, *79*
Kwon, T.H., 93, 103, *118*
Kyu Ho Park, 233, 234, 240, 242, 243, *276*

L

Lampert, R., 141, *210*
Lange, R., 103, *120*
Lanubile, F., 140, *207*
Lappala, K., 31, 32, 34, 35, 38, 40, 43, *79*
Larsen, T.J., 101–103, *119*
Lassila, K.S., 99, 100, *118*
Laugero, G., 69, *74*
Lavazza, L., 38, 67, *74*, *77*
Lawrence, P., 106, *121*

Lebeck, A.R., 213, *274*
Lee, B., 213, 242, 243, *278*
Lee, H., 67, *79*
Lee, J., 68, *79*
Lemke, A.C., 32, 37, 38, 40, 43, 68, *77*
Leonard-Barton, D., 98, 110, *118*
Letovsky, S., 141, *210*
Levine, L., 37–39, *81*, 102, 107, 113, *119*, *122*, *123*
Li, W., 138, *209*
Li, Y., 64, 65, 71, *79*
Lim, W.C., 38, *79*
Lindvall, M., 31, 34, 41, 43, 65, *74*, *79*, 131, 134, 136, 140, 147, 151, 158, 169, 178, 202, 205, 206, *209*
Linstone, H.A., 104, *121*
Lipkind, I., 213, *275*
Liskov, B., 213, *274*
Lister, T., 6, *27*
Littman, D., 141, *210*
Liu, C., 46, 67, *76*
Liu, Y.A., 213, *273*
Locke, E.A., 107, *121*
Loi, M., 67, *74*
Long, D.D.E., 248, 250, 253, *277*
Long, M.D., 32, 42, 73, *82*
Lopata, C.L., 110, 111, 113, 114, 116, *122*
Lorsch, J., 106, *121*
Lotem, A., 71, *80*
Lovato, C.Y., 113, *123*
Lucas Jr., H.C., 93, *118*
Lui, J.C.S., 213, 259, *275*
Lyle, J.R., 138, 140, *208*
Lyytinen, K., 103, *120*

M

Maansaari, J., 115, *126*
Maclean, A., 68, *80*
Mahajan, V., 102, *119*
Maheshwari, U., 213, *274*
Maier, F.H., 96, 97, *118*
Makpangou, M., 213, *275*
Malcolm, R., 115, *125*
Man Hon Wong, 213, 259, *275*
March, J.G., 33, *80*, 86, *117*
Marcolin, B.L., 102, *120*

Markus, M.L., 89, 91–93, 105, *117*, *118*
Marmor-Squires, A.B., 96, 97, *118*
Marshall, T.E., 114, 116, *123*, *126*
Martin, J., 91, *117*
Martin, R.J., 96, 97, *118*
Marwood, D., 248, 250, 251, 253, *277*
Mastelloni, G., 140, *207*
Maurer, F., 19, *27*
McCall, R., 37, 40, 42, 68, *77*, *81*
McCreight, E.M., 213, 217, 218, *274*
McCrickard, D.S., 204, *209*
McDade, S., 103, *120*
McFeeley, B., 96, *118*
McGarry, F., 38, 65, *74*, *82*
McGuire, E., 102, *119*
McMaster, T., 91, 101, 102, 104, 105, *117*, *119*
Melo, W.L., 67, *75*
Melone, N., 103, 106, *120*, *121*
Menaud, J.-M., 213, *275*
Menlo, W., 66, *76*
Merron, K., 107, *122*
Meyerson, D., 91, *117*
Mi, P., 56, 66, 67, *77*, *80*
Michel, S., 250, 253, *277*
Miller, W.R., 99, 100, *118*
Milutinovic, V., 213, 230–235, 242, *273*, *276*, *277*
Ming-Syan Chen, 213, 259, *275*
Miwa, H., 213, *275*
Modali, S., 64, 65, 71, *79*
Mogul, J.C., 248, 250, 253, *277*
Moore, G.A., 103, 104, 114, *120*
Moran, T., 68, *80*
Morasca, S., 38, *77*
Morgan, E., 114, *124*
Morgan, G., 91, *117*
Morris, A., 113, *123*
Morris, M.G., 115, *125*
Mowry, T., 233, 234, 244, *276*
Muller, E., 102, *119*
Müller, W., 34, *73*
Mumford, E., 102, *119*
Muñoz-Avila, H., 71, *80*
Munro, M.C., 100, *119*, 138, 139, *209*, *210*
Muntz, R., 250, 253, *277*
Myers, W., 114, *124*

N

Nakakoji, K., 40, *77*
Nam-Hee Kim, 213, *273*
Nanda, 233, 234, 242, 243, *276*
NASA GSFC, 49, *80*
Nash, S.H., 96, 97, *118*
Nau, D.S., 71, *80*
Neighbors, J., 37, *80*
Nelson, A.C., 115, *126*
Newman, M., 107, *121*
Nguyen, K., 250, 253, *277*
Nick, M., 31, 34, 39, 41, 43, *74*, *76*, *80*
Nilsson, A., 40, *75*
Nonaka, I., 32, 33, *80*
Nord, W.R., 106, *121*
North, J., 114, *124*

O

Object-Oriented Software Engineering, 150, *209*
Objectory Design, 150, *209*
Objectory Process, 133, 146, *209*
Objectory Requirements Analysis and Robustness Analysis, 150, *209*
Objectory Tool, 133, 140, *209*
Oddy, R.N., 43, *75*
O'Hara, A., 67, *81*
Oivo, M., 43, *80*
Oldano, G., 38, *77*
Oliva, T.A., 103, *120*
Olsen, J., 86, *117*
Olson, M.H., 115, *125*
Orazi, E., 38, *77*
Orlikowski, W.J., 91, 99, *118*
Osterweil, L.J., 50, 55, 56, 67, 68, *79*–*81*
Ostwald, J., 40, 42, 44, 68, *77*
Over, J., 67, *76*
Overgaard, G., 133, 140, 149, *208*

P

Page, G., 38, *74*
Pajerski, R., 38, *74*
Papamarcos, M., 213, 219, *274*
Park, S., 213, *274*

Parkes, C., 114, *125*
Patel, J., 213, 219, *274*
Patnayakuni, R., 113, *123*
Paulk, M.C., 66, *79*, *80*
Pearce, M., 39, *80*
Pei, C., 213, *274*
Pen-Chung Yew, 213, *274*
Pérez, C.E., 213, *273*
Perry, D.E., 67, *80*
Peters, T., 108, *122*
Peterson, R.A., 102, *119*
Pettengill, R., 138, *207*
Pfeffer, J., 108, *122*
Pfleeger, S.L., 85, *117*, 140, *209*
Pham, T., 56, 66, 67, *77*
Picco, G.P., 67, *74*
Pierre, G., 213, *275*
Pinch, T.J., 104, *121*
Pinto, J., 141, *210*
Plakal, M., 213, *273*
Plaza, E., 39, *73*
Pong, F., 213, *273*
Pont, A., 213, *273*
Popovich, S.S., 66, 67, *79*
Port, D., 45, 50, 64, 66, 71, *75*
Potter, M., 113, *123*
Poulin, J.S., 42, *80*
Povey, D., 250–253, *277*
Powell, W.W., 107, *122*
Premkumar, G., 113, *123*
Prete, C.A., 213, 217, 219, 221, 223–225, *274–276*
Pries-Heje, J., 102, *119*
Prieto-Díaz, R., 37, 39, *80*, *81*
Prina, G., 219, 221, *276*

Q

Qi Tang Lin, 213, *275*
Qing, Y., 213, *274*
Queille, J., 138, *209*

R

Rabinovich, I., 213, *274*
Rabinovich, M., 213, 248, 250, 252, 253, *274*, *277*
Radice, R., 67, *81*

Raghavendran, A., 31, 32, 34, 35, 38, 40, 43, *79*
Rai, A., 99, 113, 114, *119*, *123*
Rainer Jr., R.K., 110, 114, *122*, *123*
Rajaraman, R., 213, *274*
Ramiller, N.C., 103, 112, *120*, *122*
Ramlingam, G., 140, *210*
Rao, K., 115, *125*
Ravichandran, T., 110, 113, *122*, *123*
Rech, J., 34, *76*
Redmiles, D., 40, *77*
Redwine Jr., S.T., 96, 97, *118*
Reeves, B., 40, 42, 68, *77*
Repenning, N.P., 86, 87, *117*
Reynolds Jr., P.F., 213, *274*
Ricciardi, L., 219, 221, *276*
Rich, C.H., 32, *81*
Richardson, G.P., 88, *117*
Richardson, L., 114, *124*
Riddle, W.E., 96, 97, *118*
Rifkin, S., 99, 100, 105, 115, *119*, *121*
Risen, J., 84, *116*
Roberts Jr., T.L., 110, *122*
Robertson, E., 40, *75*
Robey, D., 93, *118*
Rodriguez, P., 249–254, *277*
Rogers, E.M., 101–103, 110, 111, 114, *119*
Rollnick, S., 99, 100, *118*
Román, A.G., 213, *273*
Rombach, D., 31, 33, 34, 38, 65, 66, *74*, *75*
Rosenbloom, P.S., 71, *77*
Rosenkopf, L., 106, *121*
Rosenstein, A., 250, 253, *277*
Roth, G., 90, *117*
Roth, N., 67, *81*
Rottman, J., 115, *126*
Rouvellou, I., 213, *275*
Royce, W.W., 146, *210*
Rubin, B., 40, *75*
Ruíz, B.H., 213, *273*
Runesson, M., 169, *209*
Rus, I., 31, 43, *79*
Ryan, T.F., 90, *117*

S

Sagie, A., 114, *124*
Sahuquillo, J., 213, *273*

Sandahl, K., 140, 202, *209*
Satterthwaite, E., 213, 217, *275*
Scacchi, W., 56, 66, 67, *77*, *80*
Scharff, E., 42, *81*
Schlabach, J., 36, *79*
Schneider, K., 42, 69, *81*
Schoen, E., 138, *207*
Scholes, J., 104, *121*
Schön, D.A., 34, *81*
Schultz, R.L., 93, *118*
Schumpeter, J.A., 96, 109, *118*, *122*
Schwab, T., 43, *77*
Schwaber, K., 65, *81*
Schwartz, M., 250, 252, 253, *277*
Schwinn, T., 42, 69, *81*
SEI, 141, *210*
Selfridge, P.G., 32, 42, 43, 73, 76, *82*
Senge, P.M., 85, 86, *117*
Sentosa, L., 39, *80*
Shahmehri, N., 140, *210*
Shaw, M., 31, *81*
Shaw, N.G., 110, *122*
Shim, S.J., 115, *126*
Shin-Dug Kim, 213, *273*
Shipman, F., 37, 40, 42, 68, *77*, *81*
Shrira, L., 213, *274*
Silva, J., 91, *117*
Simoni, R., 233, 234, *276*
Simos, M.A., 37–39, *81*
Singer, C.A., 141, *210*
Singh, J.P., 223, 228–235, 240, 242, 243, *276*
Sinnwell, M., 213, *275*
Sista, P., 259, *278*
Sleator, D., 213, 220, *276*
Smith, A.J., 213, 219, 220, 232, 234, *276*
Smith, R.H., 115, *125*
Snyder, T.R., 49, *79*
Soloway, E., 141, *210*
Sorin, D.J., 213, *273*
Spanner, C., 249–254, *277*
Spilka, R., 99, *119*
Stålhane, T., 42, 62, *75*
Stallaert, J., 113, *123*
Staudenmayer, N.A., 67, *80*
Stein, B.A., 114, *125*
Stein, E.W., 68, *81*
Stewart, L., 213, 217, *275*
Strasburg, D., 141, *210*

Straub, D.W., 114, *124*
Stroustrup, B., 146, *210*
Strubing, J., 6, *27*
Sutcu, C., 110, *122*
Sutton, R.I., 108, *122*
Sutton, S.M., 56, *81*
Swanson, E.B., 102, 103, 112, 115, *119*, *120*, *122*, *125*

T

Tait, P., 115, *125*
TakeFive Software, 200, *210*
Takeychi, H., 32, 33, *80*
Tam, K.Y., 113, *123*
Tanaka, Y., 213, *275*
Tari, Z., 213, *275*
Tartalja, I., 230, 233–235, *277*
Tautz, C., 34, 39, 43, *74*, *80*, *81*
Taylor, R.N., 38, 67, *74*, *75*
Terveen, L.G., 32, 42, 71, 73, *82*
Tewari, R., 213, 250–253, *274*, *277*
Thacker, C., 213, 217, *275*
Thangadurai, G., 213, *273*, *274*
Thapar, M., 233, 234, 242, 243, *276*
Theel, O.E., 213, *273*
Thomas, M., 65, *82*
Thunquest, G., 56, 66, *77*
Tip, F., 140, *210*
Tomasevic, M., 230–234, 242, *276*
Tornatzky, L.G., 103, 112, *120*, *122*
Toyoshima, Y., 138, *209*
Tracz, W., 61, *82*
Turver, R.J., 139, *210*
Tushman, M.L., 106, *121*
Tyre, M.J., 99, *118*

U

Ungson, G.R., 68, *82*
USC, 64, *82*

V

Van Slack, T., 97, *118*
Veenstra, J.R., 213, 220, *275*

Venkatesh, V., 115, *125*
Vessey, I., 35, 37, 40, *82*, 115, *125*
Vidgen, R.T., 91, 104, *117*
Vin, H., 250–253, *277*
Vin, H.M., 213, *274*
Vissaggio, G., 140, *207*
Vlissides, J., 37, 46, *77*
Voidrot, J., 138, *209*
Votta, L.G., 6, *27*, 67, *80*

W

Waligora, S., 38, *74*
Wallnau, K.C., 31, *75*
Walsh, J.P., 68, *82*
Walz, D.B., 38, *82*
Wang, J., 246, 248–254, *277*
Wang, T., 40, *75*
Wang, Z., 250, 252, 253, *277*
Want, W., 250, 253, *277*
Warboys, B., 102, *119*
Wartik, S., 115, *126*
Wastell, D.G., 91, 102, 104, *117*, *119*
Waterman Jr., R.H., 108, *122*
Waters, R.C., 32, *81*
Webb, L., 110, *122*
Weber, C.V., 66, *80*
Weber, R., 34, 71, *73*, *80*
Weber, W.-D., 233, 234, 244, *276*
Weick, K., 92, 93, *118*
Weikum, G., 213, *275*
Weinberg, G., 6, *27*
Wen, F., 138, *209*
Wentzel, W., 67, *77*
Whinston, A.B., 113, *123*
Whitehead, E.J., 38, *74*
Wilde, N., 138, 141, *209*, *210*
Williams, C., 213, *274*
Williams, L.R., 86, 115, *117*, *125*
Williamson, A., 114, *124*
Williamson, R., 140, *208*

Willis, R.R., 49, *79*
Wills, C.E., 213, 257, *274*, *278*
Wind, Y., 102, *119*
Winn, T., 37, *82*
Winograd, T., 42, 58, *82*
Wolfe, R.A., 113, *123*
Wolfson, O., 259, *278*
Won-Kee Hong, 213, *273*
Wood, D.A., 213, *273*, *274*
Wroblewski, D., 71, *82*

Y

Yacobellis, R.K., 38, *74*
Yadav, S.B., 110, *122*
Yahong Sui, 213, *275*
Yakemovic, K., 68, 69, *76*
Yang, H.-L., 115, *126*
Yang, J., 250, 253, *277*
Yang, Q., 213, *273*
Yau, S., 138, *210*
Ye Tung, 234, *276*
Ying, H., 213, *273*
Young, R., 68, *80*
Yourdon, E., 10, *27*
Yu, L., 64, 65, 71, *79*
Yu, P.S., 213, 259, *275*

Z

Zaharioudakis, M., 213, *274*
Zelkowitz, M.V., 38, *74*, 96, 97, 115, *118*
Zhang, L., 250, 253, *277*
Zhijung Wang, 234, *276*
Zigurs, I., 115, *126*
Zimring, C., 39, *80*
Zmud, R.W., 93, 99, 103, 113, 114, *118*, *119*, *122–124*
Zolner, J., 114, *124*
Zwass, V., 68, *81*

Subject Index

A

Access latency, 248, 253, 254
Actor Network Theory, 104
Actual Impact Set (AIS), 143
Adaptation, mutual, 98–9, 110
Adopters, categorization of, 101–2, 114
Adoption, *see* Process adoption
AHDMS protocol, 221–2
    bus utilization, 224
    cache miss ratio, 225
    memory requirements, 222, 224, 226, 227
    message complexity, 222, 223, 226
    synchronization delay, 222, 226
    transaction size, 222, 226
Amazon, 14
Analysis object model, 148, 203, 204
Artifact object model, 142, 143
Artifact storage, 11, 19, 26
Asset management, 14–15

B

Backup and recovery, 37–8
Bandwidth, 229, 253–4, 259, 260, 262
Bootstrap, 66, 95
BORE, 35, 44–66, 68–73
    activity precedence, 68
    approach overview, 48–9
    case-based planning, 71
    cases, 46, 73
    CeBASE, 64, 71
    CMMI compliance, 65
    configuration management, 71
    effort metrics, 46
    experience packaging, 61
    future work, 70–2
    implementation roles, 61–3, 71
    knowledge delivery, 56
    MBASE, 63–5, 71
    methodologies, 46
        creation of, 49–54
    methodology rules, 49
        editing, 52–3
    methodology tasks, 46
        creation of, 50–2
    model of concepts, 46, 47
    organizations, 47, 48
    pilot projects, 35, 63
    privilege manager, 57
    process discovery, 63
    process models, 72
    process-level reviews, 60
    project, 47
        execution of, 56–7
        instantiation of, 54–6
        process deviations, 57–60
    project scheduling interfaces, 46
    project tasks, 47
    Software Design Studio (SDS), 55, 65
    tailoring rules, 55–6, 62, 65, 68
    Task Manager, 44, 45
    tasks, 46
    terminology, 46–7
Broadcast (bus-based) protocols, 216–27
    adaptive hybrid protocols, 221–2
    hybrid protocols, 220–1
    invalidation based, 219–20
    selective, 223–4
    summary, 224–7, 269
    update based, 217–19
BuildTopia, 13
Bus-based protocols, *see* Broadcast (bus-based) protocols

C

Cache Array Routing Protocol, 252
Cache Digest, 252
Cachemesh, 252
Caching on World Wide Web, *see* Web caching
Capability Maturity Models, 85, 95
Capitalism, 107
CASE, 95, 115
  see also Objectory SE
CC-NUMA architecture, 228–30
CDEs, 2–3, 6–27
  asset management, 14–15
  barriers to, 25
  classification of, 12, 26–7
  collaboration, 22, 25, 26
  community building, 22, 25, 26
  coordination, 22, 25, 26
  emergence of, 8–9
  evolution of, 24–5
  features, 21–4
  information services, 15–16
  infrastructure, 16–17
  non-software domains, 12–14
  points of friction addressed by, 9–12, 21
  preparation for adoption, 26
  for software development, 8–12, 19–24
  Web communities, 17–19
CeBASE, 64, 71
Change candidates, 138
Change history analysis, 137
Change management, 11, 24, 94, 114
Changes
  primary, 138, 196
  secondary, 138, 196
Chat rooms, 17
Classes
  change-prone, 198
  coupling between, 182–3
  relations between, 182–90
    see also Inheritance relations; Inter-class relations
  size considerations, 178–82, 198
CMM, 66, 68, 112
CMMI, 66
COCOMO, 134, 156
CoCreate, 13
Cohen's Kappa value, 151

Coherence protocols, 212–73
  conclusions, 271–3
  consistency requirement variations, 272
  introduction, 212–13
  motivation, 214
  overview of classes, 270
  parameter definitions, 214–15
  see also Broadcast (bus-based) protocols; Message-passing (directory based) protocols; Web caching schemes; Web coherence; Wireless protocols
Collab.net, 19
Collaborative development environments, *see* CDEs
Communication
  group, 9, 10, 11
  in process adoption, 110
Communities of practice, 41, 42
Competency-destroying technology, 106
Competency-enhancing technology, 106
Competitive snooping algorithm, 220
ComponentSource, 14, 15
Computer-aided software engineering, *see* CASE
Consumer product development, 9
Cost estimation models, 134, 156, 200–1
Creative destruction, 109
CRISP, 252
Customer intimacy, 105

D

Decision support, case-based, 39
Dependency analysis, 136, 138–40
Design environments, domain-specific, 36, 37, 38, 40–1
Design object models, 148, 169–78, 202, 203, 204
  abstraction level, 169–71, 173, 174, 176–7
Design rationale techniques, 68–9
Designer Assistant, 42
Destruction, creative, 109
developerWorks, 14, 15
DevX, 19
Diffusion, 87, 88, 101–5, 110, 115
  criticisms of theory, 103–5
DIGIT, 103

SUBJECT INDEX 291

Directory based protocols, *see* Message-passing (directory based) protocols
Directory organizations
  fully-mapped, 231–2, 235–41
    cache-based, 232, 237–40
    centralized, 231
    flat, 231, 232, 235–7
    hierarchical, 231
    hybrid, 232, 240–1
    memory-based, 232
  hierarchy of, 234
  partially-mapped, 232–4, 241–6
    dir_i organization, 232
    dir_i-B organization, 233, 242–4
    dir_i-CV_K organization, 233, 244–6
    dir_i-NB organization, 233, 242, 243
Distributed Internet Cache, 252
Domain abstractions, 36, 37, 40
Domain analysis, 36, 37, 38, 39–40
Domain lifecycle, 35–7
Domain Name Services (DNS), 254
Domain object model, 148, 203, 204
Domain-Oriented Design Environments (DODEs), 40
Dragon protocol, 217–19
  bus utilization, 224
  cache miss ratio, 225
  memory requirements, 218, 219
  messaging complexity, 218, 219, 221
  saturation by, 224, 228
  synchronization delay, 218, 219
  transaction size, 218, 219, 226

E

Eclipse, 7, 8
Edit-history, 196, 197, 200
Efficient Distributed Write Protocol (EDWP), 220–1
EMACS, 193
Endeavors system, 67
Ericsson Radio Systems (ERA), 131, 143–4
  see also PMR-project
Estimated Impact Set (EIS), 142, 143
ETVX method, 67
Eureka, 42
Experience factory, 33–4, 35, 38, 72, 85
Experience packaging, 34
External rereads (XRR) metric, 220, 221
eXtreme programming, 85, 86, 112

F

Factor studies, 110–15
Firefly protocol, 217
Flashline, 14
Formalization, 113
Frameworks, 38, 40–1
Friction, points of, 9–11, 21
Fully Distributed Internet Cache, 252

G

Groove, 18–19

H

Hyper-Text Transfer Protocol (HTTP), 254, 255

I

Cadence, 13
IDEAL model, 96
IDEs, 3, 5, 7
Illinois–MESI protocol, *see* MESI protocol
Impact Analysis (IA), 130–1, 136–43
  dependency analysis, 136, 138–40
  effectiveness evaluation, 142–3
  framework for, 141–2
  ripple effect analysis, 138–40
  software change process model, 137–8
  traceability approaches, 140–1
  see also RDIA
Impact factors, 203–5
Impact model, 142
Imperialism, 104
Incremental update invalidation, 265, 266, 267
  memory requirements, 266
  messaging complexity, 265, 266
  synchronization delay, 265, 266
  transaction size, 266
Incremental update propagation, 265–6, 267
  memory requirements, 266
  messaging complexity, 265, 266
  synchronization delay, 265, 266
  transaction size, 266
Information services, 15–16

Inheritance relations, 170, 171, 172, 177, 182
    changed vs. unchanged, 187, 189
    changes in, 174–5
    investigating for change, 199
    predicted vs. non-predicted, 188, 189
Innovation, 94, 101, 111–12
Instant messaging (IM), 16–17
Institutionalization, 107
Integrated development environments, *see* IDEs
Inter-class relations, 171, 172, 175–6, 177, 185–6
    definition, 172
Interaction theory, 90
Interconnection networks, 229
Interface object model, 142, 143
Internal object model, 142
Internet Cache Protocol, 252
Internet Protocol (IP), 254
Interpretivism, 90–1
ISO 9000, 66, 85, 95, 112
Iterative reuse model, 149

K

Knowing-doing gap, 108–9
Knowledge acquisition, 40, 43, 71
Knowledge creation, 33, 38, 42, 44, 49
Knowledge feedback, 43–4
Knowledge lifecycle, experience-based, 32–3
Knowledge management, experience-based, 32–41

L

Latency, 108–9
Leadership, 94–5, 109, 114–15
Lotus Notes, 17–18

M

Mailing lists, 17
Market demands, 113
MBASE, 63–5, 71
Member function definitions
    changed, 159
    predicted, 158
Memory blocks
    local, 231
    remote, 231
MESI protocol, 219
    bus utilization, 224
    cache miss ratio, 225
    in directory-based systems, 234, 238
    memory requirements, 219–20, 227, 235
    messaging complexity, 219–20, 221
    synchronization delay, 219–20
    transaction size, 219–20, 226
Message boards, 17
Message-passing (directory based) protocols, 227–46
    CC-NUMA architecture, 228–30
    directory-based organizations, *see* Directory organizations
    summary, 246, 247, 269–70
Migratory data, 221–2
MILOS, 19
Mobile computing network environment, 260–1
MSDN, 14, 15
Multicast mechanism, 273
Mutual adaptation, 98–9, 110

N

NetMeeting, 6, 17
Nodes, definitions of
    cluster owner, 240
    dirty, 230
    exclusive, 231
    home, 230
    local (requesting), 231
    owner, 231
Normative pressure, 87
NUMA-Q, 238–40
    see also SCI protocol

O

Object-oriented frameworks, 37
Objectory, 133, 146–50
    dependent objects function, 149
    input, 147–8
    models, 148–9
    output, 148
    Premium Analysis & Design, 146
    use, 147
        during RDIA, 149

SUBJECT INDEX

Objectory SE, 149–50, 191, 192, 193
  improvements, 150, 203–4
OneSpace, 13
Ontologies, 90
Open source development, 8–9, 20
Operational excellence, 105
Organization, characteristics of, 113
Organizational learning, 34–5, 38, 39, 72

P

Pair programmimg, 85, 86
Passive Shared Copy Removal protocol, *see* PSCR protocol
Passive sharing, 223
Path creation, 109
Path dependence, 94, 109–10
Piggyback Cache Validation (PCV), 257
Piggyback Server Invalidation (PSI), 257
PlaceWare, 17
PMR-project, 131, 132–3, 143–50, 207
  implementation, 146
  introduction, 132–3
  project developers, 150
  software development process model (SDPM), 146–7
  system structure, 144–5
  see also Objectory; RDIA
Pointer overflow, 233
Positivism, 90
Procedural Hierarchy of Issue structures, 68–9
Process adoption, 84–116
  case studies, 115
  communication, 110
  cyclic nature, 99
  definition, 93
  double-bubble process, 99–100
  factor studies, 110–15
  fields touched by implementation research, 94–5
  Markus model, 89–93
  non-linear (messy) models, 98–100
  quantitative estimates, 115–16
  Repenning model, 86–9
  stage/phase models, 96–7
  user acceptance, 115
  see also Diffusion; Resistance
Process languages, 67, 68

Process-centered Software Engineering Environments (PSEEs), 66–7
Product adoption, 95–6
Product innovativeness, 105
Project dashboards, 11, 21
PSCR protocol, 223–4
  bus utilization, 224–5
  cache miss ratio, 225
  memory requirements, 223, 224, 226, 227
  message complexity, 223, 226
  saturation by, 228
  synchronization delay, 223, 226
  transaction size, 223, 226

Q

QIP, 34, 48, 49, 71
Quality Improvement Paradigm, *see* QIP

R

Rational Developer Network (RDN), 15
Rational Unified Process (RUP), 3, 26, 50, 65, 68, 112
RDIA, 130–207
  additional work, 154
  class relation considerations, 182–90
  class size considerations, 178–82, 198
  conclusions, 206–7
  conservative prediction, 199
  constraints, 136
  cost estimation models, 134, 156, 200–1
  developers' opinions, 190–2, 194–5
    comments on, 193, 195–6
  edit-history, 196, 197, 200
  evaluation on class level, 151–6
  evaluation on member function level, 156–62
  evaluation per requirement, 163–9
    relative rank-order of requirements, 165–8
  evaluations of release projects, 197–8
  explanation building, 196–7
  impact factors, 203–5
  improvements, 192, 196, 197–202
  porting of operating system requirement, 154
  purpose, 135–6
  quantitative results summary, 193–4
  release-to-class view, 198–9

research effort, 196
research questions, 134–5
software evolution planning problem, 133–4
strengths, 190–1
tool support, 193, 197, 200, 207
underprediction factor statistics, 162, 165
weaknesses, 191
see also Design object models; PMR-project
Read Write Broadcast (RWB) protocol, 220
Reality, social construction of, 95
Reasoning, case-based, 39
Reduced State Transition (RST) protocol, 217
Reductionism, 103–4
Reinforcement, 87
Relations, inter-class, *see* Inter-class relations
Repositories, 34, 35
case-based, 36, 37, 38
experience-based, 43
Requirements analysis, 147–8
Requirements-Driven Impact Analysis, *see* RDIA
Resilience, 4
Resistance, 90, 93, 94, 105–9
theories of, 91, 92
Reusable Asset Specification (RAS), 26
Ripple effects, 136
analysis of, 138–40

S

Saturation, 224, 228
Scalable Coherence Interface, *see* SCI protocol
Scalable multiprocessors, 229
SCCS, 192, 193, 200, 207
SCI protocol, 238–40
memory requirements, 239
message complexity, 239–40
synchronization delay, 239, 240
transaction size, 239
SCRUM, 65
SDPM, 146–7
SGI Origin, 234, 235
coherence protocol
memory requirements, 237, 240
message complexity, 236–7, 241
synchronization delay, 236, 237
transaction size, 237, 241

SGI Origin 2000, 245
SGI Origin 2002, 245
SharePoint, 19
Slashdot, 18
Slicing, 138–40
complement slice, 139
decomposition slice, 138
SNIFF, 192, 193, 200
Snooping, 217, 220, 222, 262
Soft Systems Methodology, 104
Software Architecture Analysis Method (SAAM), 203
Software change process model, 137–8
Software Design Studio (SDS), 55, 65
Software development
experience-based, 30–73
conclusions, 72–3
software process frameworks, 66–7
software process modeling, 66–8
tool support, 41–4
see also BORE; Knowledge management, experience-based
release-oriented, 130
social dynamics of, 6–8
see also CDEs
Software process automation, 56
Software process frameworks, 66
Software process modeling, 66–8
Software reuse, 42, 66
SourceForge, 19–20
SPICE, 66
Stakeholder negotiation, 10, 11
Stanford Flash, 235–7
see also SGI Origin
Starfire project, 9
Start up costs, 9, 10, 11
Starting Impact Set (SIS), 142
Summary Cache, 252
Symmetric Multi-Processor organization, 228
System Set, 142

T

Technology
competency-destroying, 106
competency-enhancing, 106
social shaping of, 95, 104
Technology churn, 4
TheServerSide, 15, 16

SUBJECT INDEX

Time starvation, 10, 11
Tool designers, 38, 40
Traceability, 136, 137, 140–1, 203

U

Unified Modeling Language (UML), 3, 26
Uniform Resource Locator (URL), 254
Update invalidation (UI) coherence, 261, 263–4, 267
  memory requirements, 264
  messaging complexity, 263, 264
  synchronization delay, 263, 264
  transaction size, 264
  see also Incremental update invalidation
Update propagation (UP) coherence, 261, 264–5, 267
  memory requirements, 265
  messaging complexity, 264, 265
  synchronization delay, 264, 265
  transaction size, 265
  see also Incremental update propagation
Update-Once protocol, 221
  bus utilization, 224
  cache miss ratio, 225
  memory requirements, 221, 222, 224, 226, 227
  message complexity, 221, 222, 223, 226
  synchronization delay, 221, 222, 226
  transaction size, 221, 222, 226
Use-case models, 147, 148, 149, 202, 203, 204
User acceptance, 115

V

Video conferencing, 17
Visual Studio, 7, 8

W

Web caching schemes, 246–58
  advantages, 248
  client caches, 248, 250
  coherence in, see Web coherence
  distributed, 249, 251–2
  hierarchical, 249, 250–1
  hybrid, 249, 252–3
  institutional-level caches, 250, 251
  proxy caches, 248
  server caches, 248
  web site mirroring, 249–50
  see also Web coherence
Web coherence, 253–8
  access latency issues, 253, 254
  communication link bandwidths, 253–4
  memory requirements, 253
  message complexity, 254
  piggyback coherence techniques, 257–8, 271
  strongly consistent cache coherence, 254, 255, 256
    client validation, 255, 256
    server invalidation, 255, 256
  summary, 258, 270–1
  weakly consistent cache coherence, 254, 255, 256–8
    Adaptive Time-To-Live (TTL), 256
Web communities, 17–19
Web Monkey, 15
Web site mirroring, 249–50
WebEx, 17
Whiteboards, 6, 17, 21
WikiWeb, 18
Wireless protocols, 259–67
  asynchronous operation mode, 261
  bandwidth limitations, 259, 260, 262
  design requirements, 261–2
  disconnection factor, 259
  future development, 272
  mobility factor, 259
  summary, 266–7, 268, 271
  synchronous operation mode, 261
  update broadcast parameter definitions, 263
  see also Incremental update invalidation; Incremental update propagation; Update invalidation (UI) coherence; Update propagation (UP) coherence
Work product collaboration, 9, 10, 11
Working space organization, 7, 9, 10
Write-Once protocol, 221
Write-run length (WRL) metric, 220, 221
WRL metric, 220, 221

X

XRR metric, 220, 221

Y

Yahoo groups, 18

Contents of Volumes in This Series

Volume 40

Program Understanding: Models and Experiments
    A. VON MAYRHAUSER AND A. M. VANS
Software Prototyping
    ALAN M. DAVIS
Rapid Prototyping of Microelectronic Systems
    APOSTOLOS DOLLAS AND J. D. STERLING BABCOCK
Cache Coherence in Multiprocessors: A Survey
    MAZIN S. YOUSIF, M. J. THAZHUTHAVEETIL, AND C. R. DAS
The Adequacy of Office Models
    CHANDRA S. AMARAVADI, JOEY F. GEORGE, OLIVIA R. LIU SHENG, AND JAY F. NUNAMAKER

Volume 41

Directions in Software Process Research
    H. DIETER ROMBACH AND MARTIN VERLAGE
The Experience Factory and Its Relationship to Other Quality Approaches
    VICTOR R. BASILI
CASE Adoption: A Process, Not an Event
    JOCK A. RADER
On the Necessary Conditions for the Composition of Integrated Software Engineering Environments
    DAVID J. CARNEY AND ALAN W. BROWN
Software Quality, Software Process, and Software Testing
    DICK HAMLET
Advances in Benchmarking Techniques: New Standards and Quantitative Metrics
    THOMAS CONTE AND WEN-MEI W. HWU
An Evolutionary Path for Transaction Processing Systems
    CARLTON PU, AVRAHAM LEFF, AND SHU-WEI, F. CHEN

Volume 42

Nonfunctional Requirements of Real-Time Systems
    TEREZA G. KIRNER AND ALAN M. DAVIS
A Review of Software Inspections
    ADAM PORTER, HARVEY SIY, AND LAWRENCE VOTTA
Advances in Software Reliability Engineering
    JOHN D. MUSA AND WILLA EHRLICH
Network Interconnection and Protocol Conversion
    MING T. LIU
A Universal Model of Legged Locomotion Gaits
    S. T. VENKATARAMAN

Volume 43

Program Slicing
  DAVID W. BINKLEY AND KEITH BRIAN GALLAGHER
Language Features for the Interconnection of Software Components
  RENATE MOTSCHNIG-PITRIK AND ROLAND T. MITTERMEIR
Using Model Checking to Analyze Requirements and Designs
  JOANNE ATLEE, MARSHA CHECHIK, AND JOHN GANNON
Information Technology and Productivity: A Review of the Literature
  ERIK BRYNJOLFSSON AND SHINKYU YANG
The Complexity of Problems
  WILLIAM GASARCH
3-D Computer Vision Using Structured Light: Design, Calibration, and Implementation Issues
  FRED W. DEPIERO AND MOHAN M. TRIVEDI

Volume 44

Managing the Risks in Information Systems and Technology (IT)
  ROBERT N. CHARETTE
Software Cost Estimation: A Review of Models, Process and Practice
  FIONA WALKERDEN AND ROSS JEFFERY
Experimentation in Software Engineering
  SHARI LAWRENCE PFLEEGER
Parallel Computer Construction Outside the United States
  RALPH DUNCAN
Control of Information Distribution and Access
  RALF HAUSER
Asynchronous Transfer Mode: An Engineering Network Standard for High Speed Communications
  RONALD J. VETTER
Communication Complexity
  EYAL KUSHILEVITZ

Volume 45

Control in Multi-threaded Information Systems
  PABLO A. STRAUB AND CARLOS A. HURTADO
Parallelization of DOALL and DOACROSS Loops—a Survey
  A. R. HURSON, JOFORD T. LIM, KRISHNA M. KAVI, AND BEN LEE
Programming Irregular Applications: Runtime Support, Compilation and Tools
  JOEL SALTZ, GAGAN AGRAWAL, CHIALIN CHANG, RAJA DAS, GUY EDJLALI, PAUL HAVLAK, YUAN-SHIN HWANG, BONGKI MOON, RAVI PONNUSAMY, SHAMIK SHARMA, ALAN SUSSMAN, AND MUSTAFA UYSAL
Optimization Via Evolutionary Processes
  SRILATA RAMAN AND L. M. PATNAIK
Software Reliability and Readiness Assessment Based on the Non-homogeneous Poisson Process
  AMRIT L. GOEL AND KUNE-ZANG YANG
Computer-supported Cooperative Work and Groupware
  JONATHAN GRUDIN AND STEVEN E. POLTROCK
Technology and Schools
  GLEN L. BULL

CONTENTS OF VOLUMES IN THIS SERIES

Volume 46

Software Process Appraisal and Improvement: Models and Standards
  MARK C. PAULK
A Software Process Engineering Framework
  JYRKI KONTIO
Gaining Business Value from IT Investments
  PAMELA SIMMONS
Reliability Measurement, Analysis, and Improvement for Large Software Systems
  JEFF TIAN
Role-based Access Control
  RAVI SANDHU
Multithreaded Systems
  KRISHNA M. KAVI, BEN LEE, AND ALLI R. HURSON
Coordination Models and Language
  GEORGE A. PAPADOPOULOS AND FARHAD ARBAB
Multidisciplinary Problem Solving Environments for Computational Science
  ELIAS N. HOUSTIS, JOHN R. RICE, AND NAREN RAMAKRISHNAN

Volume 47

Natural Language Processing: A Human-Computer Interaction Perspective
  BILL MANARIS
Cognitive Adaptive Computer Help (COACH): A Case Study
  EDWIN J. SELKER
Cellular Automata Models of Self-replicating Systems
  JAMES A. REGGIA, HUI-HSIEN CHOU, AND JASON D. LOHN
Ultrasound Visualization
  THOMAS R. NELSON
Patterns and System Development
  BRANDON GOLDFEDDER
High Performance Digital Video Servers: Storage and Retrieval of Compressed Scalable Video
  SEUNGYUP PAEK AND SHIH-FU CHANG
Software Acquisition: The Custom/Package and Insource/Outsource Dimensions
  PAUL NELSON, ABRAHAM SEIDMANN, AND WILLIAM RICHMOND

Volume 48

Architectures and Patterns for Developing High-performance, Real-time ORB Endsystems
  DOUGLAS C. SCHMIDT, DAVID L. LEVINE, AND CHRIS CLEELAND
Heterogeneous Data Access in a Mobile Environment – Issues and Solutions
  J. B. LIM AND A. R. HURSON
The World Wide Web
  HAL BERGHEL AND DOUGLAS BLANK
Progress in Internet Security
  RANDALL J. ATKINSON AND J. ERIC KLINKER
Digital Libraries: Social Issues and Technological Advances
  HSINCHUN CHEN AND ANDREA L. HOUSTON
Architectures for Mobile Robot Control
  JULIO K. ROSENBLATT AND JAMES A. HENDLER

Volume 49

A Survey of Current Paradigms in Machine Translation
    BONNIE J. DORR, PAMELA W. JORDAN, AND JOHN W. BENOIT
Formality in Specification and Modeling: Developments in Software Engineering Practice
    J. S. FITZGERALD
3-D Visualization of Software Structure
    MATHEW L. STAPLES AND JAMES M. BIEMAN
Using Domain Models for System Testing
    A. VON MAYRHAUSER AND R. MRAZ
Exception-handling Design Patterns
    WILLIAM G. BAIL
Managing Control Asynchrony on SIMD Machines—a Survey
    NAEL B. ABU-GHAZALEH AND PHILIP A. WILSEY
A Taxonomy of Distributed Real-time Control Systems
    J. R. ACRE, L. P. CLARE, AND S. SASTRY

Volume 50

Index Part I
Subject Index, Volumes 1–49

Volume 51

Index Part II
Author Index
Cumulative list of Titles
Table of Contents, Volumes 1–49

Volume 52

Eras of Business Computing
    ALAN R. HEVNER AND DONALD J. BERNDT
Numerical Weather Prediction
    FERDINAND BAER
Machine Translation
    SERGEI NIRENBURG AND YORICK WILKS
The Games Computers (and People) Play
    JONATHAN SCHAEFFER
From Single Word to Natural Dialogue
    NEILS OLE BENSON AND LAILA DYBKJAER
Embedded Microprocessors: Evolution, Trends and Challenges
    MANFRED SCHLETT

Volume 53

Shared-Memory Multiprocessing: Current State and Future Directions
    PER STEUSTRÖM, ERIK HAGERSTEU, DAVID I. LITA, MARGARET MARTONOSI, AND MADAN VERNGOPAL

Shared Memory and Distributed Shared Memory Systems: A Survey
    KRISHNA KAUI, HYONG-SHIK KIM, BEU LEE, AND A. R. HURSON
Resource-Aware Meta Computing
    JEFFREY K. HOLLINGSWORTH, PETER J. KELCHER, AND KYUNG D. RYU
Knowledge Management
    WILLIAM W. AGRESTI
A Methodology for Evaluating Predictive Metrics
    JASRETT ROSENBERG
An Empirical Review of Software Process Assessments
    KHALED EL EMAM AND DENNIS R. GOLDENSON
State of the Art in Electronic Payment Systems
    N. ASOKAN, P. JANSON, M. STEIVES, AND M. WAIDNES
Defective Software: An Overview of Legal Remedies and Technical Measures Available to Consumers
    COLLEEN KOTYK VOSSLER AND JEFFREY VOAS

Volume 54

An Overview of Components and Component-Based Development
    ALAN W. BROWN
Working with UML: A Software Design Process Based on Inspections for the Unified Modeling Language
    GUILHERME H. TRAVASSOS, FORREST SHULL, AND JEFFREY CARVER
Enterprise JavaBeans and Microsoft Transaction Server: Frameworks for Distributed Enterprise Components
    AVRAHAM LEFF, JOHN PROKOPEK, JAMES T. RAYFIELD, AND IGNACIO SILVA-LEPE
Maintenance Process and Product Evaluation Using Reliability, Risk, and Test Metrics
    NORMAN F. SCHNEIDEWIND
Computer Technology Changes and Purchasing Strategies
    GERALD V. POST
Secure Outsourcing of Scientific Computations
    MIKHAIL J. ATALLAH, K.N. PANTAZOPOULOS, JOHN R. RICE, AND EUGENE SPAFFORD

Volume 55

The Virtual University: A State of the Art
    LINDA HARASIM
The Net, the Web and the Children
    W. NEVILLE HOLMES
Source Selection and Ranking in the WebSemantics Architecture Using Quality of Data Metadata
    GEORGE A. MIHAILA, LOUIQA RASCHID, AND MARIA-ESTER VIDAL
Mining Scientific Data
    NAREN RAMAKRISHNAN AND ANANTH Y. GRAMA
History and Contributions of Theoretical Computer Science
    JOHN E. SAVAGE, ALAN L. SALEM, AND CARL SMITH
Security Policies
    ROSS ANDERSON, FRANK STAJANO, AND JONG-HYEON LEE
Transistors and 1C Design
    YUAN TAUR

Volume 56

Software Evolution and the Staged Model of the Software Lifecycle
    KEITH H. BENNETT, VACLAV T. RAJLICH, AND NORMAN WILDE
Embedded Software
    EDWARD A. LEE
Empirical Studies of Quality Models in Object-Oriented Systems
    LIONEL C. BRIAND AND JÜRGEN WÜST
Software Fault Prevention by Language Choice: Why C Is Not My Favorite Language
    RICHARD J. FATEMAN
Quantum Computing and Communication
    PAUL E. BLACK, D. RICHARD KUHN, AND CARL J. WILLIAMS
Exception Handling
    PETER A. BUHR, ASHIF HARJI, AND W. Y. RUSSELL MOK
Breaking the Robustness Barrier: Recent Progress on the Design of the Robust Multimodal System
    SHARON OVIATT
Using Data Mining to Discover the Preferences of Computer Criminals
    DONALD E. BROWN AND LOUISE F. GUNDERSON

Volume 57

On the Nature and Importance of Archiving in the Digital Age
    HELEN R. TIBBO
Preserving Digital Records and the Life Cycle of Information
    SU-SHING CHEN
Managing Historical XML Data
    SUDARSHAN S. CHAWATHE
Adding Compression to Next-Generation Text Retrieval Systems
    NIVIO ZIVIANI AND EDLENO SILVA DE MOURA
Are Scripting Languages Any Good? A Validation of Perl, Python, Rexx, and Tcl against C, C++, and Java
    LUTZ PRECHELT
Issues and Approaches for Developing Learner-Centered Technology
    CHRIS QUINTANA, JOSEPH KRAJCIK, AND ELLIOT SOLOWAY
Personalizing Interactions with Information Systems
    SAVERIO PERUGINI AND NAREN RAMAKRISHNAN

Volume 58

Software Development Productivity
    KATRINA D. MAXWELL
Transformation-Oriented Programming: A Development Methodology for High Assurance Software
    VICTOR L. WINTER, STEVE ROACH, AND GREG WICKSTROM
Bounded Model Checking
    ARMIN BIERE, ALESSANDRO CIMATTI, EDMUND M. CLARKE, OFER STRICHMAN, AND
        YUNSHAN ZHU
Advances in GUI Testing
    ATIF M. MEMON
Software Inspections
    MARC ROPER, ALASTAIR DUNSMORE, AND MURRAY WOOD

Software Fault Tolerance Forestalls Crashes: To Err Is Human; To Forgive Is Fault Tolerant
    LAWRENCE BERNSTEIN
Advances in the Provisions of System and Software Security—Thirty Years of Progress
    RAYFORD B. VAUGHN

ISBN 0-12-012159-X